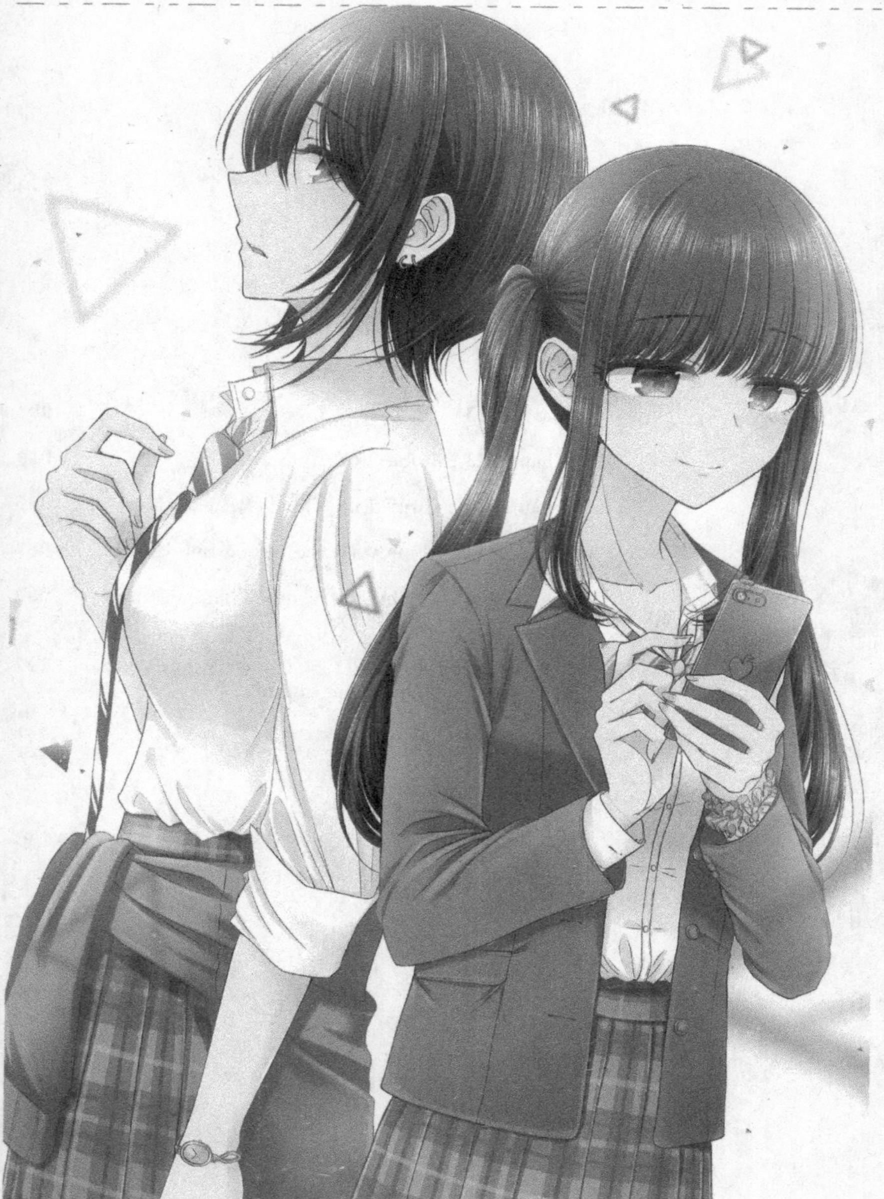

f a i l e d   p r i n c e s s e s   v o l u m e   t h r e e

contents

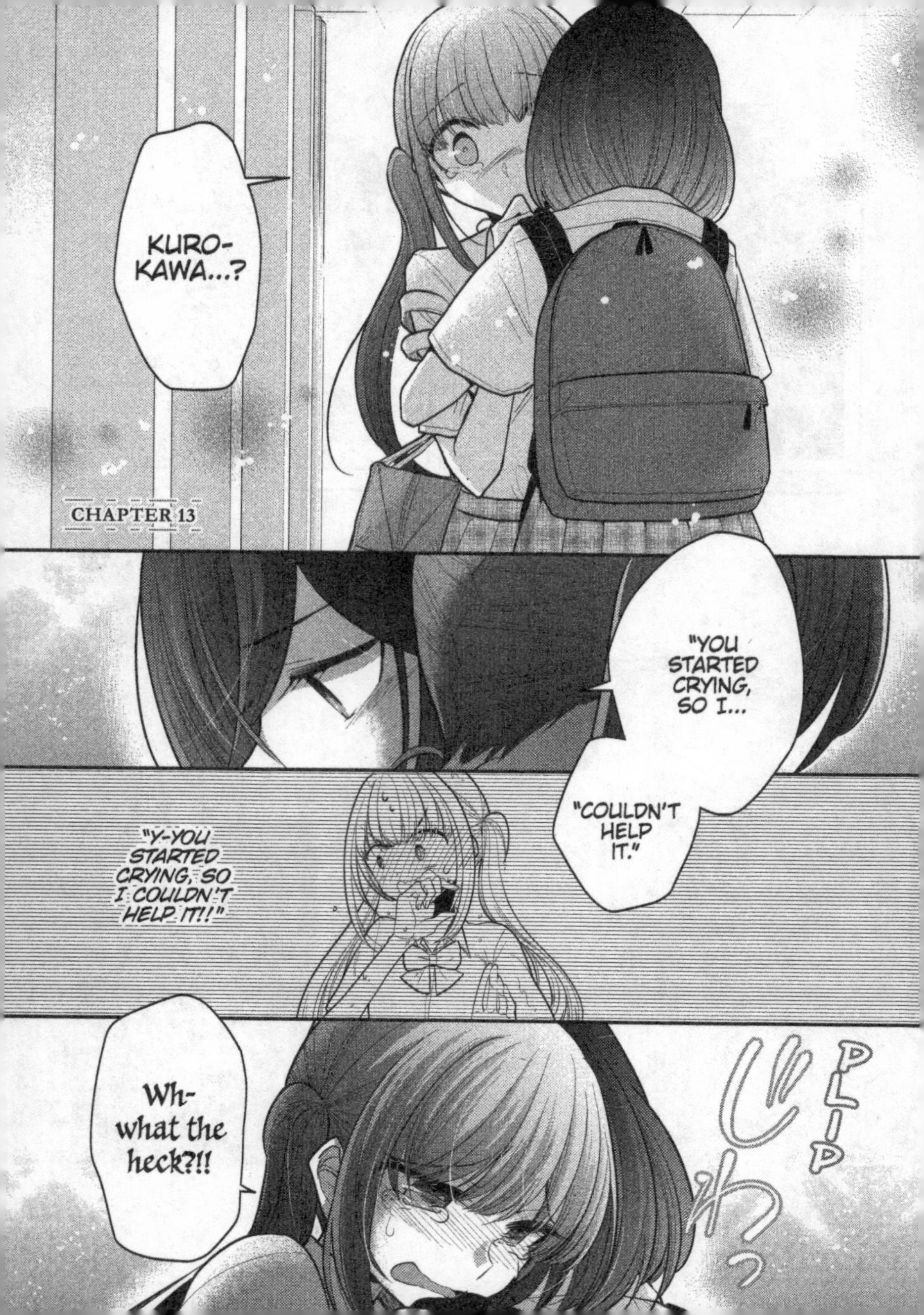
KURO-KAWA...?
CHAPTER 13
"YOU STARTED CRYING, SO I...
"COULDN'T HELP IT."
"Y-YOU STARTED CRYING, SO I COULDN'T HELP IT!!"
PLIP
Wh- what the heck?!!

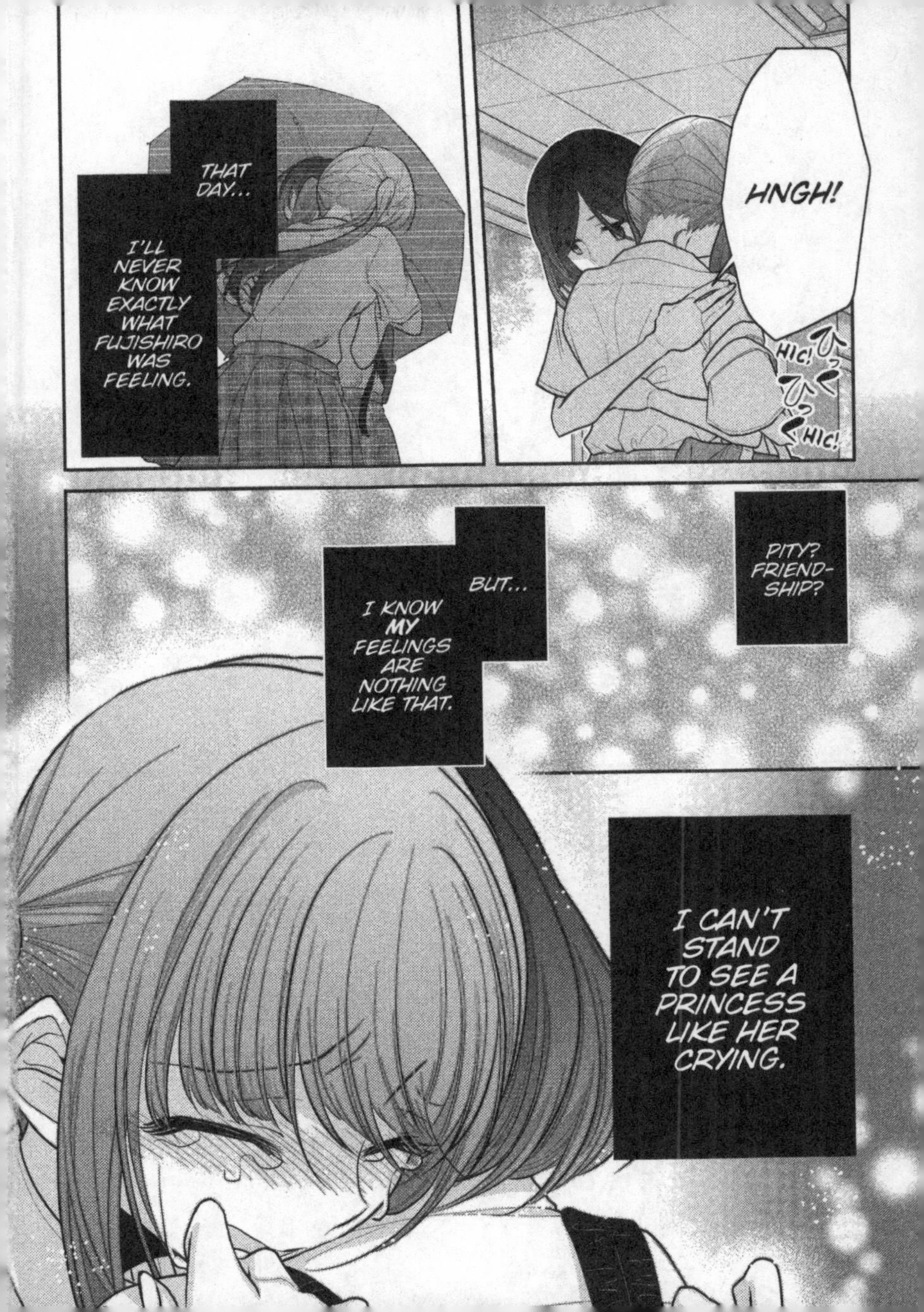
HNGH!
HIC!
HIC!
THAT DAY...
I'LL NEVER KNOW EXACTLY WHAT FUJISHIRO WAS FEELING.
PITY? FRIEND-SHIP?
BUT...
I KNOW **MY** FEELINGS ARE NOTHING LIKE THAT.
I CAN'T STAND TO SEE A PRINCESS LIKE HER CRYING.

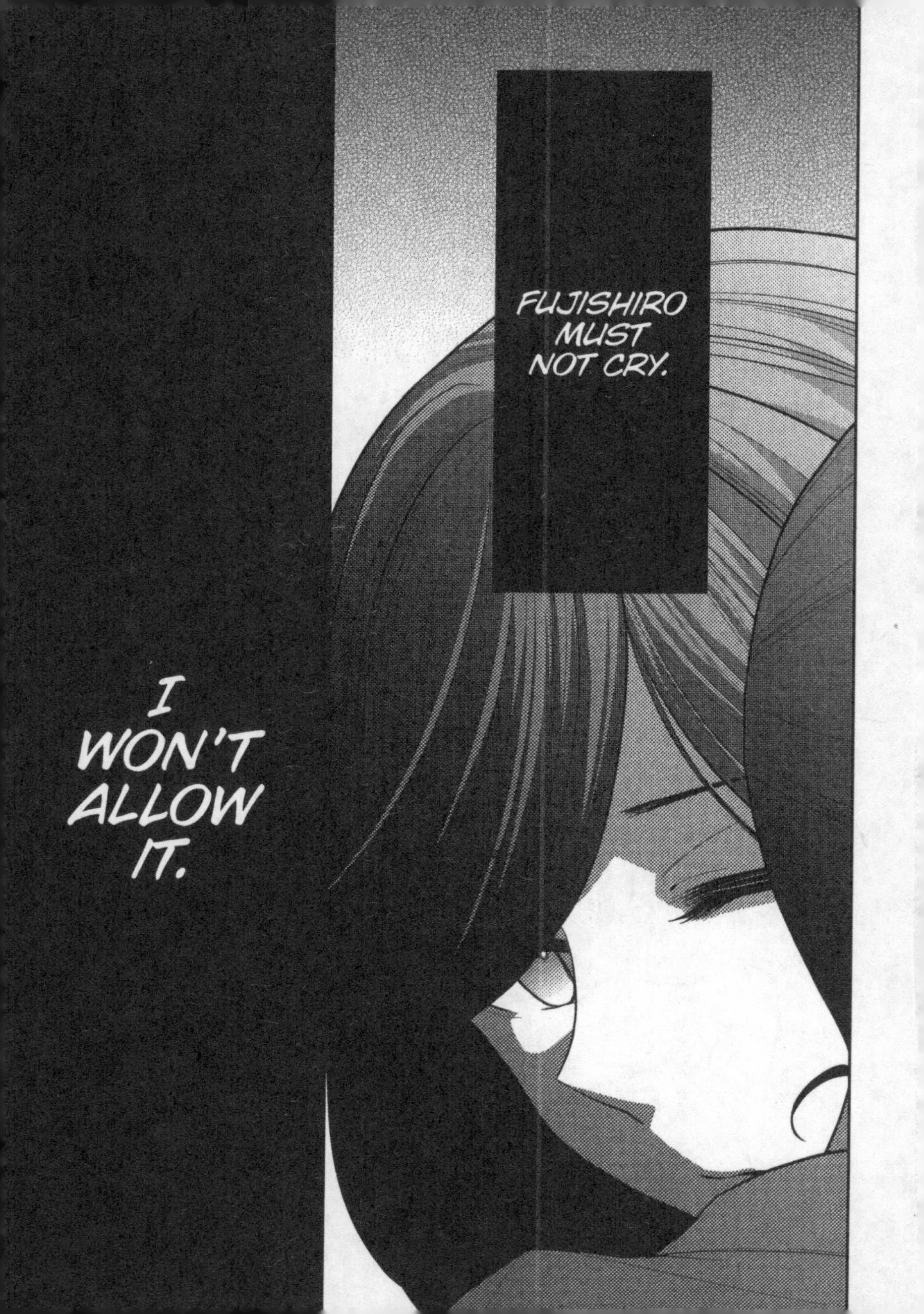
FUJISHIRO MUST NOT CRY.
I WON'T ALLOW IT.

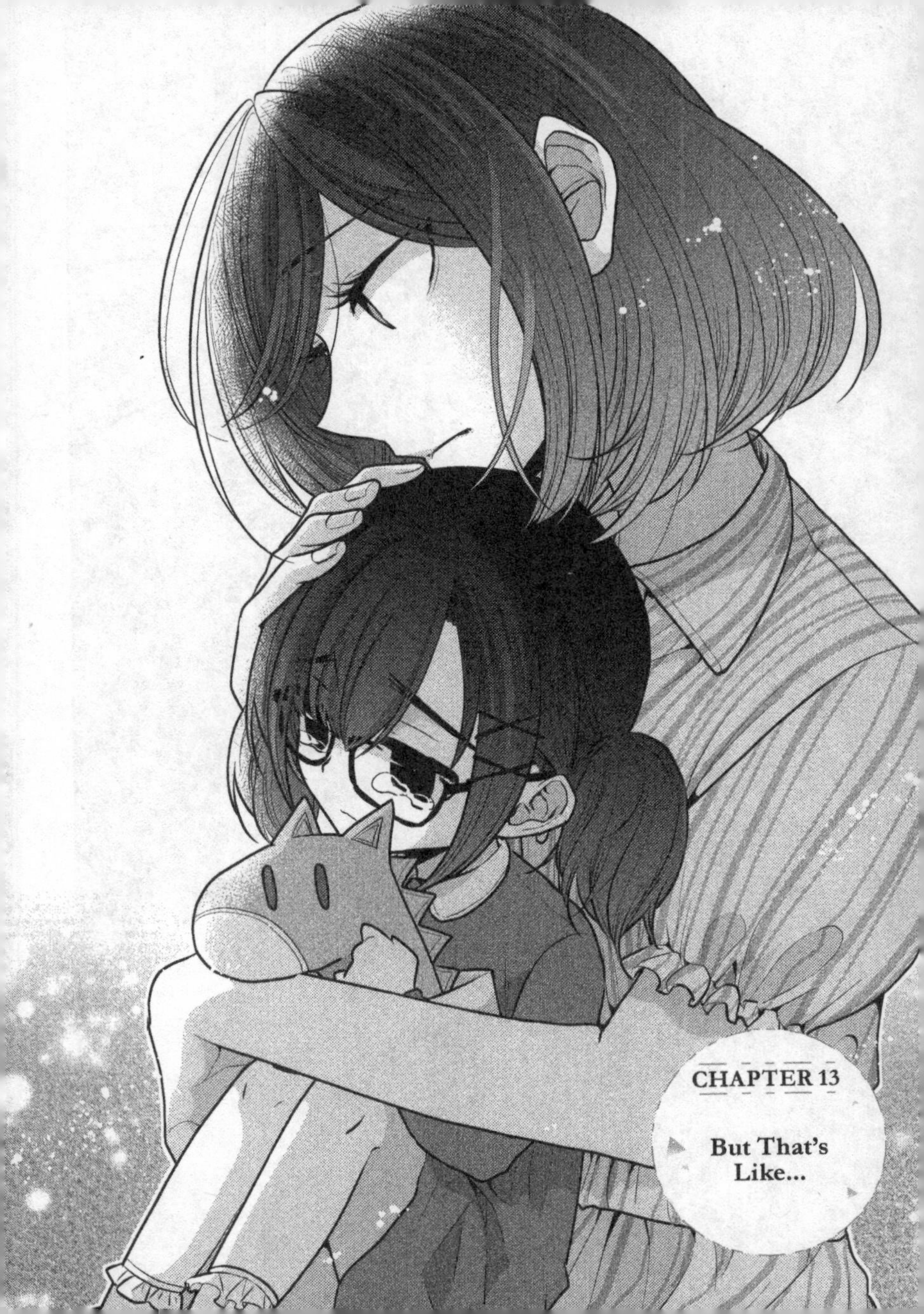
CHAPTER 13
But That's Like...

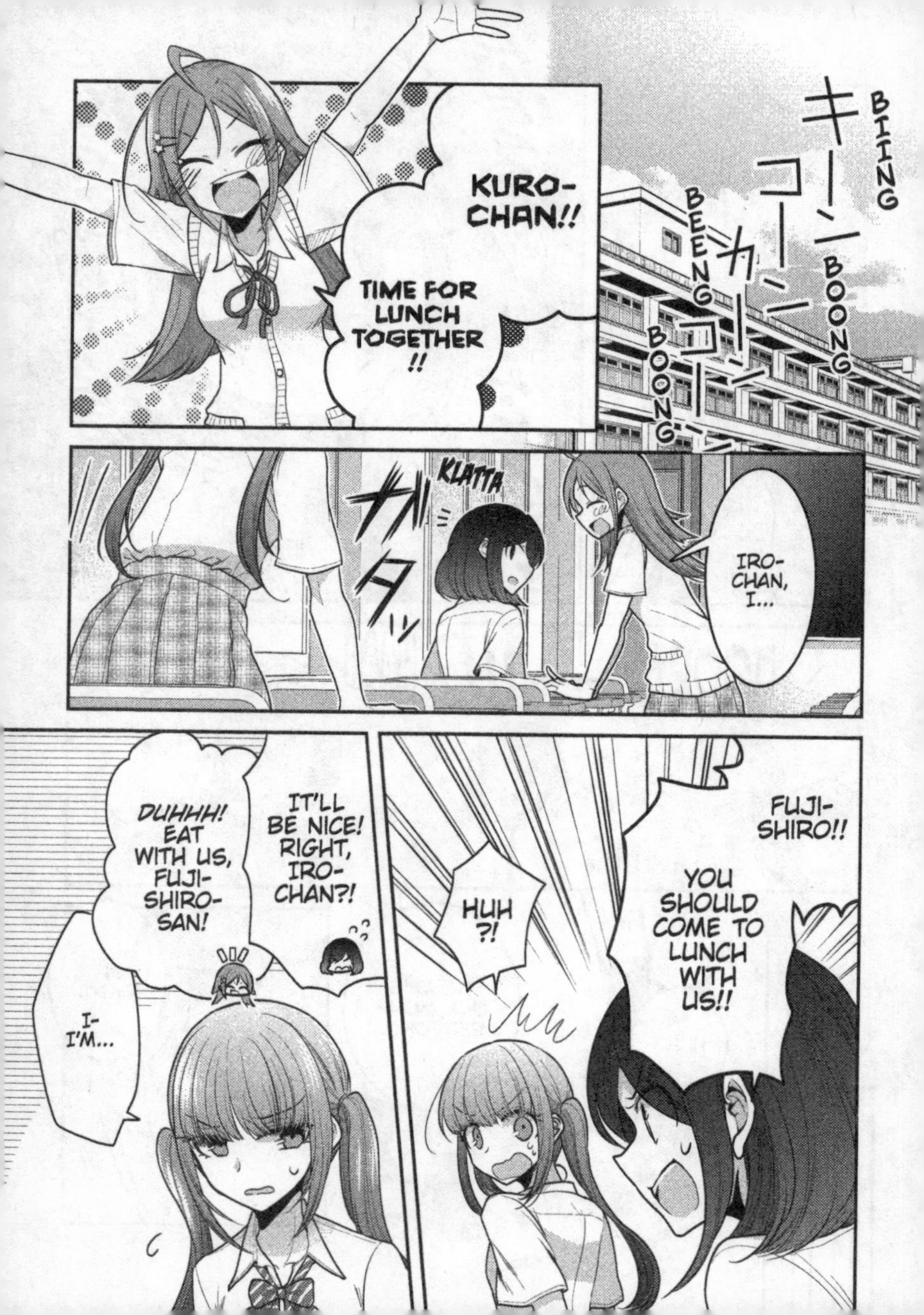

BIIING
BOONG
BEENG
BOONG
KURO-CHAN!!
TIME FOR LUNCH TOGETHER!!
KLATTA
IRO-CHAN, I...
FUJI-SHIRO!!
YOU SHOULD COME TO LUNCH WITH US!!
HUH?!
IT'LL BE NICE! RIGHT, IRO-CHAN?!
DUHHH! EAT WITH US, FUJI-SHIRO-SAN!
I- I'M...

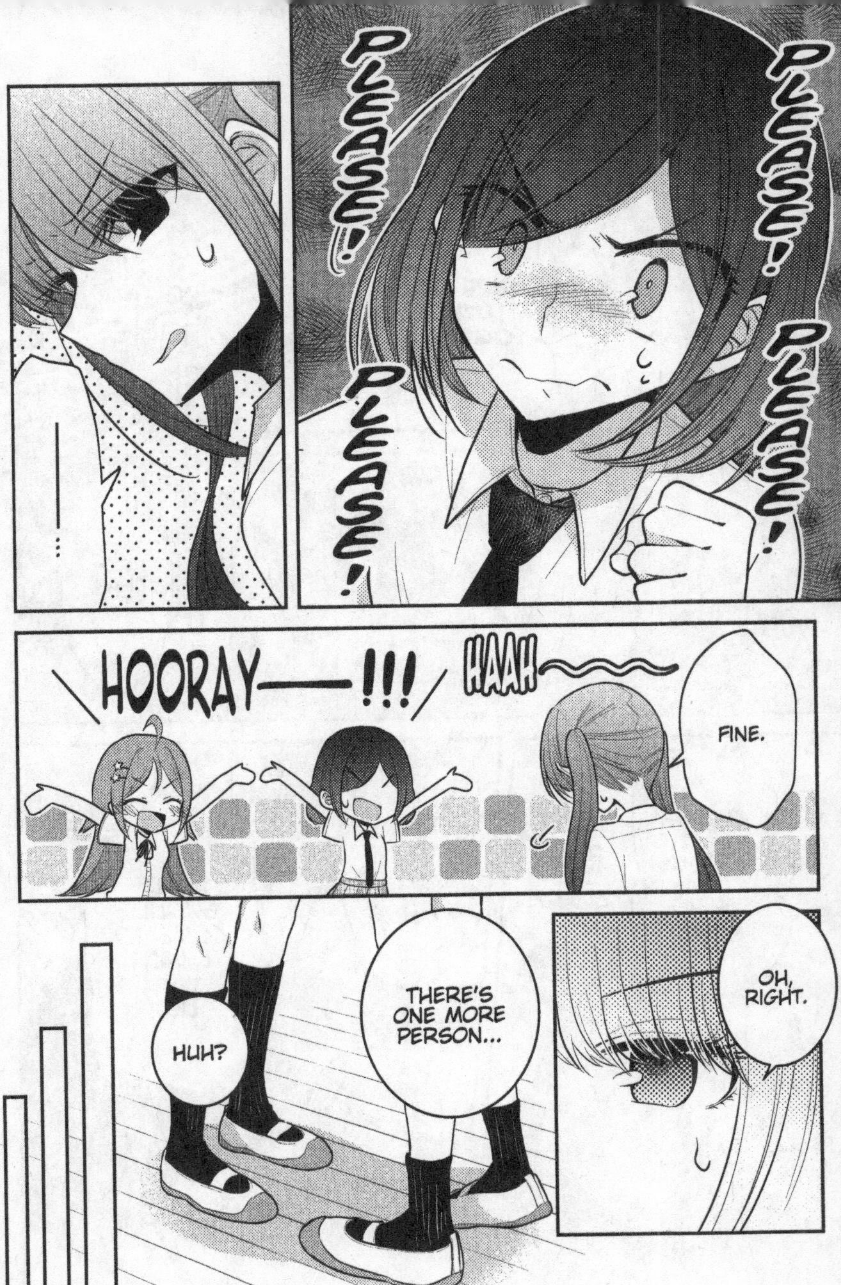
PLEASE! PLEASE!
PLEASE! PLEASE!
—...
FINE.
HAAH~~~
HOORAY——!!!
OH, RIGHT.
THERE'S ONE MORE PERSON...
HUH?

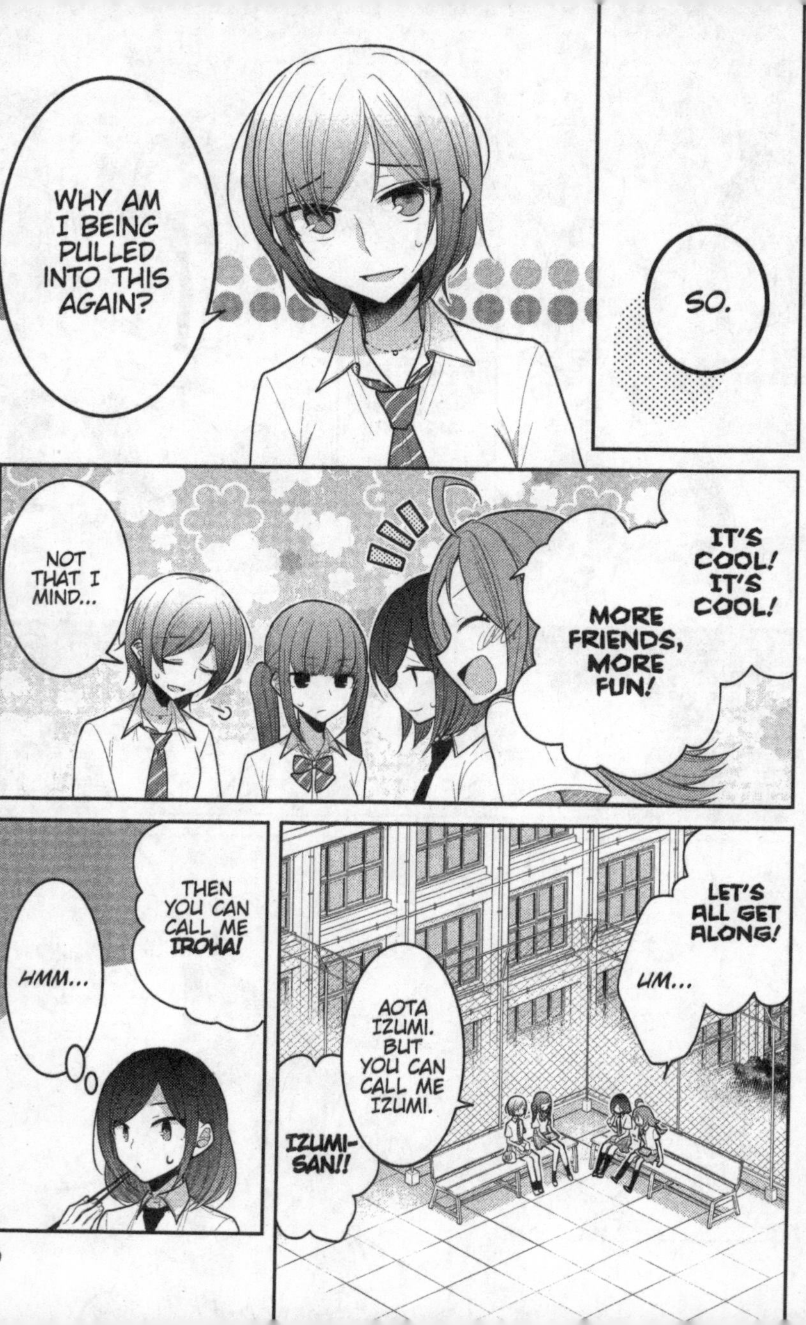
SO.
WHY AM I BEING PULLED INTO THIS AGAIN?
IT'S COOL! IT'S COOL!
MORE FRIENDS, MORE FUN!
NOT THAT I MIND...
LET'S ALL GET ALONG!
UM...
AOTA IZUMI. BUT YOU CAN CALL ME IZUMI.
IZUMI-SAN!!
THEN YOU CAN CALL ME IROHA!
HMM...

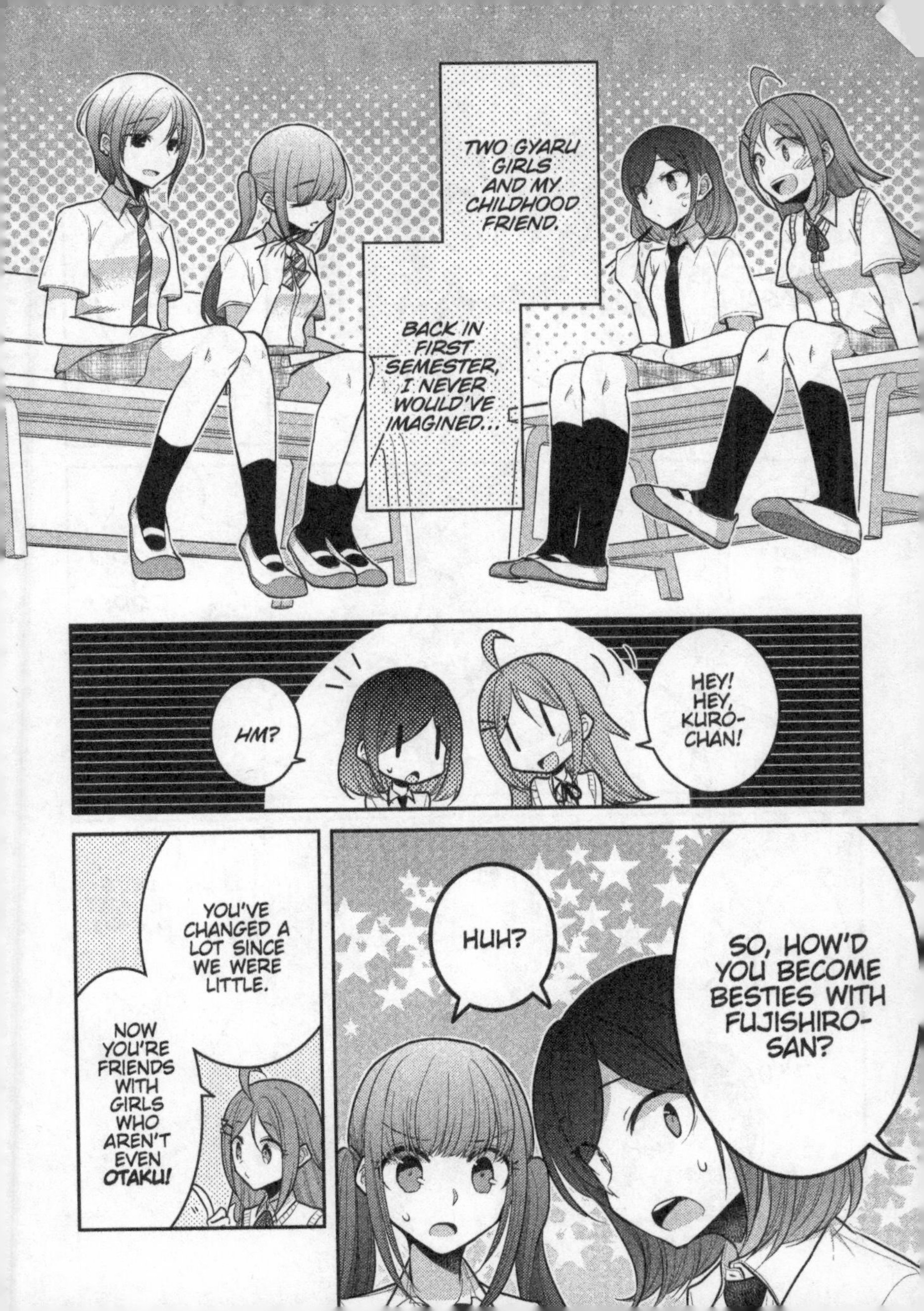
TWO GYARU GIRLS AND MY CHILDHOOD FRIEND.
BACK IN FIRST SEMESTER, I NEVER WOULD'VE IMAGINED...
HEY! HEY, KURO-CHAN!
HM?
SO, HOW'D YOU BECOME BESTIES WITH FUJISHIRO-SAN?
HUH?
YOU'VE CHANGED A LOT SINCE WE WERE LITTLE.
NOW YOU'RE FRIENDS WITH GIRLS WHO AREN'T EVEN OTAKU!

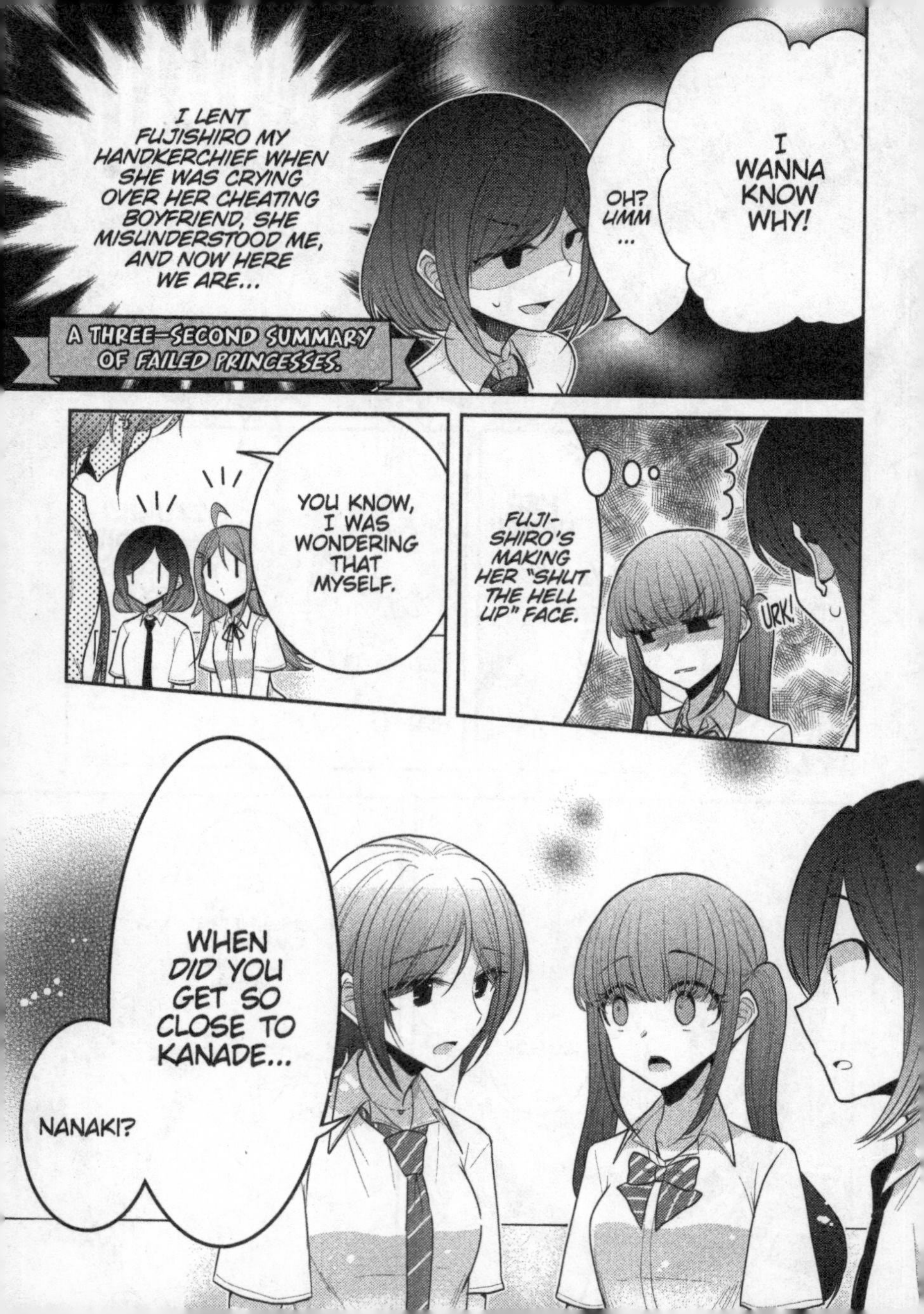
I WANNA KNOW WHY!
OH? UMM ...
I LENT FUJISHIRO MY HANDKERCHIEF WHEN SHE WAS CRYING OVER HER CHEATING BOYFRIEND, SHE MISUNDERSTOOD ME, AND NOW HERE WE ARE...
A THREE-SECOND SUMMARY OF FAILED PRINCESSES.
FUJI-SHIRO'S MAKING HER "SHUT THE HELL UP" FACE.
URK!
YOU KNOW, I WAS WONDERING THAT MYSELF.
WHEN DID YOU GET SO CLOSE TO KANADE...
NANAKI?

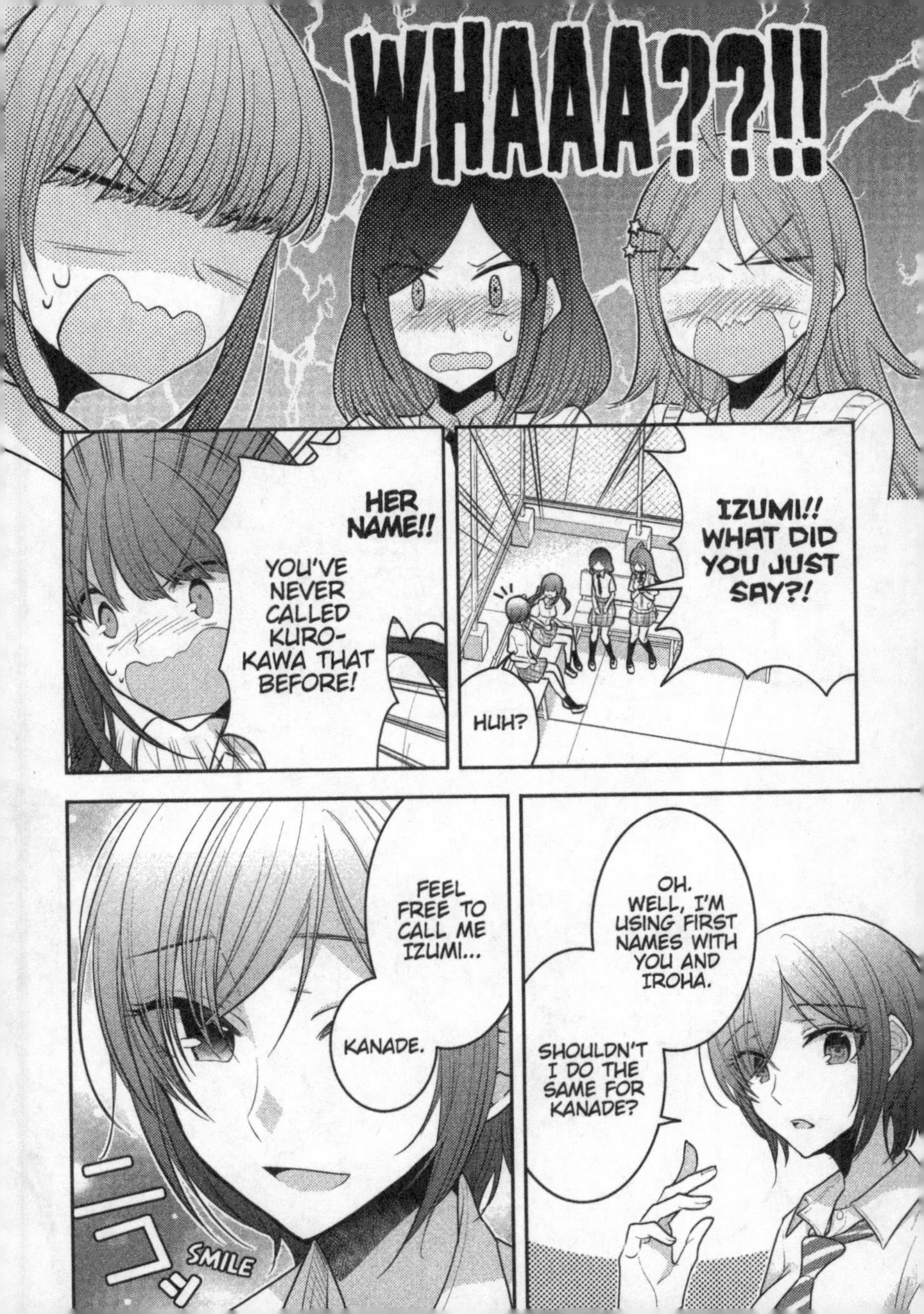
WHAAA??!!
IZUMI!! WHAT DID YOU JUST SAY?!
HUH?
HER NAME!!
YOU'VE NEVER CALLED KURO-KAWA THAT BEFORE!
OH. WELL, I'M USING FIRST NAMES WITH YOU AND IROHA.
SHOULDN'T I DO THE SAME FOR KANADE?
FEEL FREE TO CALL ME IZUMI...
KANADE.
SMILE

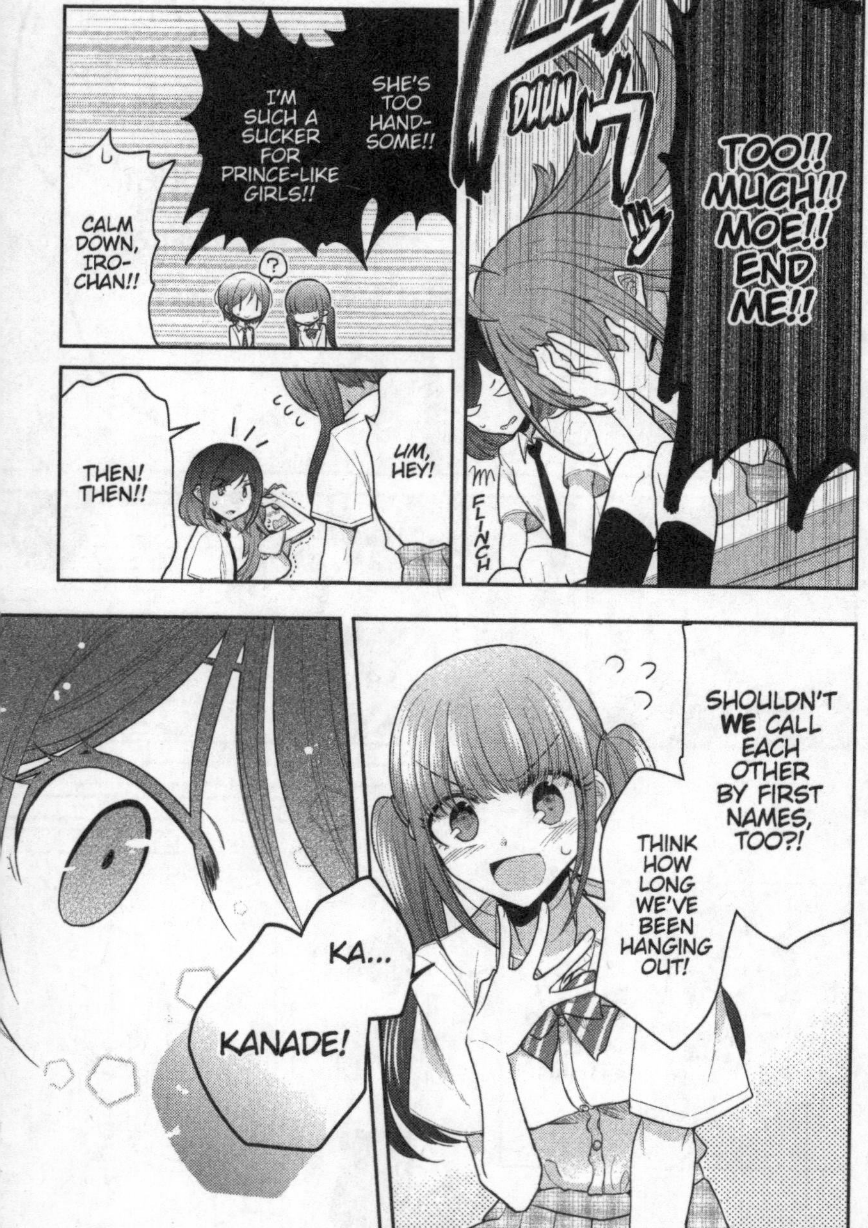
DUUN
TOO!! MUCH!! MOE!! END ME!!
FLINCH
SHE'S TOO HAND-SOME!!
I'M SUCH A SUCKER FOR PRINCE-LIKE GIRLS!!
CALM DOWN, IRO-CHAN!!
?
UM, HEY!
THEN! THEN!!
SHOULDN'T WE CALL EACH OTHER BY FIRST NAMES, TOO?!
THINK HOW LONG WE'VE BEEN HANGING OUT!
KA...
KANADE!

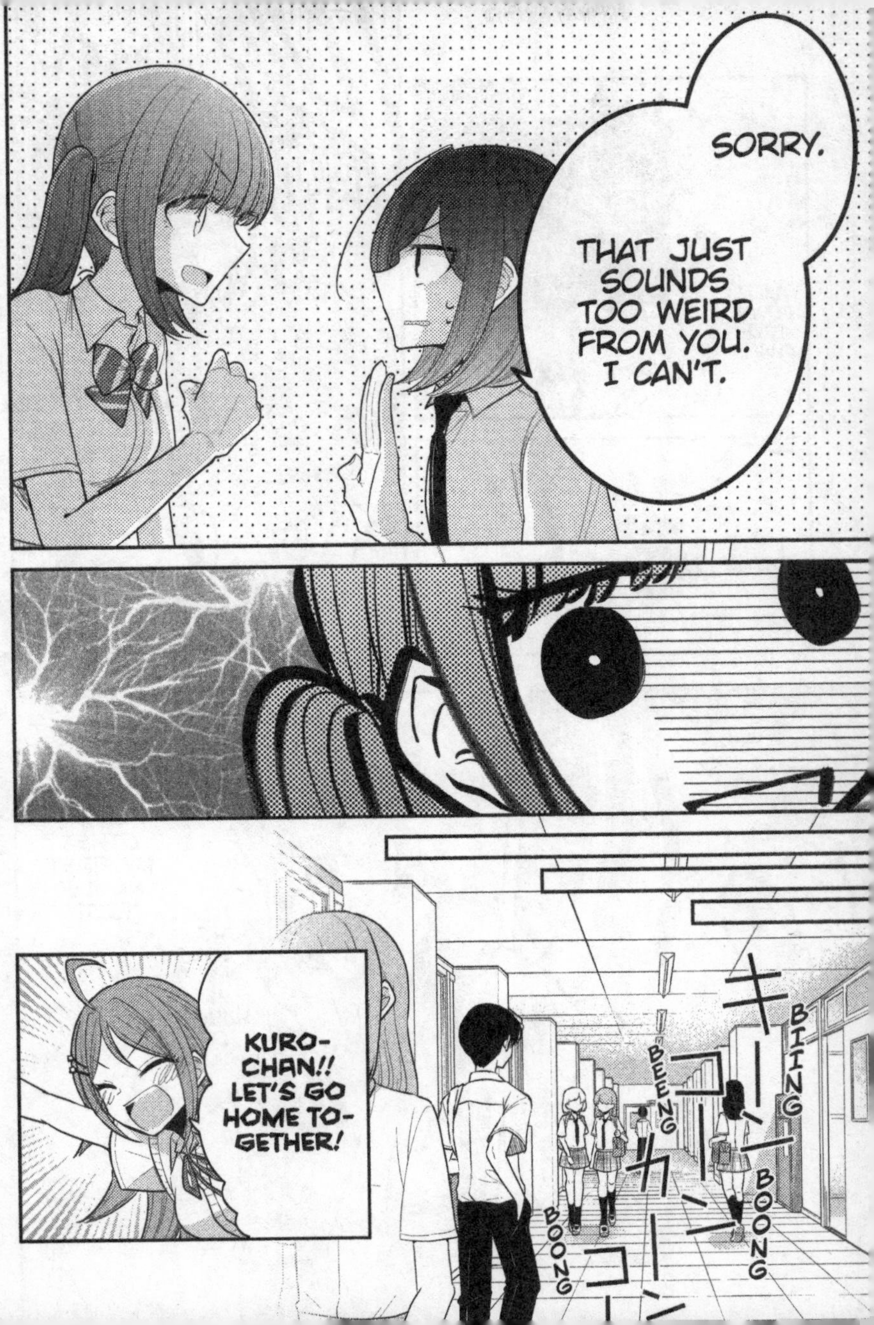
SORRY.
THAT JUST SOUNDS TOO WEIRD FROM YOU. I CAN'T.
BIING
BEENG
BOONG
BOONG
KURO-CHAN!! LET'S GO HOME TO-GETHER!

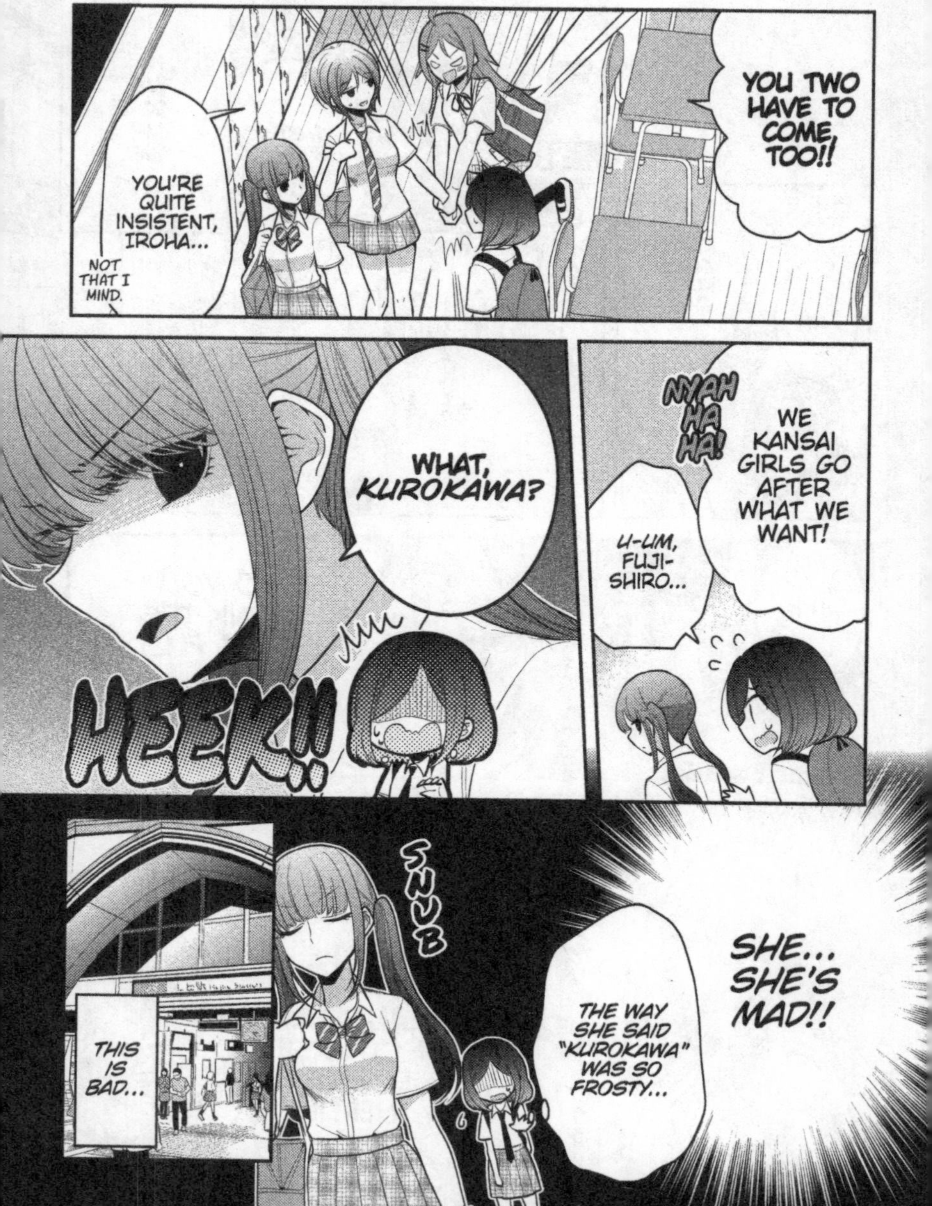
YOU TWO HAVE TO COME, TOO!!
YOU'RE QUITE INSISTENT, IROHA...
NOT THAT I MIND.
NYAH HA HA!
WE KANSAI GIRLS GO AFTER WHAT WE WANT!
U-UM, FUJI-SHIRO...
WHAT, KUROKAWA?
HEEK!!
SHE... SHE'S MAD!!
THE WAY SHE SAID "KUROKAWA" WAS SO FROSTY...
SNUB
THIS IS BAD...

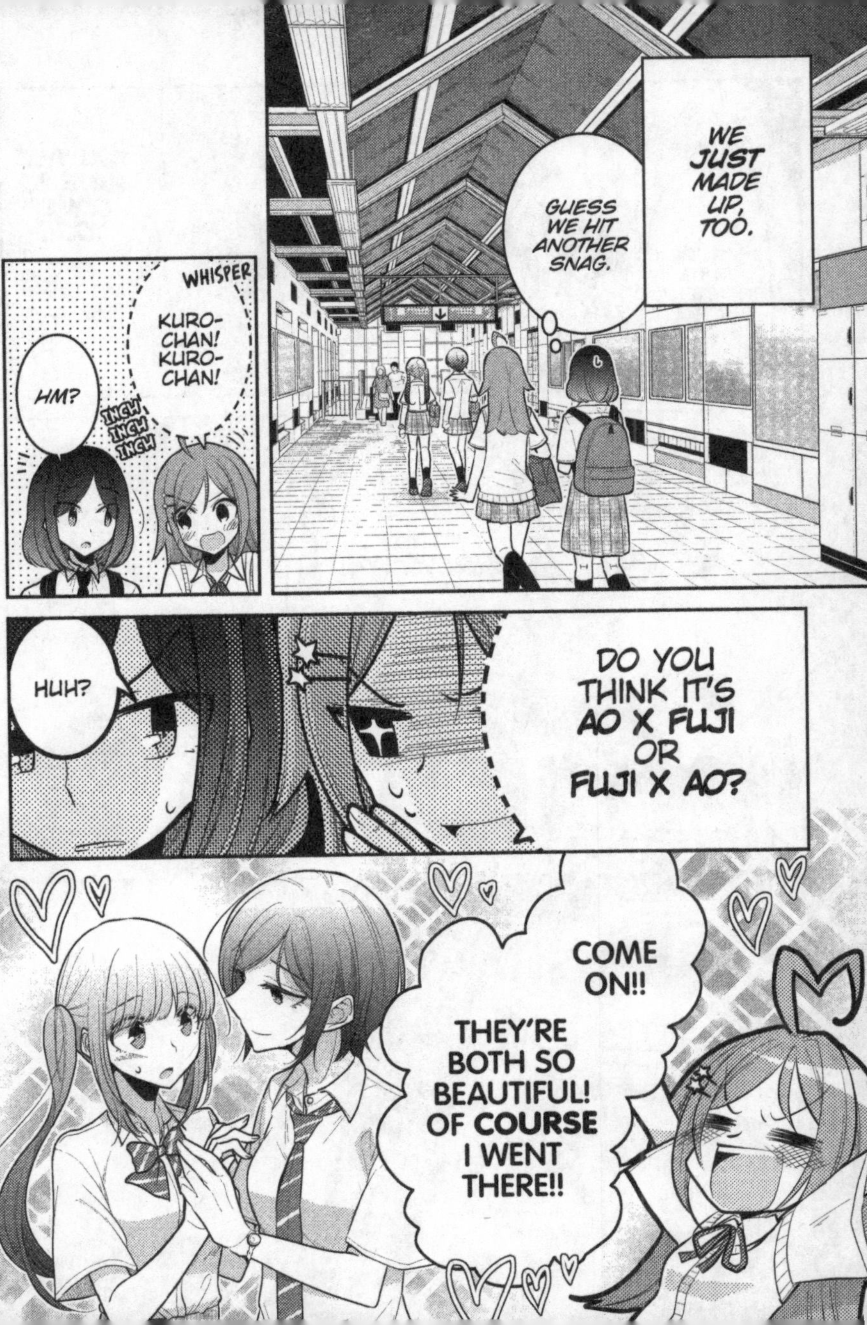
WE JUST MADE UP, TOO.
GUESS WE HIT ANOTHER SNAG.
WHISPER
KURO-CHAN! KURO-CHAN!
INCH INCH INCH
HM?
DO YOU THINK IT'S AO X FUJI OR FUJI X AO?
HUH?
COME ON!!
THEY'RE BOTH SO BEAUTIFUL! OF COURSE I WENT THERE!!

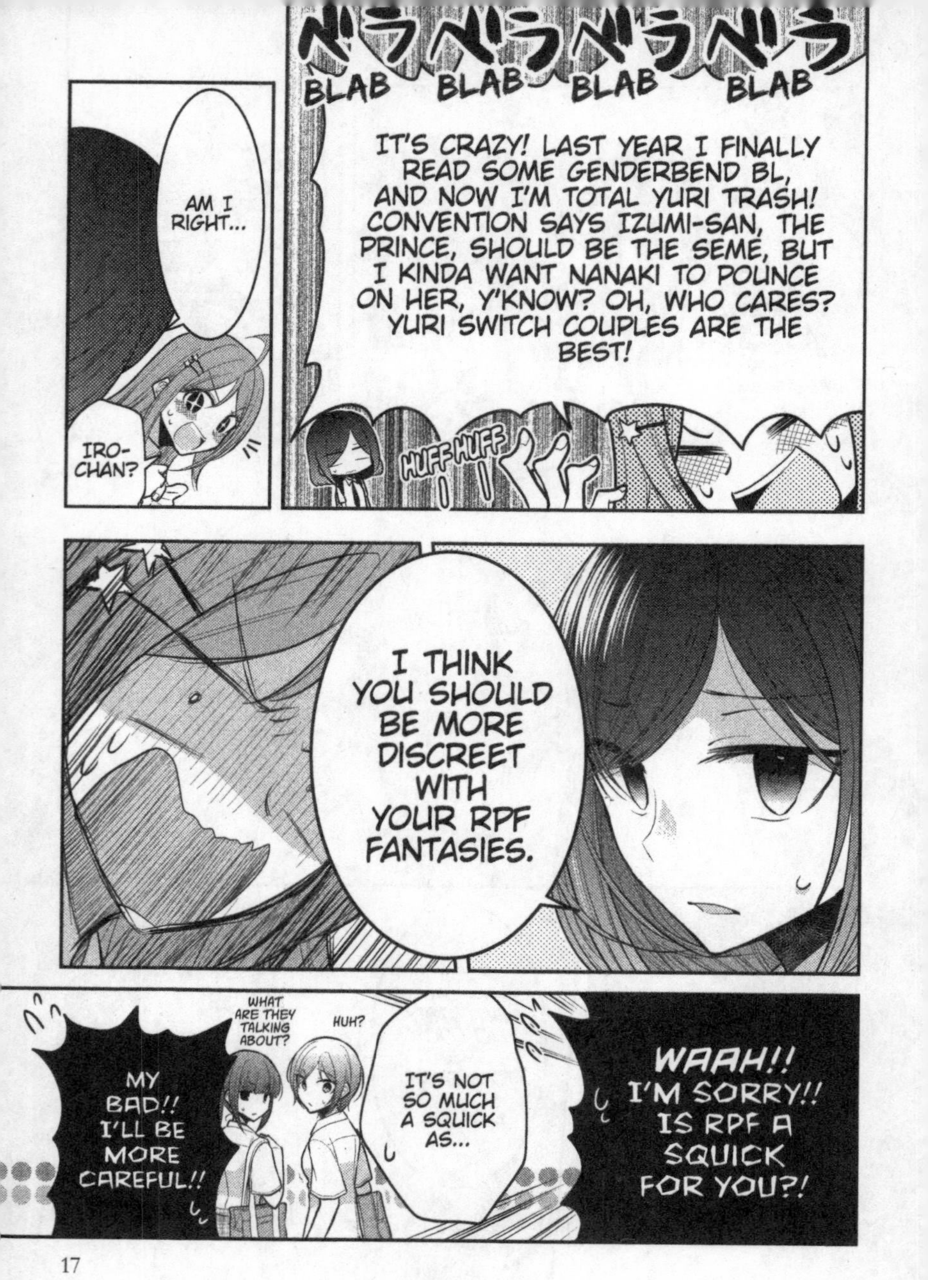
ベラベラベラベラ
BLAB BLAB BLAB BLAB
IT'S CRAZY! LAST YEAR I FINALLY READ SOME GENDERBEND BL, AND NOW I'M TOTAL YURI TRASH! CONVENTION SAYS IZUMI-SAN, THE PRINCE, SHOULD BE THE SEME, BUT I KINDA WANT NANAKI TO POUNCE ON HER, Y'KNOW? OH, WHO CARES? YURI SWITCH COUPLES ARE THE BEST!
HUFF HUFF
AM I RIGHT...
IRO-CHAN?
I THINK YOU SHOULD BE MORE DISCREET WITH YOUR RPF FANTASIES.
WAAH!! I'M SORRY!! IS RPF A SQUICK FOR YOU?!
IT'S NOT SO MUCH A SQUICK AS...
HUH?
WHAT ARE THEY TALKING ABOUT?
MY BAD!! I'LL BE MORE CAREFUL!!

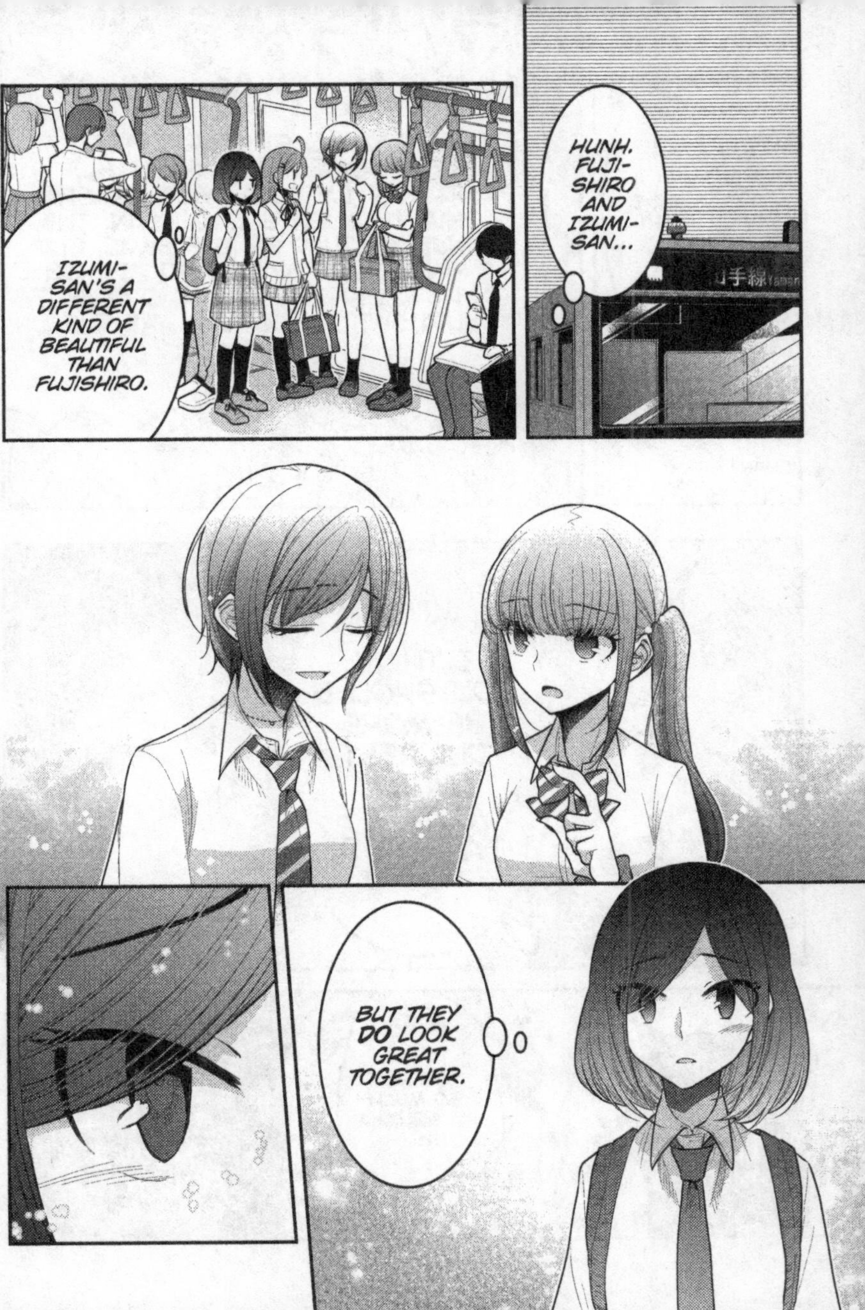
HUNH. FUJISHIRO AND IZUMI-SAN...
IZUMI-SAN'S A DIFFERENT KIND OF BEAUTIFUL THAN FUJISHIRO.
BUT THEY DO LOOK GREAT TOGETHER.

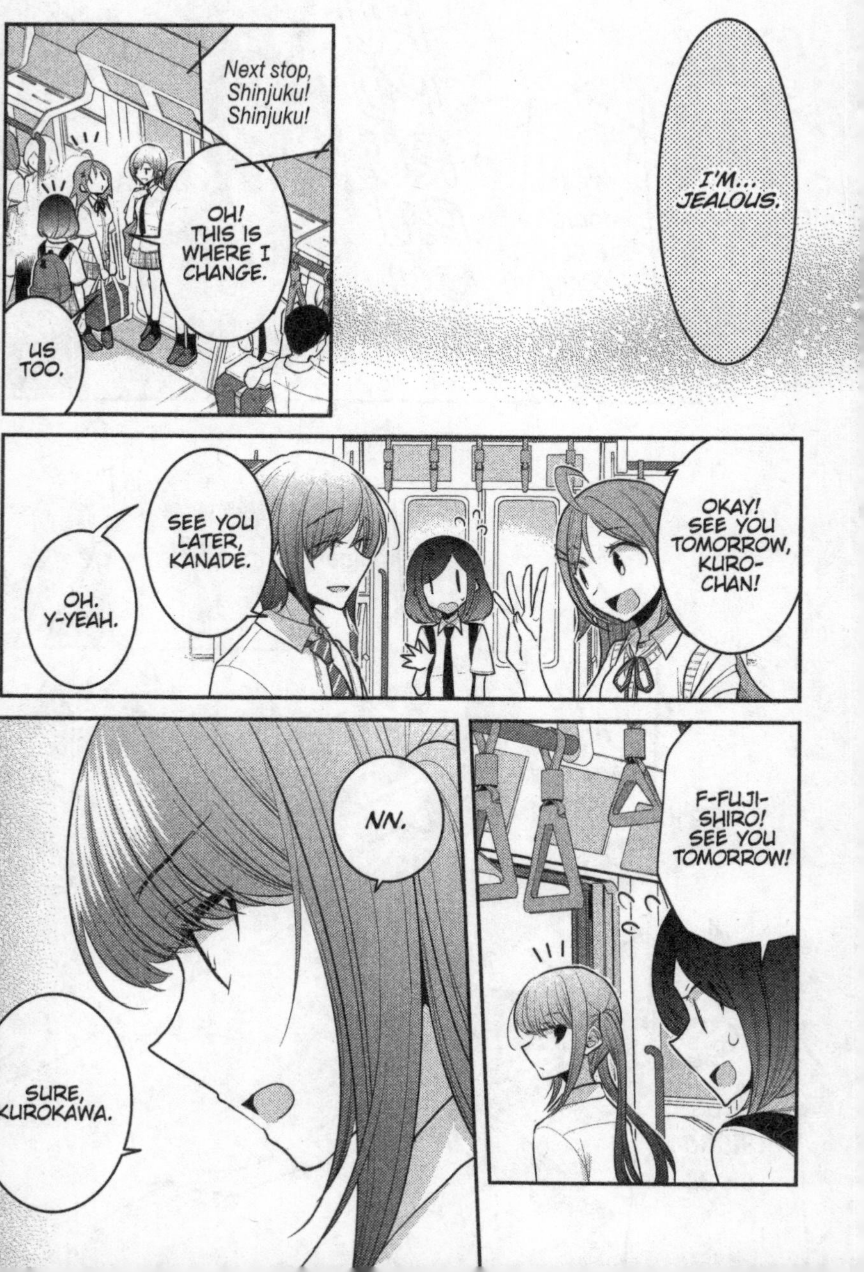
I'M... JEALOUS.
Next stop, Shinjuku! Shinjuku!
OH! THIS IS WHERE I CHANGE.
US TOO.
OKAY! SEE YOU TOMORROW, KURO-CHAN!
SEE YOU LATER, KANADE.
OH. Y-YEAH.
F-FUJI-SHIRO! SEE YOU TOMORROW!
NN.
SURE, KUROKAWA.

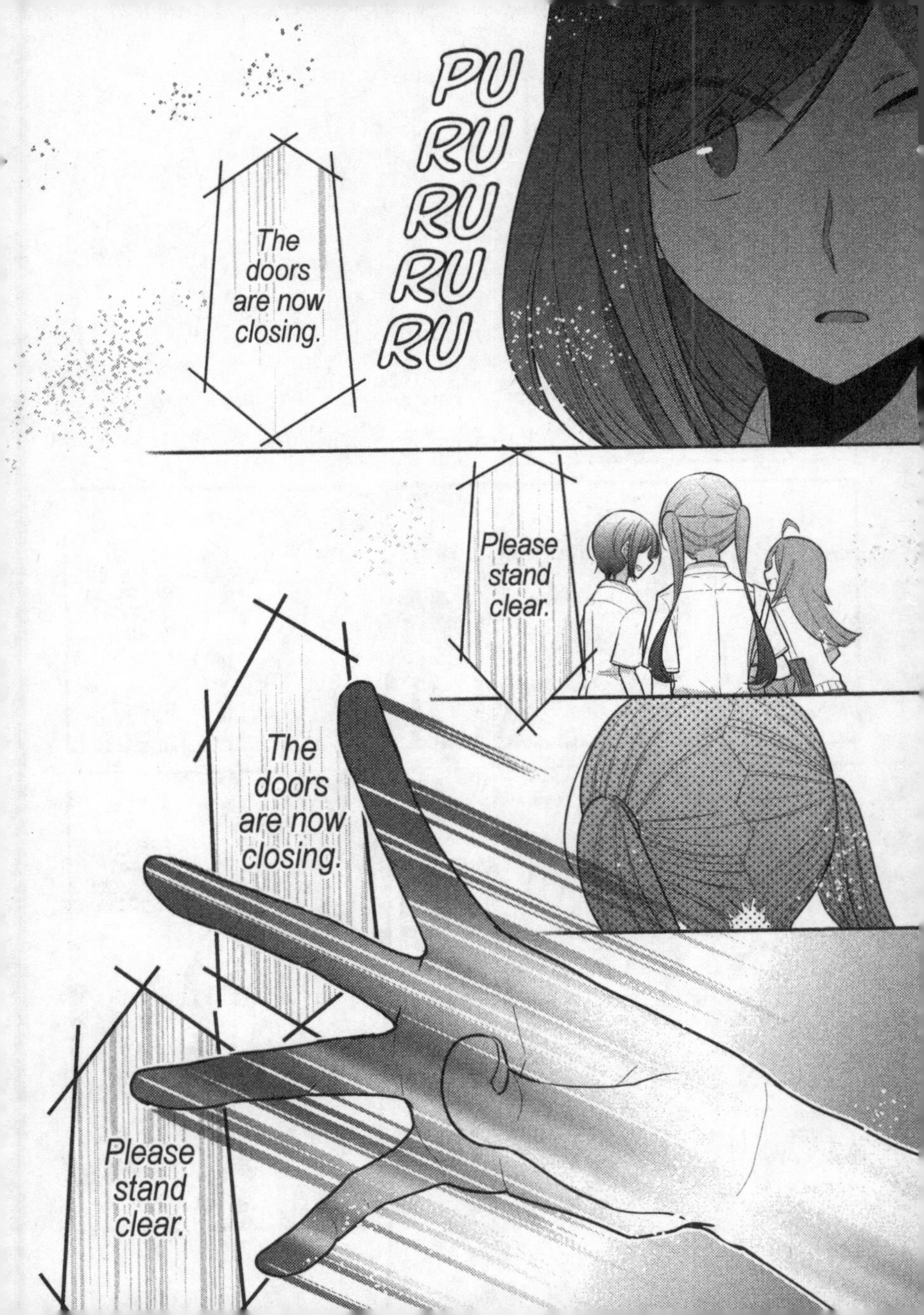
PU RU RU RU RU
The doors are now closing.
Please stand clear.
The doors are now closing.
Please stand clear.

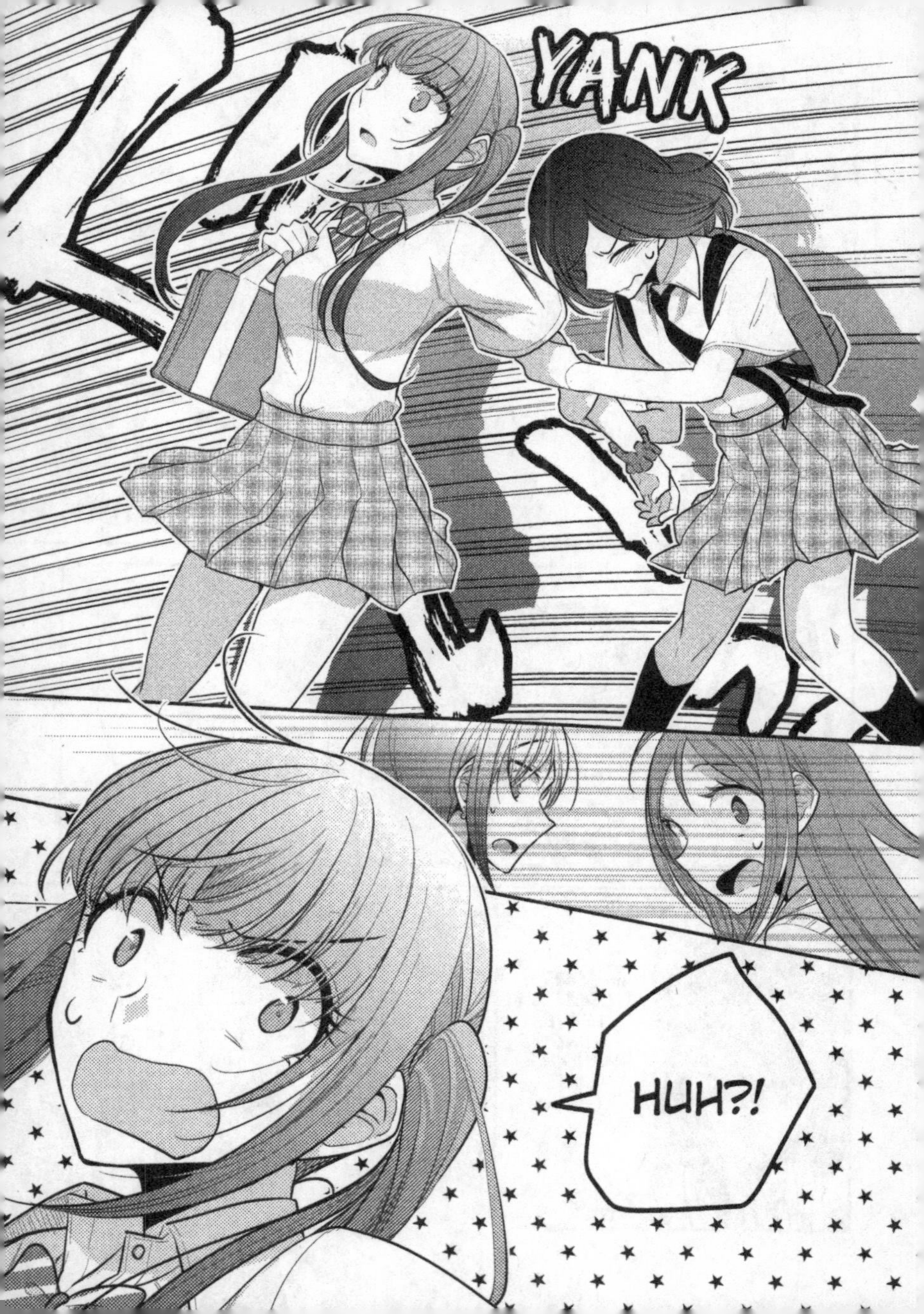
YANK
HUH?!

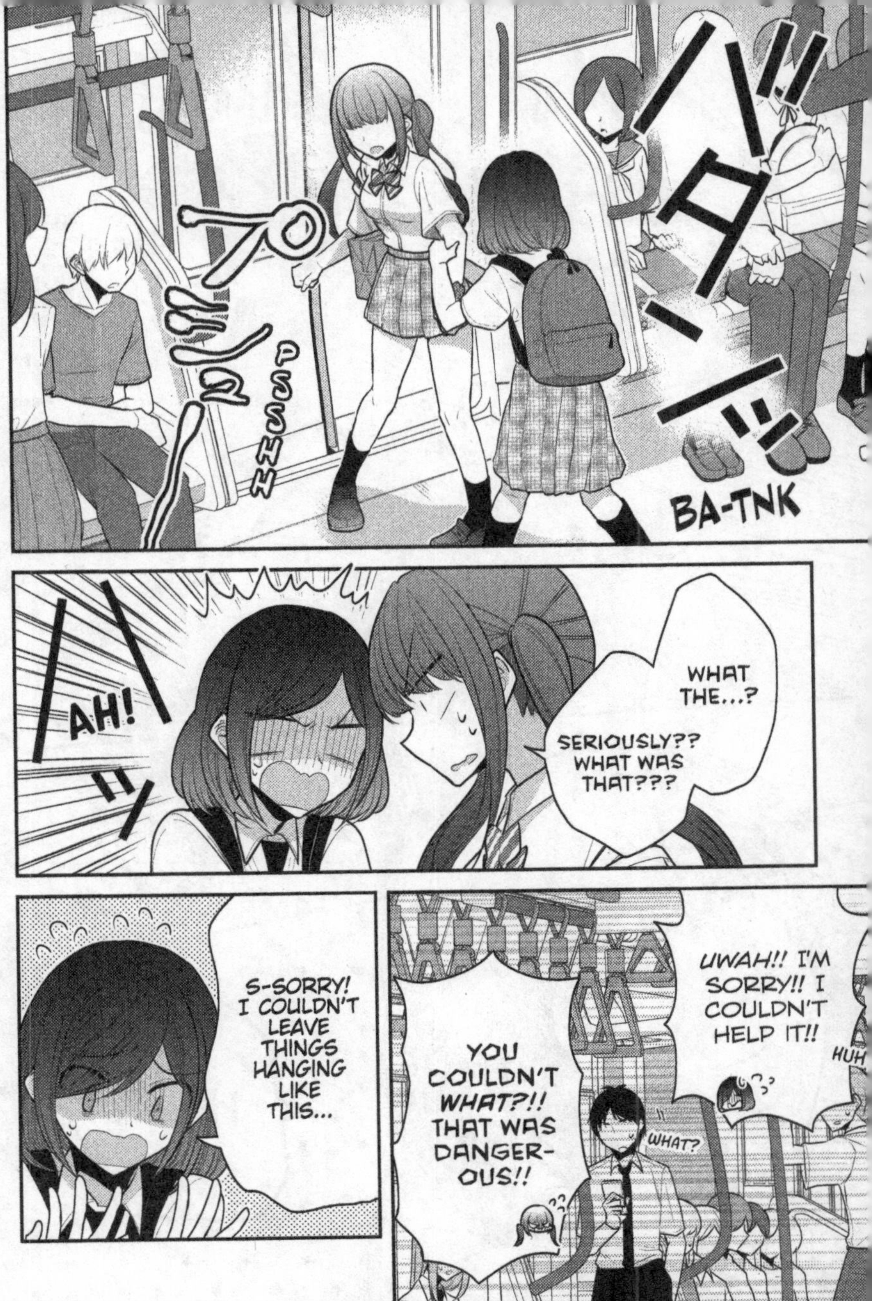
BA-TNK
PSSHHH
WHAT THE...?
SERIOUSLY?? WHAT WAS THAT???
AH!
UWAH!! I'M SORRY!! I COULDN'T HELP IT!!
HUH
YOU COULDN'T WHAT?!! THAT WAS DANGER-OUS!!
WHAT?
S-SORRY! I COULDN'T LEAVE THINGS HANGING LIKE THIS...

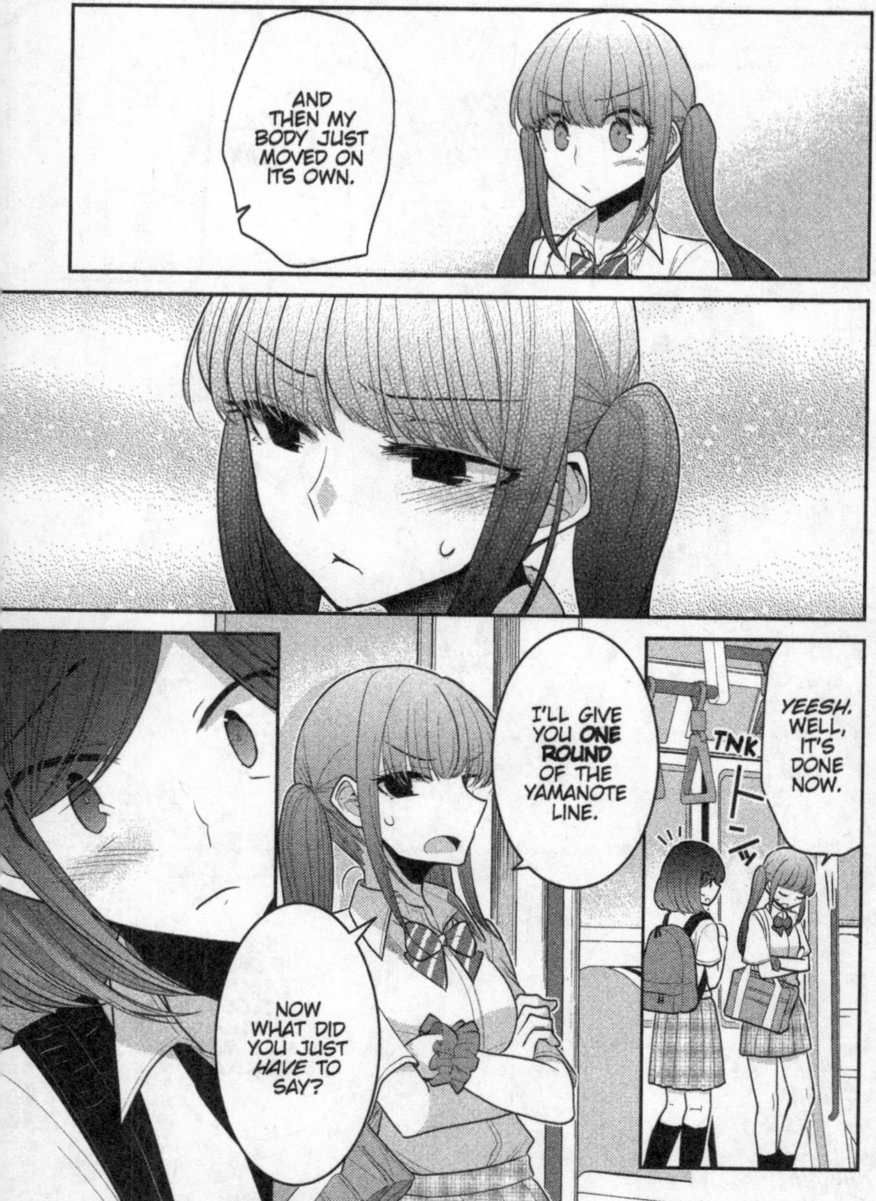
AND THEN MY BODY JUST MOVED ON ITS OWN.
TNK
YEESH. WELL, IT'S DONE NOW.
I'LL GIVE YOU **ONE ROUND** OF THE YAMANOTE LINE.
NOW WHAT DID YOU JUST *HAVE* TO SAY?

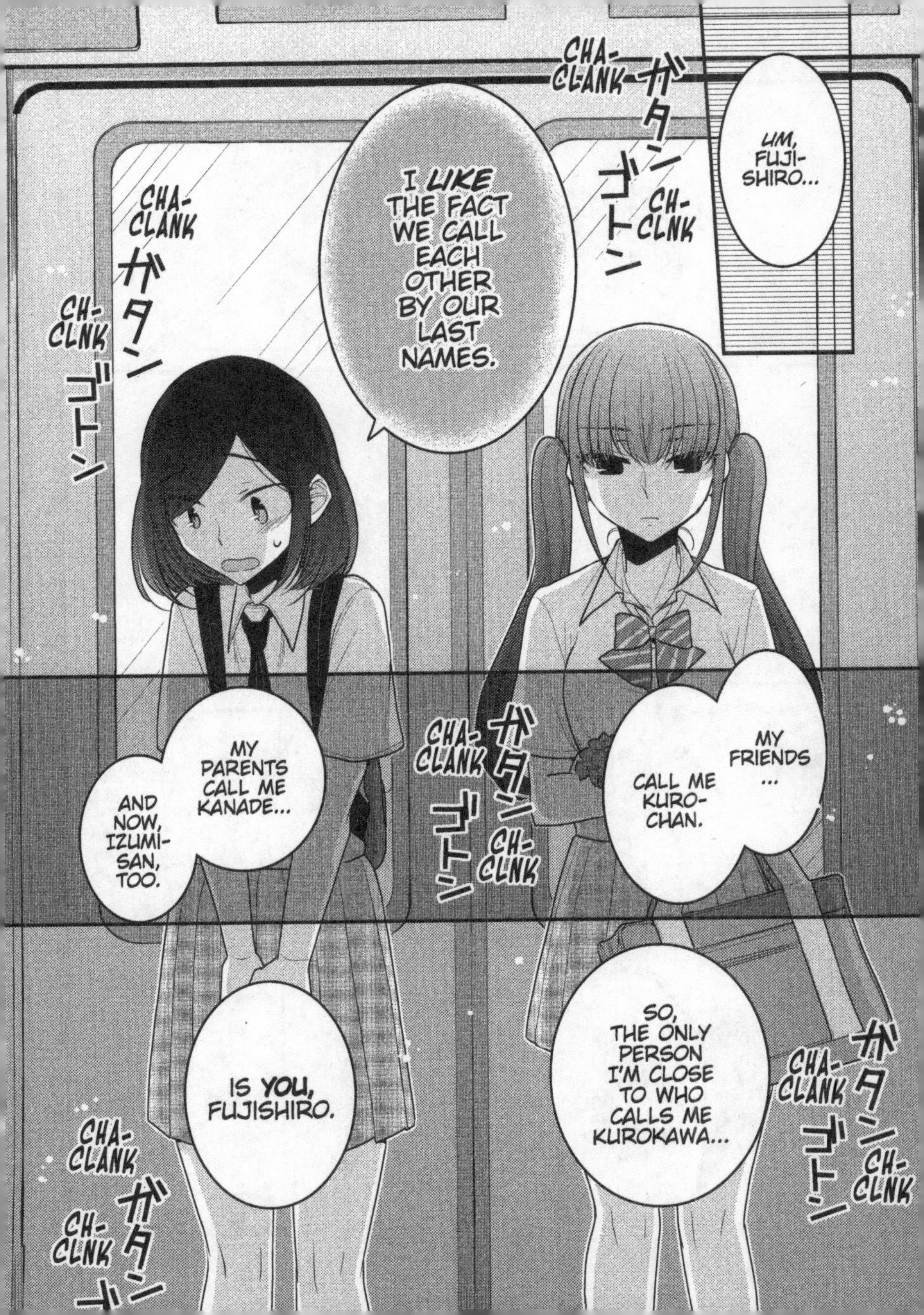
CHA-CLANK
ガタン
UM, FUJI-SHIRO...
CH-CLNK
ゴトン
I LIKE THE FACT WE CALL EACH OTHER BY OUR LAST NAMES.
CHA-CLANK
ガタン
CH-CLNK
ゴトン
MY FRIENDS ...
CALL ME KURO-CHAN.
CHA-CLANK
ガタン
CH-CLNK
ゴトン
MY PARENTS CALL ME KANADE...
AND NOW, IZUMI-SAN, TOO.
CHA-CLANK
ガタン
CH-CLNK
ゴトン
SO, THE ONLY PERSON I'M CLOSE TO WHO CALLS ME KUROKAWA...
IS YOU, FUJISHIRO.
CHA-CLANK
ガタン
CH-CLNK

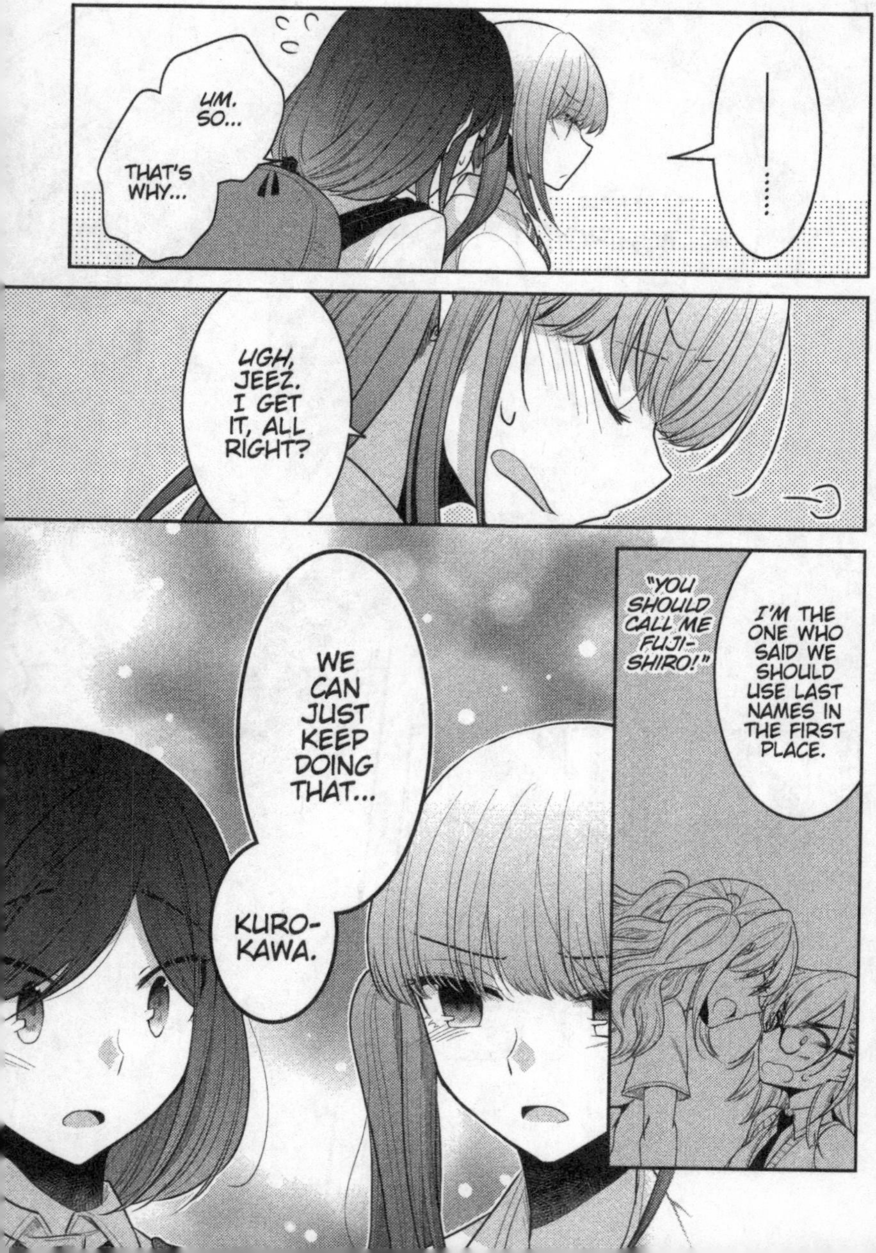
—......
UM. SO...
THAT'S WHY...
UGH, JEEZ. I GET IT, ALL RIGHT?
I'M THE ONE WHO SAID WE SHOULD USE LAST NAMES IN THE FIRST PLACE.
"YOU SHOULD CALL ME FUJI-SHIRO!"
WE CAN JUST KEEP DOING THAT...
KURO-KAWA.

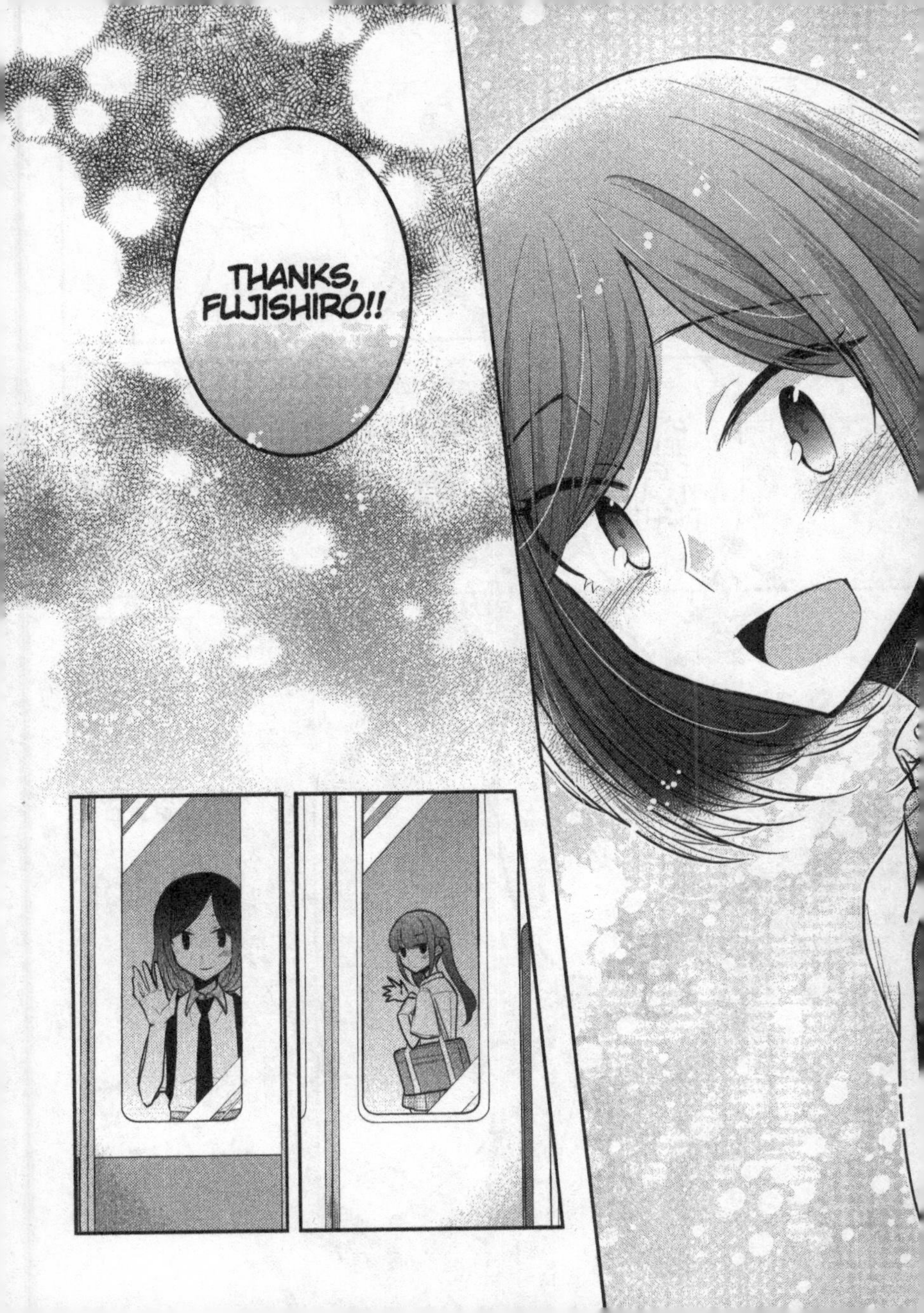
THANKS, FUJISHIRO!!

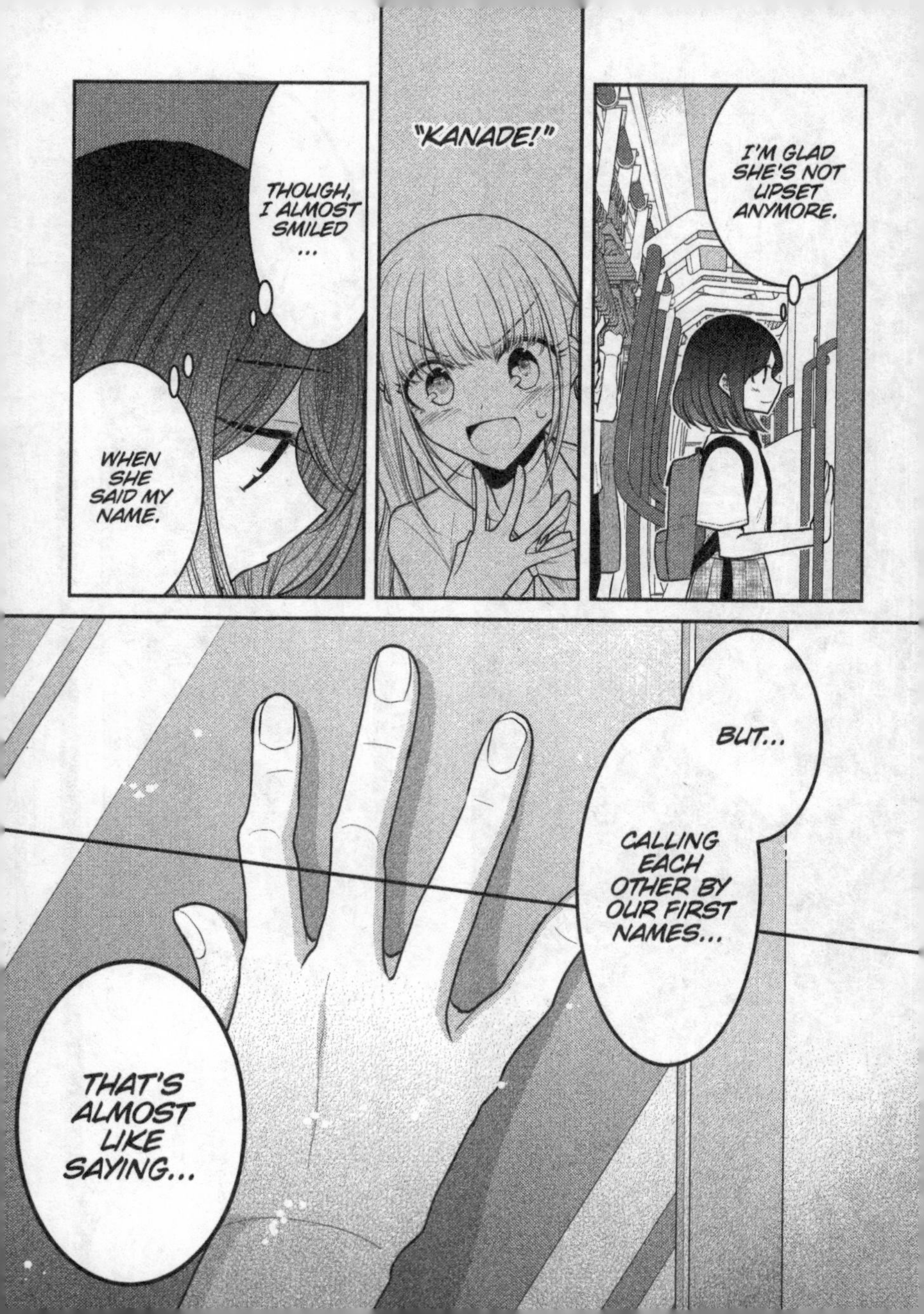
I'M GLAD SHE'S NOT UPSET ANYMORE.
"KANADE!"
THOUGH, I ALMOST SMILED ...
WHEN SHE SAID MY NAME.
BUT...
CALLING EACH OTHER BY OUR FIRST NAMES...
THAT'S ALMOST LIKE SAYING...

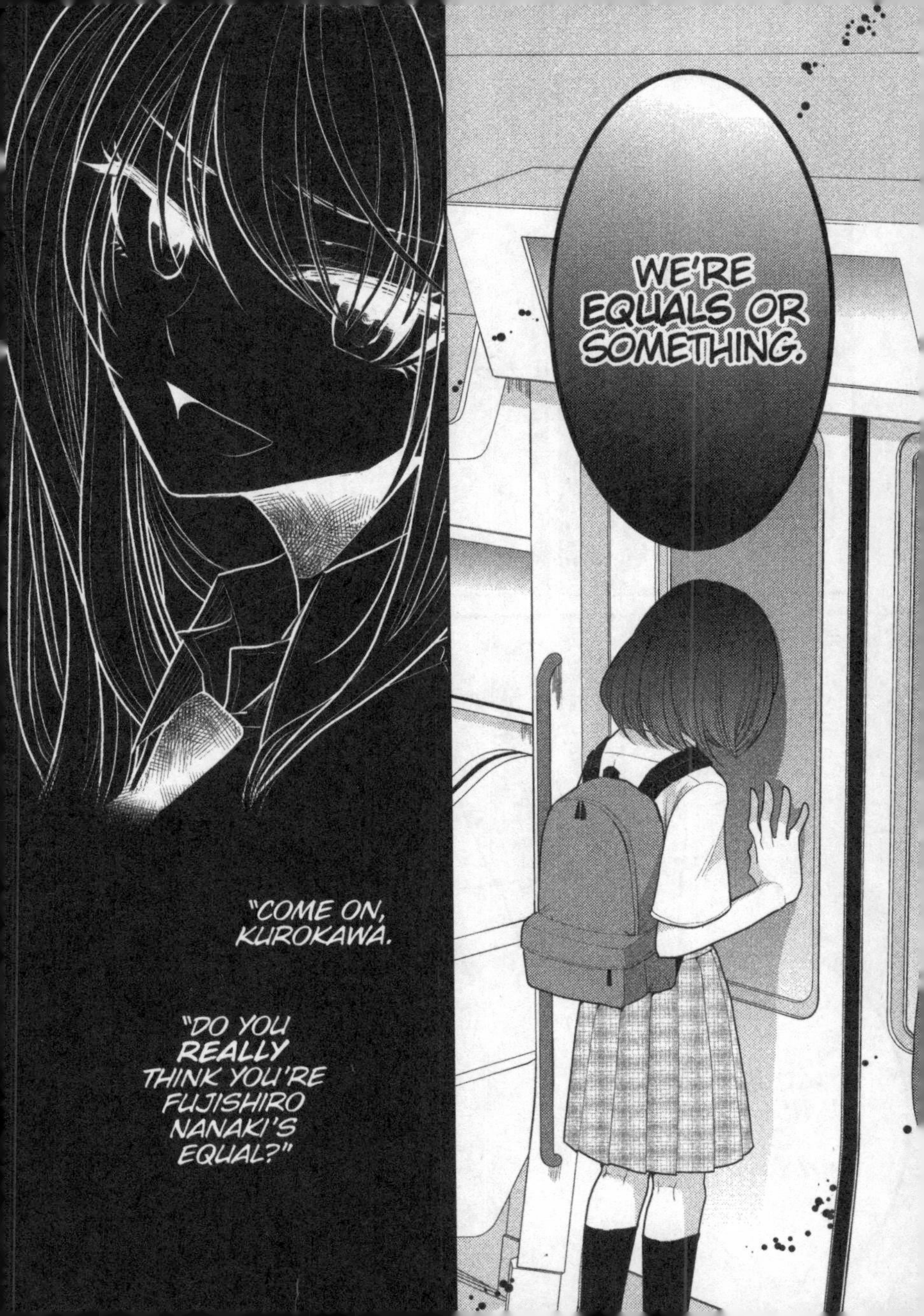
WE'RE EQUALS OR SOMETHING.
"COME ON, KUROKAWA.
"DO YOU REALLY THINK YOU'RE FUJISHIRO NANAKI'S EQUAL?"

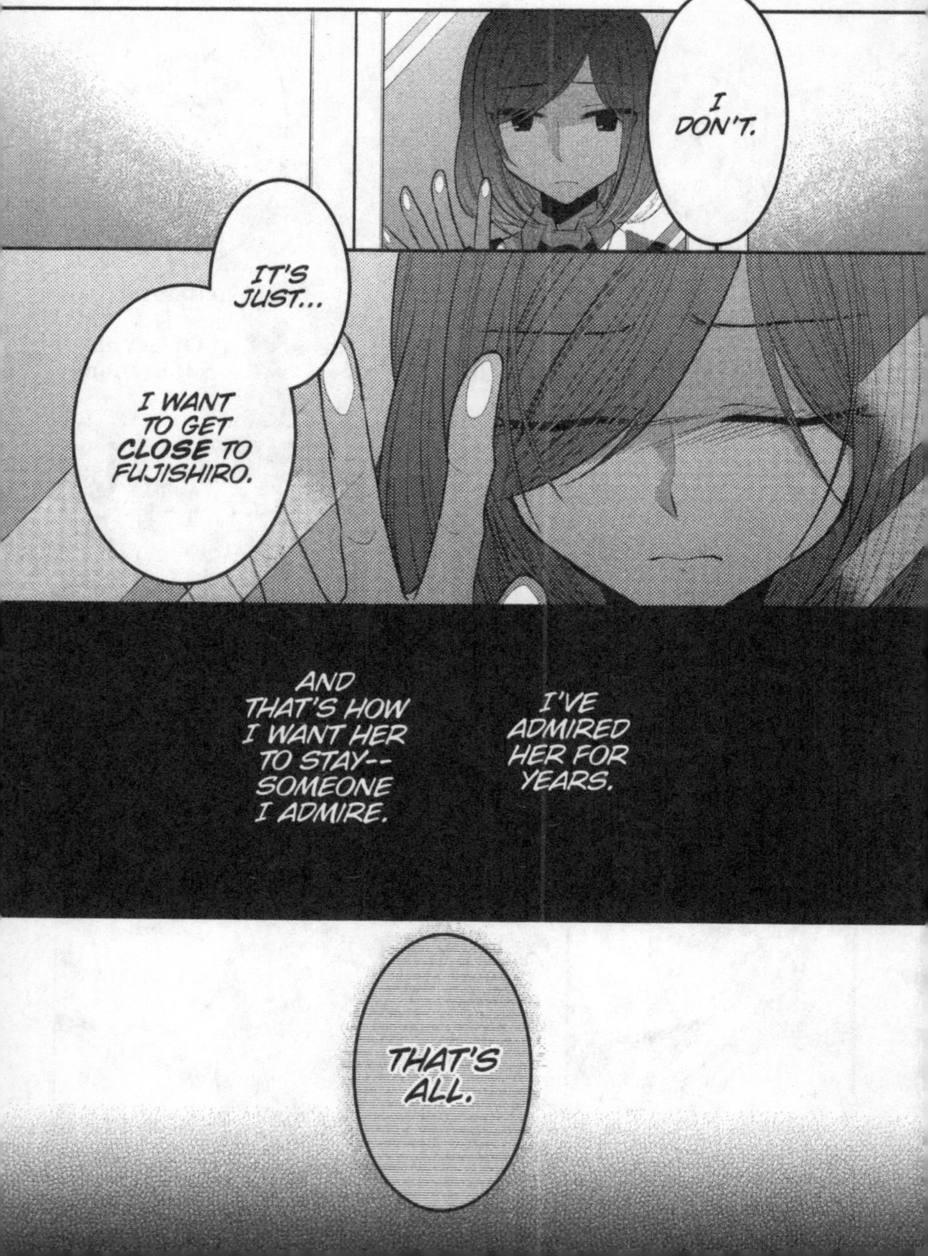
I DON'T.
IT'S JUST...
I WANT TO GET CLOSE TO FUJISHIRO.
I'VE ADMIRED HER FOR YEARS.
AND THAT'S HOW I WANT HER TO STAY-- SOMEONE I ADMIRE.
THAT'S ALL.

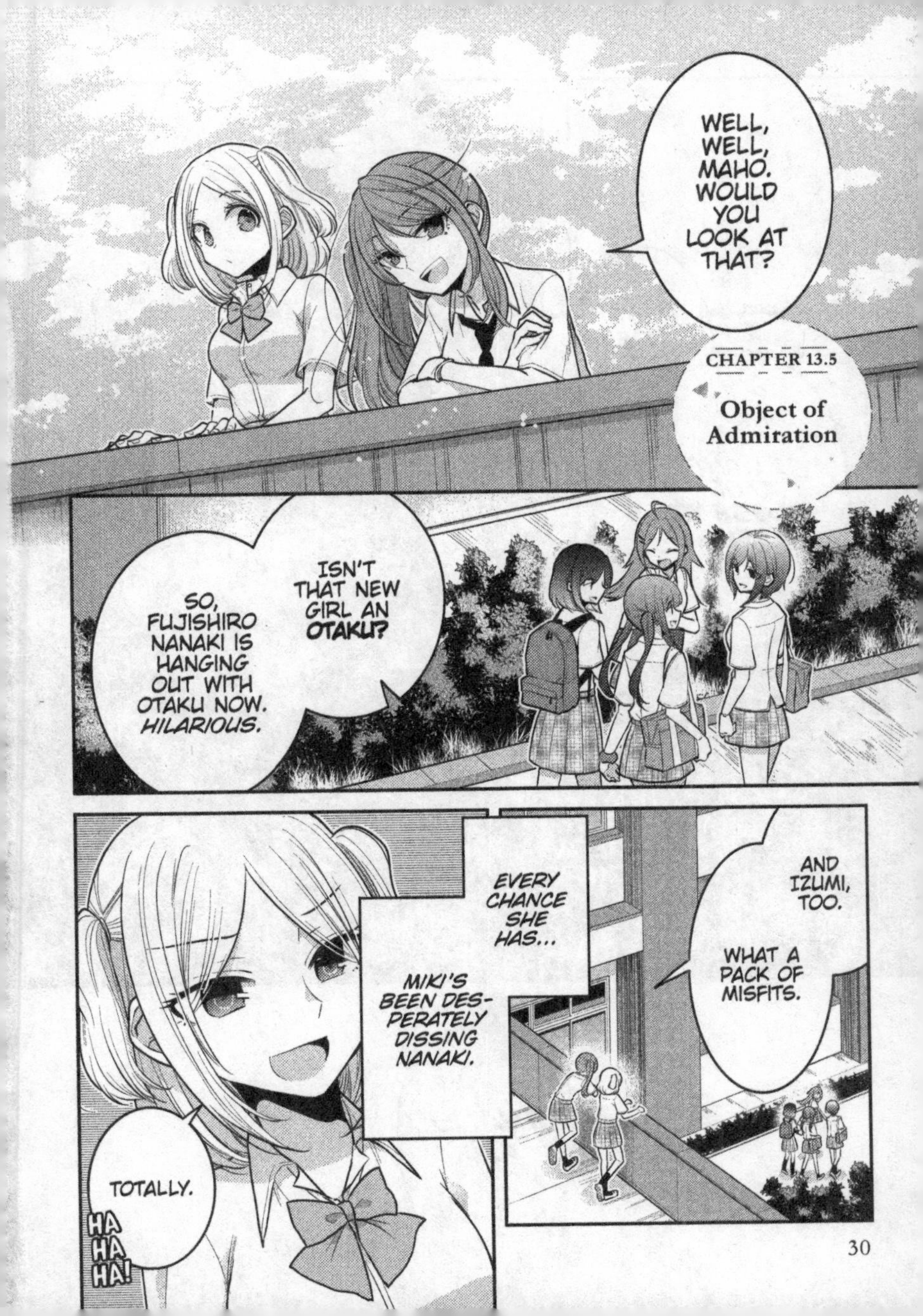
WELL, WELL, MAHO. WOULD YOU LOOK AT THAT?
CHAPTER 13.5
Object of Admiration
ISN'T THAT NEW GIRL AN **OTAKU?**
SO, FUJISHIRO NANAKI IS HANGING OUT WITH OTAKU NOW. *HILARIOUS.*
AND IZUMI, TOO.
WHAT A PACK OF MISFITS.
EVERY CHANCE SHE HAS...
MIKI'S BEEN DES-PERATELY DISSING NANAKI.
TOTALLY.
HA HA HA!

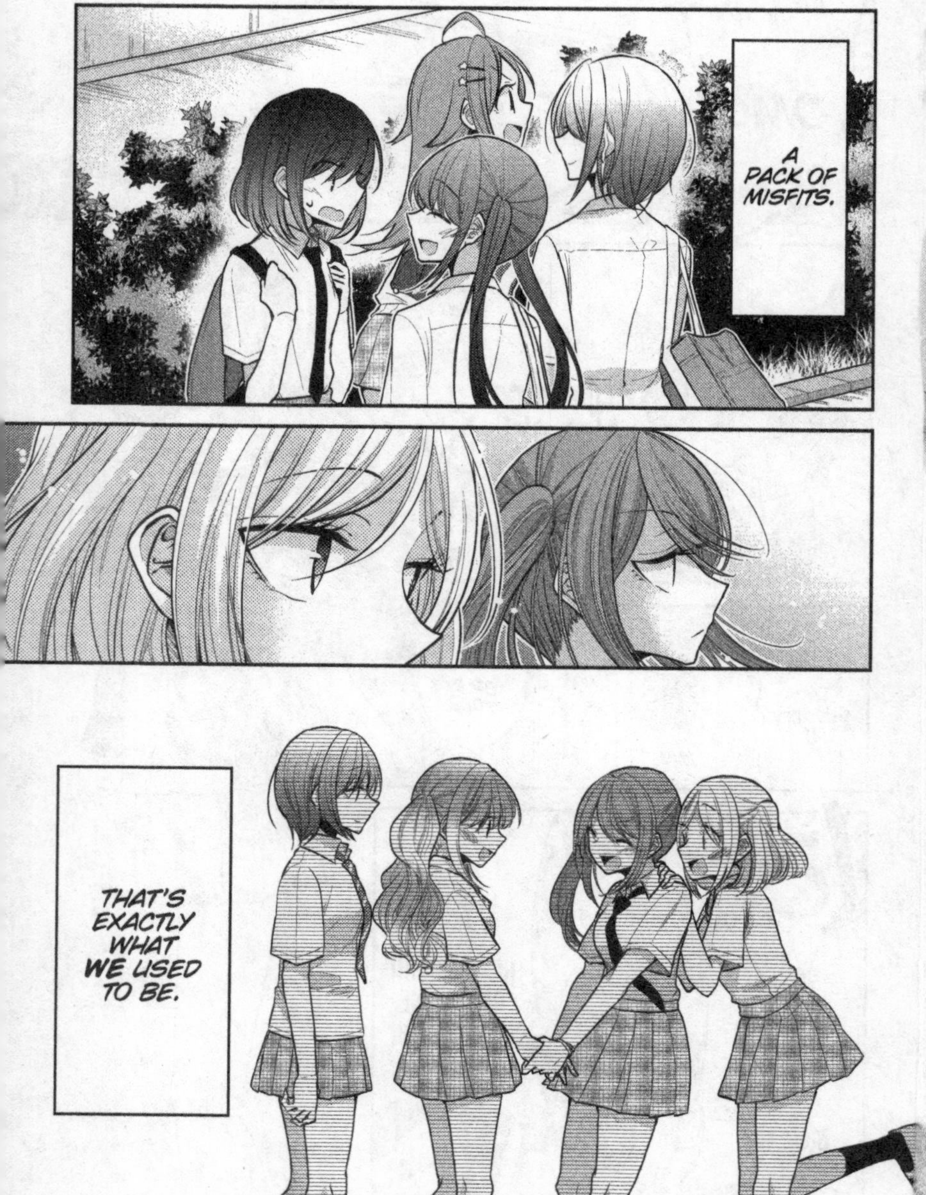
A PACK OF MISFITS.
THAT'S EXACTLY WHAT WE USED TO BE.

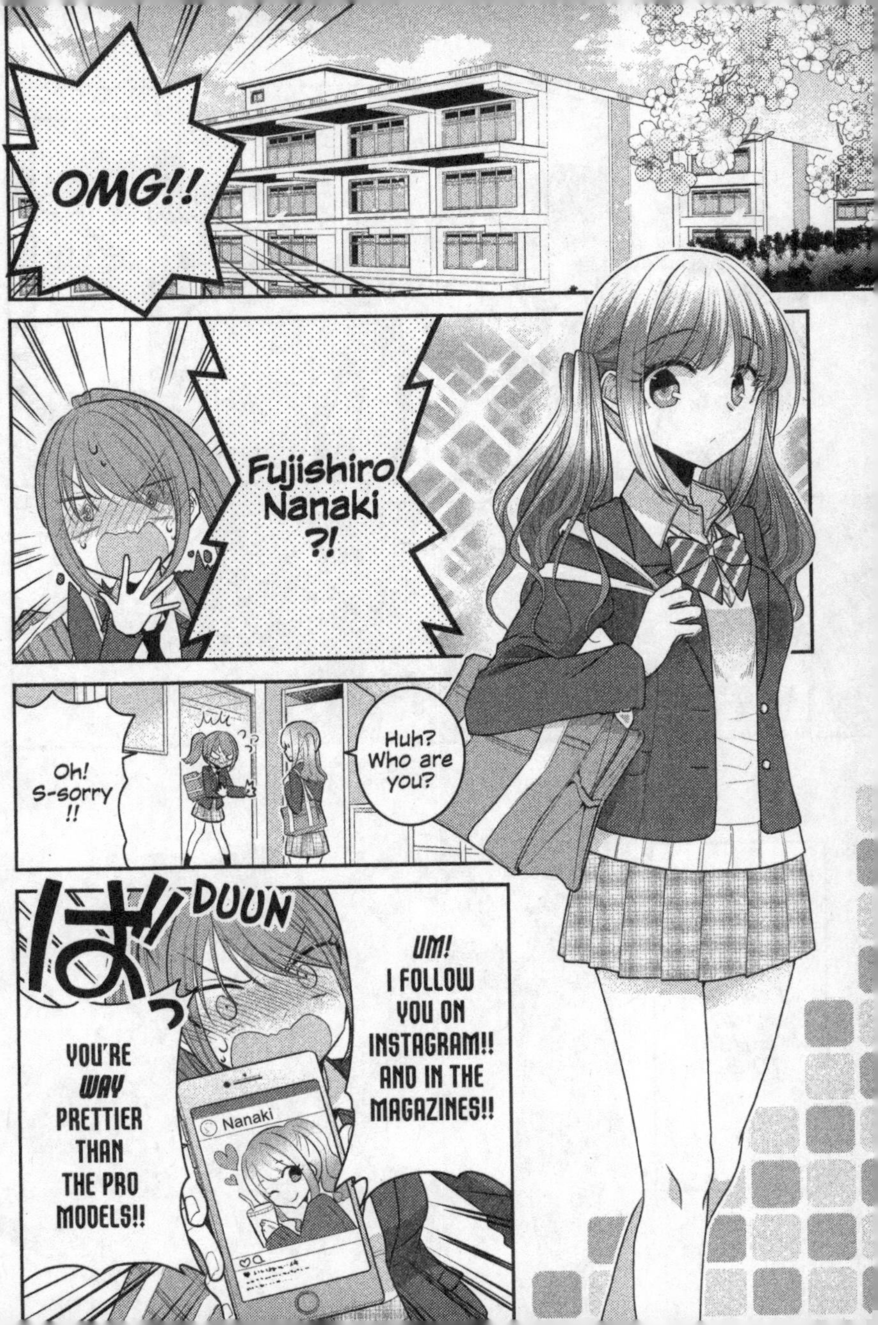
OMG!!
Fujishiro Nanaki ?!
Huh? Who are you?
Oh! S-sorry !!
ぱ!!っ
DUUN
UM! I FOLLOW YOU ON INSTAGRAM!! AND IN THE MAGAZINES!!
YOU'RE WAY PRETTIER THAN THE PRO MODELS!!
Nanaki

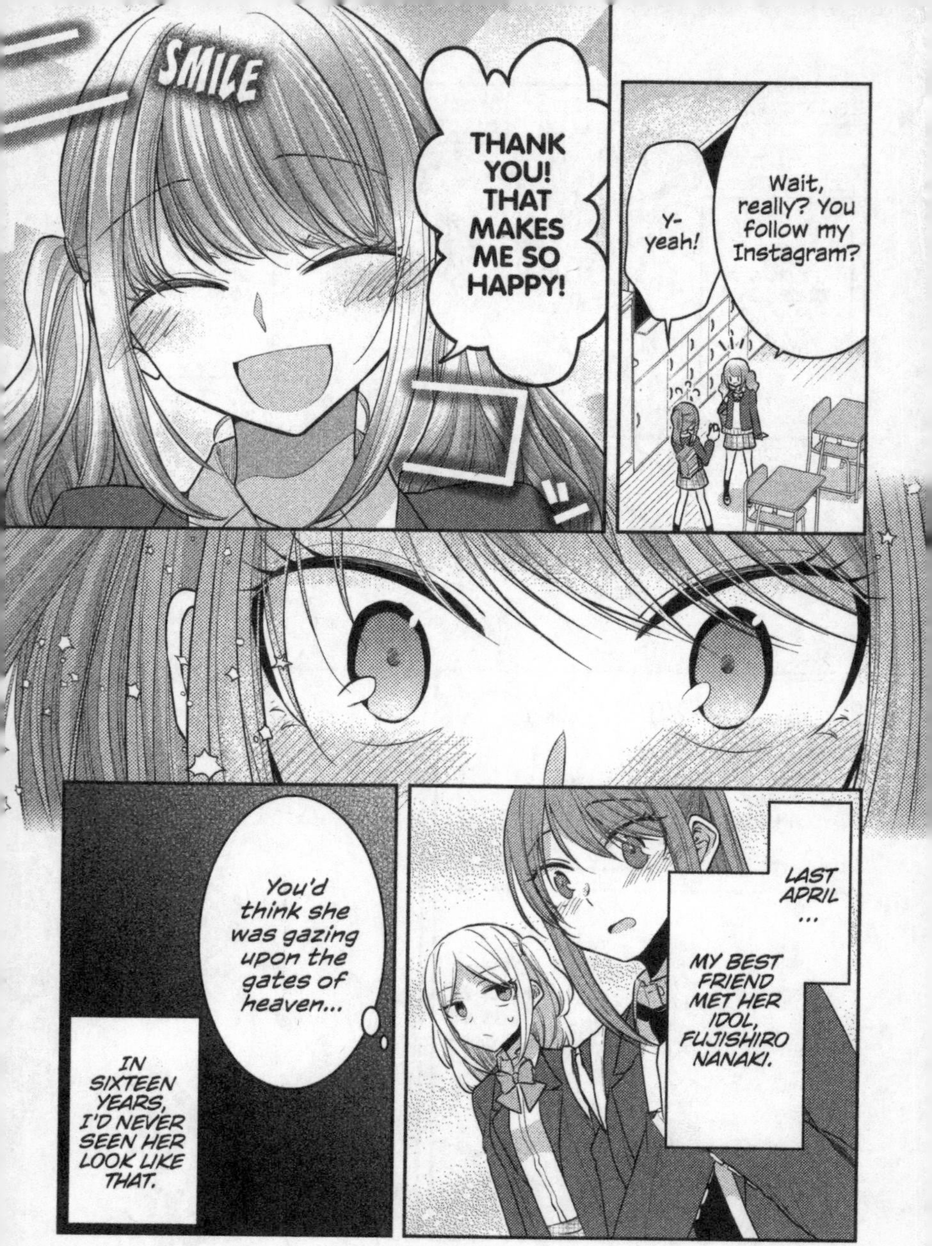
Wait, really? You follow my Instagram?
Y-yeah!
SMILE
THANK YOU! THAT MAKES ME SO HAPPY!
LAST APRIL...
MY BEST FRIEND MET HER IDOL, FUJISHIRO NANAKI.
You'd think she was gazing upon the gates of heaven...
IN SIXTEEN YEARS, I'D NEVER SEEN HER LOOK LIKE THAT.

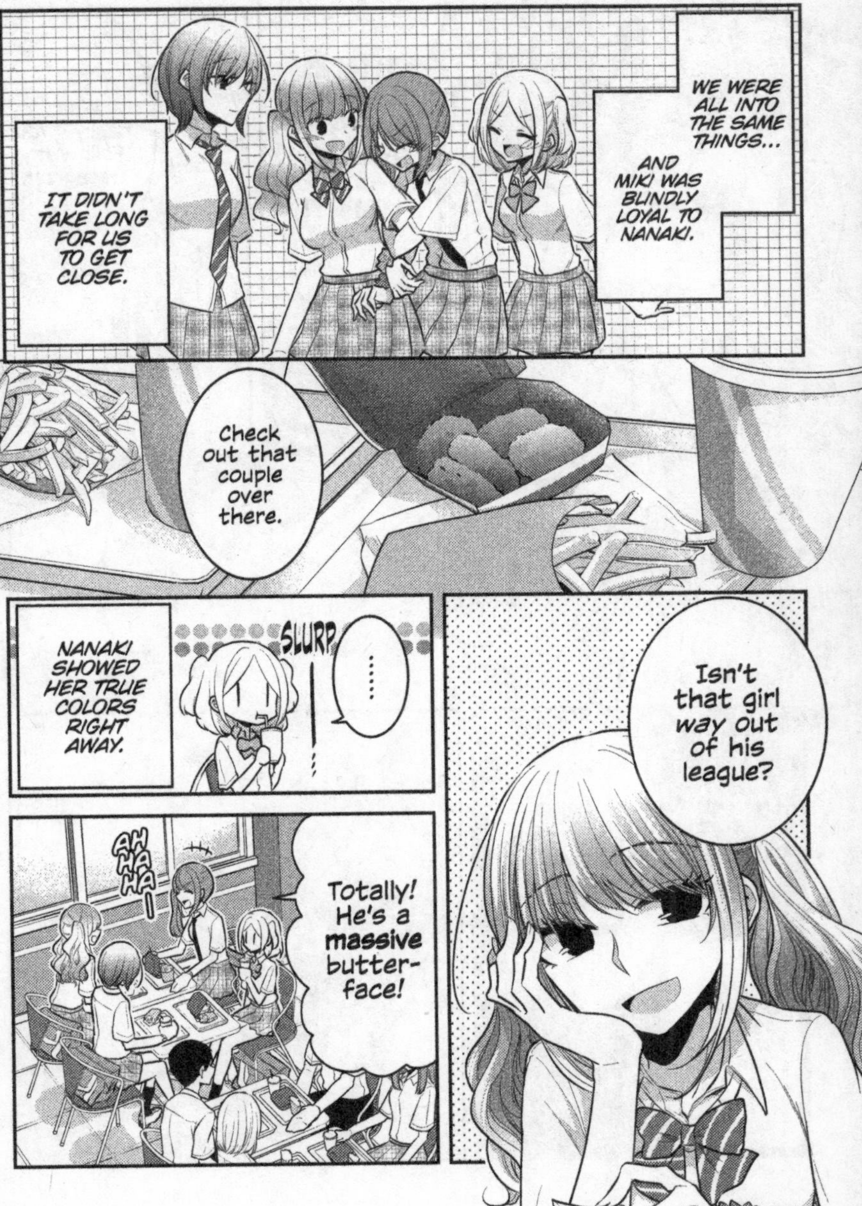

WE WERE ALL INTO THE SAME THINGS...
AND MIKI WAS BLINDLY LOYAL TO NANAKI.
IT DIDN'T TAKE LONG FOR US TO GET CLOSE.
Check out that couple over there.
Isn't that girl way out of his league?
NANAKI SHOWED HER TRUE COLORS RIGHT AWAY.
......
SLURP
Totally! He's a **massive** butter-face!
AH HA HA HA!

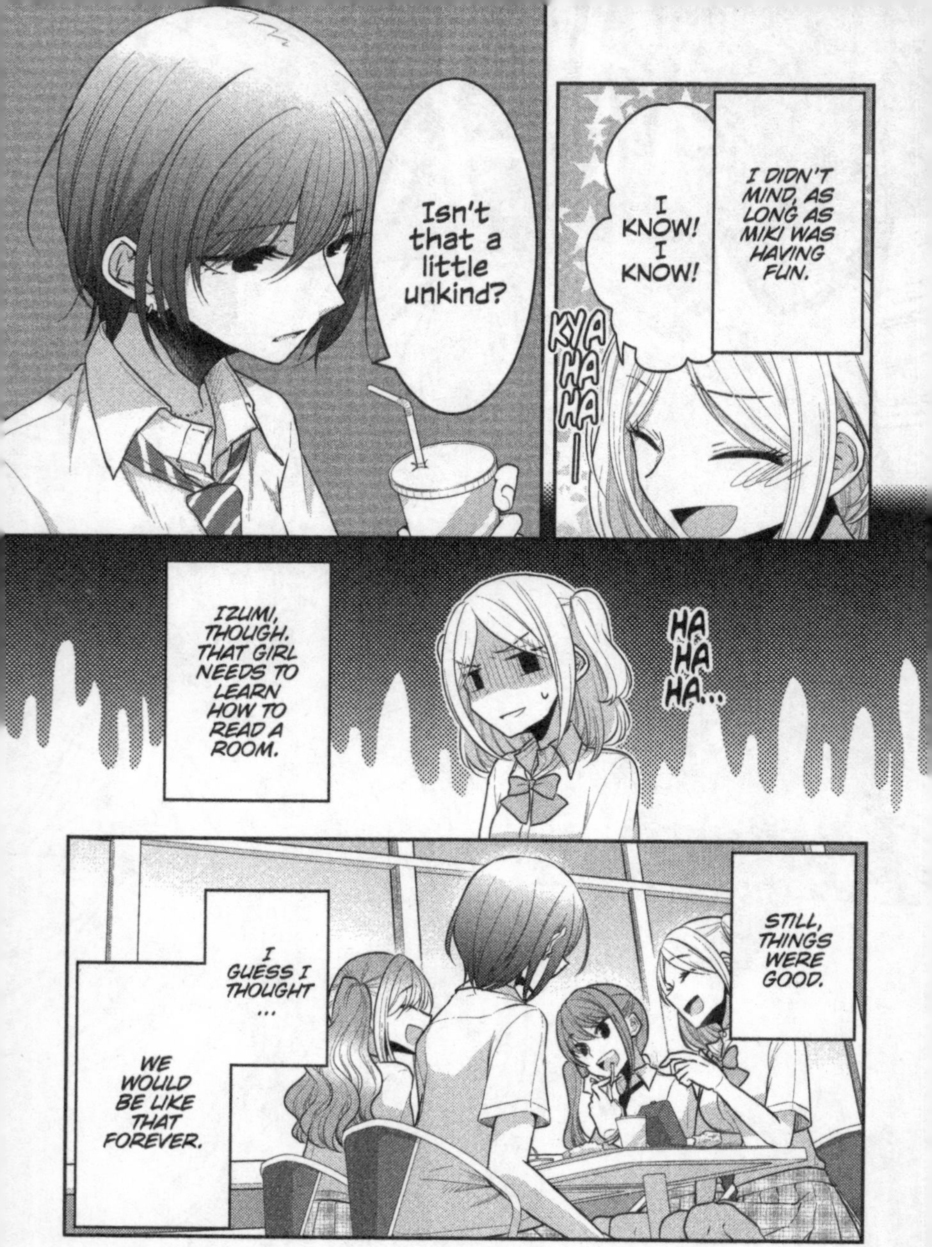
I DIDN'T MIND, AS LONG AS MIKI WAS HAVING FUN.
I KNOW! I KNOW!
KYA HA HA HA —
Isn't that a little unkind?
IZUMI, THOUGH. THAT GIRL NEEDS TO LEARN HOW TO READ A ROOM.
HA HA HA...
STILL, THINGS WERE GOOD.
I GUESS I THOUGHT...
WE WOULD BE LIKE THAT FOREVER.

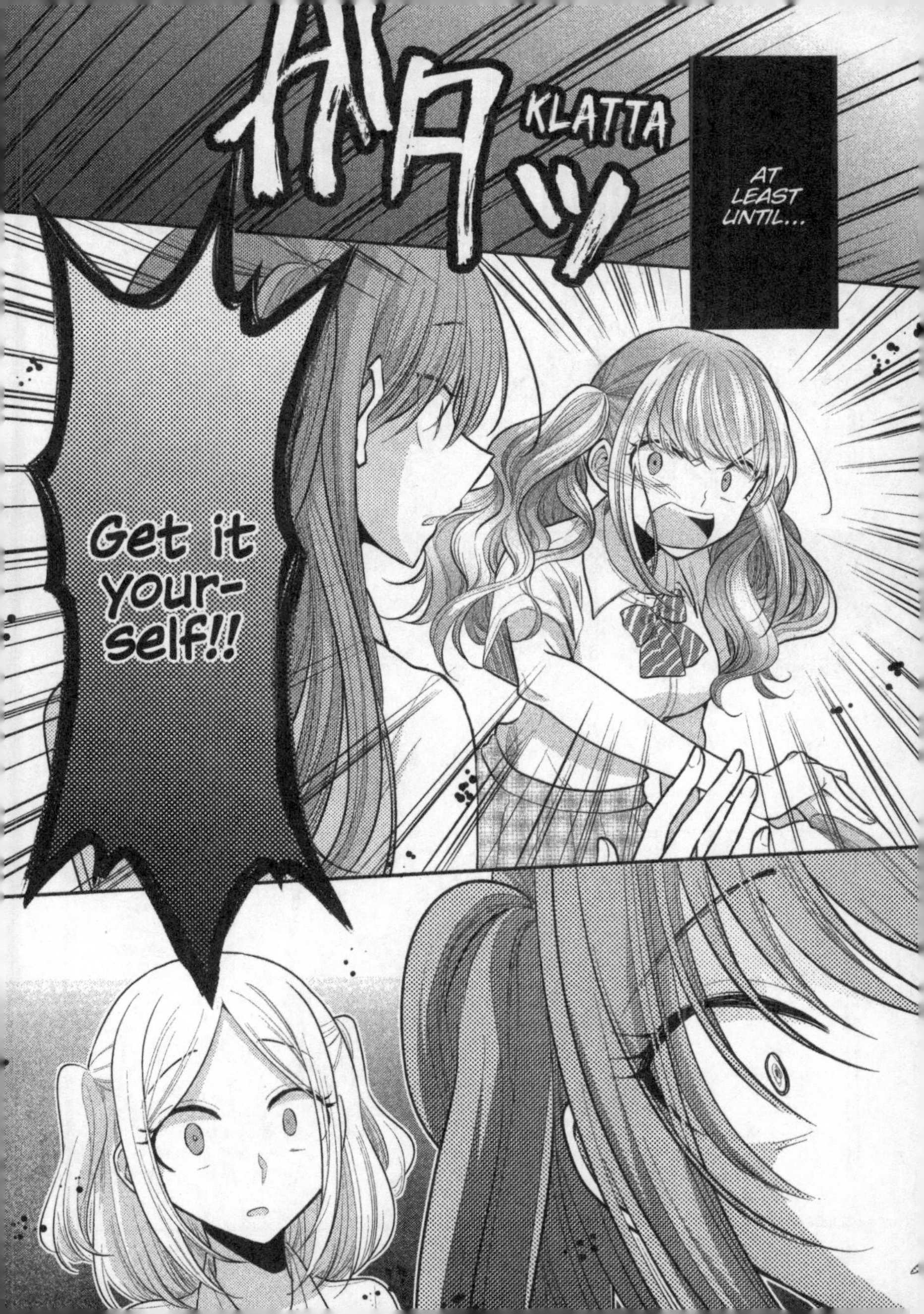
AT LEAST UNTIL...
KLATTA
Get it your-self!!

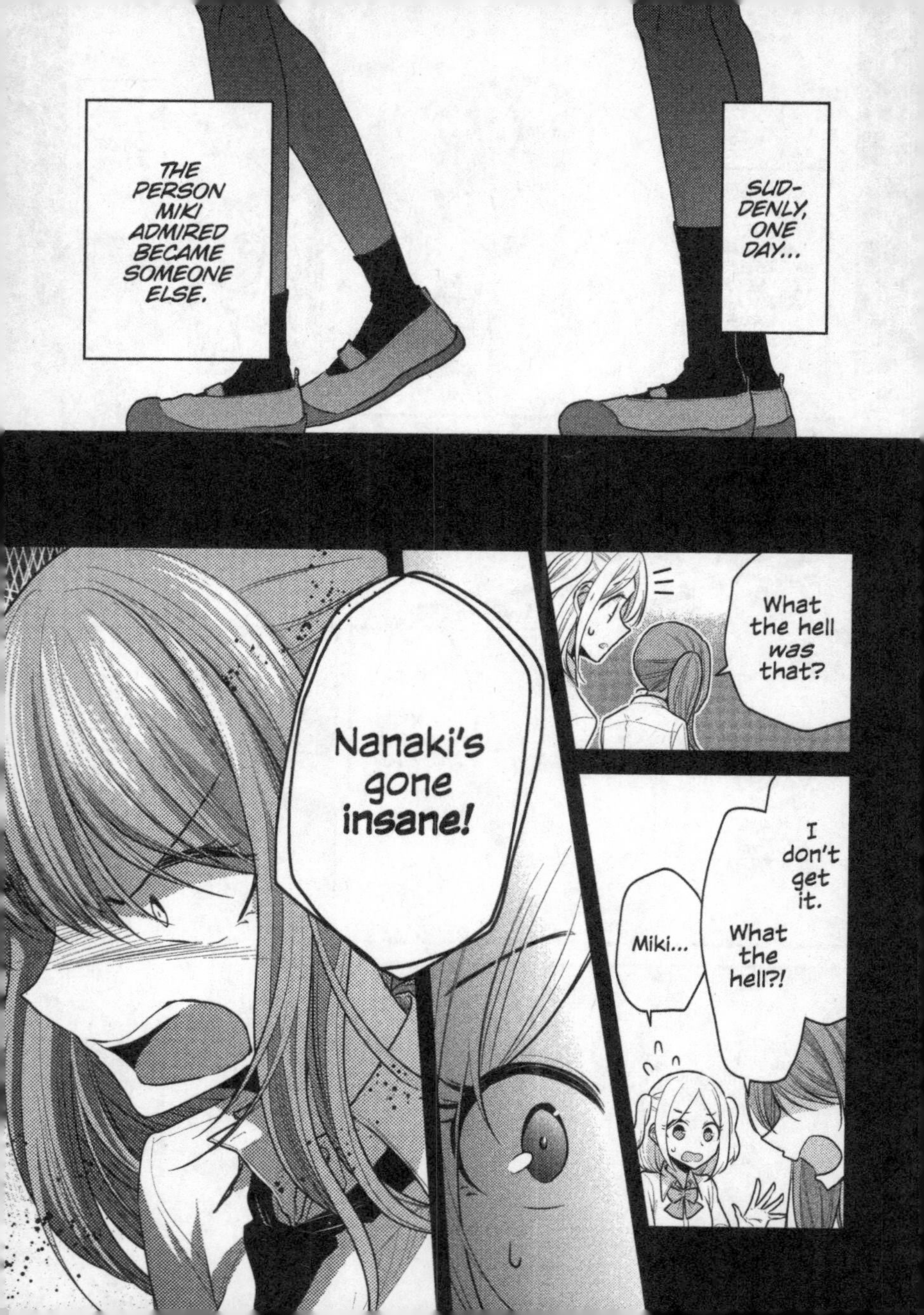
SUDDENLY, ONE DAY...
THE PERSON MIKI ADMIRED BECAME SOMEONE ELSE.
What the hell was that?
I don't get it.
What the hell?!
Miki...
Nanaki's gone insane!

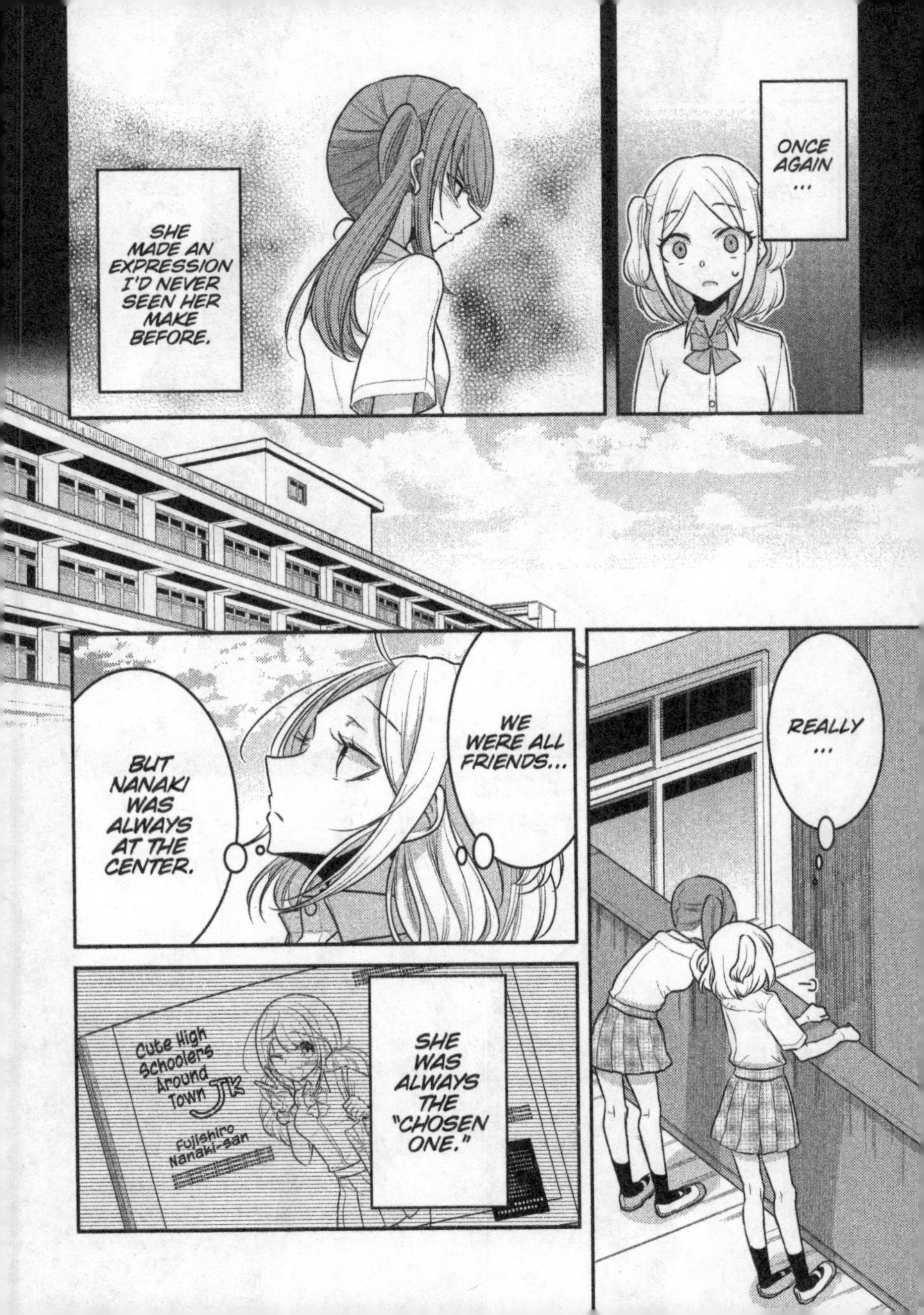
ONCE AGAIN ...
SHE MADE AN EXPRESSION I'D NEVER SEEN HER MAKE BEFORE.
REALLY ...
WE WERE ALL FRIENDS...
BUT NANAKI WAS ALWAYS AT THE CENTER.
SHE WAS ALWAYS THE "CHOSEN ONE."
Cute High Schoolers Around Town
Fujishiro Nanaki-san

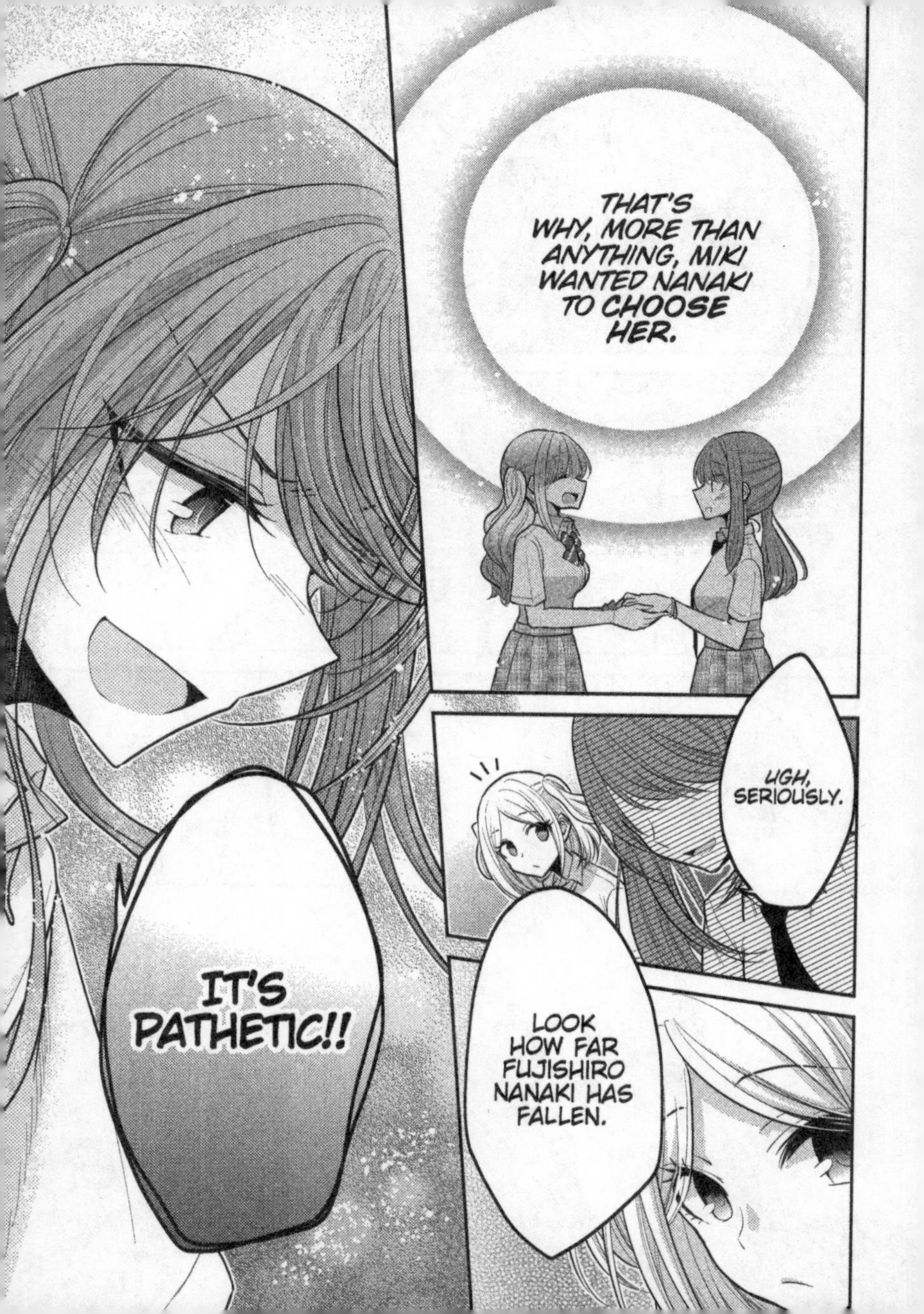
THAT'S WHY, MORE THAN ANYTHING, MIKI WANTED NANAKI TO CHOOSE HER.
UGH, SERIOUSLY.
LOOK HOW FAR FUJISHIRO NANAKI HAS FALLEN.
IT'S PATHETIC!!

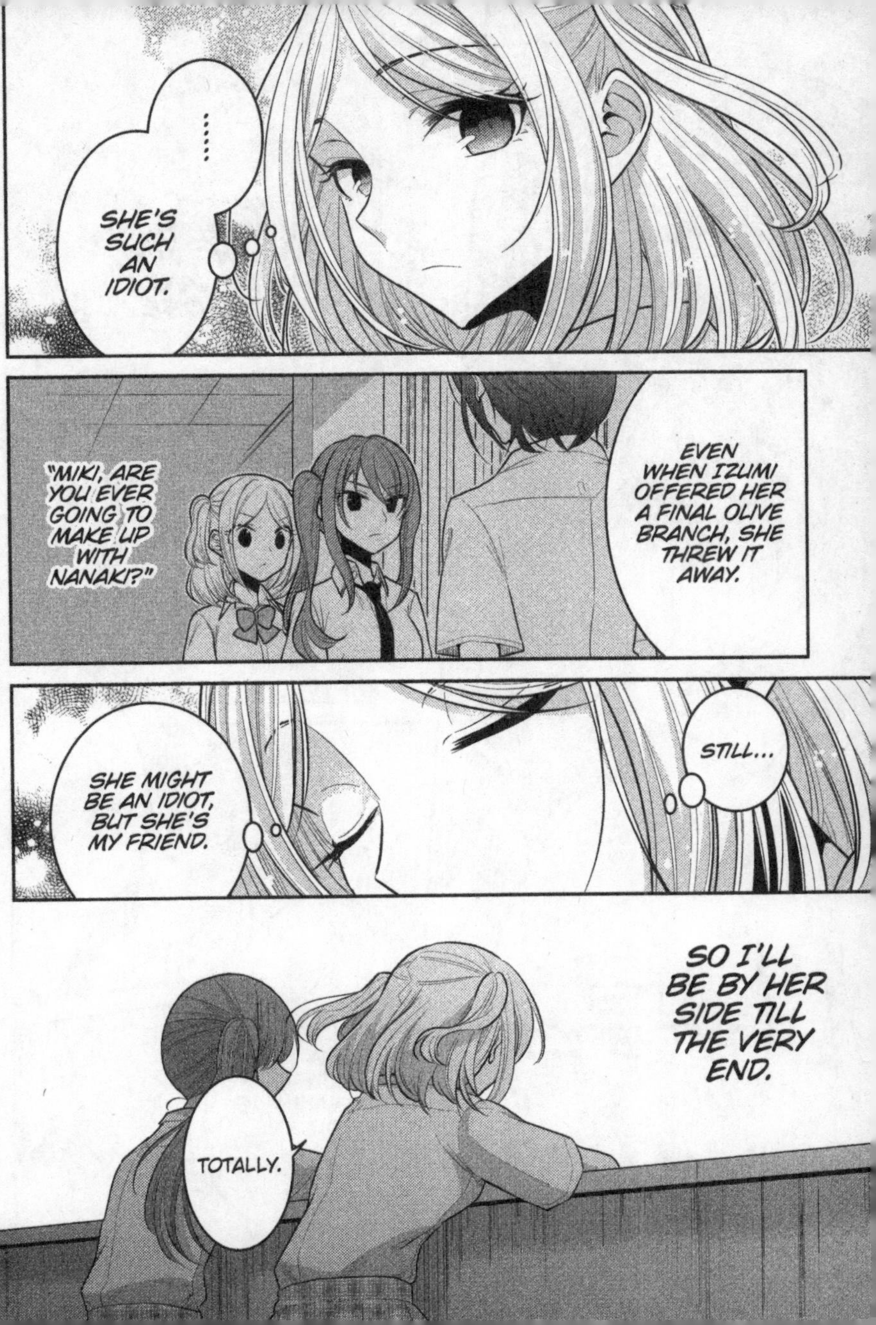
......
SHE'S SUCH AN IDIOT.
EVEN WHEN IZUMI OFFERED HER A FINAL OLIVE BRANCH, SHE THREW IT AWAY.
"MIKI, ARE YOU EVER GOING TO MAKE UP WITH NANAKI?"
STILL...
SHE MIGHT BE AN IDIOT, BUT SHE'S MY FRIEND.
SO I'LL BE BY HER SIDE TILL THE VERY END.
TOTALLY.

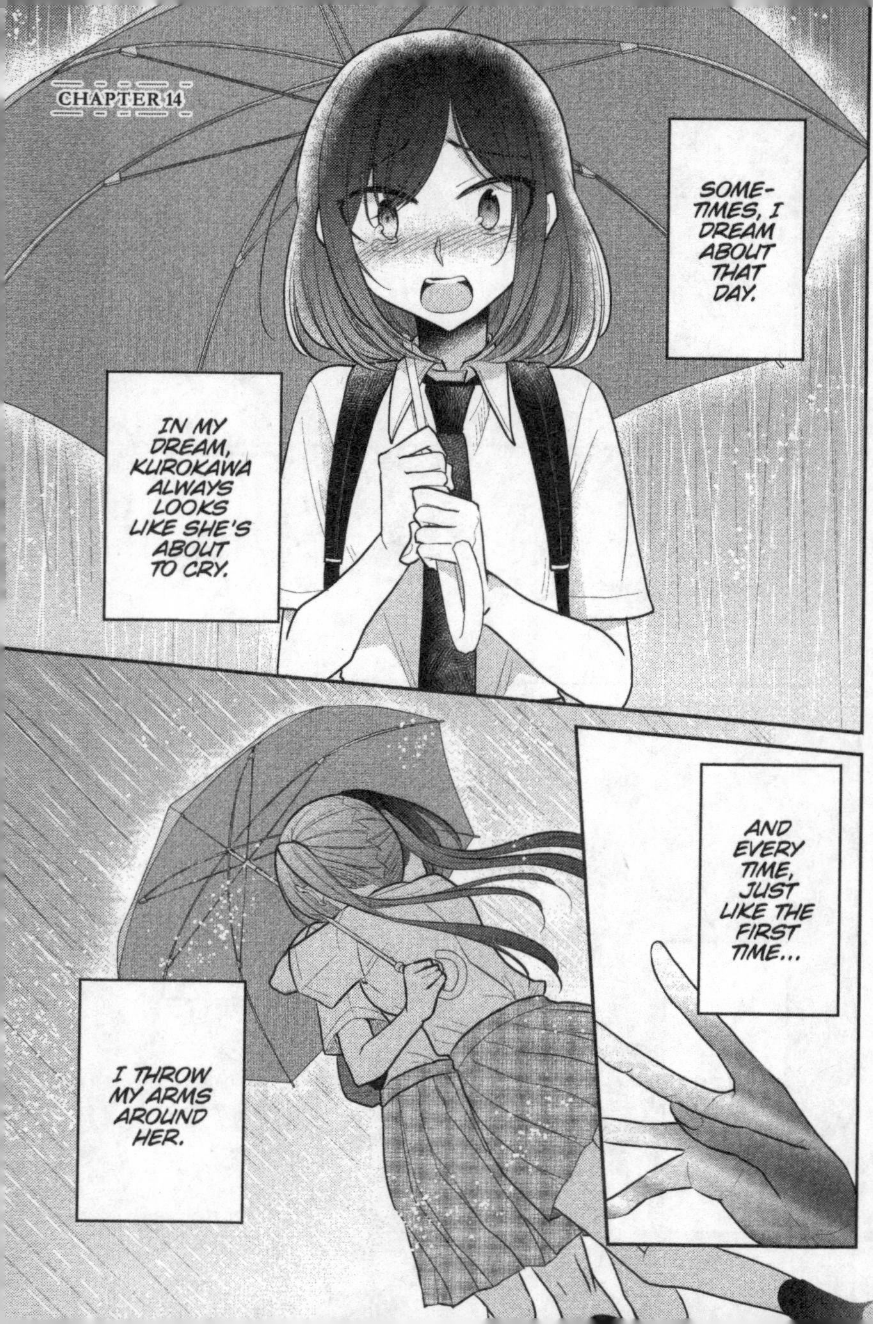
CHAPTER 14
SOME-TIMES, I DREAM ABOUT THAT DAY.
IN MY DREAM, KUROKAWA ALWAYS LOOKS LIKE SHE'S ABOUT TO CRY.
AND EVERY TIME, JUST LIKE THE FIRST TIME...
I THROW MY ARMS AROUND HER.

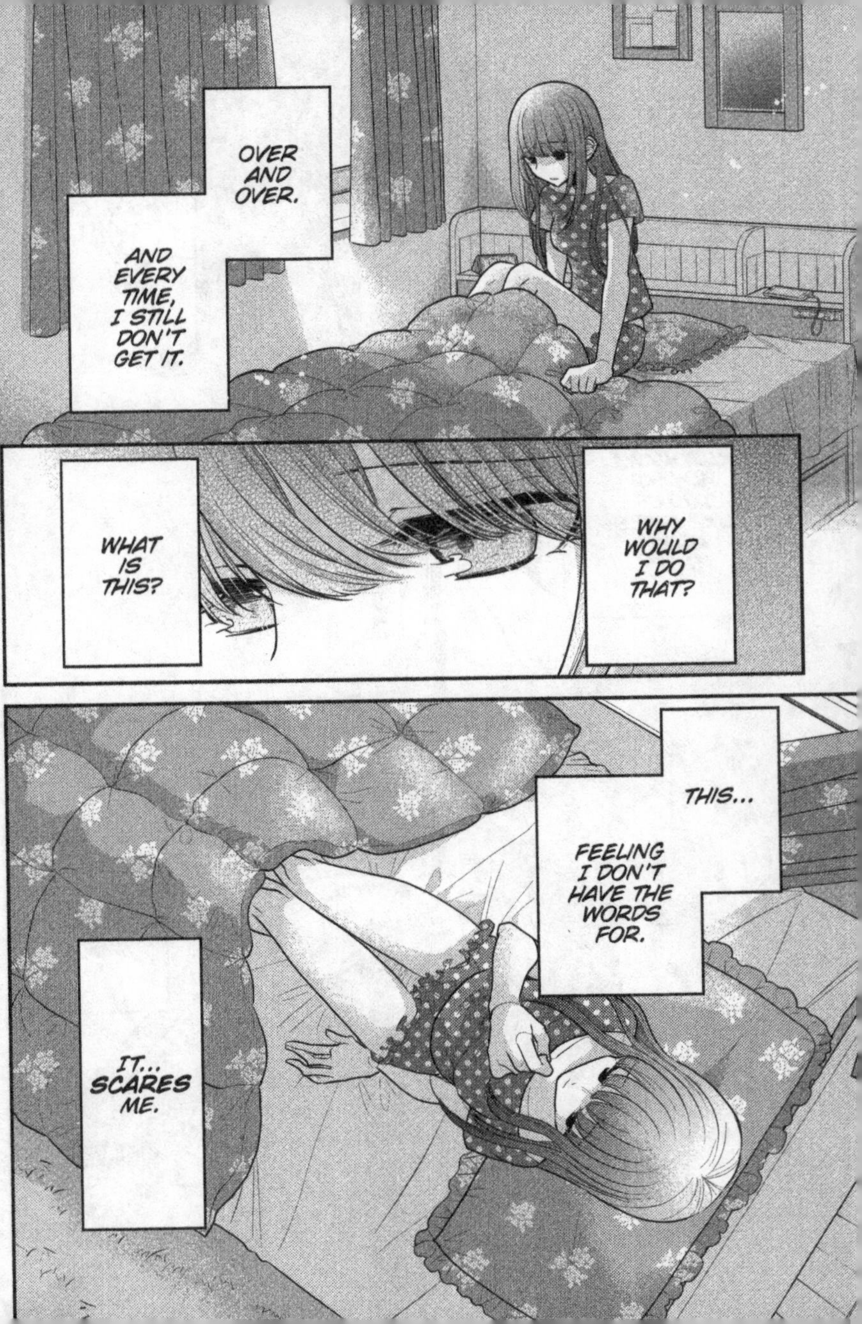
OVER AND OVER.
AND EVERY TIME, I STILL DON'T GET IT.
WHY WOULD I DO THAT?
WHAT IS THIS?
THIS...
FEELING I DON'T HAVE THE WORDS FOR.
IT... SCARES ME.

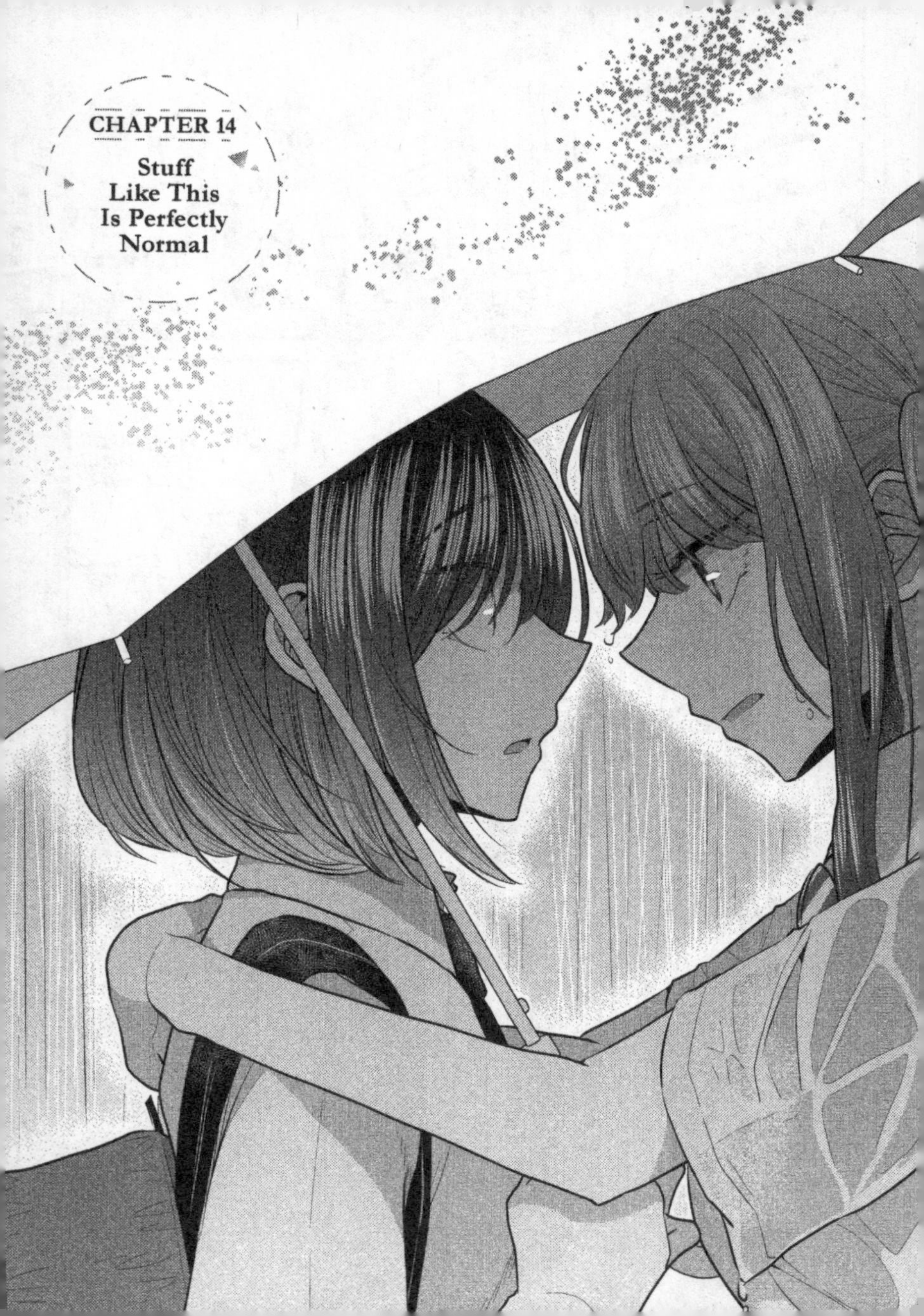
CHAPTER 14
Stuff Like This Is Perfectly Normal

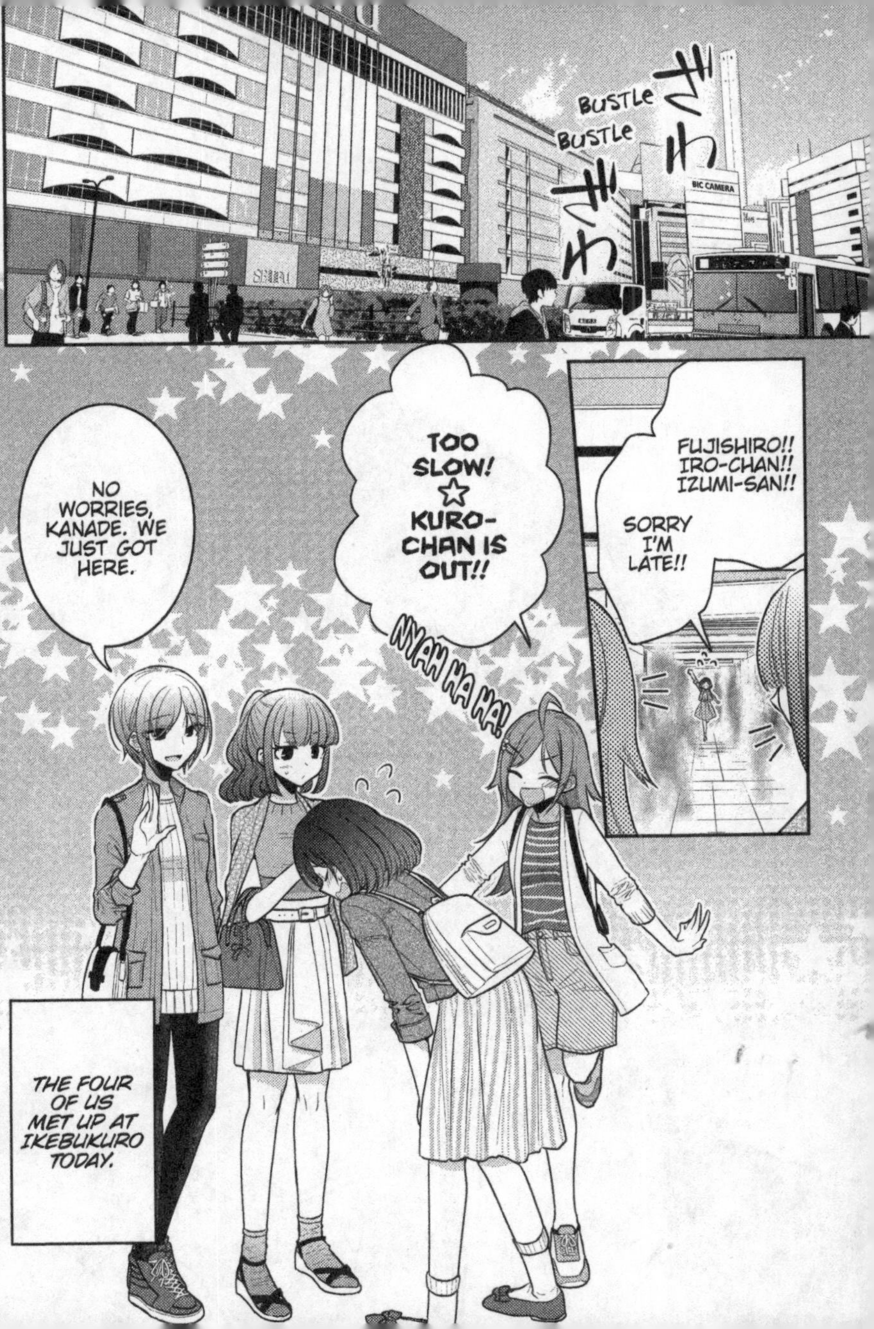
ざわ
BUSTLE
ざわ
BUSTLE
BIC CAMERA
FUJISHIRO!! IRO-CHAN!! IZUMI-SAN!!
SORRY I'M LATE!!
TOO SLOW! ☆ KURO-CHAN IS OUT!!
NYAH HA HA!
NO WORRIES, KANADE. WE JUST GOT HERE.
THE FOUR OF US MET UP AT IKEBUKURO TODAY.

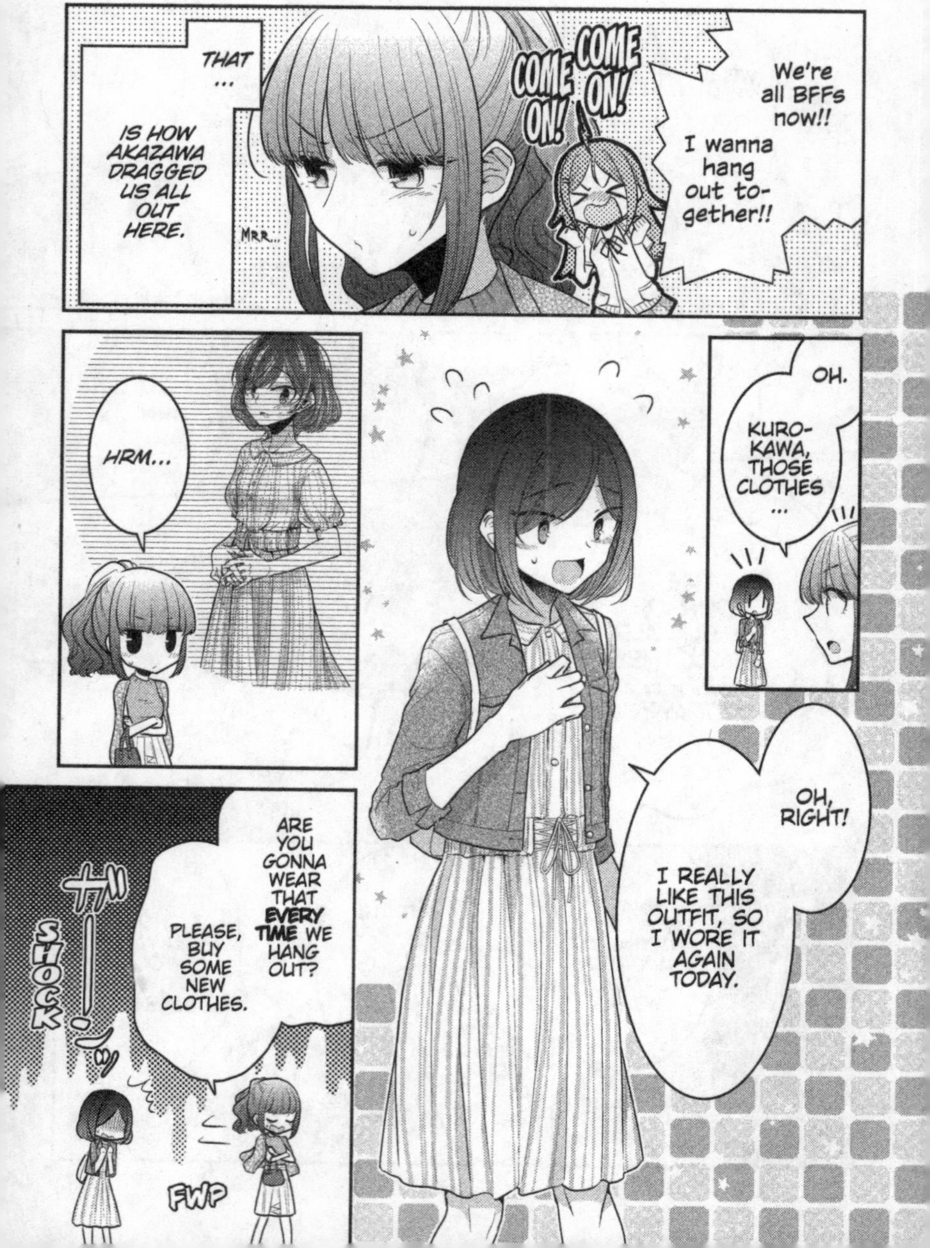
We're all BFFs now!!
I wanna hang out to-gether!!
COME ON! COME ON!
MRR...
THAT ...
IS HOW AKAZAWA DRAGGED US ALL OUT HERE.
OH.
KURO-KAWA, THOSE CLOTHES ...
OH, RIGHT!
I REALLY LIKE THIS OUTFIT, SO I WORE IT AGAIN TODAY.
HRM...
ARE YOU GONNA WEAR THAT **EVERY TIME** WE HANG OUT?
PLEASE, BUY SOME NEW CLOTHES.
SHOCK!
FWP

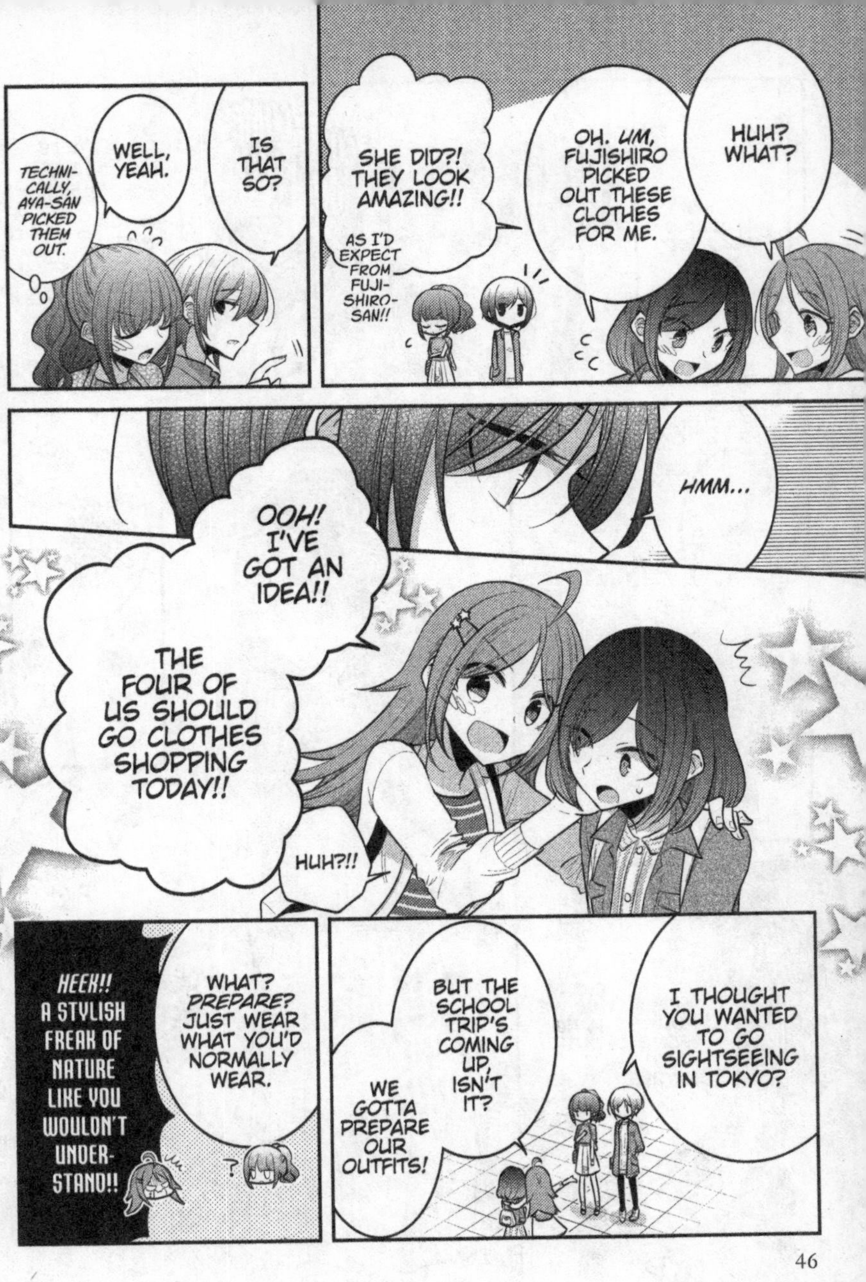
HUH? WHAT?
OH. UM, FUJISHIRO PICKED OUT THESE CLOTHES FOR ME.
SHE DID?! THEY LOOK AMAZING!!
AS I'D EXPECT FROM FUJI-SHIRO-SAN!!
IS THAT SO?
WELL, YEAH.
TECHNI-CALLY, AYA-SAN PICKED THEM OUT.
HMM...
OOH! I'VE GOT AN IDEA!!
THE FOUR OF US SHOULD GO CLOTHES SHOPPING TODAY!!
HUH?!!
I THOUGHT YOU WANTED TO GO SIGHTSEEING IN TOKYO?
BUT THE SCHOOL TRIP'S COMING UP, ISN'T IT?
WE GOTTA PREPARE OUR OUTFITS!
WHAT? PREPARE? JUST WEAR WHAT YOU'D NORMALLY WEAR.
HEEK!! A STYLISH FREAK OF NATURE LIKE YOU WOULDN'T UNDER-STAND!!

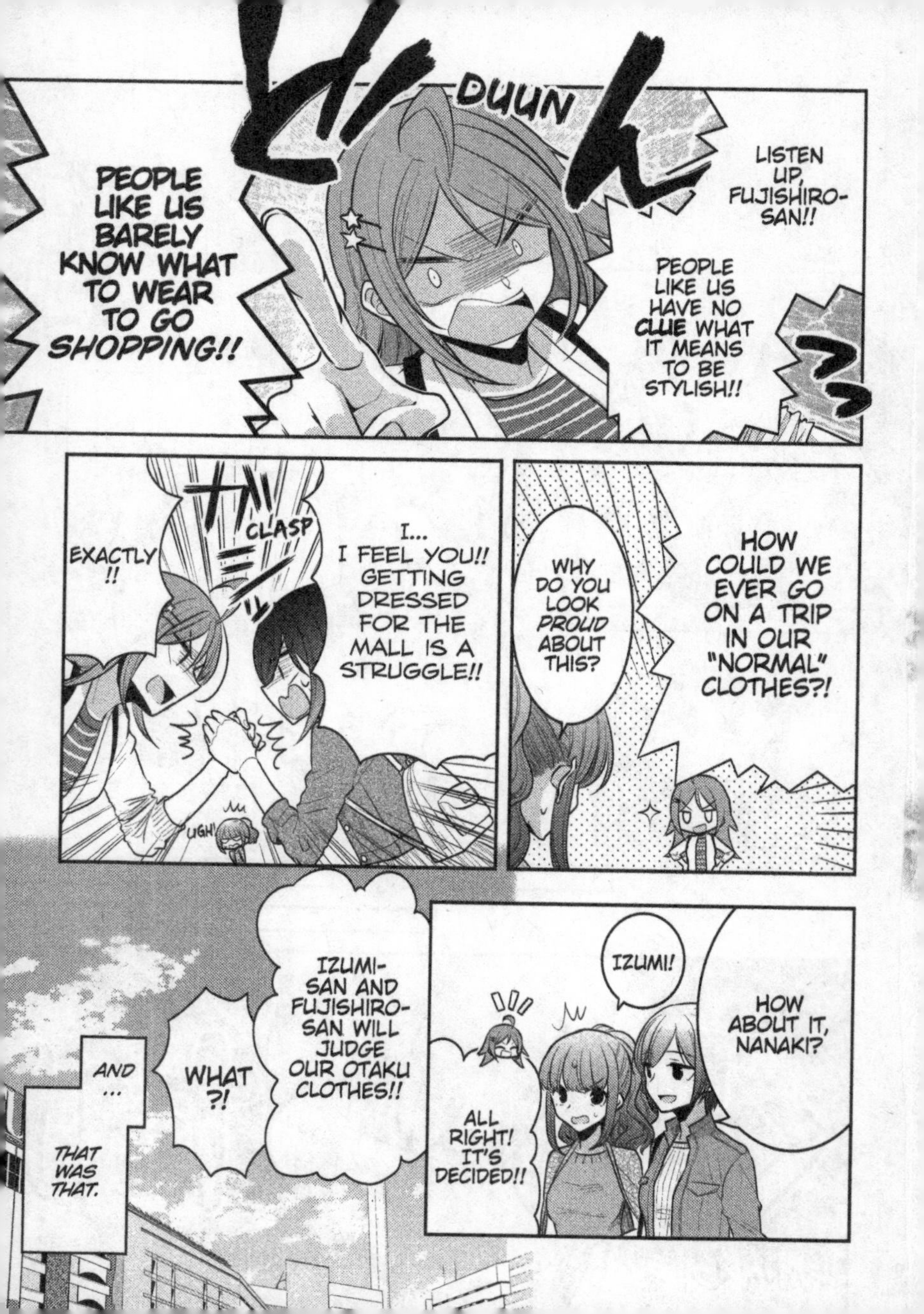
DUUN
LISTEN UP, FUJISHIRO-SAN!!
PEOPLE LIKE US HAVE NO CLUE WHAT IT MEANS TO BE STYLISH!!
PEOPLE LIKE US BARELY KNOW WHAT TO WEAR TO GO SHOPPING!!
HOW COULD WE EVER GO ON A TRIP IN OUR "NORMAL" CLOTHES?!
WHY DO YOU LOOK PROUD ABOUT THIS?
CLASP
I... I FEEL YOU!! GETTING DRESSED FOR THE MALL IS A STRUGGLE!!
EXACTLY!!
UGH!
HOW ABOUT IT, NANAKI?
IZUMI!
ALL RIGHT! IT'S DECIDED!!
IZUMI-SAN AND FUJISHIRO-SAN WILL JUDGE OUR OTAKU CLOTHES!!
WHAT?!
AND...
THAT WAS THAT.

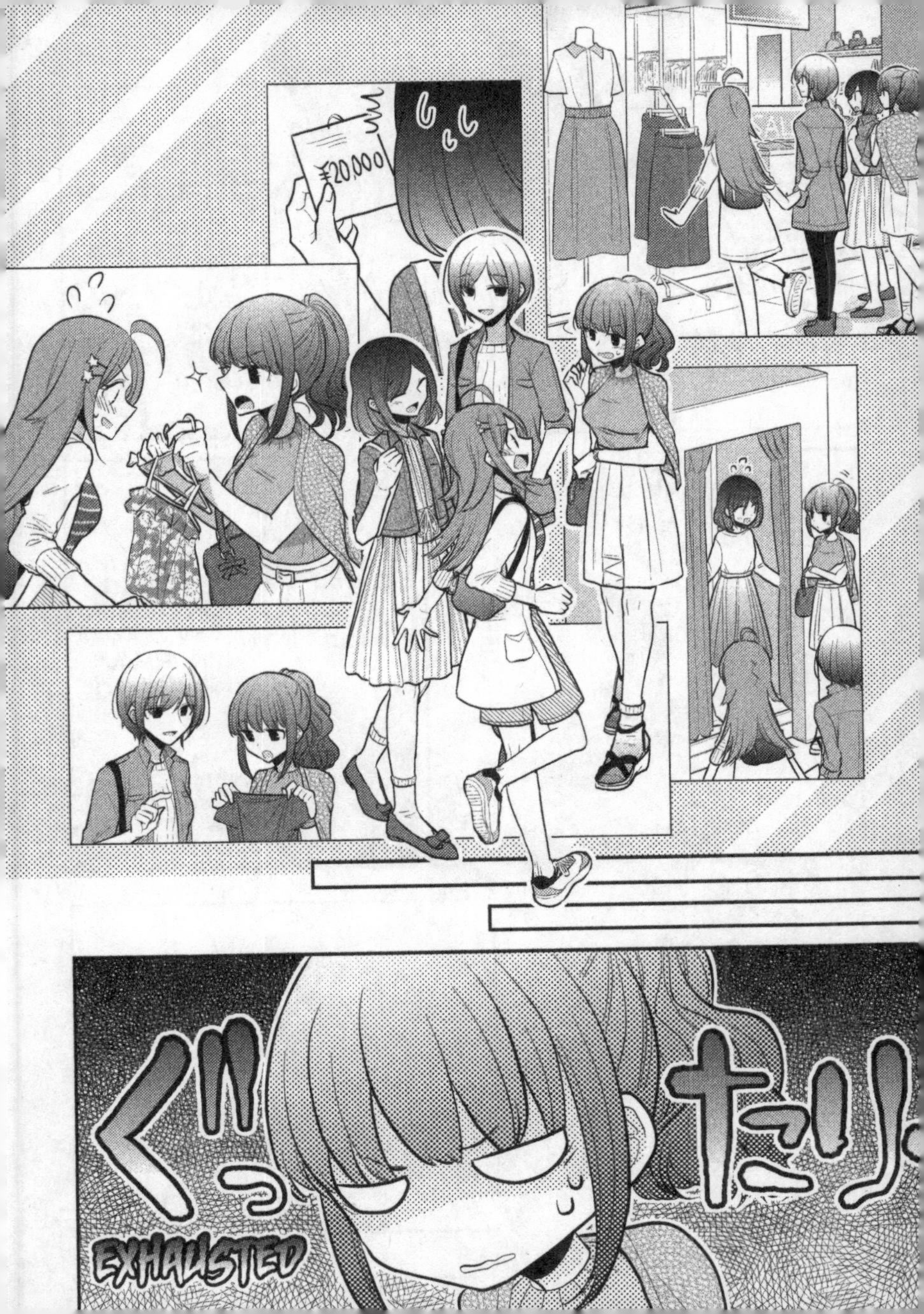
¥20,000
ぐったり
EXHAUSTED

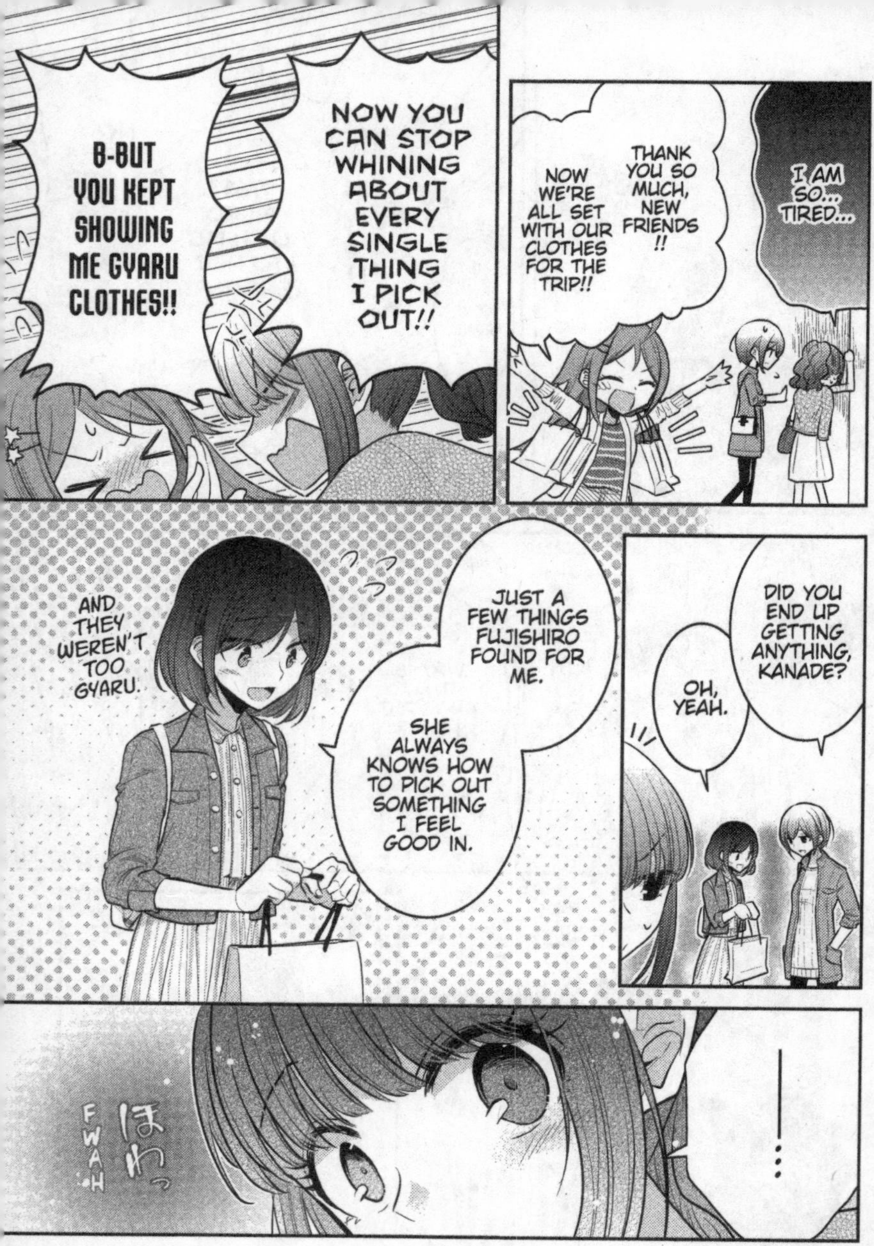
I AM SO... TIRED...
THANK YOU SO MUCH, NEW FRIENDS!!
NOW WE'RE ALL SET WITH OUR CLOTHES FOR THE TRIP!!
NOW YOU CAN STOP WHINING ABOUT EVERY SINGLE THING I PICK OUT!!
B-BUT YOU KEPT SHOWING ME GYARU CLOTHES!!
DID YOU END UP GETTING ANYTHING, KANADE?
OH, YEAH.
JUST A FEW THINGS FUJISHIRO FOUND FOR ME.
SHE ALWAYS KNOWS HOW TO PICK OUT SOMETHING I FEEL GOOD IN.
AND THEY WEREN'T TOO GYARU.
—...
ほわっ
FWAH

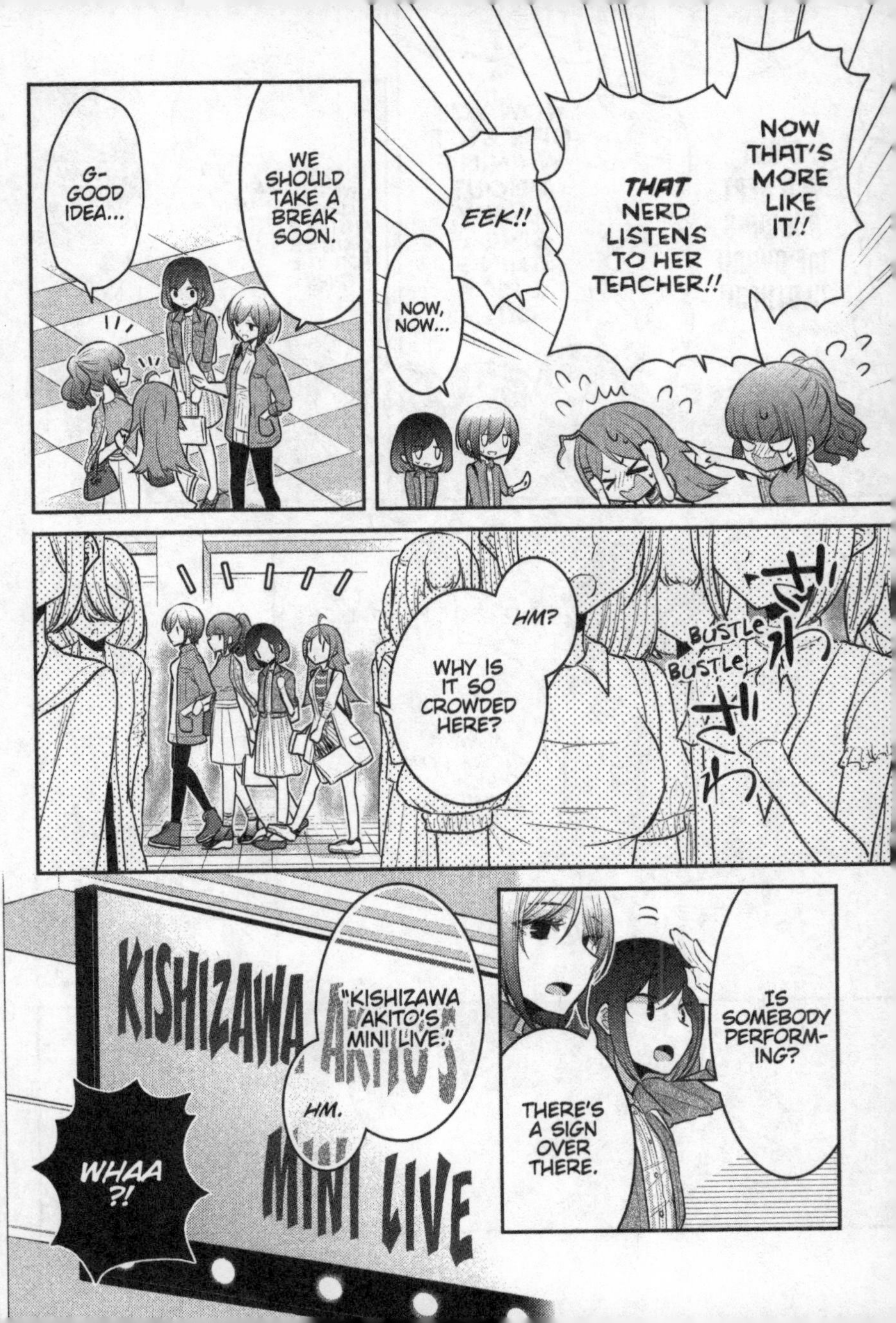
NOW THAT'S MORE LIKE IT!!
THAT NERD LISTENS TO HER TEACHER!!
EEK!!
NOW, NOW...
WE SHOULD TAKE A BREAK SOON.
G-GOOD IDEA...
HM?
WHY IS IT SO CROWDED HERE?
BUSTLE BUSTLE
IS SOMEBODY PERFORM-ING?
THERE'S A SIGN OVER THERE.
"KISHIZAWA AKITO'S MINI LIVE."
HM.
KISHIZAWA AKITO'S MINI LIVE
WHAA?!

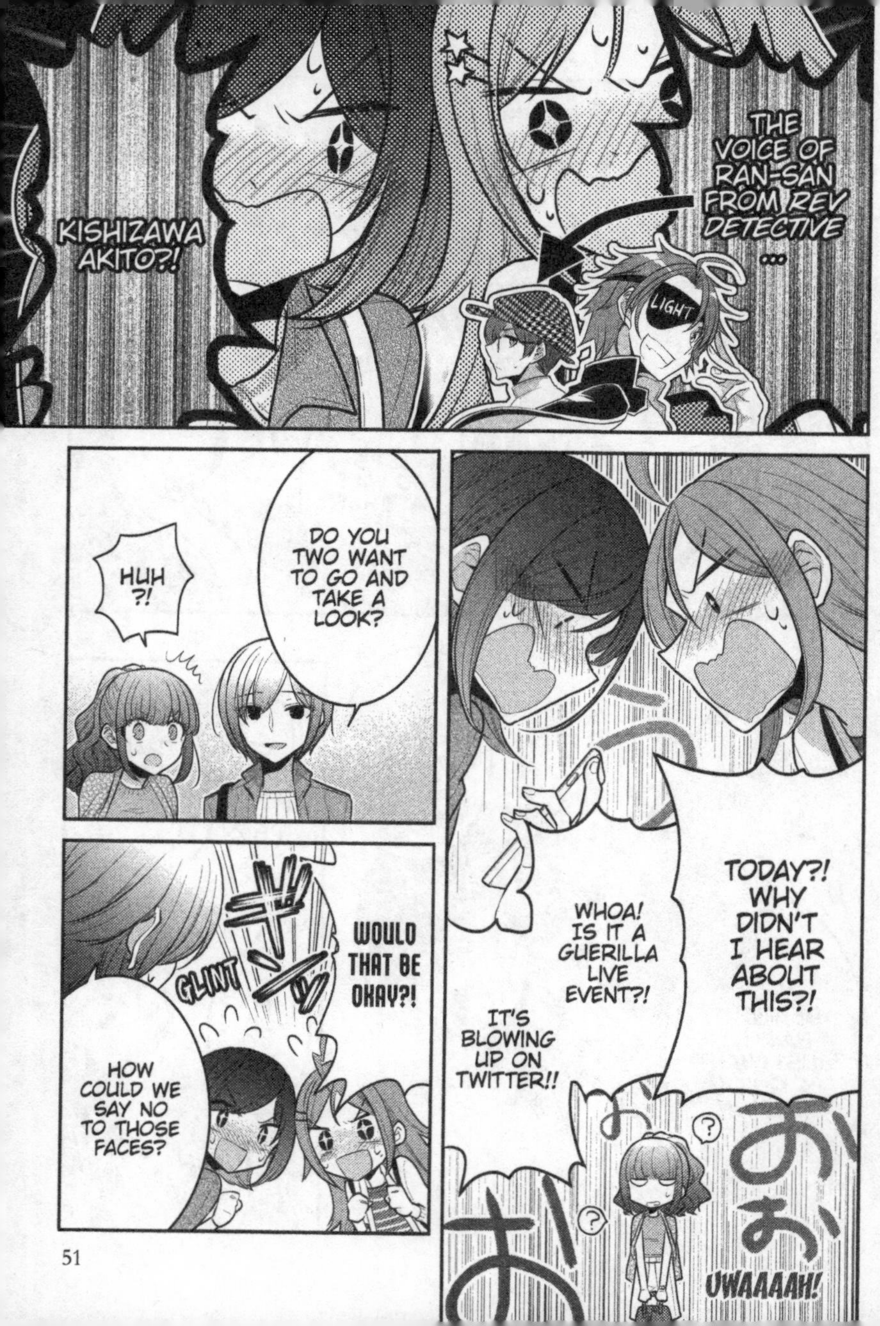
THE VOICE OF RAN-SAN FROM *REV DETECTIVE*...
KISHIZAWA AKITO?!
LIGHT
TODAY?! WHY DIDN'T I HEAR ABOUT THIS?!
WHOA! IS IT A GUERILLA LIVE EVENT?!
IT'S BLOWING UP ON TWITTER!!
UWAAAAH!
DO YOU TWO WANT TO GO AND TAKE A LOOK?
HUH?!
WOULD THAT BE OKAY?!
GLINT
HOW COULD WE SAY NO TO THOSE FACES?

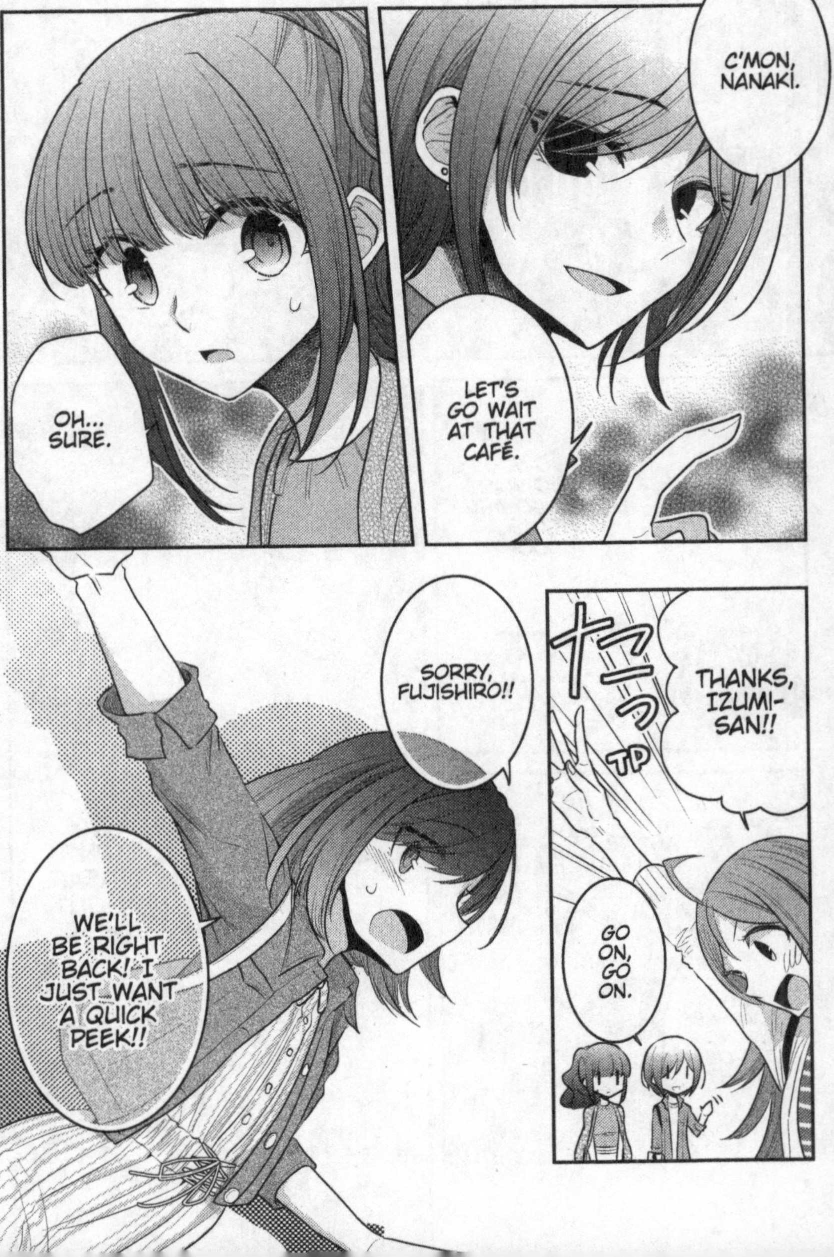
C'MON, NANAKI.
LET'S GO WAIT AT THAT CAFÉ.
OH... SURE.
THANKS, IZUMI-SAN!!
TP
GO ON, GO ON.
SORRY, FUJISHIRO!!
WE'LL BE RIGHT BACK! I JUST WANT A QUICK PEEK!!

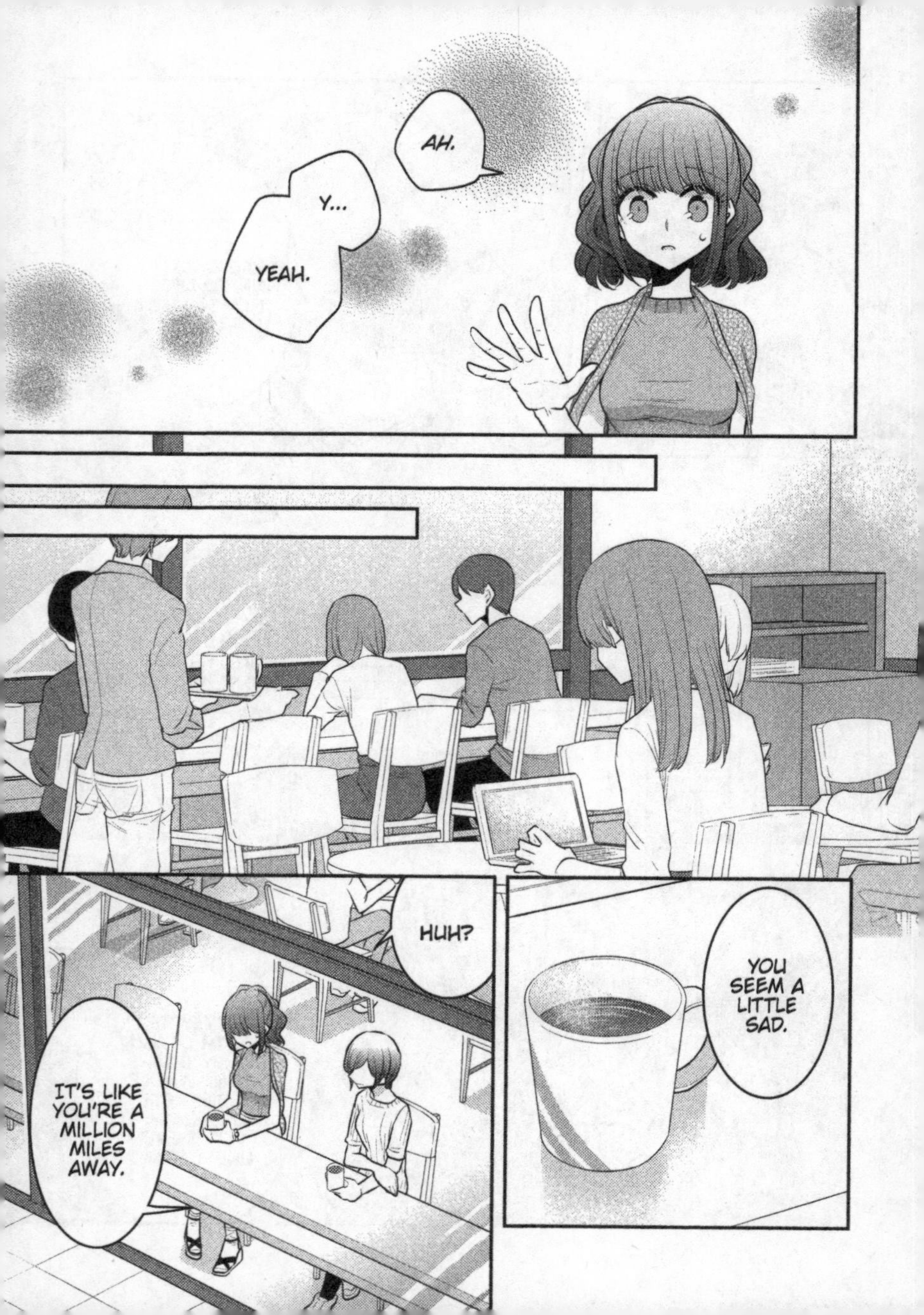
AH.
Y... YEAH.
YOU SEEM A LITTLE SAD.
HUH?
IT'S LIKE YOU'RE A MILLION MILES AWAY.

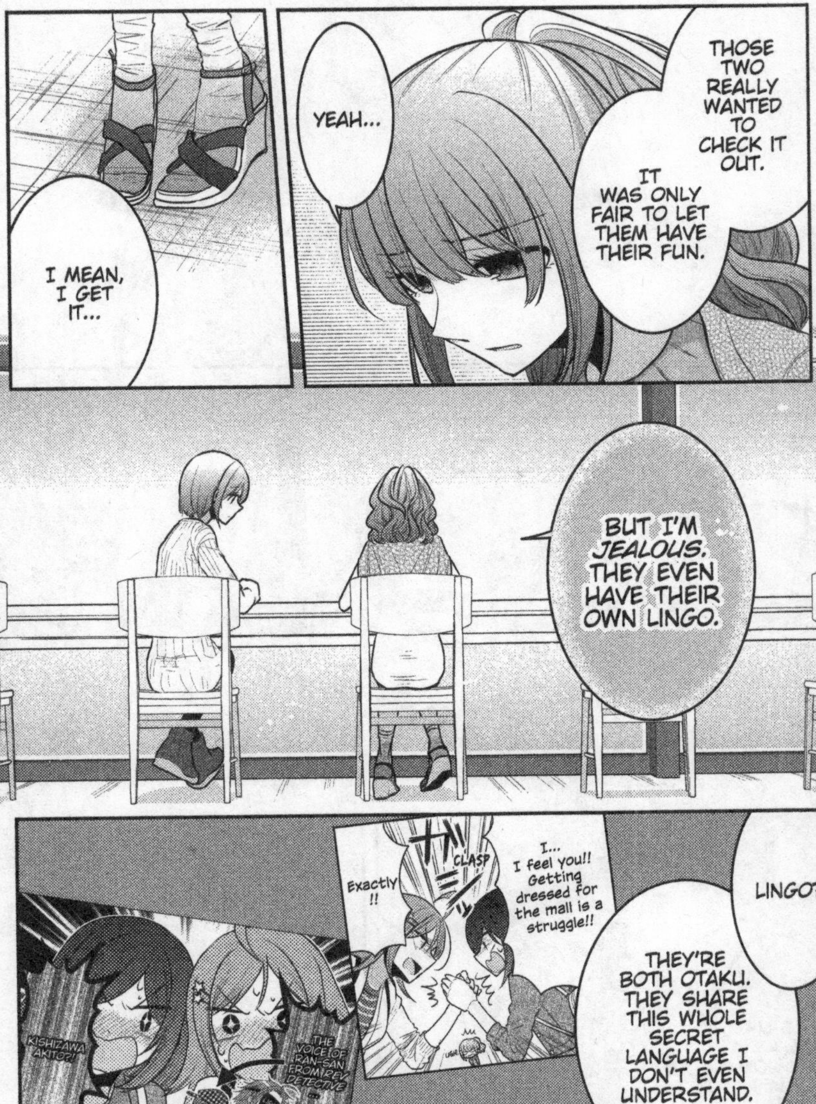
THOSE TWO REALLY WANTED TO CHECK IT OUT.
IT WAS ONLY FAIR TO LET THEM HAVE THEIR FUN.
YEAH...
I MEAN, I GET IT...
BUT I'M JEALOUS. THEY EVEN HAVE THEIR OWN LINGO.
LINGO?
THEY'RE BOTH OTAKU. THEY SHARE THIS WHOLE SECRET LANGUAGE I DON'T EVEN UNDERSTAND.
I... I feel you!! Getting dressed for the mall is a struggle!!
CLASP
Exactly!!
KISHIZAWA AKITO?!
THE VOICE OF RAN-SAN FROM REV DETECTIVE...

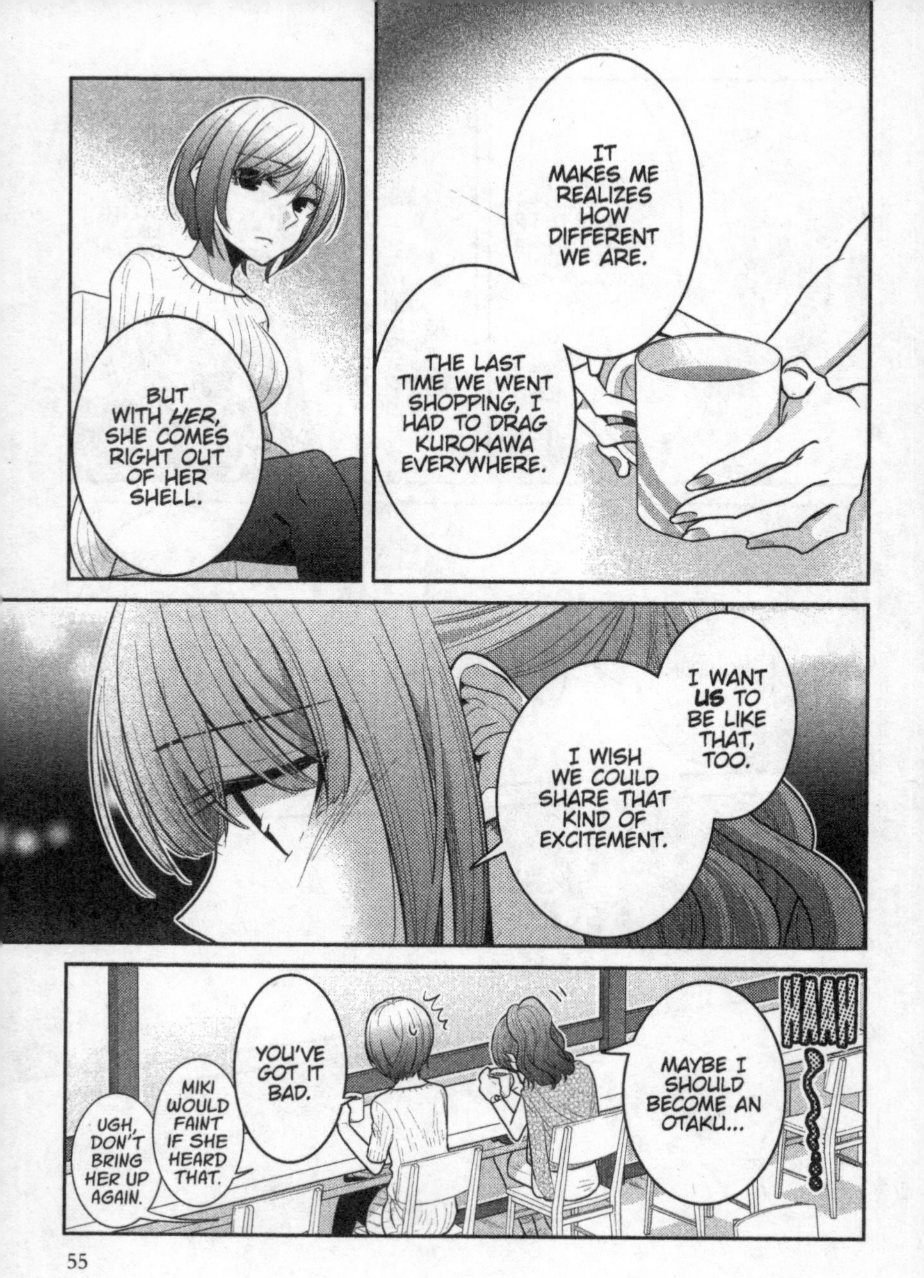
IT MAKES ME REALIZES HOW DIFFERENT WE ARE.
THE LAST TIME WE WENT SHOPPING, I HAD TO DRAG KUROKAWA EVERYWHERE.
BUT WITH *HER*, SHE COMES RIGHT OUT OF HER SHELL.
I WANT **US** TO BE LIKE THAT, TOO.
I WISH WE COULD SHARE THAT KIND OF EXCITEMENT.
KAAH
MAYBE I SHOULD BECOME AN OTAKU...
YOU'VE GOT IT BAD.
MIKI WOULD FAINT IF SHE HEARD THAT.
UGH, DON'T BRING HER UP AGAIN.

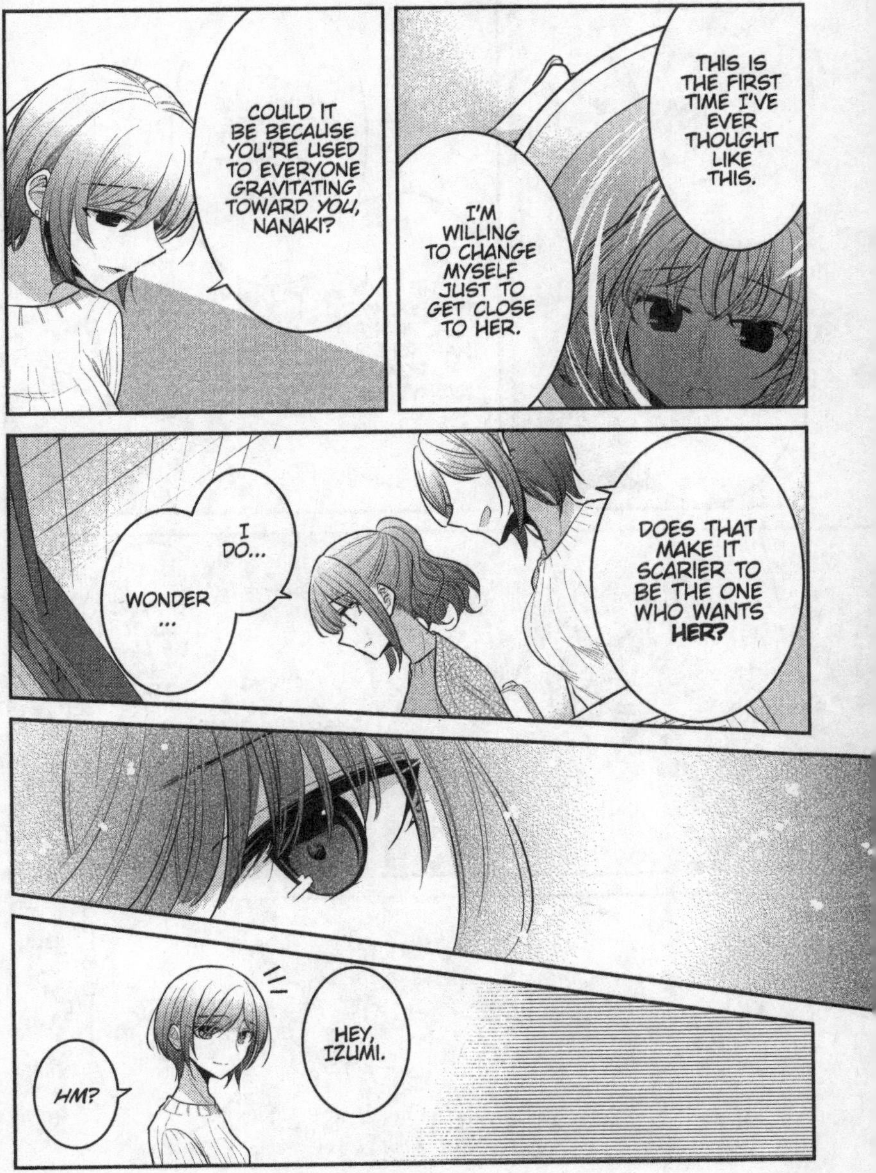
THIS IS THE FIRST TIME I'VE EVER THOUGHT LIKE THIS.
I'M WILLING TO CHANGE MYSELF JUST TO GET CLOSE TO HER.
COULD IT BE BECAUSE YOU'RE USED TO EVERYONE GRAVITATING TOWARD *YOU*, NANAKI?
DOES THAT MAKE IT SCARIER TO BE THE ONE WHO WANTS **HER**?
I DO... WONDER...
HEY, IZUMI.
HM?

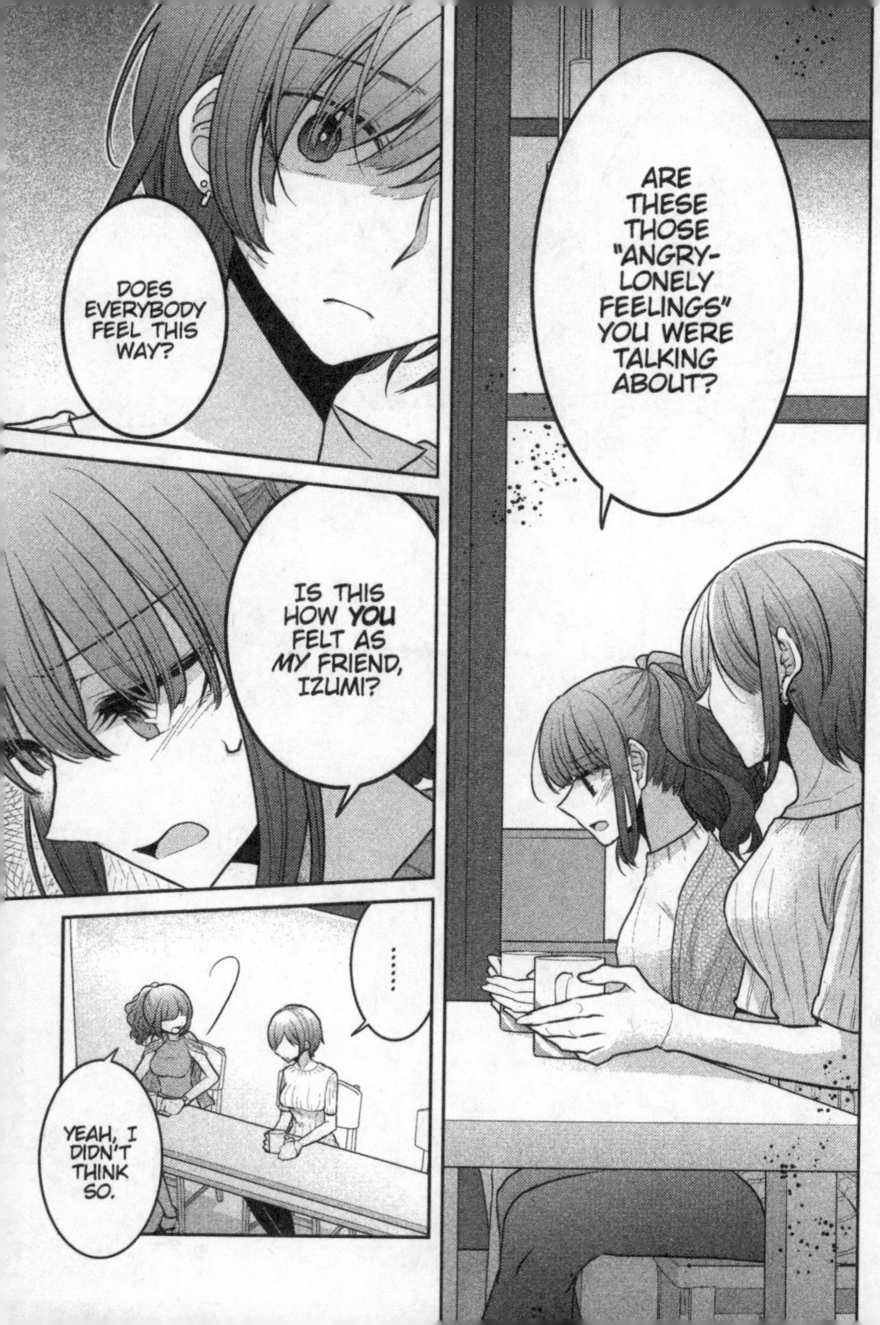
ARE THESE THOSE "ANGRY-LONELY FEELINGS" YOU WERE TALKING ABOUT?
DOES EVERYBODY FEEL THIS WAY?
IS THIS HOW **YOU** FELT AS *MY* FRIEND, IZUMI?
......
YEAH, I DIDN'T THINK SO.

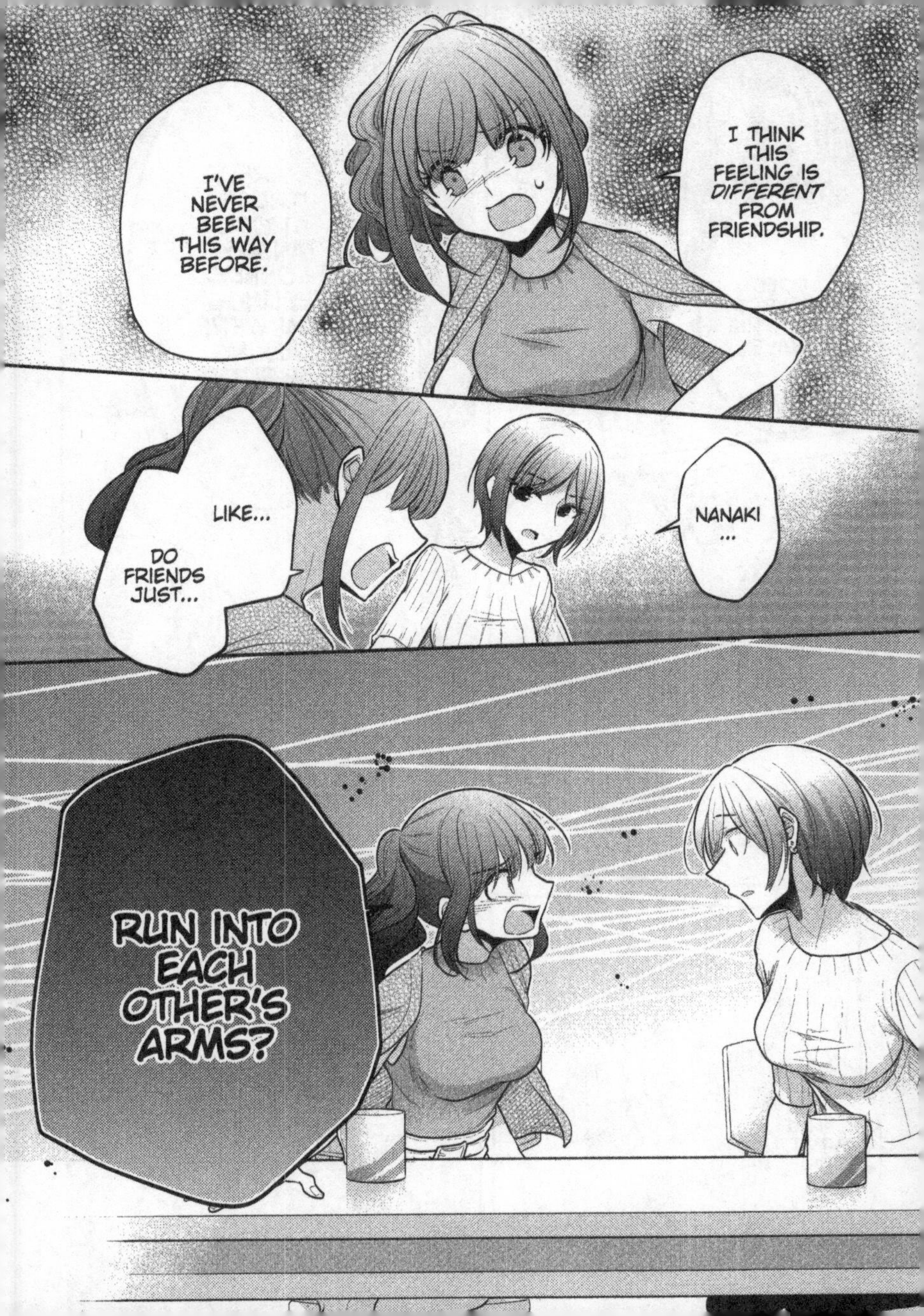
I THINK THIS FEELING IS *DIFFERENT* FROM FRIENDSHIP.
I'VE NEVER BEEN THIS WAY BEFORE.
NANAKI...
LIKE...
DO FRIENDS JUST...
RUN INTO EACH OTHER'S ARMS?

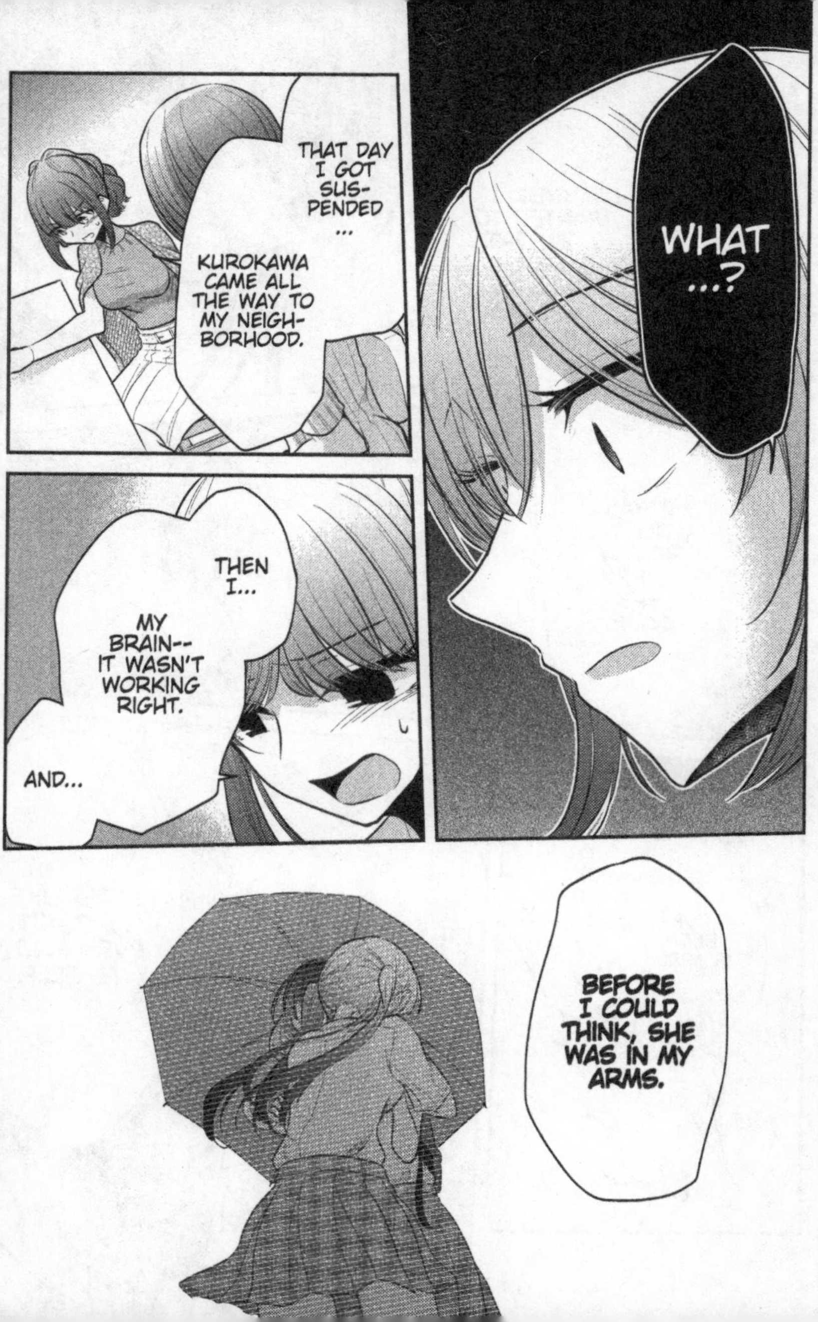
WHAT ...?
THAT DAY I GOT SUS-PENDED ...
KUROKAWA CAME ALL THE WAY TO MY NEIGH-BORHOOD.
THEN I...
MY BRAIN-- IT WASN'T WORKING RIGHT.
AND...
BEFORE I COULD THINK, SHE WAS IN MY ARMS.

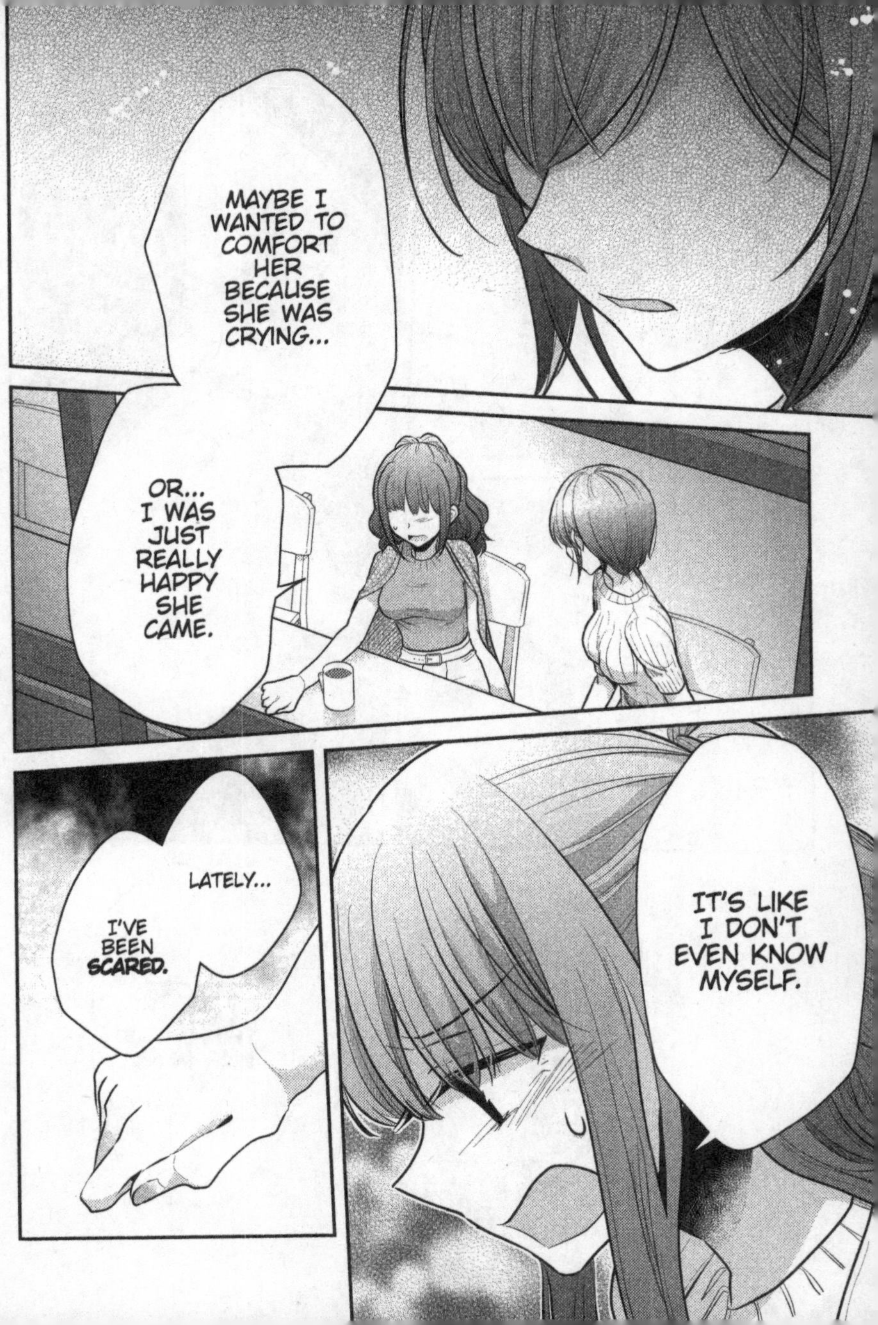
MAYBE I WANTED TO COMFORT HER BECAUSE SHE WAS CRYING...
OR... I WAS JUST REALLY HAPPY SHE CAME.
IT'S LIKE I DON'T EVEN KNOW MYSELF.
LATELY...
I'VE BEEN SCARED.

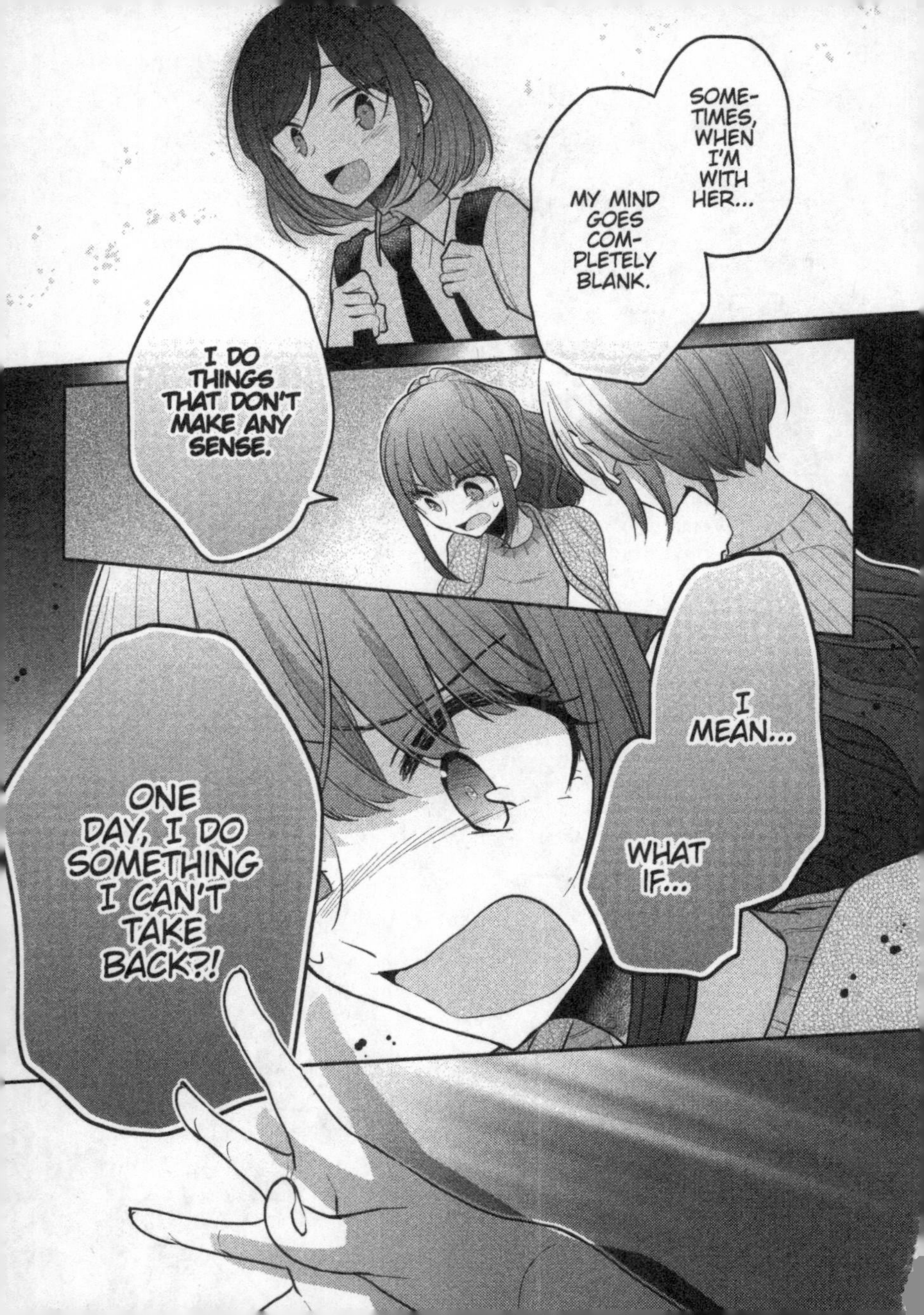
SOME-TIMES, WHEN I'M WITH HER...
MY MIND GOES COM-PLETELY BLANK.
I DO THINGS THAT DON'T MAKE ANY SENSE.
I MEAN...
WHAT IF...
ONE DAY, I DO SOMETHING I CAN'T TAKE BACK?!

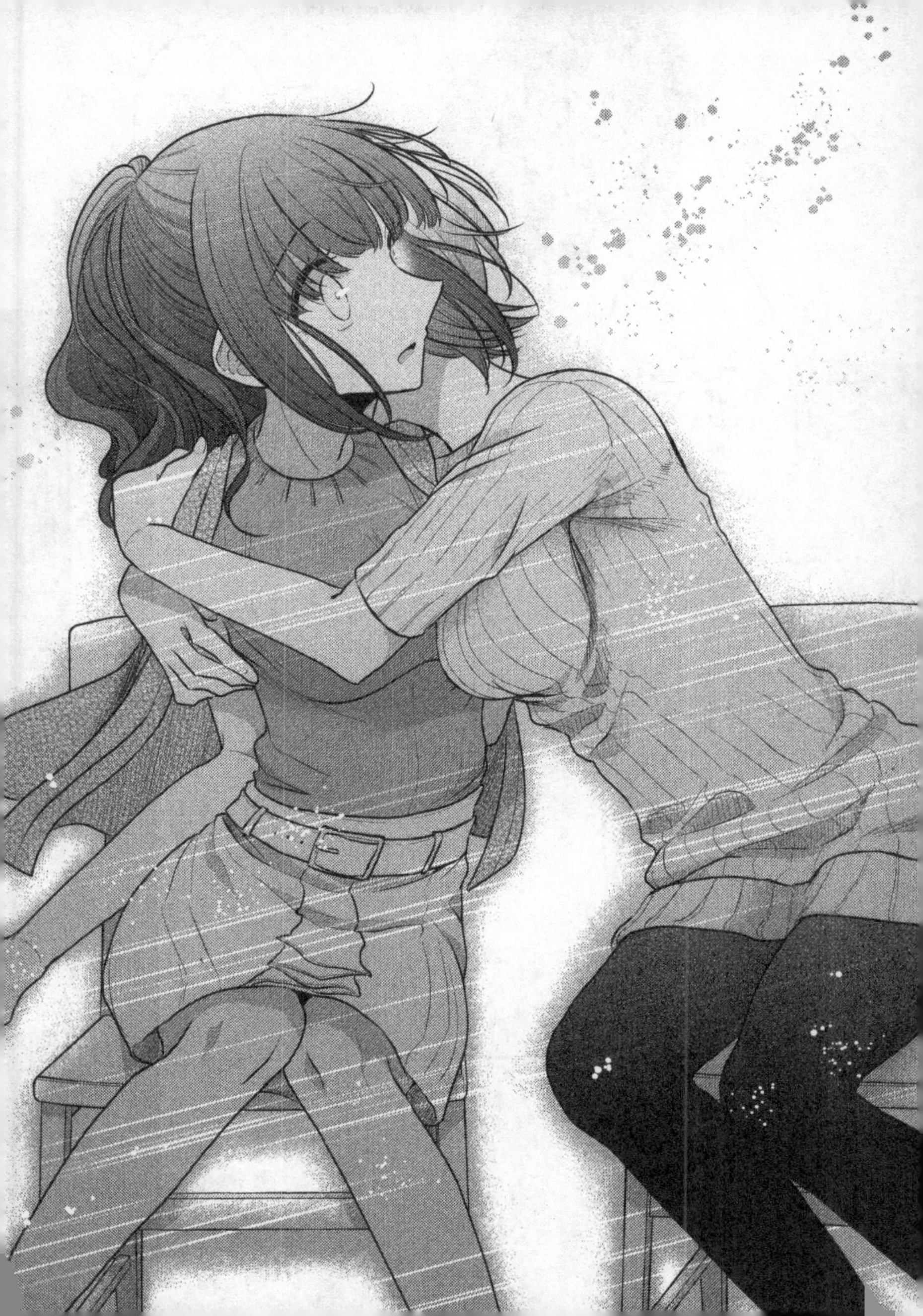

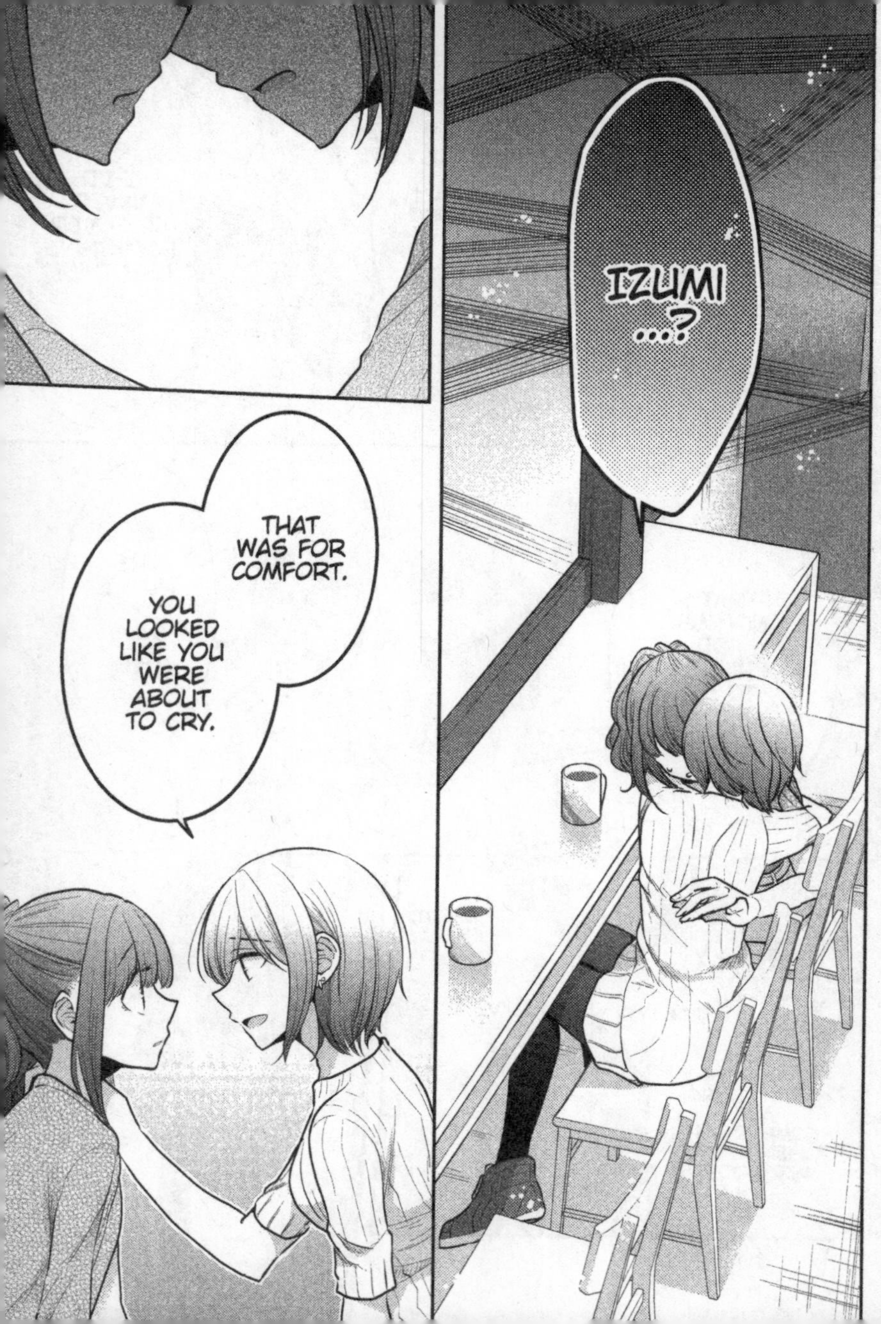
IZUMI ...?
THAT WAS FOR COMFORT.
YOU LOOKED LIKE YOU WERE ABOUT TO CRY.

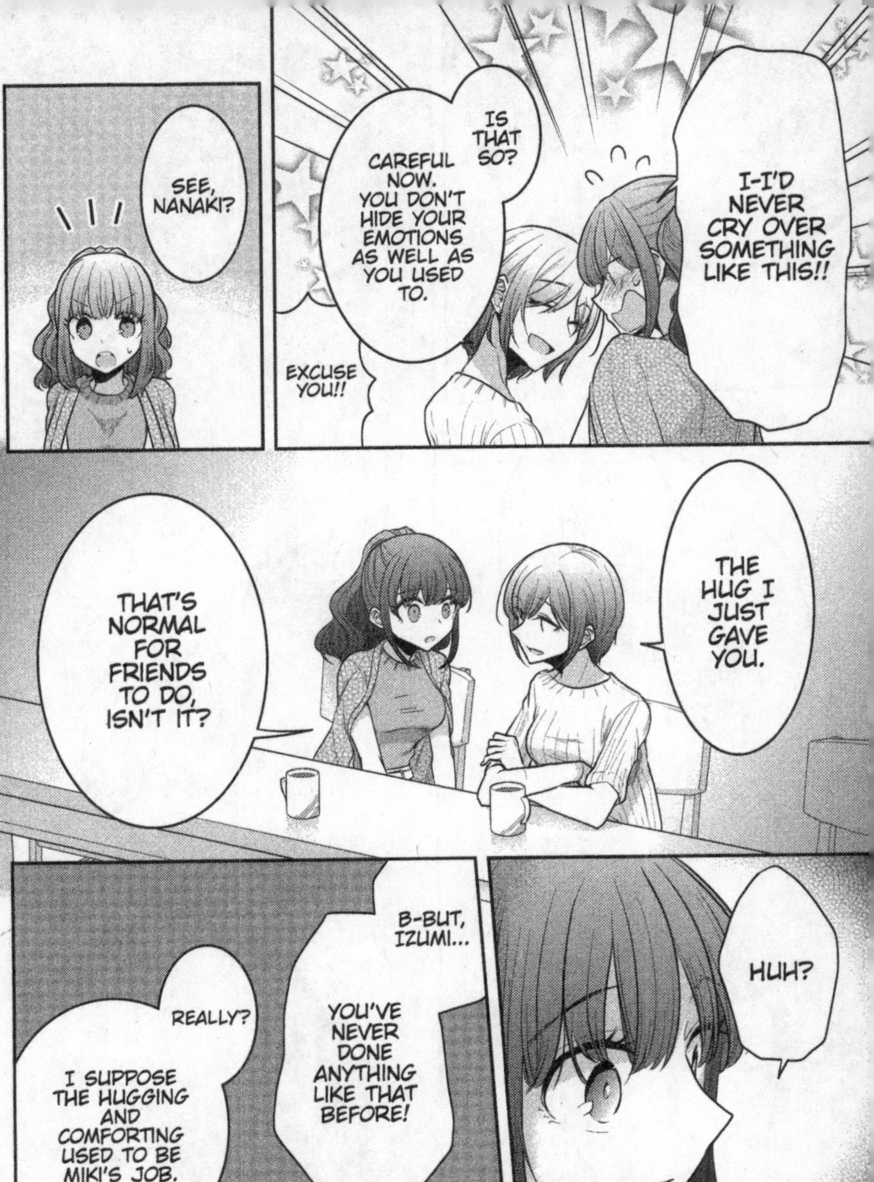
I-I'D NEVER CRY OVER SOMETHING LIKE THIS!!
IS THAT SO?
CAREFUL NOW. YOU DON'T HIDE YOUR EMOTIONS AS WELL AS YOU USED TO.
EXCUSE YOU!!
SEE, NANAKI?
THE HUG I JUST GAVE YOU.
THAT'S NORMAL FOR FRIENDS TO DO, ISN'T IT?
HUH?
B-BUT, IZUMI...
YOU'VE NEVER DONE ANYTHING LIKE THAT BEFORE!
REALLY?
I SUPPOSE THE HUGGING AND COMFORTING USED TO BE MIKI'S JOB.

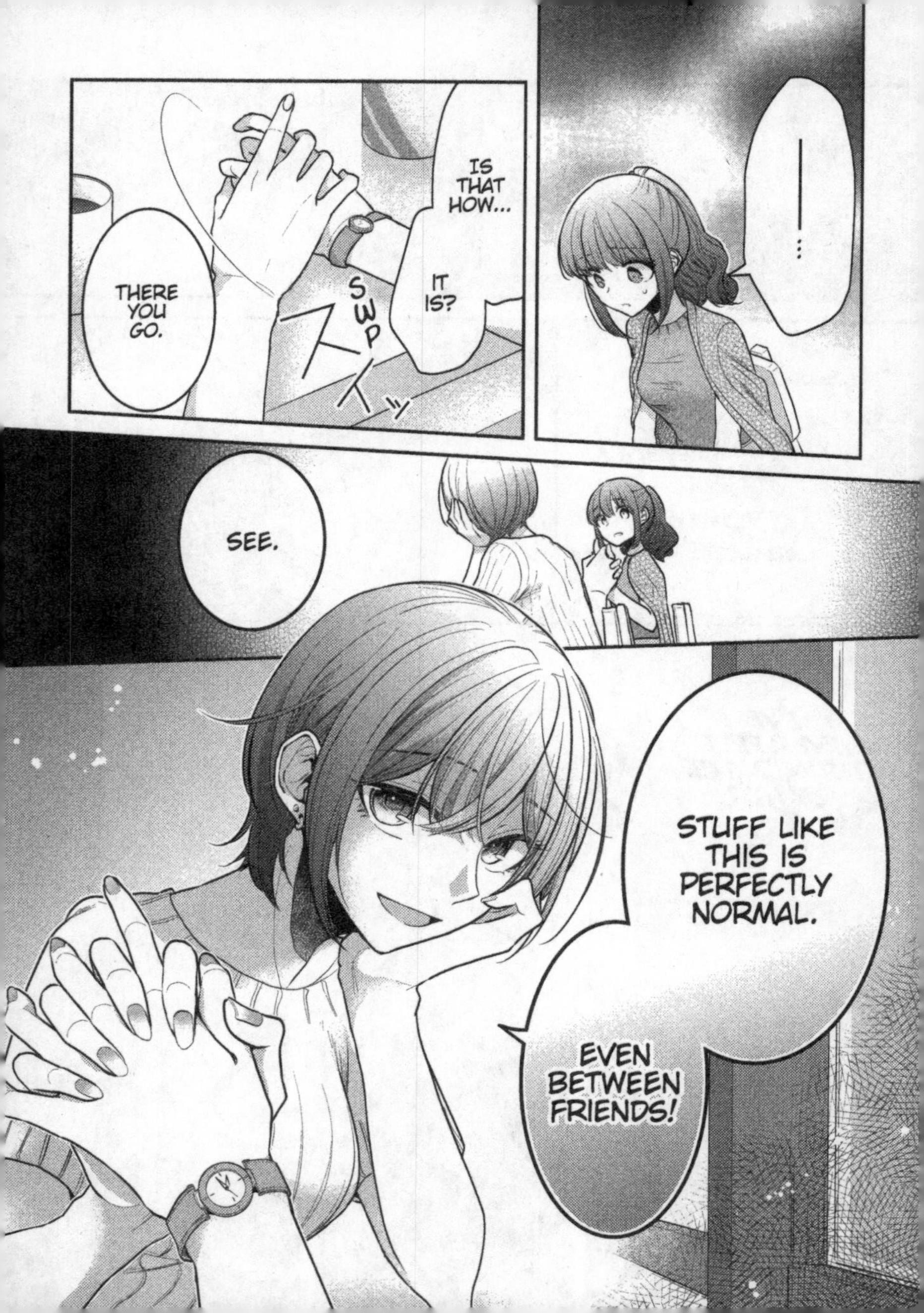

—...
IS THAT HOW... IT IS?
SWP
THERE YOU GO.
SEE.
STUFF LIKE THIS IS PERFECTLY NORMAL.
EVEN BETWEEN FRIENDS!

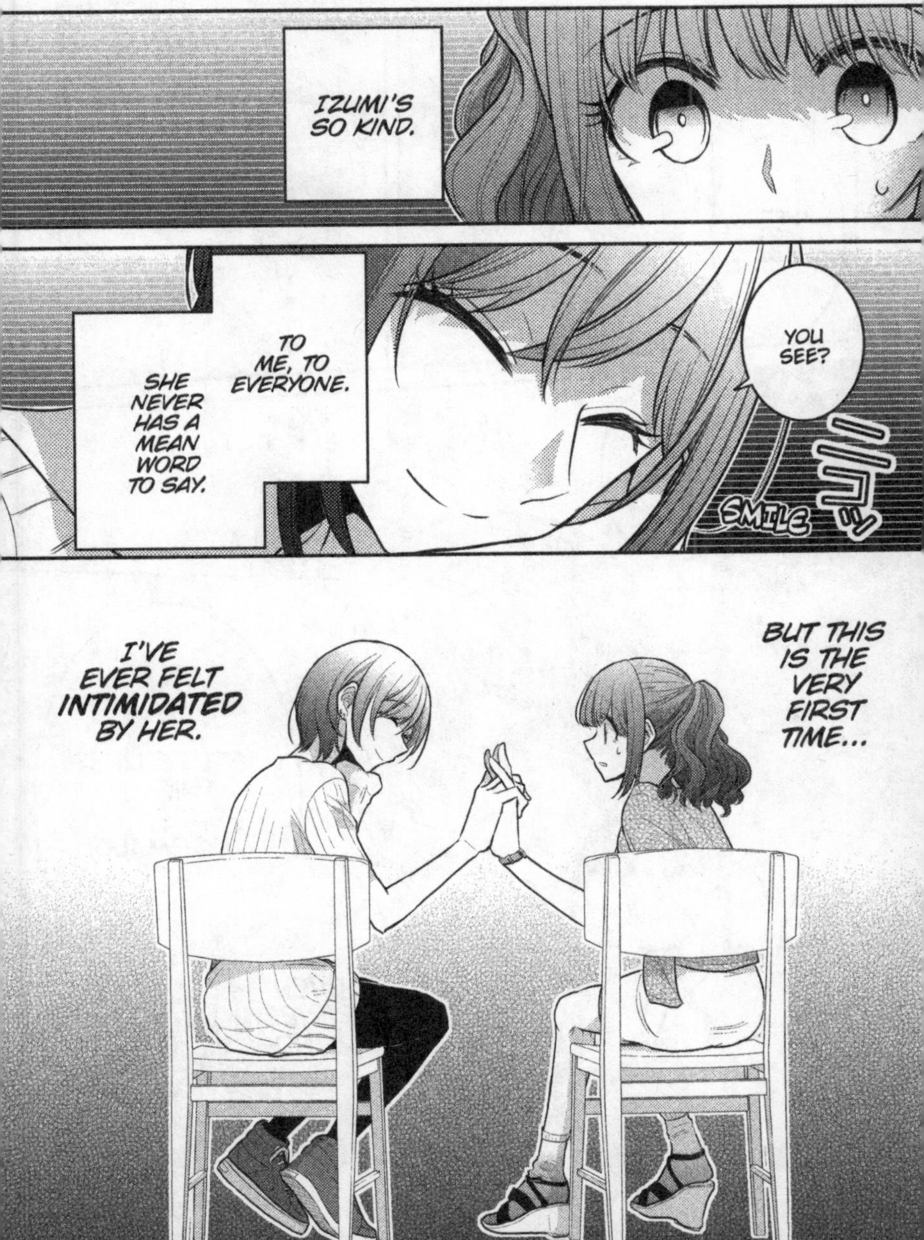
IZUMI'S SO KIND.
YOU SEE?
ニコッ
SMILE
TO ME, TO EVERYONE.
SHE NEVER HAS A MEAN WORD TO SAY.
BUT THIS IS THE VERY FIRST TIME...
I'VE EVER FELT INTIMIDATED BY HER.

CHAPTER 15

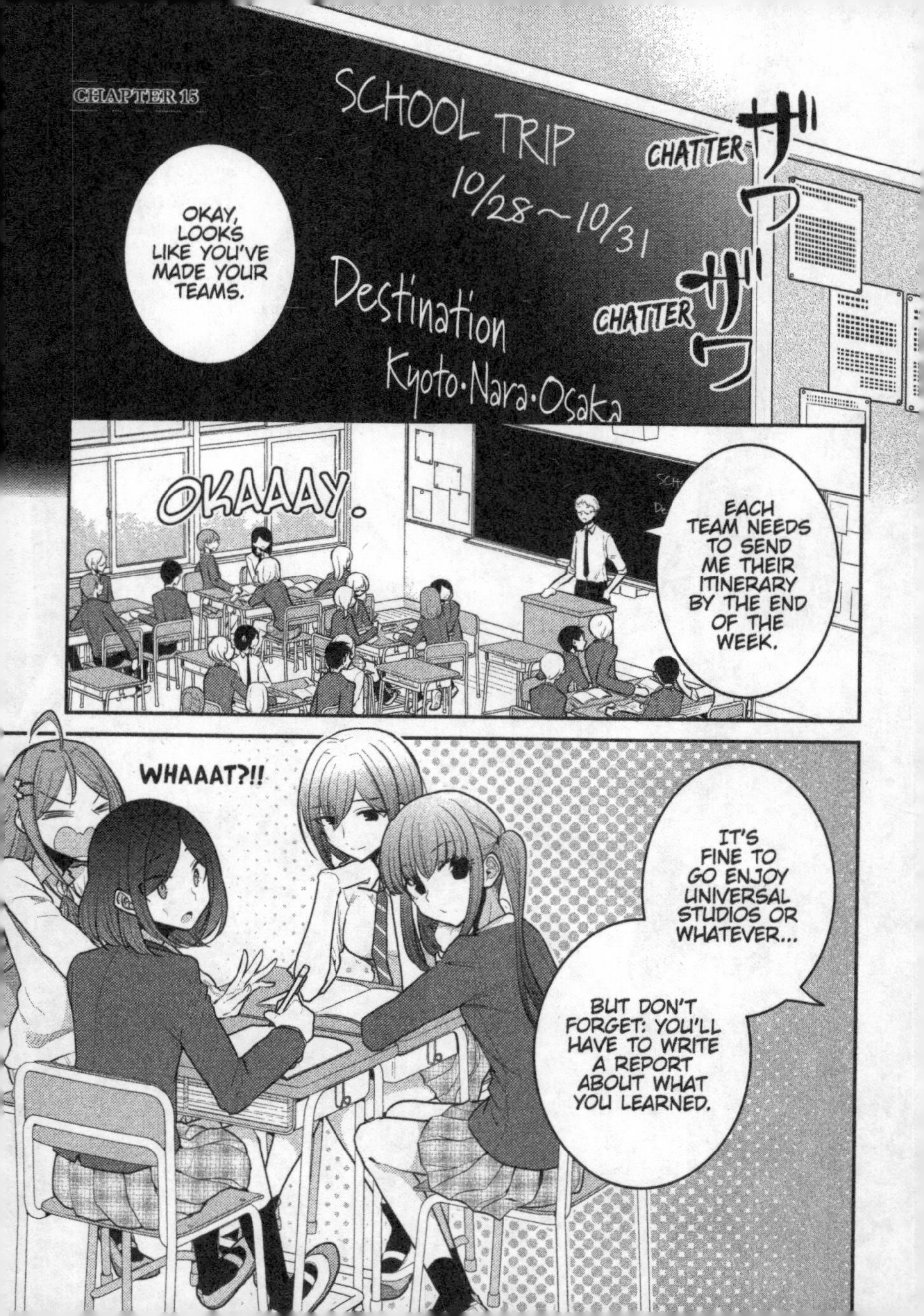

SCHOOL TRIP
10/28～10/31
Destination
Kyoto・Nara・Osaka
CHATTER ザワ
CHATTER ザワ
OKAY, LOOKS LIKE YOU'VE MADE YOUR TEAMS.
EACH TEAM NEEDS TO SEND ME THEIR ITINERARY BY THE END OF THE WEEK.
OKAAAY.
IT'S FINE TO GO ENJOY UNIVERSAL STUDIOS OR WHATEVER...
BUT DON'T FORGET: YOU'LL HAVE TO WRITE A REPORT ABOUT WHAT YOU LEARNED.
WHAAAT?!!

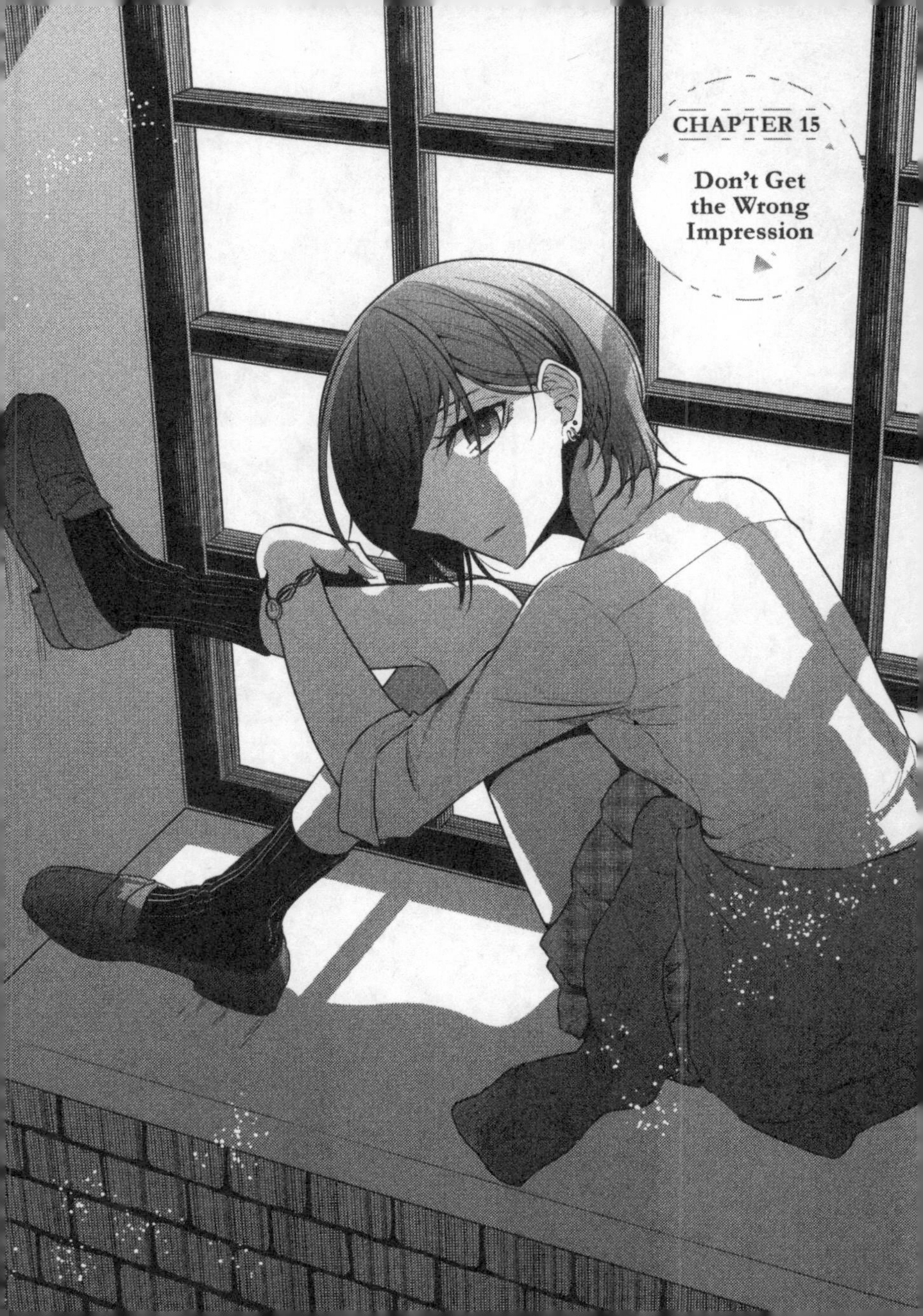
CHAPTER 15
Don't Get the Wrong Impression

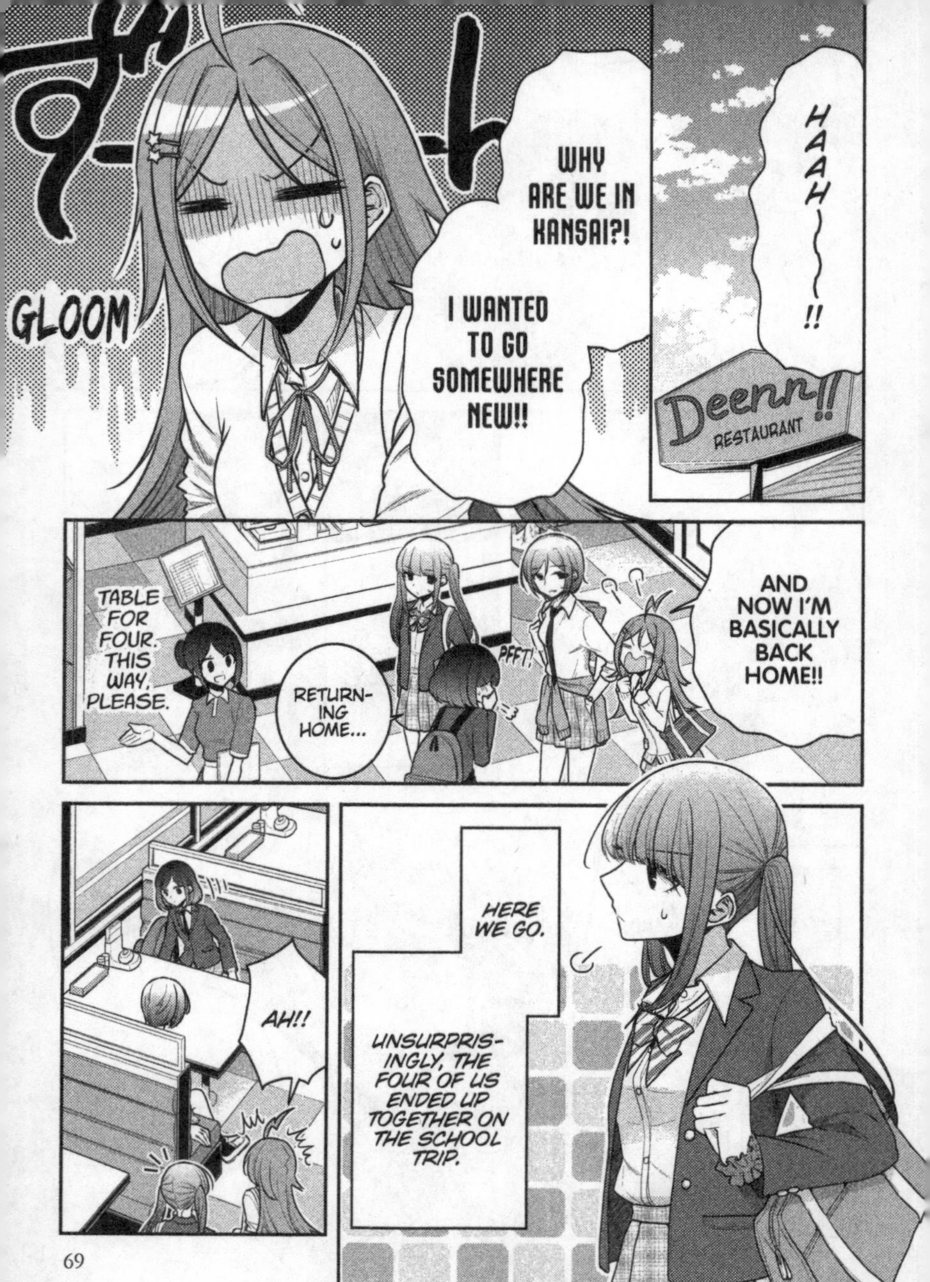
HAAAH~~!!
Deenn!!
RESTAURANT
WHY ARE WE IN KANSAI?!
I WANTED TO GO SOMEWHERE NEW!!
GLOOM
AND NOW I'M BASICALLY BACK HOME!!
PFFT!
RETURN-ING HOME...
TABLE FOR FOUR. THIS WAY, PLEASE.
HERE WE GO.
UNSURPRIS-INGLY, THE FOUR OF US ENDED UP TOGETHER ON THE SCHOOL TRIP.
AH!!

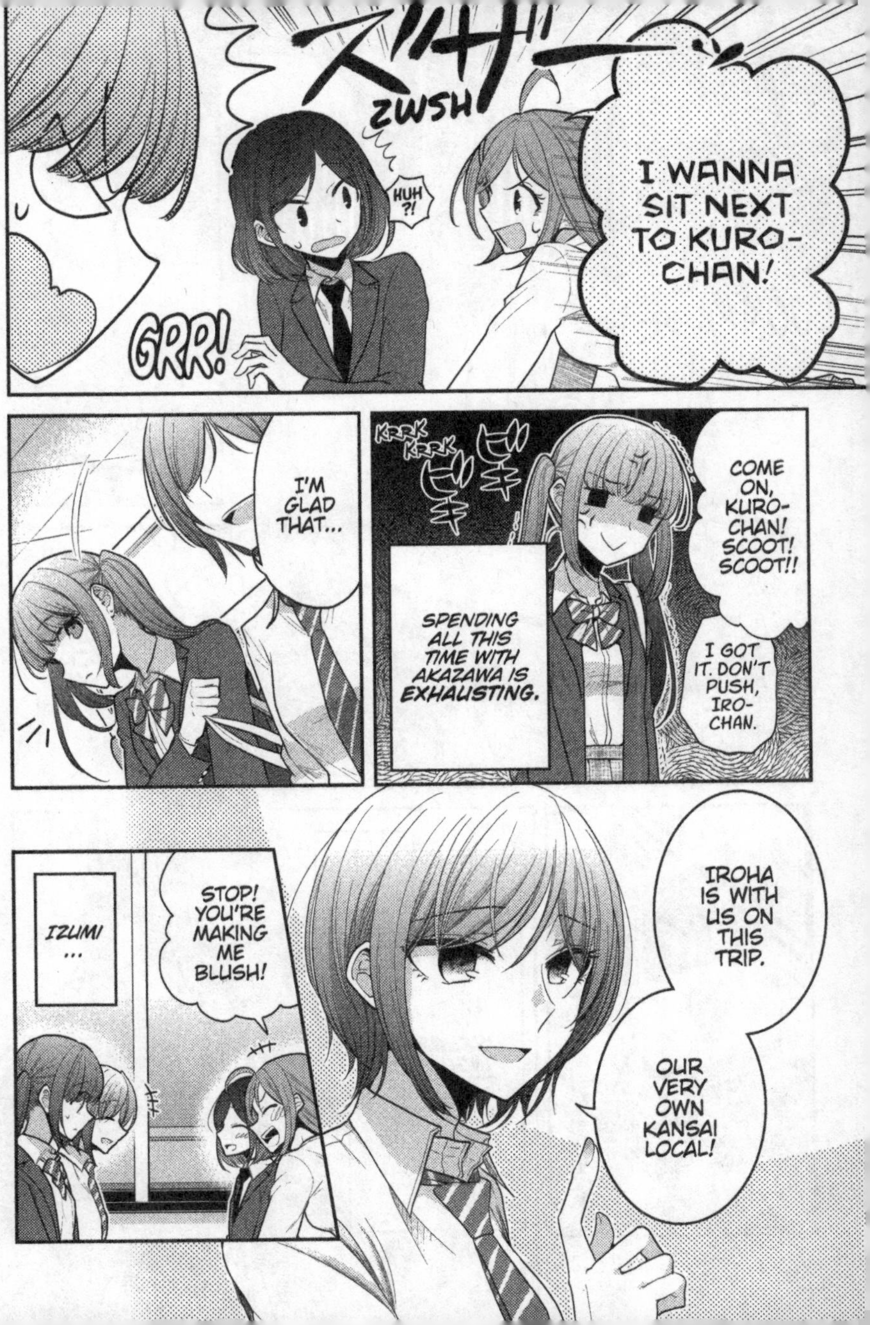
I WANNA SIT NEXT TO KURO-CHAN!
ZWSH
HUH ?!
GRR!
COME ON, KURO-CHAN! SCOOT! SCOOT!!
KRRK KRRK
I GOT IT. DON'T PUSH, IRO-CHAN.
SPENDING ALL THIS TIME WITH AKAZAWA IS EXHAUSTING.
I'M GLAD THAT...
IROHA IS WITH US ON THIS TRIP.
OUR VERY OWN KANSAI LOCAL!
STOP! YOU'RE MAKING ME BLUSH!
IZUMI ...

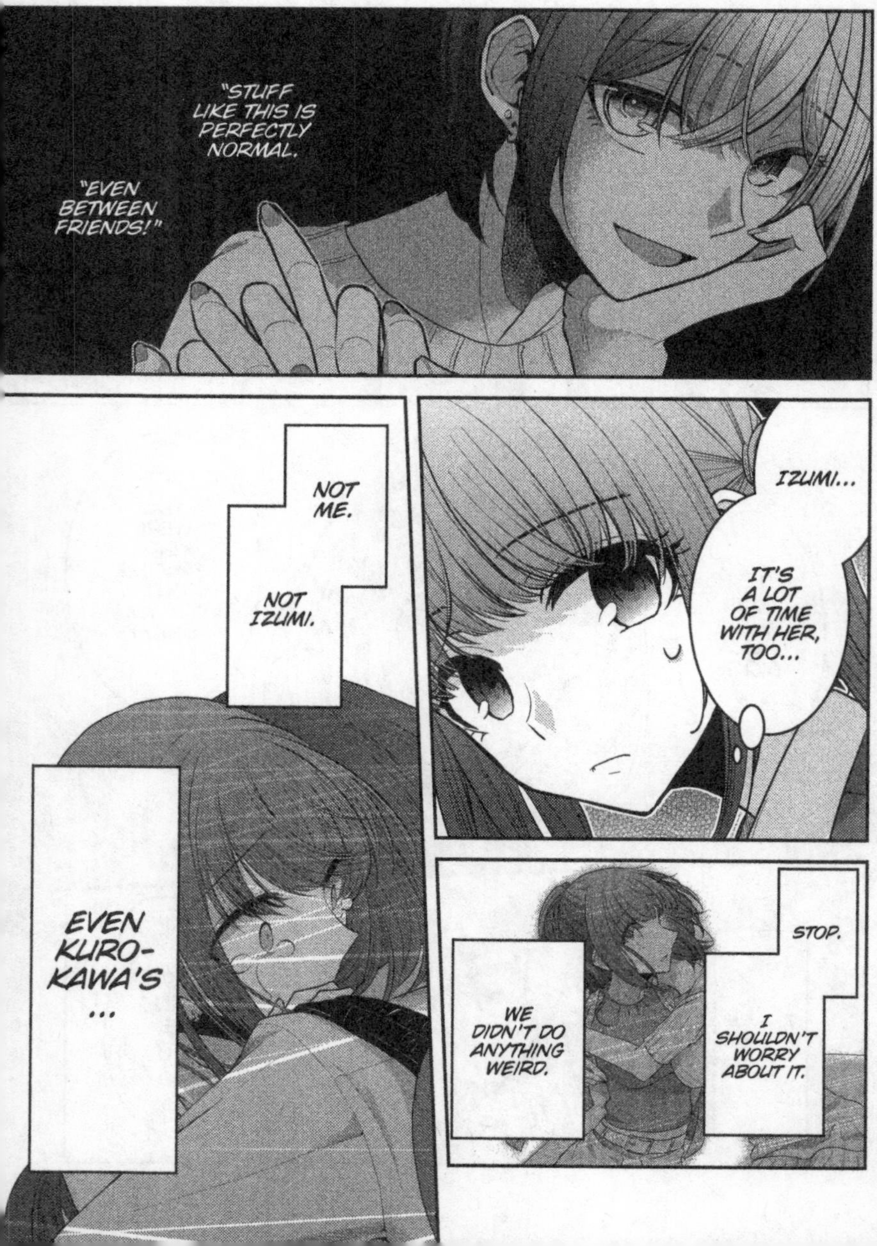
"STUFF LIKE THIS IS PERFECTLY NORMAL.
"EVEN BETWEEN FRIENDS!"
IZUMI...
IT'S A LOT OF TIME WITH HER, TOO...
STOP.
I SHOULDN'T WORRY ABOUT IT.
WE DIDN'T DO ANYTHING WEIRD.
NOT ME.
NOT IZUMI.
EVEN KURO-KAWA'S...

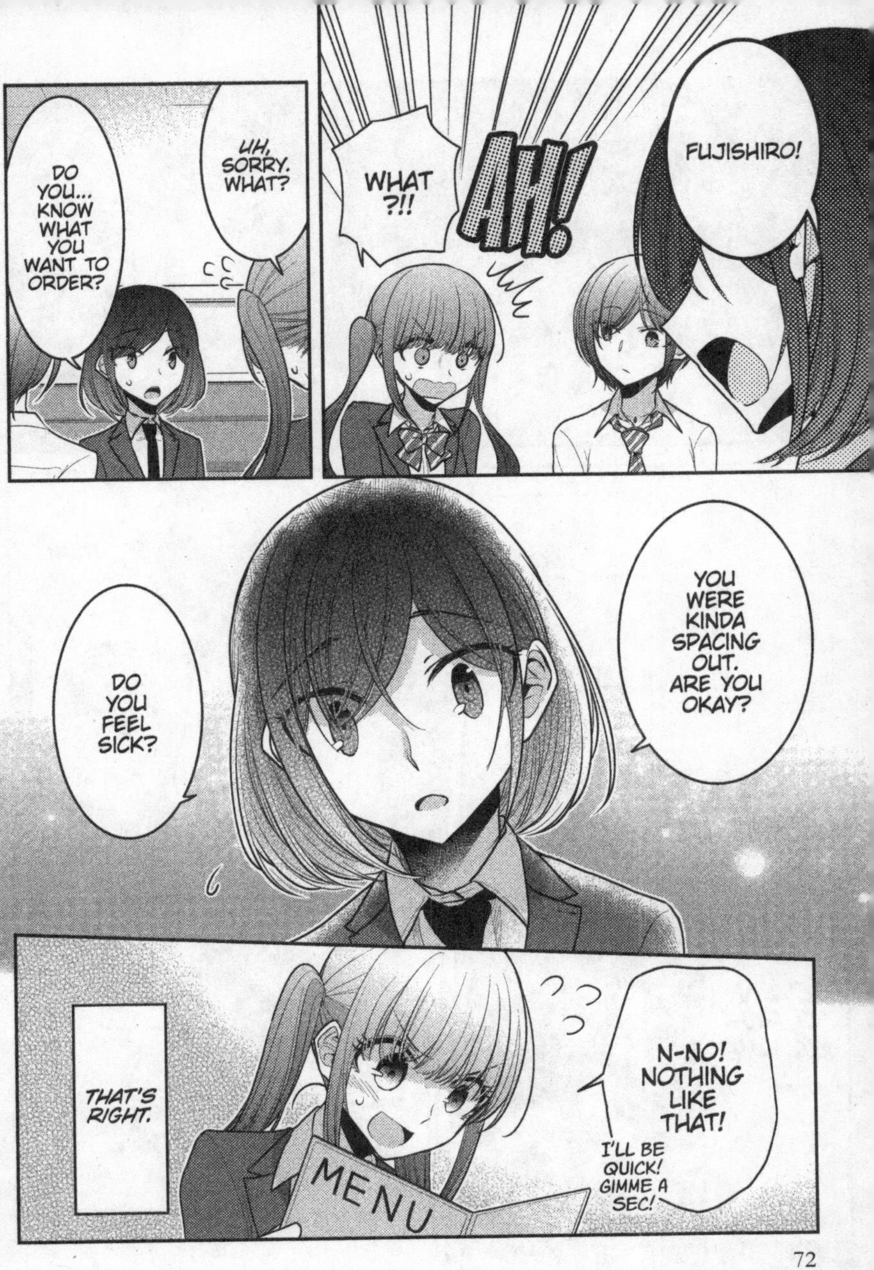
FUJISHIRO!
AH!
WHAT?!!
UH, SORRY. WHAT?
DO YOU... KNOW WHAT YOU WANT TO ORDER?
YOU WERE KINDA SPACING OUT. ARE YOU OKAY?
DO YOU FEEL SICK?
N-NO! NOTHING LIKE THAT!
I'LL BE QUICK! GIMME A SEC!
MENU
THAT'S RIGHT.

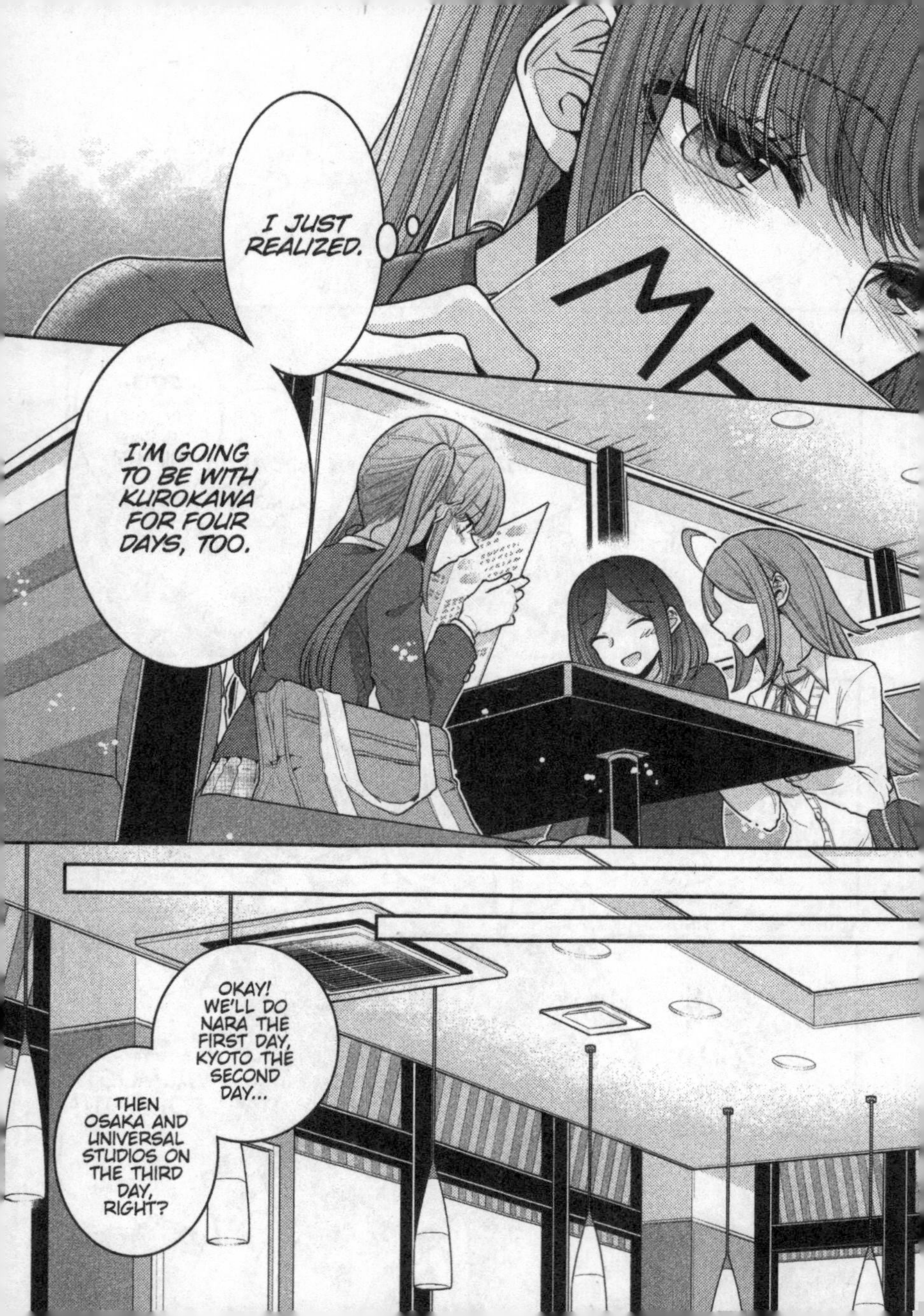
I JUST REALIZED.
I'M GOING TO BE WITH KUROKAWA FOR FOUR DAYS, TOO.
OKAY! WE'LL DO NARA THE FIRST DAY, KYOTO THE SECOND DAY...
THEN OSAKA AND UNIVERSAL STUDIOS ON THE THIRD DAY, RIGHT?

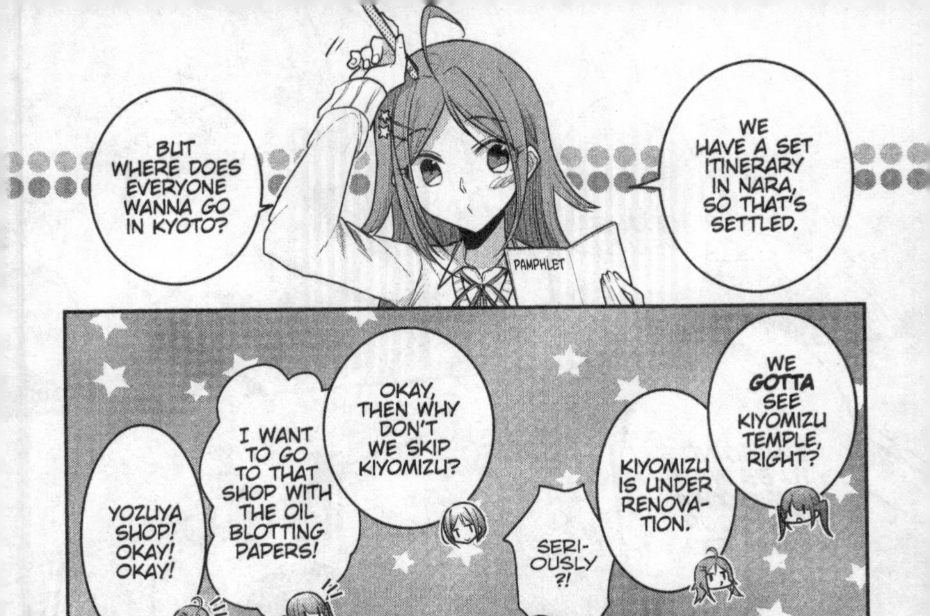
WE HAVE A SET ITINERARY IN NARA, SO THAT'S SETTLED.
BUT WHERE DOES EVERYONE WANNA GO IN KYOTO?
PAMPHLET
WE **GOTTA** SEE KIYOMIZU TEMPLE, RIGHT?
KIYOMIZU IS UNDER RENOVA-TION.
SERI-OUSLY ?!
OKAY, THEN WHY DON'T WE SKIP KIYOMIZU?
I WANT TO GO TO THAT SHOP WITH THE OIL BLOTTING PAPERS!
YOZUYA SHOP! OKAY! OKAY!
WHAT ABOUT YOU TWO?
I'D LIKE TO SEE GINKAKUJI.
GINKAKUJI OVER KINKAKUJI*? YOU MUST BE HARDCORE!

*Ginkakuji translates to the "silver pavilion" and Kinkakuji the "golden pavilion."

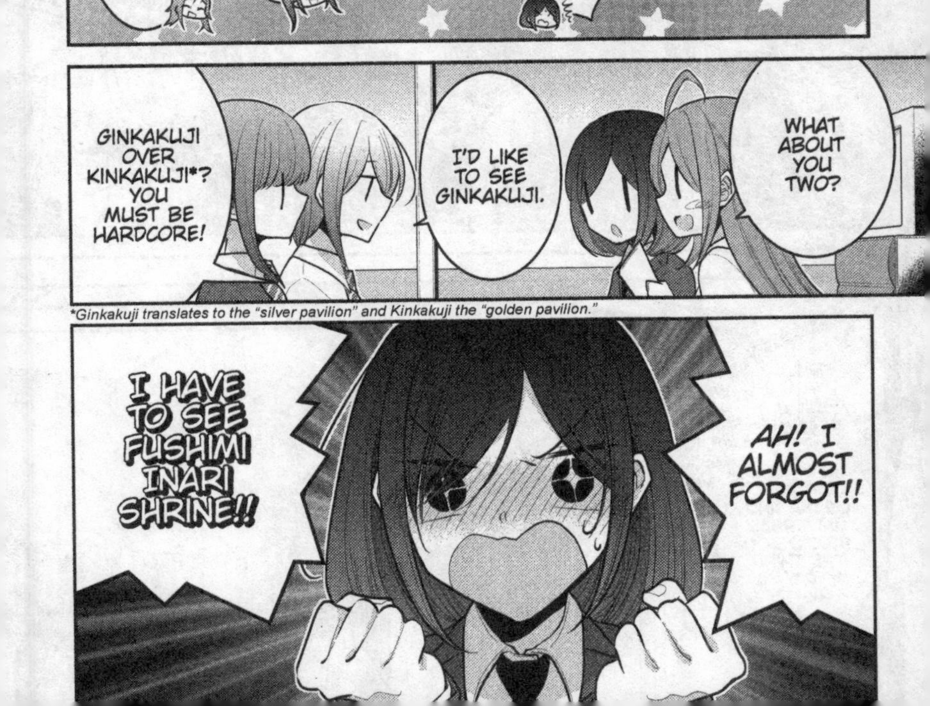
AH! I ALMOST FORGOT!!
I HAVE TO SEE FUSHIMI INARI SHRINE!!

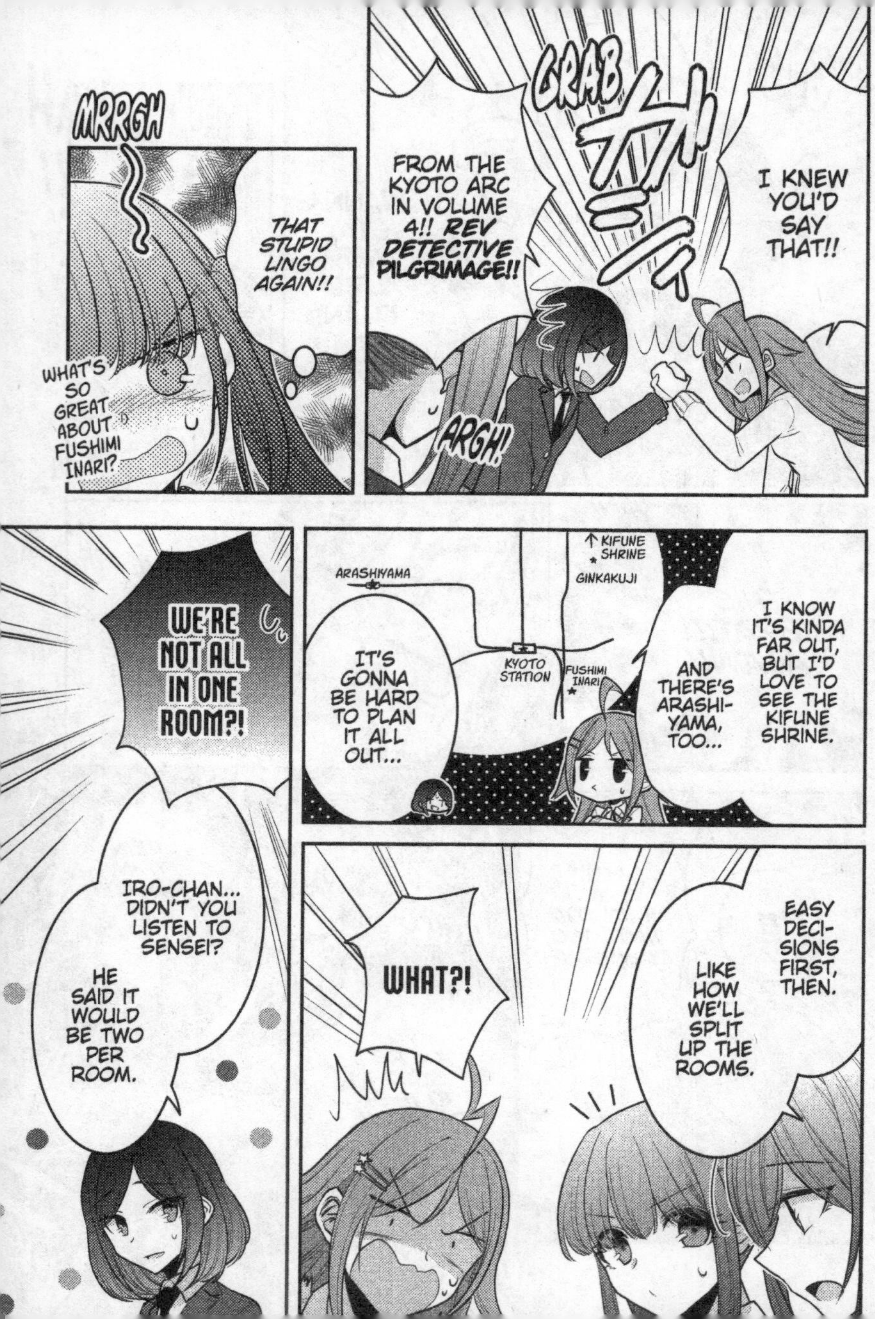

GRAB
I KNEW YOU'D SAY THAT!!
FROM THE KYOTO ARC IN VOLUME 4!! ***REV DETECTIVE PILGRIMAGE!!***
ARGH!
MRRGH
THAT STUPID LINGO AGAIN!!
WHAT'S SO GREAT ABOUT FUSHIMI INARI?
KIFUNE SHRINE
GINKAKUJI
ARASHIYAMA
KYOTO STATION
FUSHIMI INARI
I KNOW IT'S KINDA FAR OUT, BUT I'D LOVE TO SEE THE KIFUNE SHRINE.
AND THERE'S ARASHIYAMA, TOO...
IT'S GONNA BE HARD TO PLAN IT ALL OUT...
EASY DECISIONS FIRST, THEN.
LIKE HOW WE'LL SPLIT UP THE ROOMS.
WHAT?!
WE'RE NOT ALL IN ONE ROOM?!
IRO-CHAN... DIDN'T YOU LISTEN TO SENSEI?
HE SAID IT WOULD BE TWO PER ROOM.

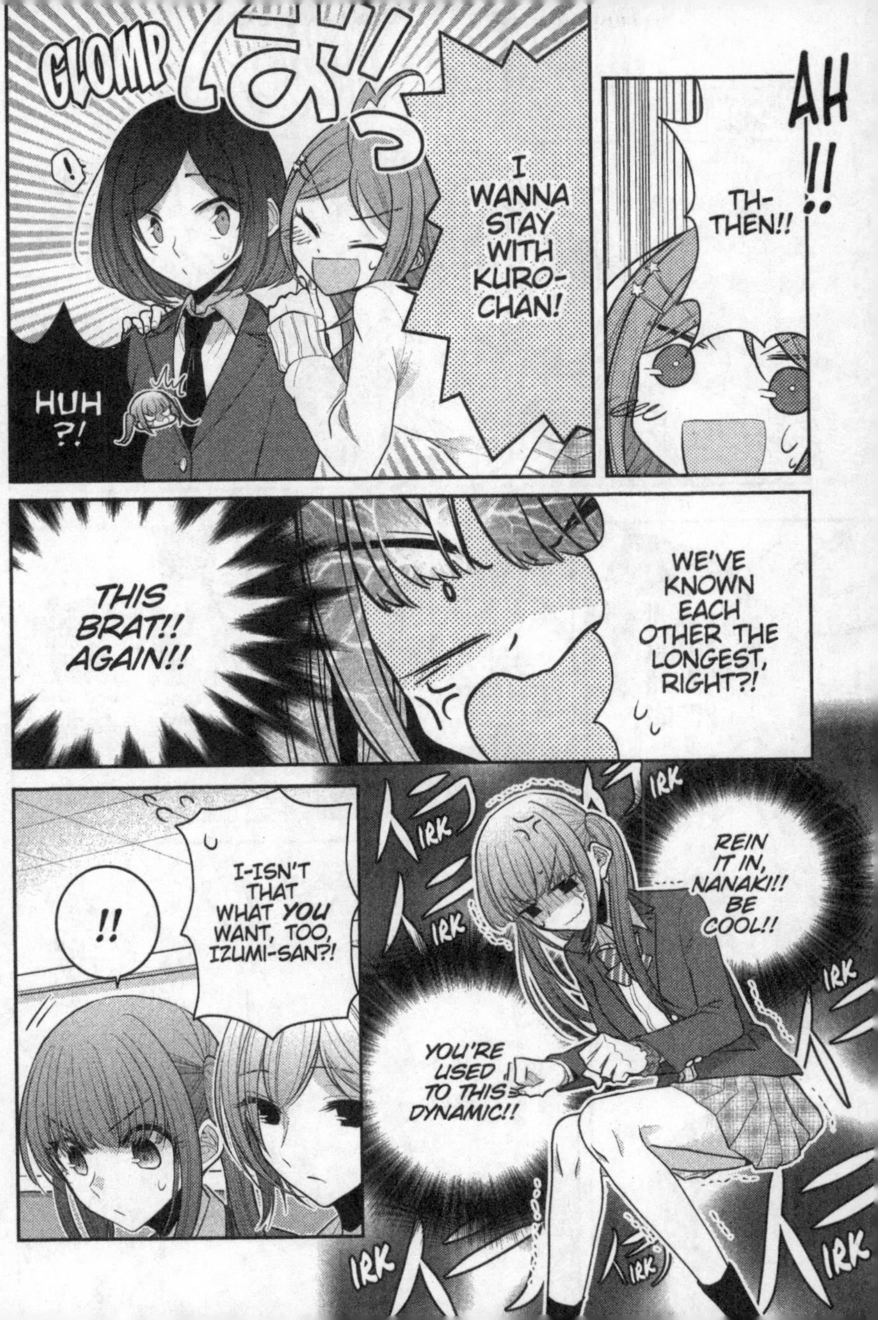
AH!!
TH- THEN!!
I WANNA STAY WITH KURO-CHAN!
GLOMP
!
HUH?!
WE'VE KNOWN EACH OTHER THE LONGEST, RIGHT?!
THIS BRAT!! AGAIN!!
IRK
REIN IT IN, NANAKI!! BE COOL!!
IRK
IRK
IRK
YOU'RE USED TO THIS DYNAMIC!!
IRK
IRK
IRK
I-ISN'T THAT WHAT YOU WANT, TOO, IZUMI-SAN?!
!!

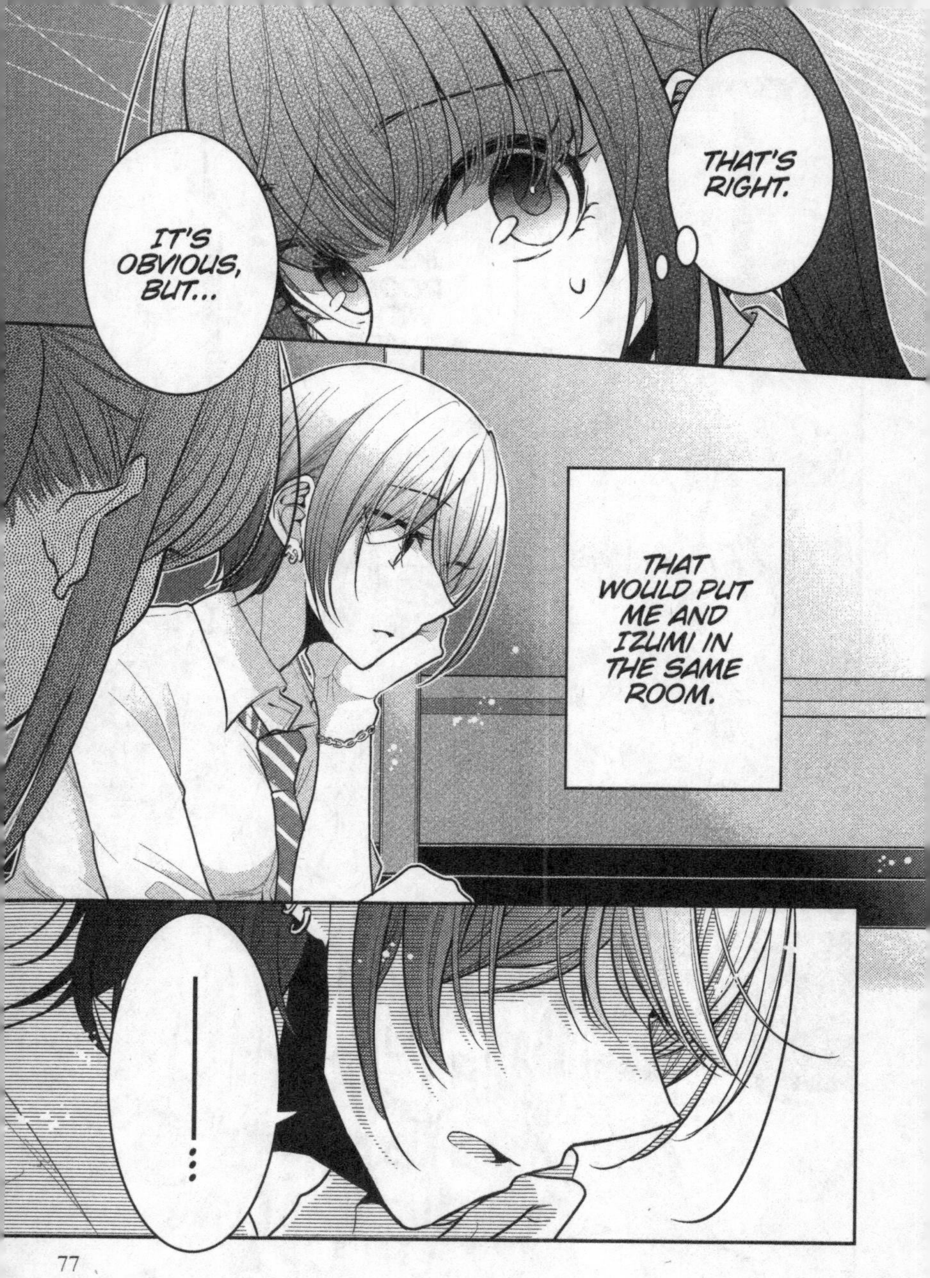
THAT'S RIGHT.
IT'S OBVIOUS, BUT...
THAT WOULD PUT ME AND IZUMI IN THE SAME ROOM.
—...

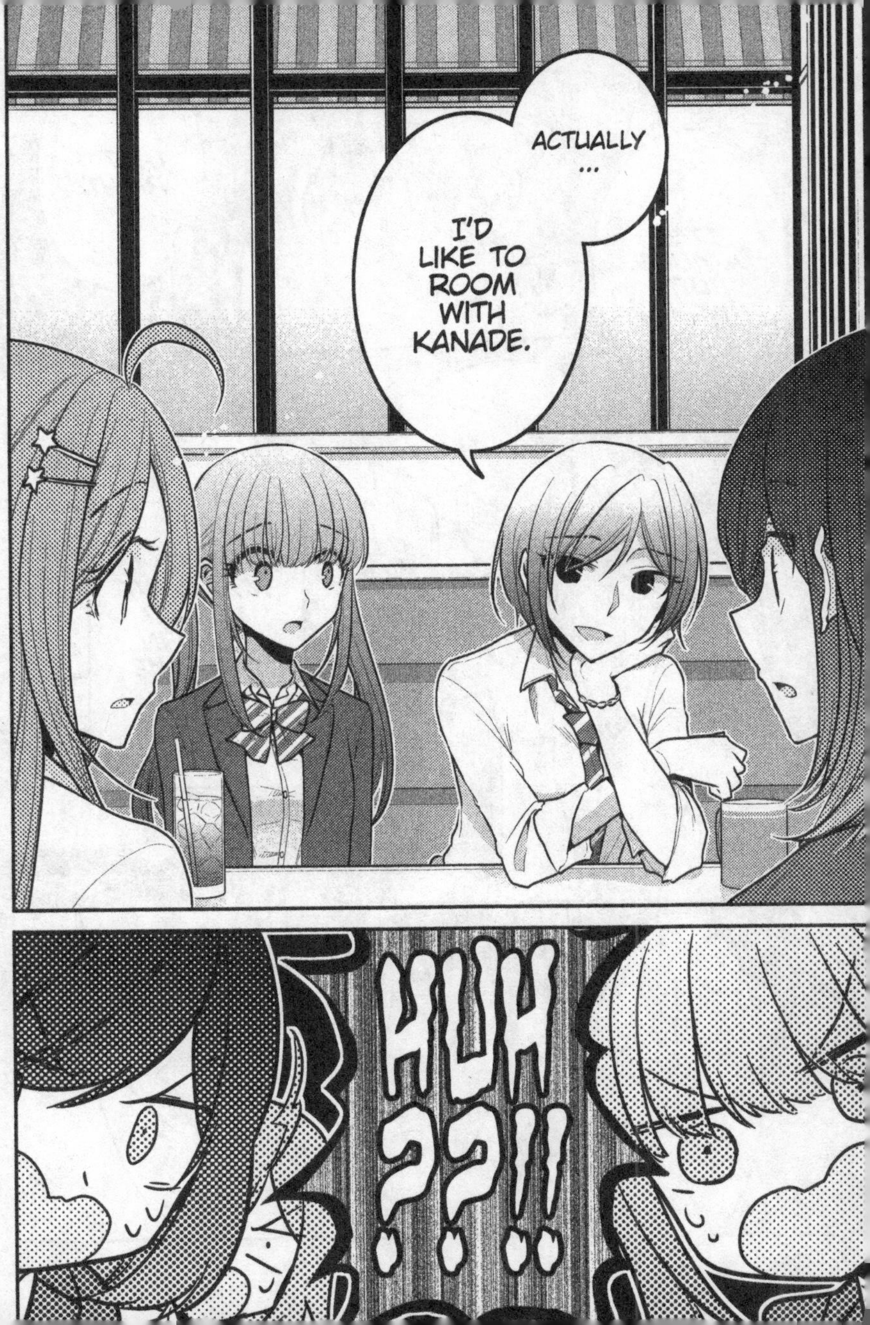
ACTUALLY ... I'D LIKE TO ROOM WITH KANADE.
HUH ??!!

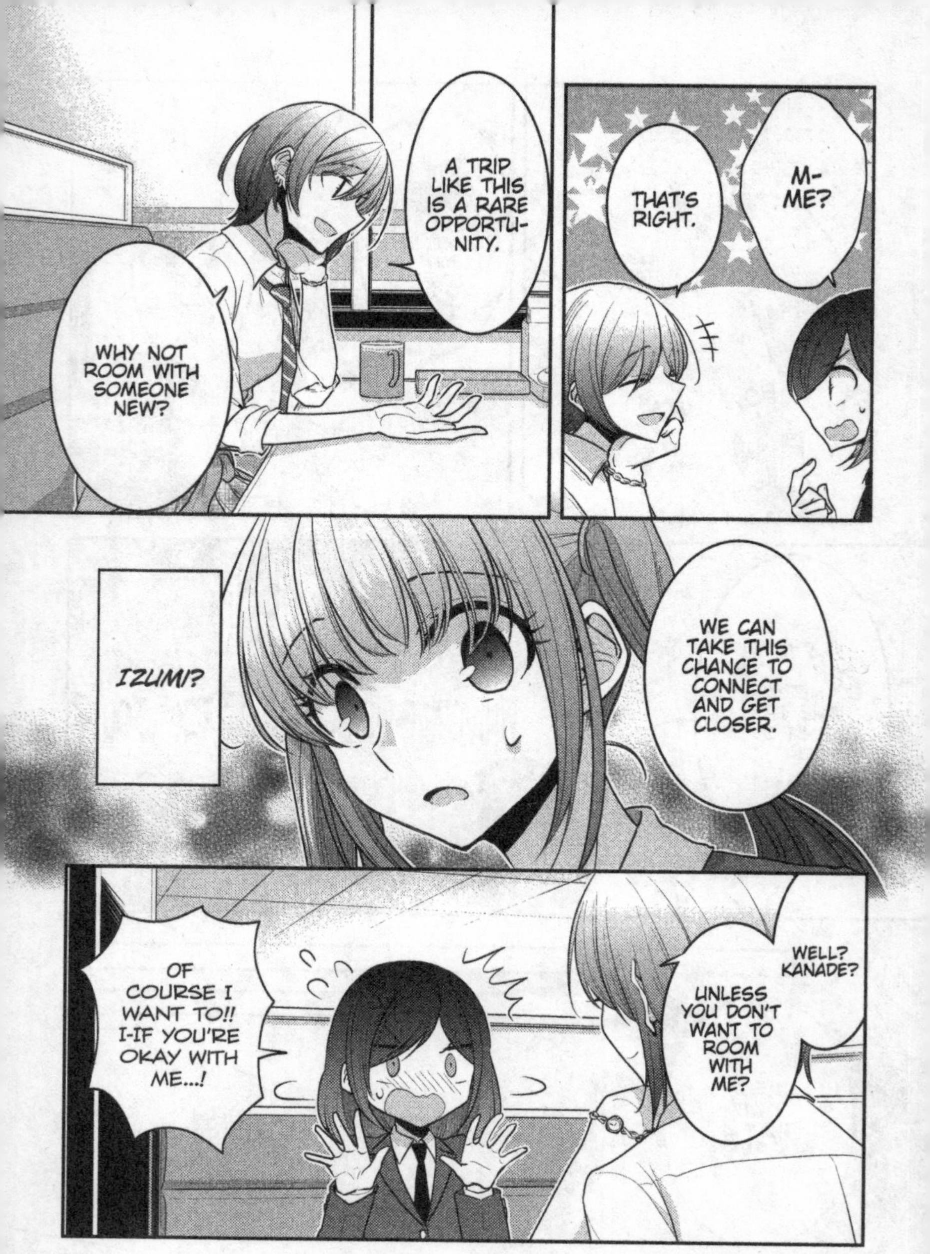
M-ME?
THAT'S RIGHT.
A TRIP LIKE THIS IS A RARE OPPORTU-NITY.
WHY NOT ROOM WITH SOMEONE NEW?
WE CAN TAKE THIS CHANCE TO CONNECT AND GET CLOSER.
IZUMI?
WELL? KANADE?
UNLESS YOU DON'T WANT TO ROOM WITH ME?
OF COURSE I WANT TO!! I-IF YOU'RE OKAY WITH ME...!

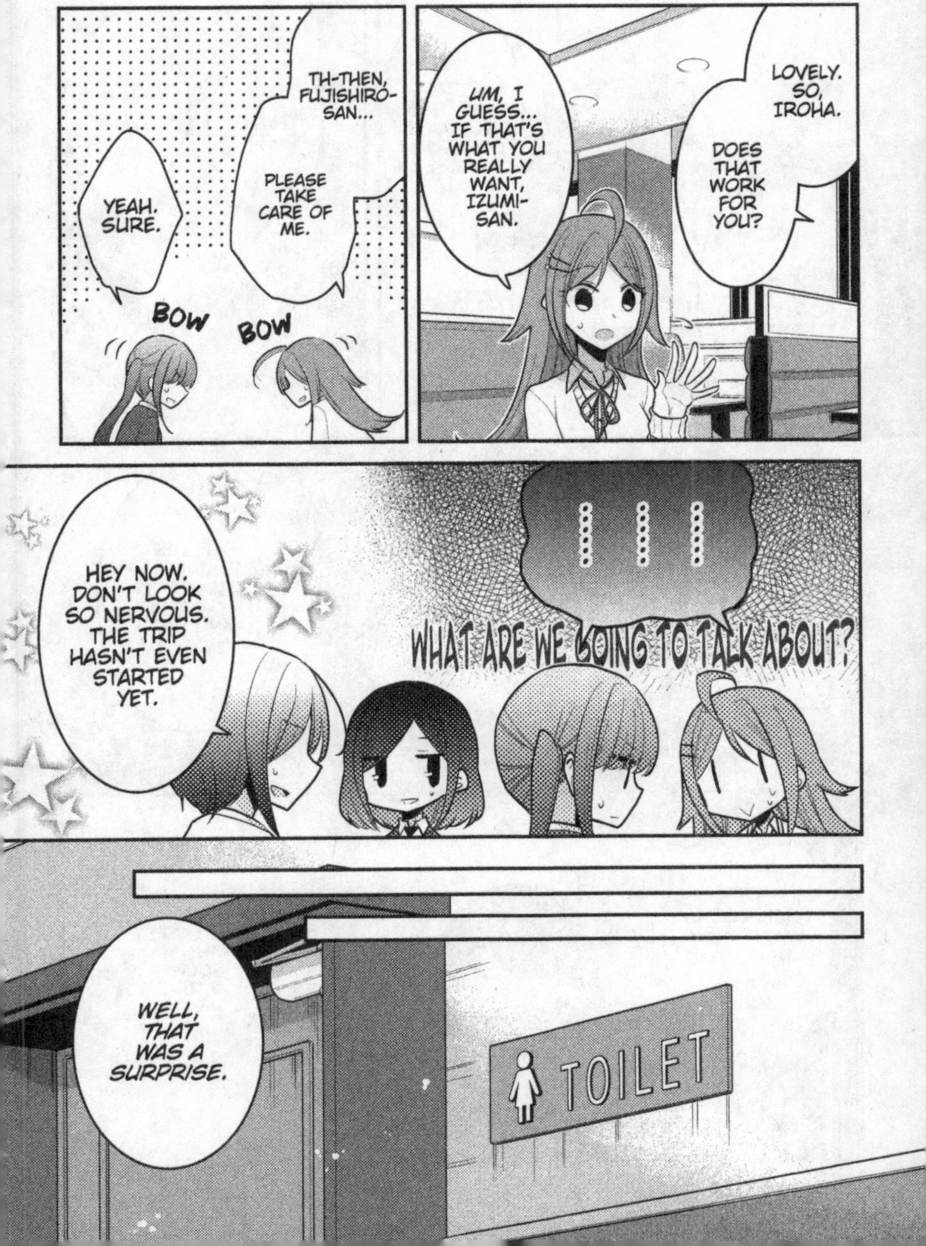
LOVELY. SO, IROHA.
DOES THAT WORK FOR YOU?
UM, I GUESS... IF THAT'S WHAT YOU REALLY WANT, IZUMI-SAN.
TH-THEN, FUJISHIRO-SAN...
PLEASE TAKE CARE OF ME.
YEAH. SURE.
BOW
BOW
....
WHAT ARE WE GOING TO TALK ABOUT?
HEY NOW. DON'T LOOK SO NERVOUS. THE TRIP HASN'T EVEN STARTED YET.
WELL, THAT WAS A SURPRISE.
TOILET

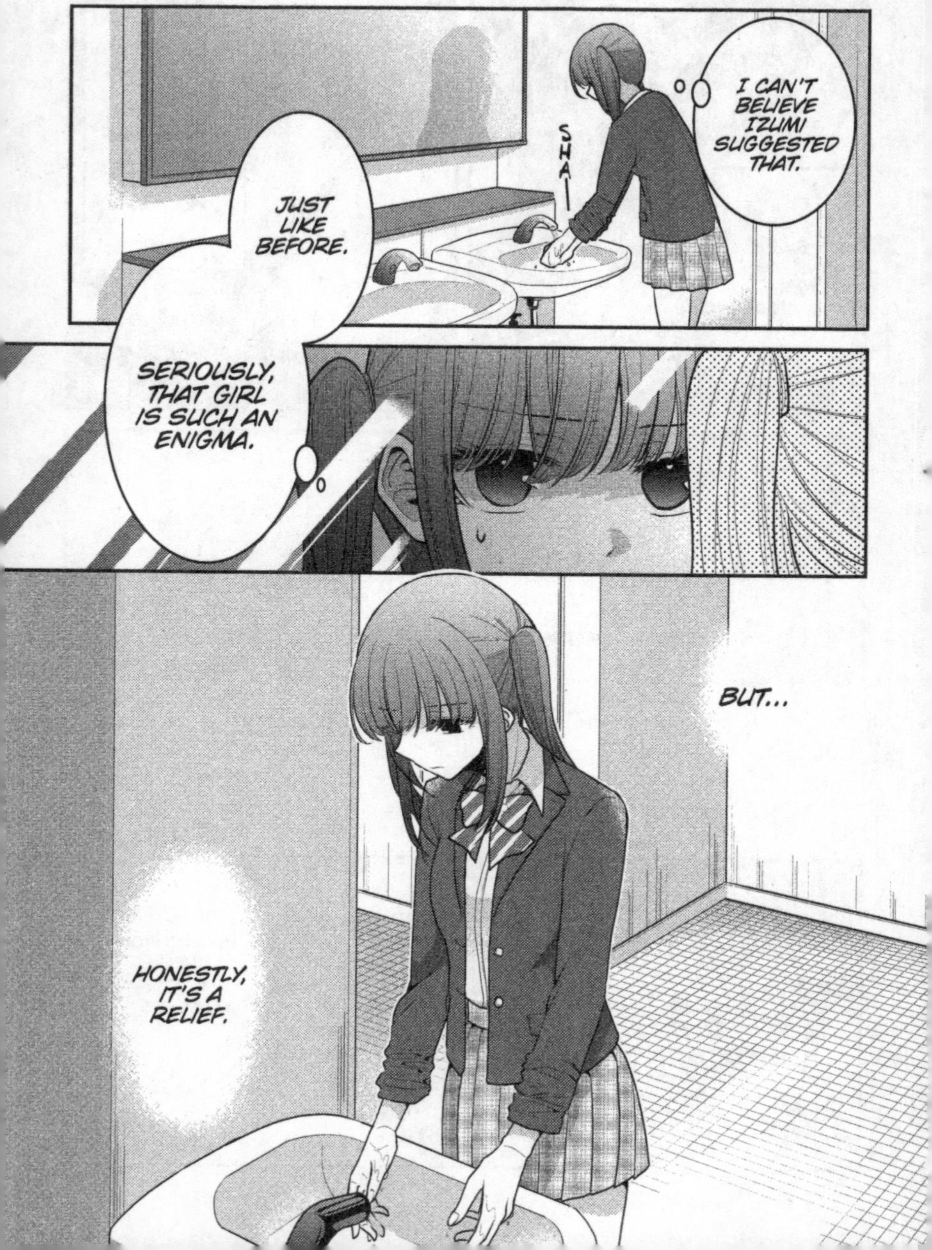
I CAN'T BELIEVE IZUMI SUGGESTED THAT.
SHA
JUST LIKE BEFORE.
SERIOUSLY, THAT GIRL IS SUCH AN ENIGMA.
BUT...
HONESTLY, IT'S A RELIEF.

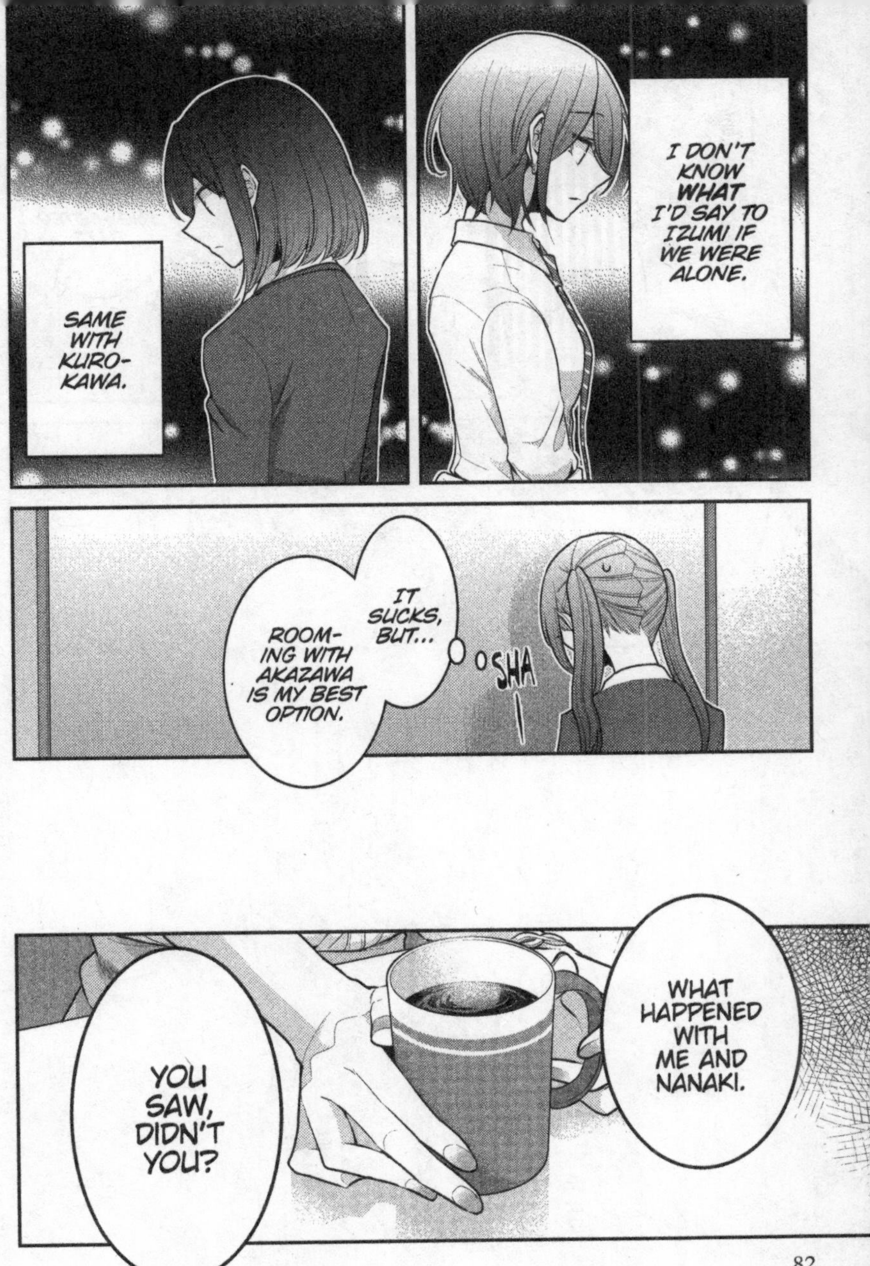
I DON'T KNOW WHAT I'D SAY TO IZUMI IF WE WERE ALONE.
SAME WITH KUROKAWA.
SHA
IT SUCKS, BUT... ROOMING WITH AKAZAWA IS MY BEST OPTION.
WHAT HAPPENED WITH ME AND NANAKI.
YOU SAW, DIDN'T YOU?

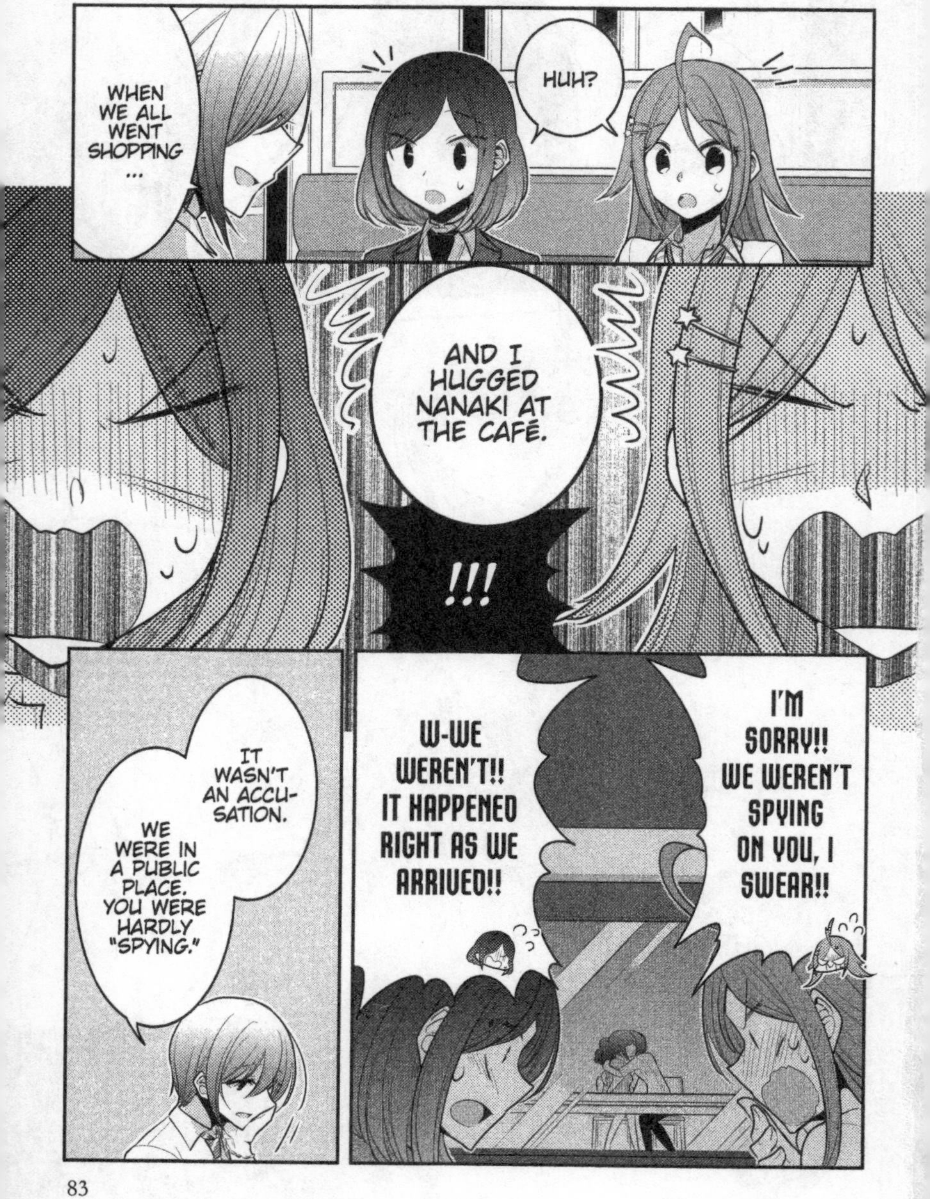
HUH?
WHEN WE ALL WENT SHOPPING ...
AND I HUGGED NANAKI AT THE CAFÉ.
!!!
I'M SORRY!! WE WEREN'T SPYING ON YOU, I SWEAR!!
W-WE WEREN'T!! IT HAPPENED RIGHT AS WE ARRIVED!!
IT WASN'T AN ACCU-SATION.
WE WERE IN A PUBLIC PLACE. YOU WERE HARDLY "SPYING."

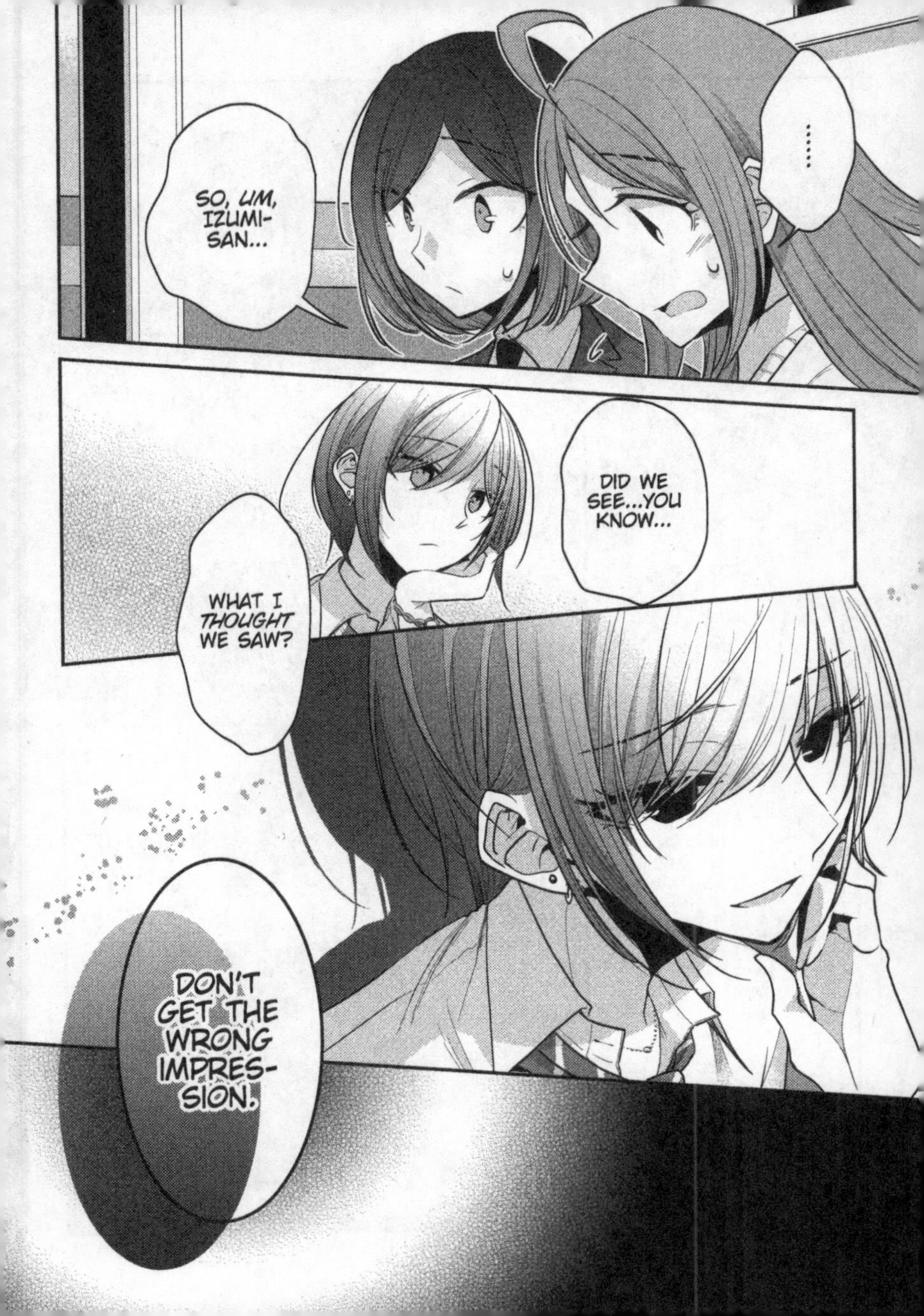
......
SO, UM, IZUMI-SAN...
DID WE SEE...YOU KNOW...
WHAT I *THOUGHT* WE SAW?
DON'T GET THE WRONG IMPRES-SION.

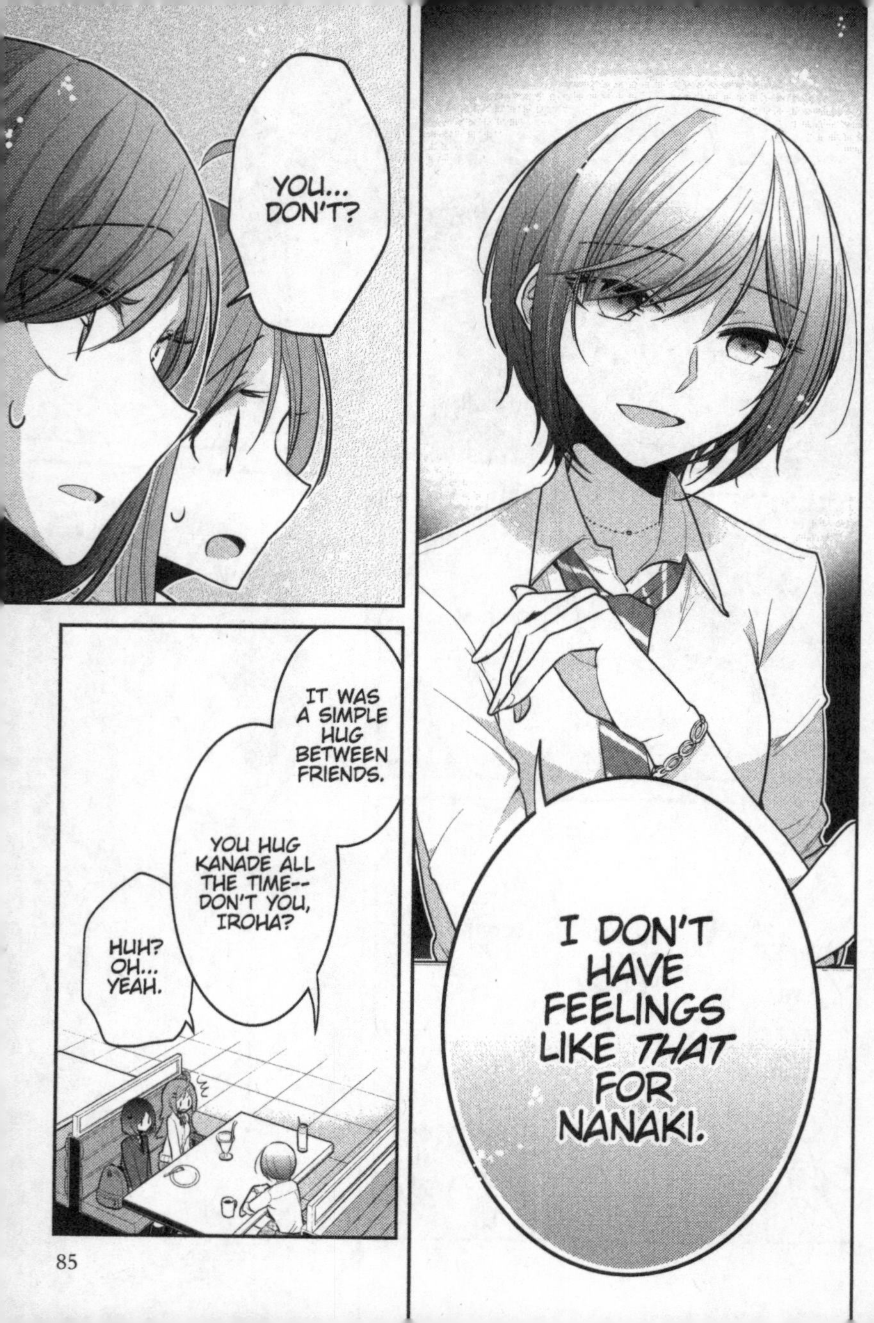
I DON'T HAVE FEELINGS LIKE *THAT* FOR NANAKI.
YOU... DON'T?
IT WAS A SIMPLE HUG BETWEEN FRIENDS.
YOU HUG KANADE ALL THE TIME-- DON'T YOU, IROHA?
HUH? OH... YEAH.

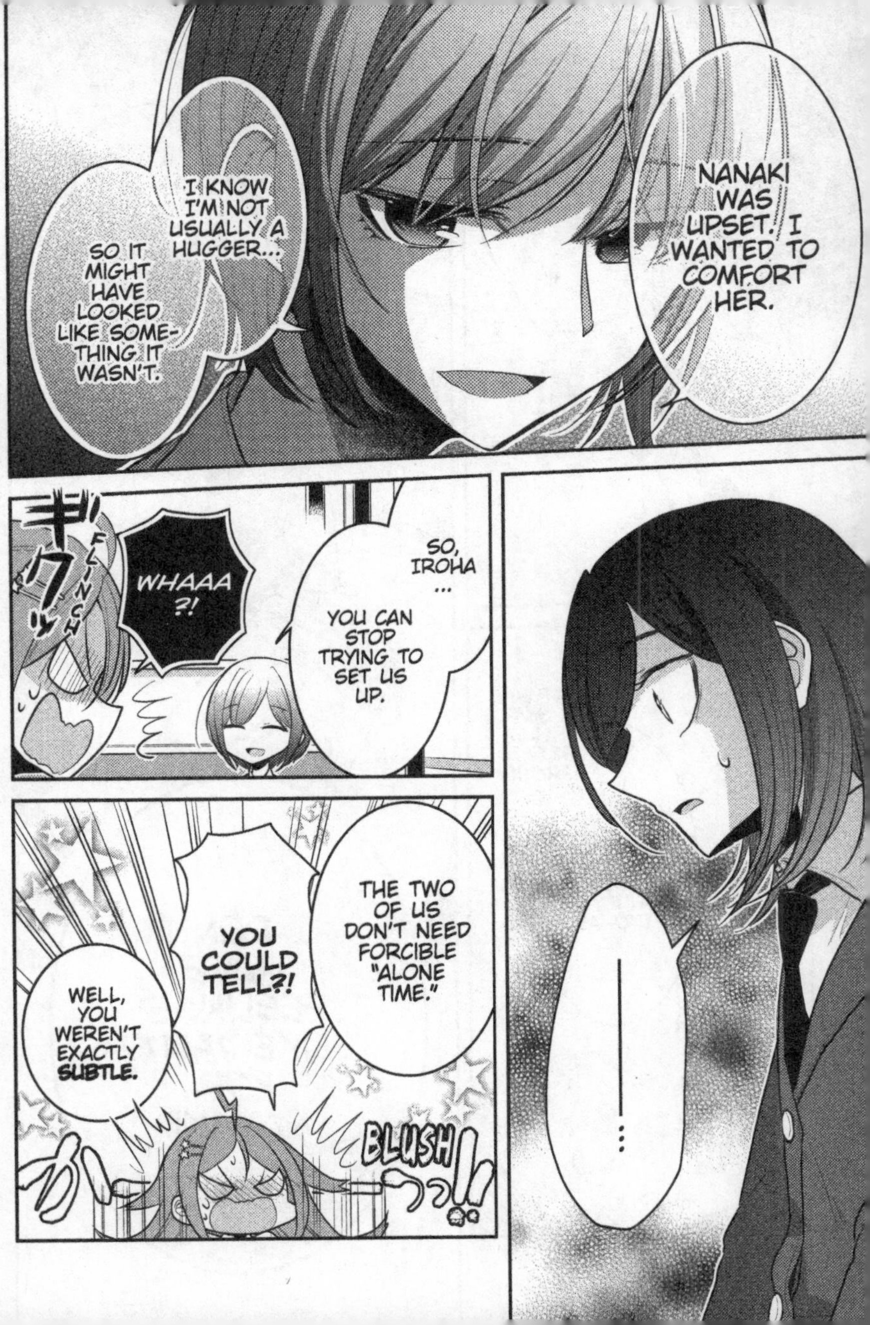
NANAKI WAS UPSET. I WANTED TO COMFORT HER.
I KNOW I'M NOT USUALLY A HUGGER...
SO IT MIGHT HAVE LOOKED LIKE SOME-THING IT WASN'T.
—...
SO, IROHA...
YOU CAN STOP TRYING TO SET US UP.
WHAAA?!
FLINCH
THE TWO OF US DON'T NEED FORCIBLE "ALONE TIME."
YOU COULD TELL?!
WELL, YOU WEREN'T EXACTLY SUBTLE.
BLUSH

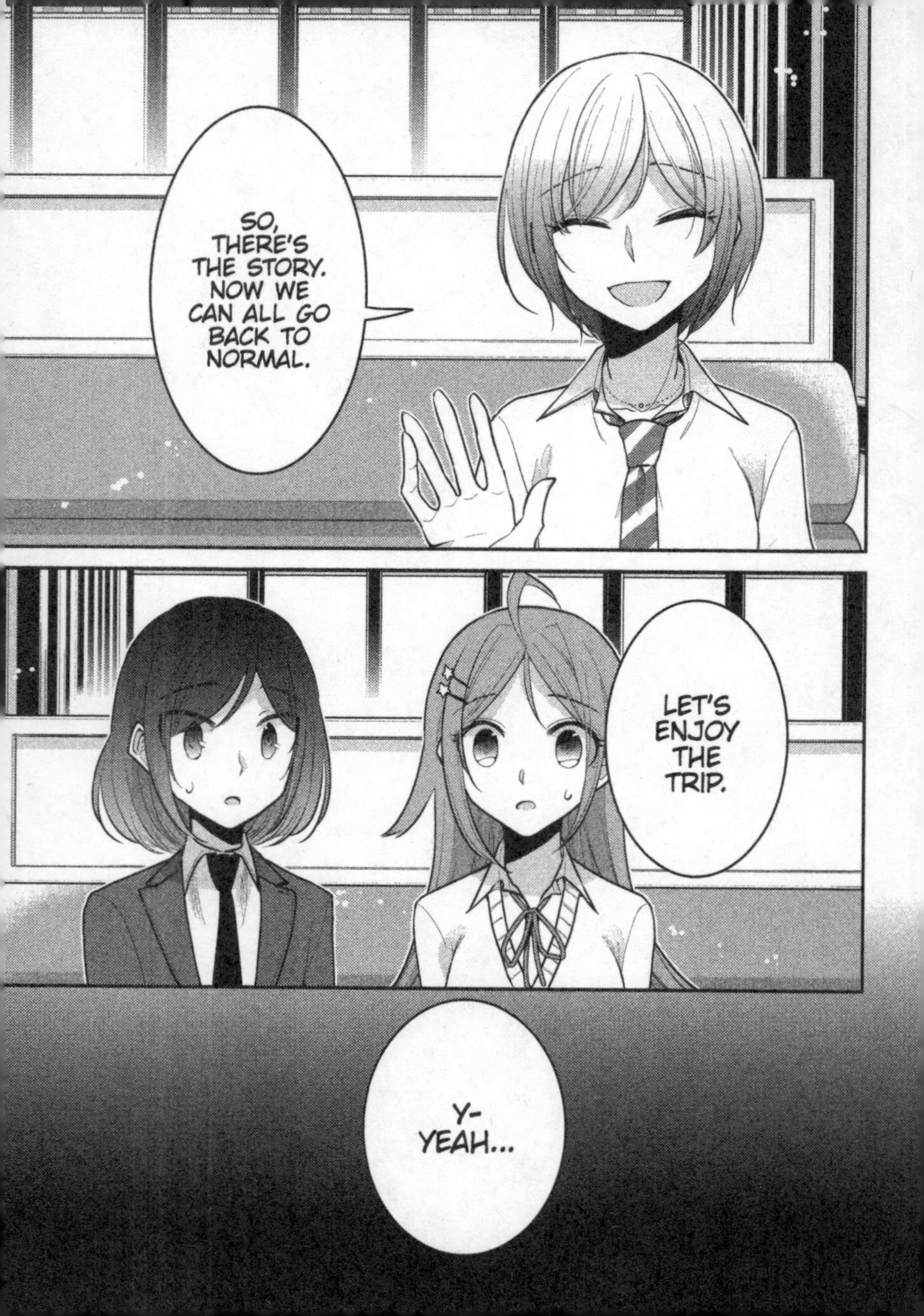
SO, THERE'S THE STORY. NOW WE CAN ALL GO BACK TO NORMAL.
LET'S ENJOY THE TRIP.
Y-YEAH...

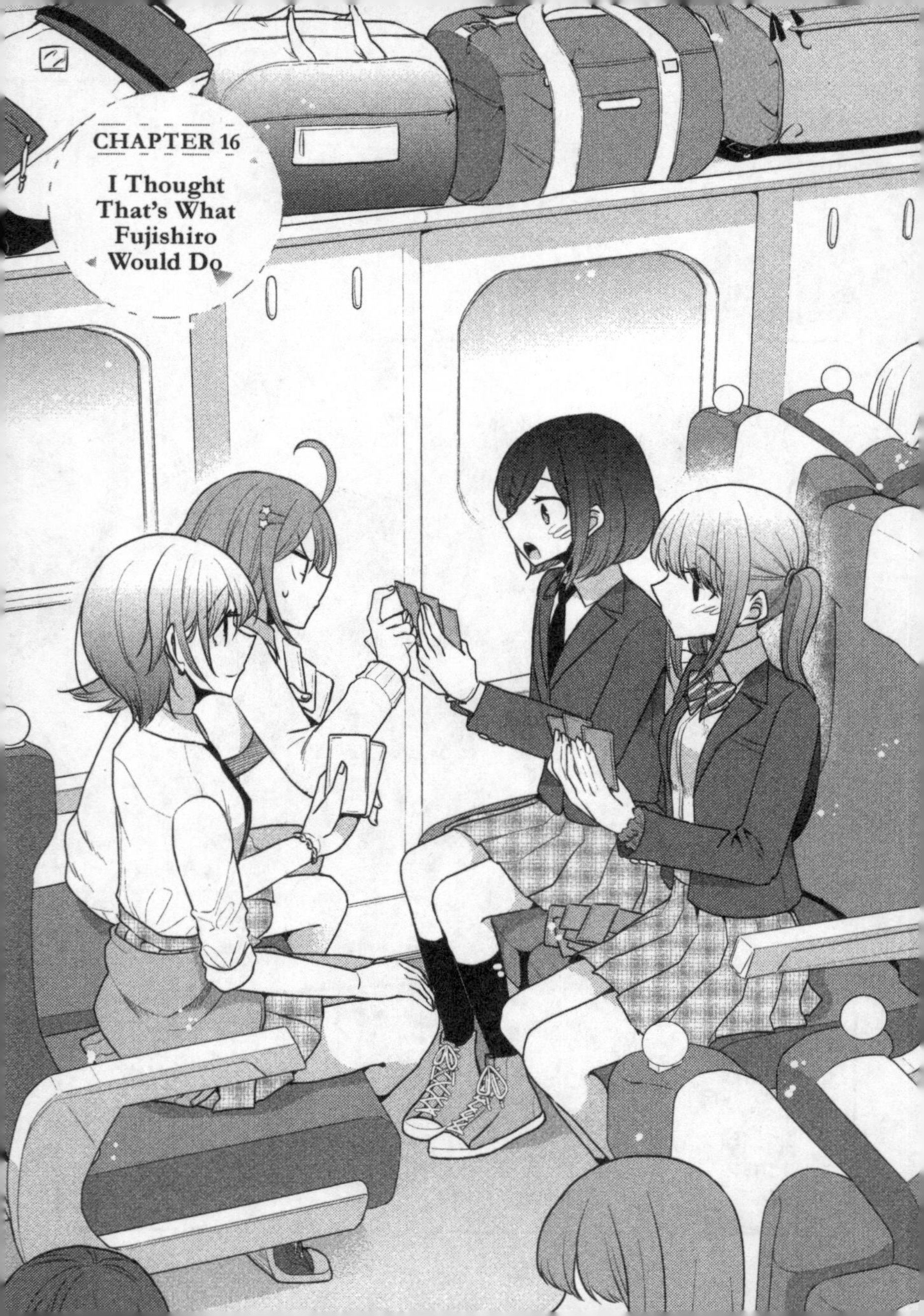
CHAPTER 16
I Thought That's What Fujishiro Would Do

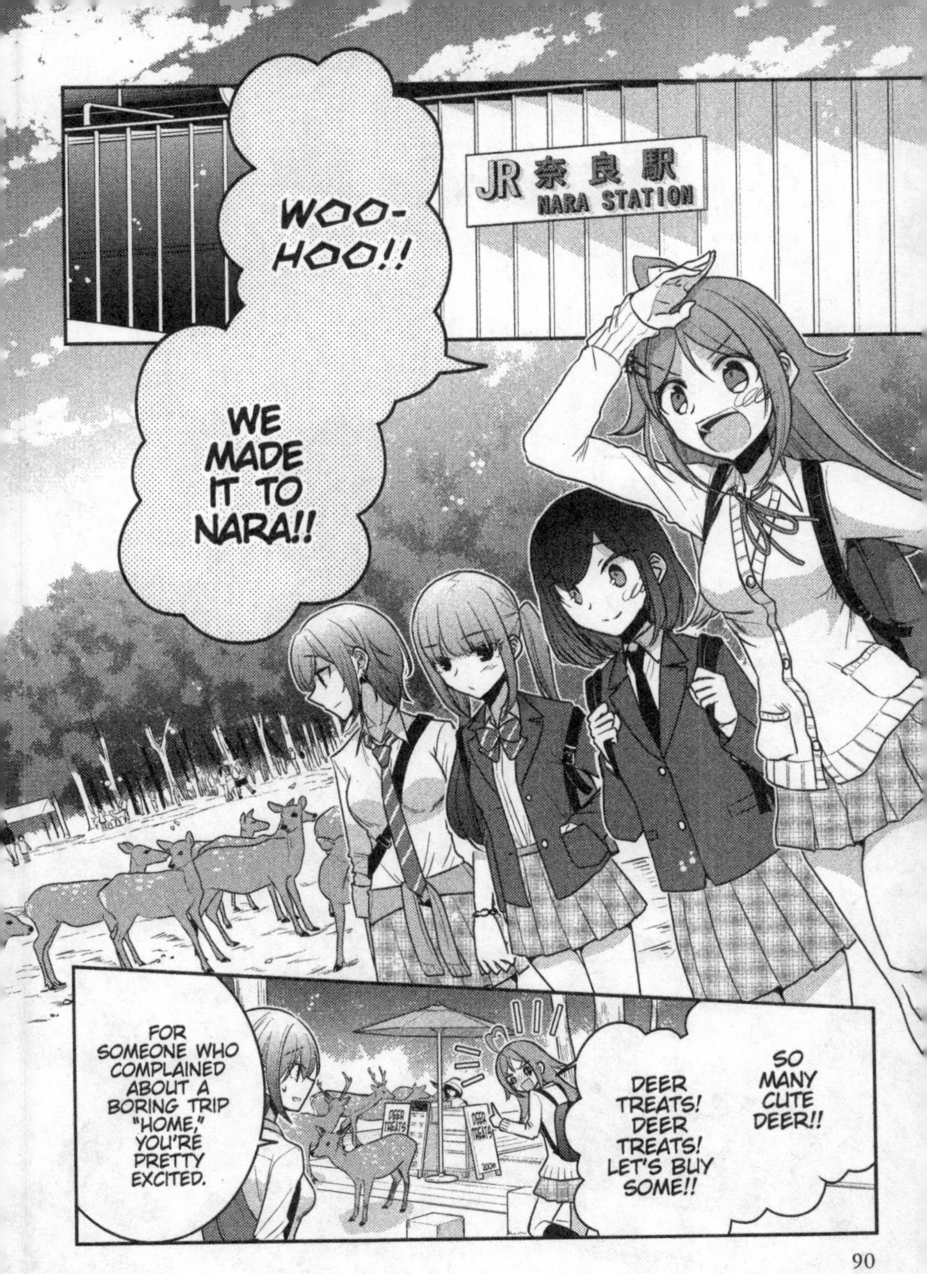
JR 奈良駅
NARA STATION
WOO-HOO!!
WE MADE IT TO NARA!!
SO MANY CUTE DEER!!
DEER TREATS! DEER TREATS! LET'S BUY SOME!!
DEER TREATS
DEER TREATS
FOR SOMEONE WHO COMPLAINED ABOUT A BORING TRIP "HOME," YOU'RE PRETTY EXCITED.

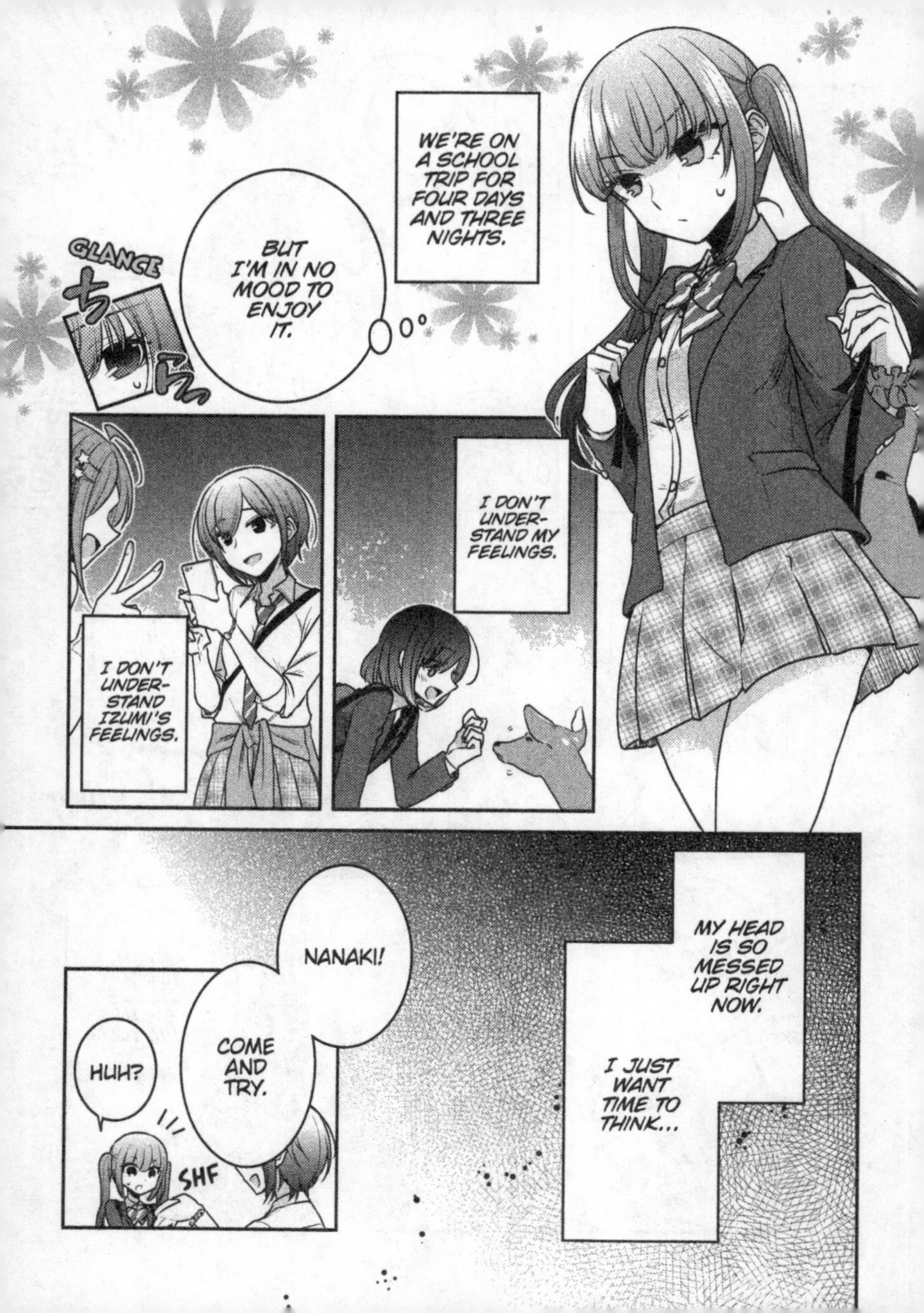

WE'RE ON A SCHOOL TRIP FOR FOUR DAYS AND THREE NIGHTS.
BUT I'M IN NO MOOD TO ENJOY IT.
GLANCE
I DON'T UNDERSTAND MY FEELINGS.
I DON'T UNDERSTAND IZUMI'S FEELINGS.
MY HEAD IS SO MESSED UP RIGHT NOW.
I JUST WANT TIME TO THINK...
NANAKI!
COME AND TRY.
HUH?
SHF

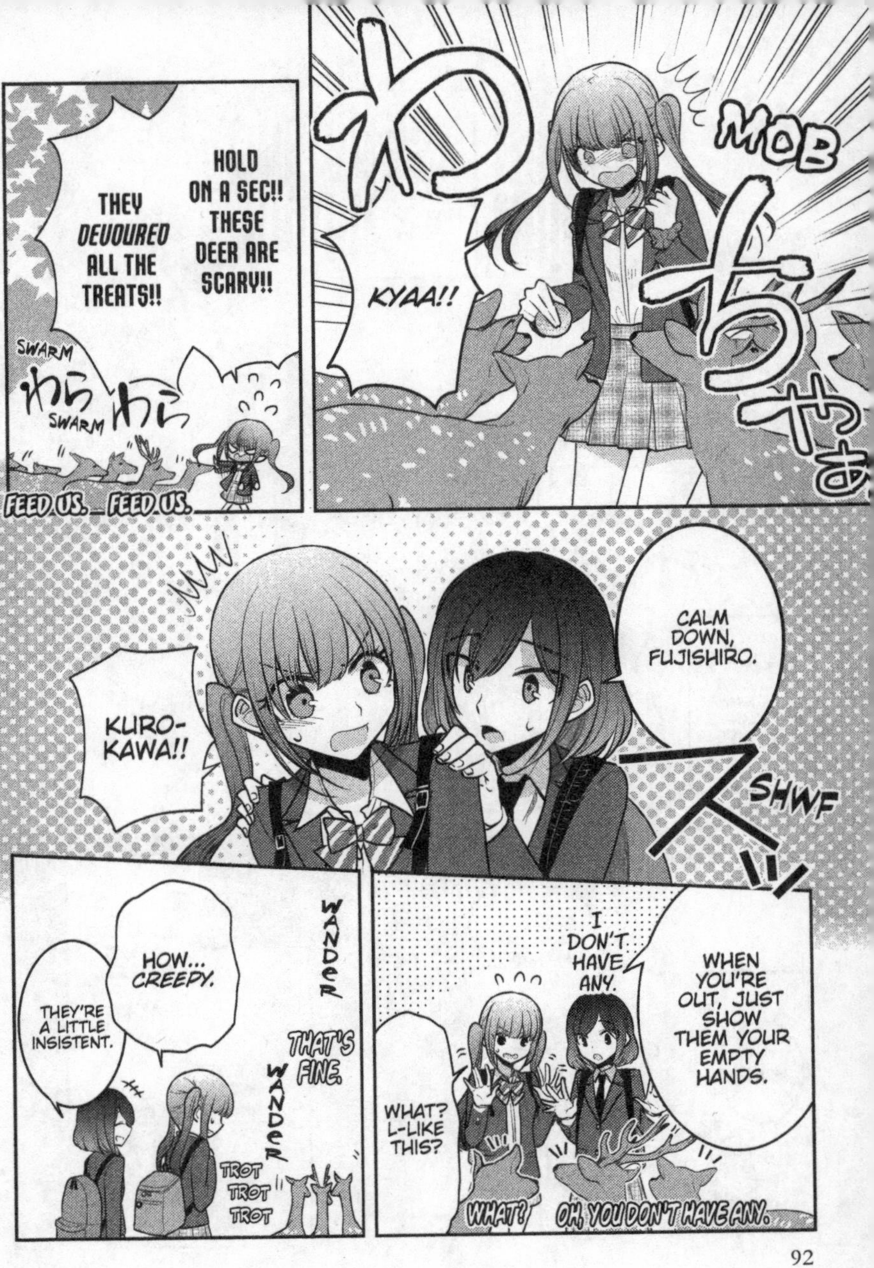
KYAA!!
わ
MOB
ちゃあ
HOLD ON A SEC!! THESE DEER ARE SCARY!!
THEY DEVOURED ALL THE TREATS!!
SWARM
わら
SWARM
わら
FEED US... FEED US.
CALM DOWN, FUJISHIRO.
ス
SHWF
ッ
KURO-KAWA!!
WHEN YOU'RE OUT, JUST SHOW THEM YOUR EMPTY HANDS.
I DON'T HAVE ANY.
WHAT? L-LIKE THIS?
OH, YOU DON'T HAVE ANY.
WHAT?
WANDER
THAT'S FINE.
WANDER
HOW... CREEPY.
THEY'RE A LITTLE INSISTENT.
TROT
TROT
TROT

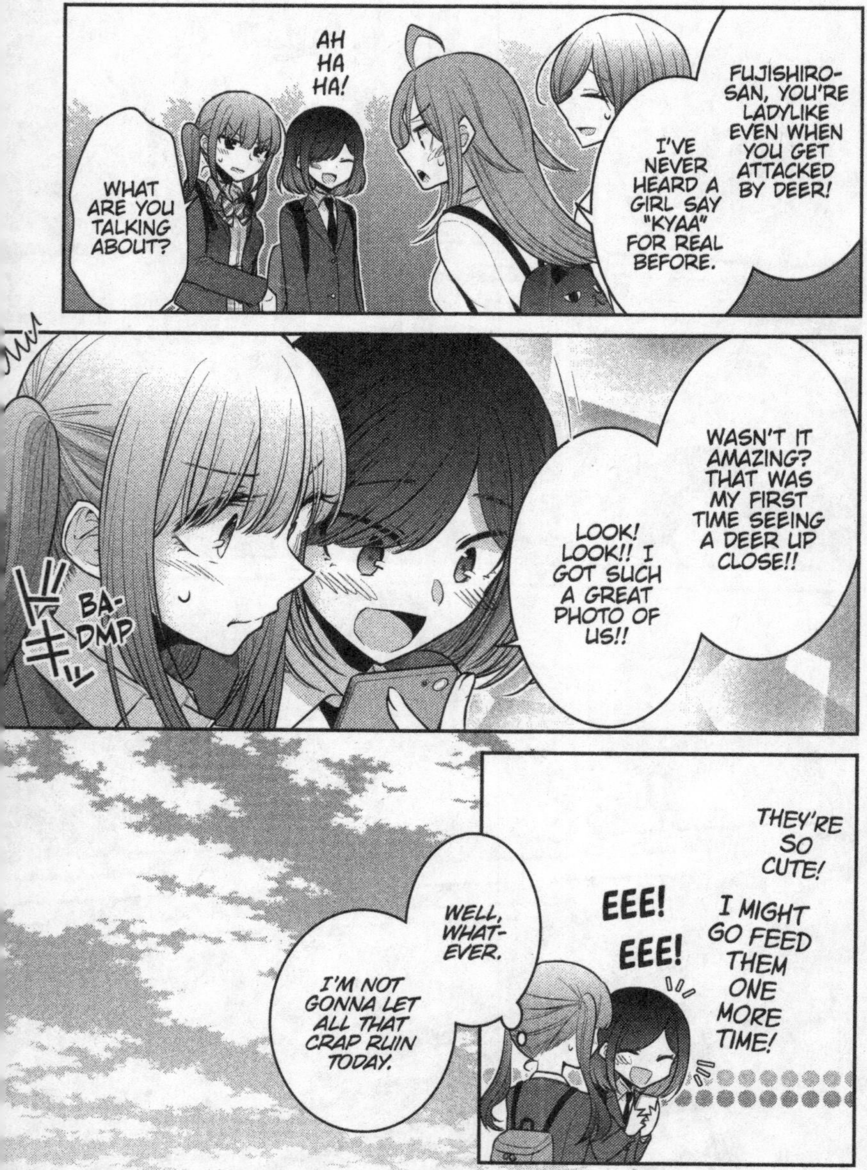
FUJISHIRO-SAN, YOU'RE LADYLIKE EVEN WHEN YOU GET ATTACKED BY DEER!
I'VE NEVER HEARD A GIRL SAY "KYAA" FOR REAL BEFORE.
AH HA HA!
WHAT ARE YOU TALKING ABOUT?
WASN'T IT AMAZING? THAT WAS MY FIRST TIME SEEING A DEER UP CLOSE!!
LOOK! LOOK!! I GOT SUCH A GREAT PHOTO OF US!!
BA-DMP
ドキッ
THEY'RE SO CUTE!
I MIGHT GO FEED THEM ONE MORE TIME!
EEE!
EEE!
WELL, WHATEVER.
I'M NOT GONNA LET ALL THAT CRAP RUIN TODAY.

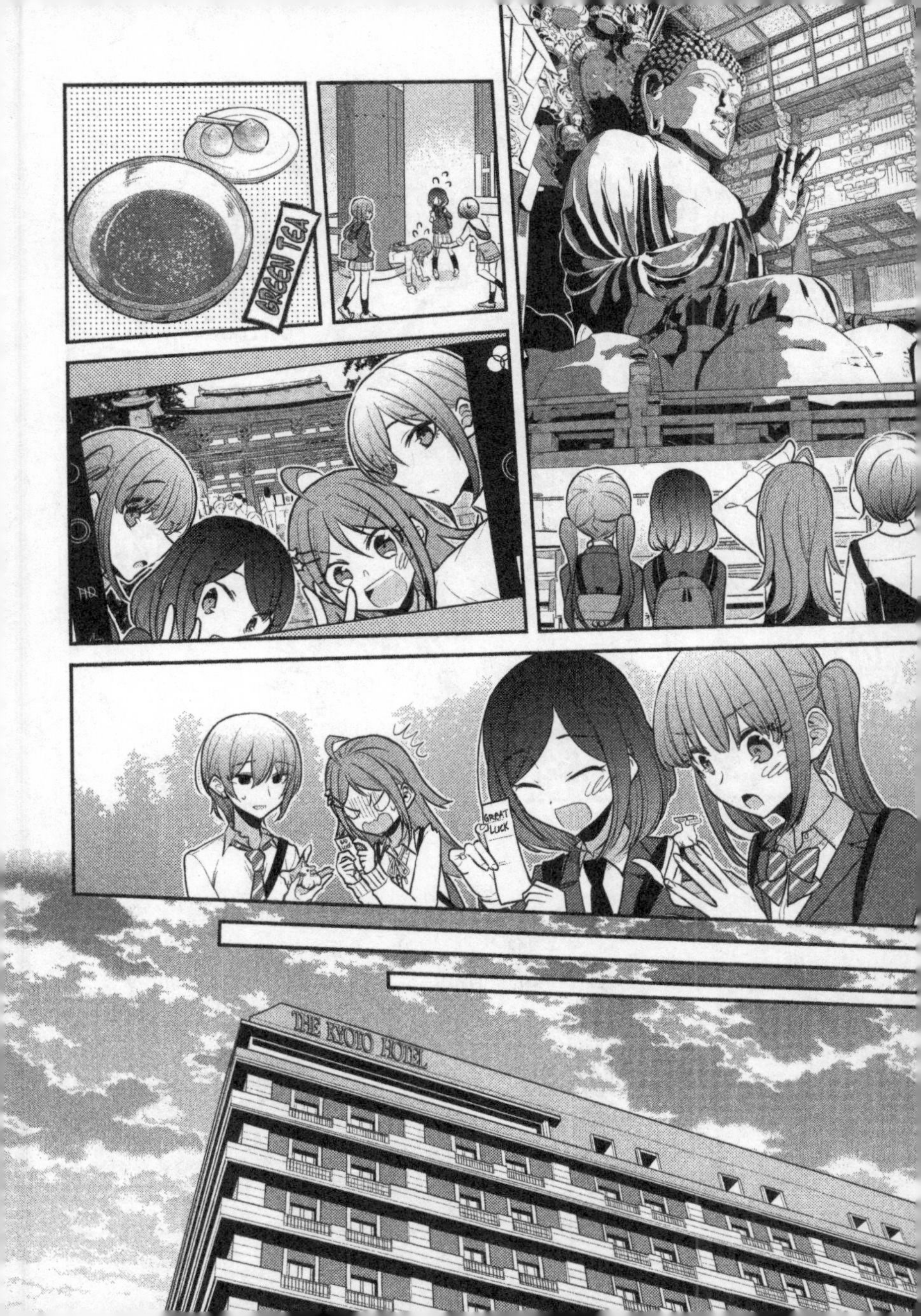
GREEN TEA
GREAT LUCK
BAD LUCK
THE KYOTO HOTEL

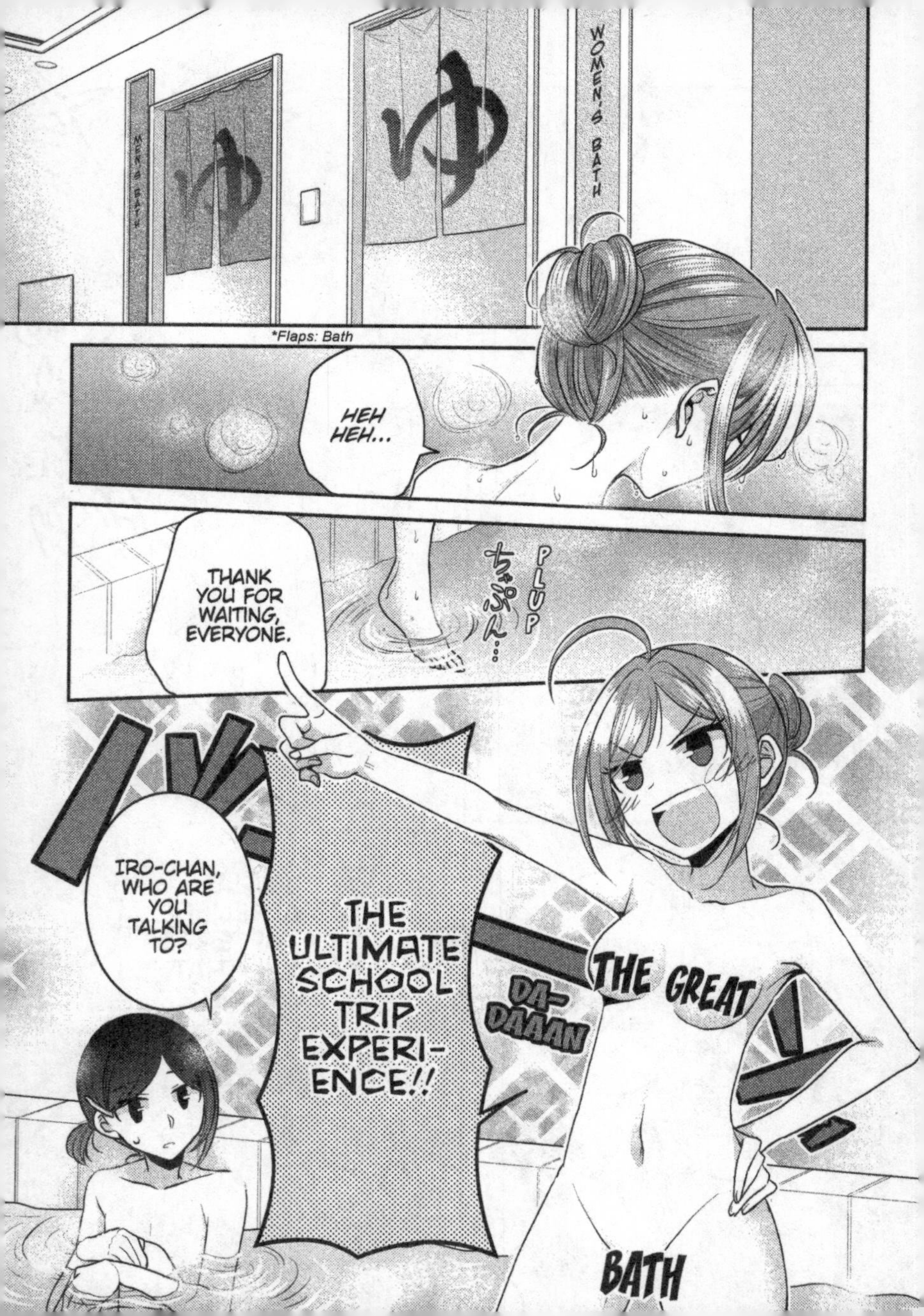
WOMEN'S BATH
MEN'S BATH
*Flaps: Bath
HEH HEH...
PLUP
ちゃぷん…
THANK YOU FOR WAITING, EVERYONE.
THE GREAT BATH
DA-DAAAN
THE ULTIMATE SCHOOL TRIP EXPERIENCE!!
IRO-CHAN, WHO ARE YOU TALKING TO?

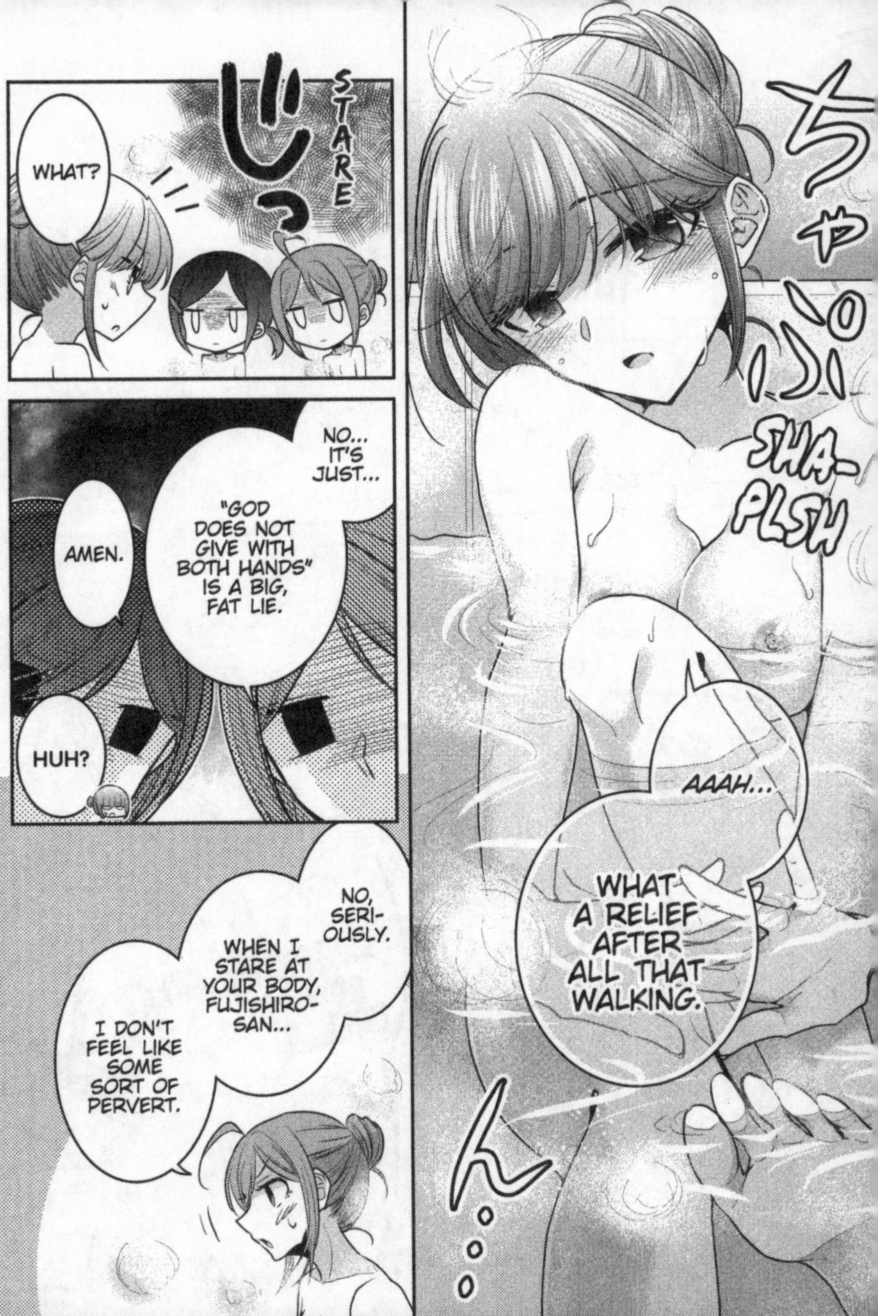
ちゃぷん
SHA-PLSH
AAAH...
WHAT A RELIEF AFTER ALL THAT WALKING.
ん...
じっ
STARE
WHAT?
NO... IT'S JUST...
"GOD DOES NOT GIVE WITH BOTH HANDS" IS A BIG, FAT LIE.
AMEN.
HUH?
NO, SERIOUSLY.
WHEN I STARE AT YOUR BODY, FUJISHIRO-SAN...
I DON'T FEEL LIKE SOME SORT OF PERVERT.

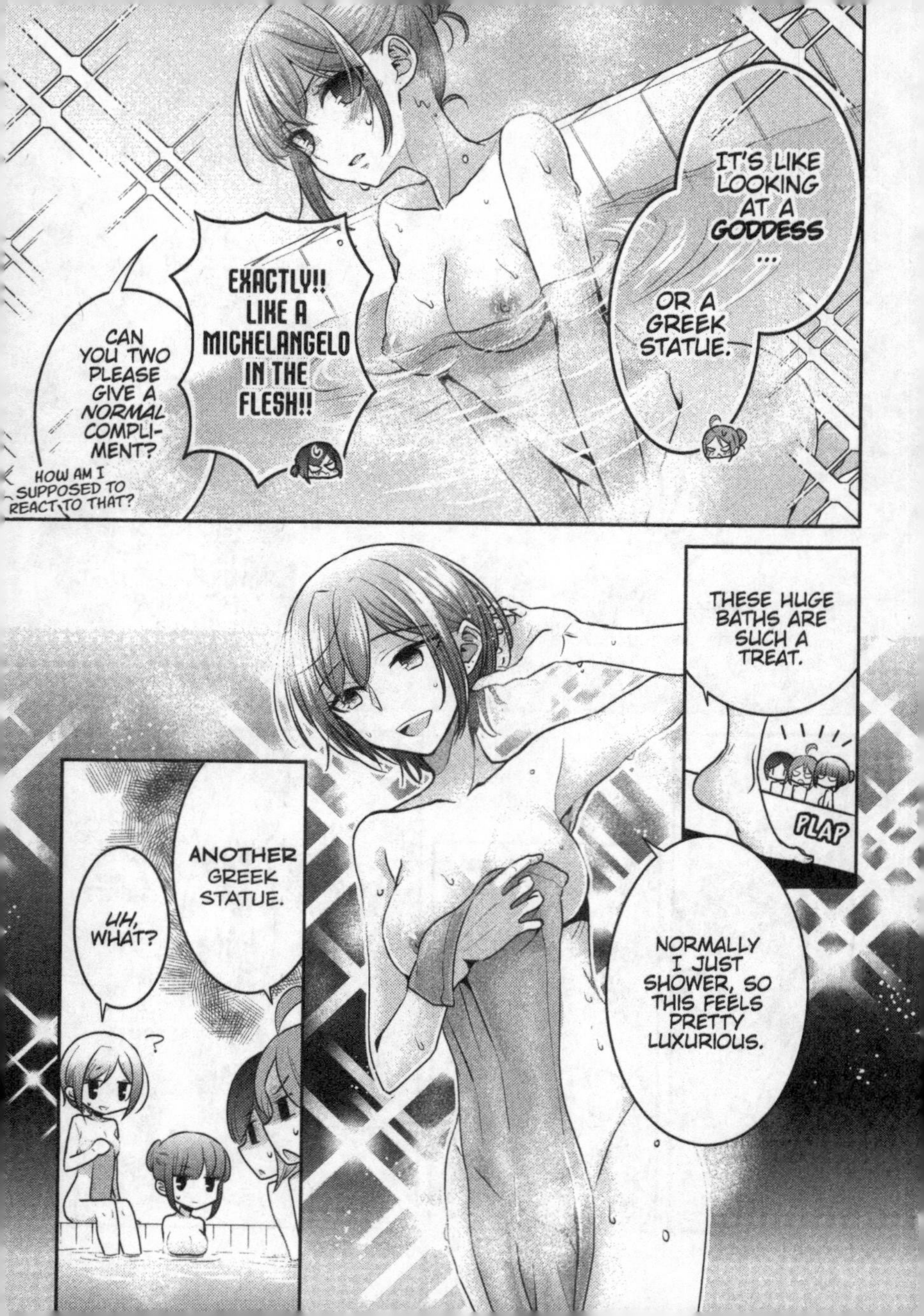
IT'S LIKE LOOKING AT A GODDESS ...
OR A GREEK STATUE.
EXACTLY!! LIKE A MICHELANGELO IN THE FLESH!!
CAN YOU TWO PLEASE GIVE A *NORMAL* COMPLIMENT?
HOW AM I SUPPOSED TO REACT TO THAT?
THESE HUGE BATHS ARE SUCH A TREAT.
PLAP
NORMALLY I JUST SHOWER, SO THIS FEELS PRETTY LUXURIOUS.
ANOTHER GREEK STATUE.
UH, WHAT?
?

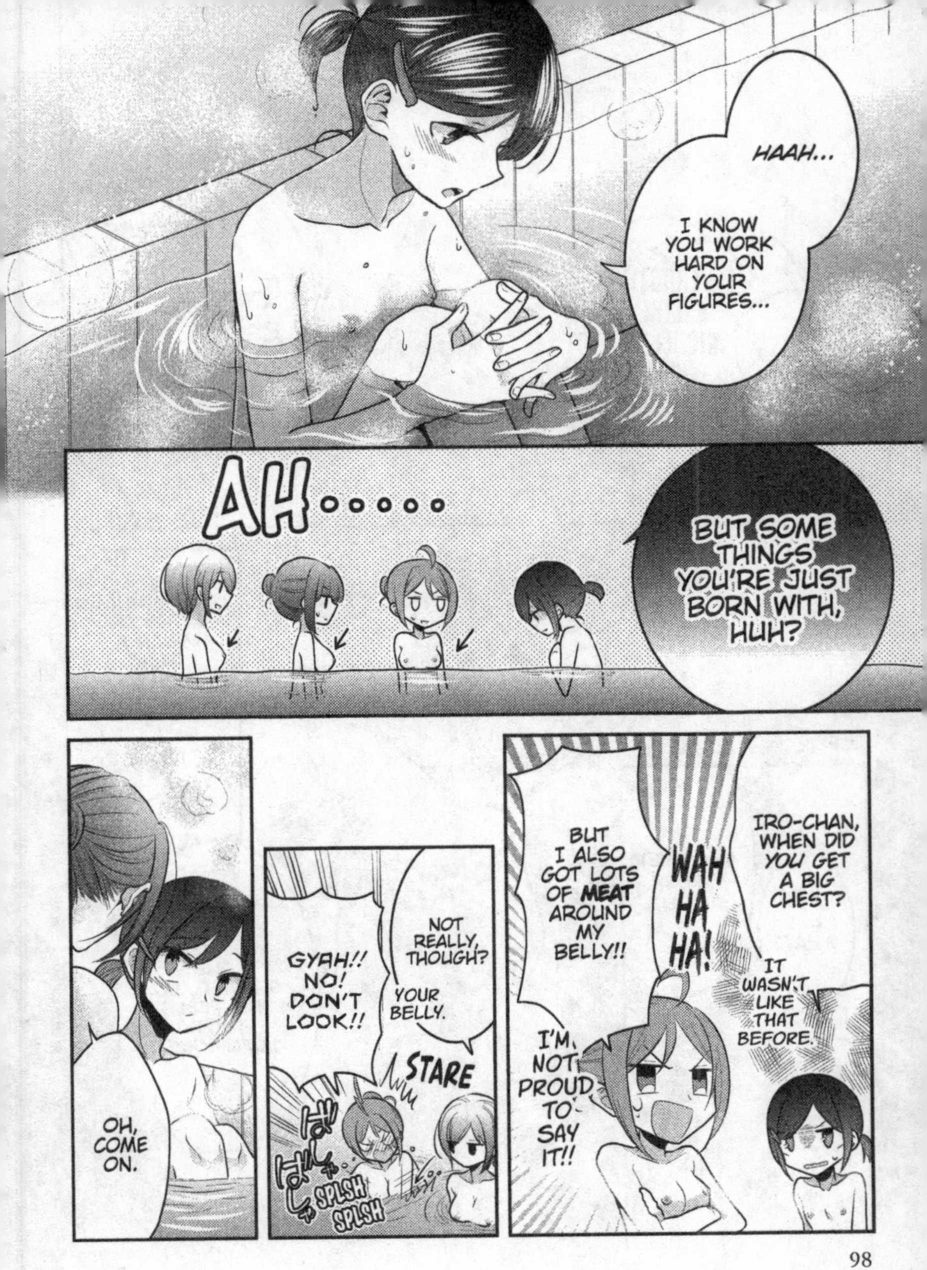
HAAH...
I KNOW YOU WORK HARD ON YOUR FIGURES...
BUT SOME THINGS YOU'RE JUST BORN WITH, HUH?
AH......
IRO-CHAN, WHEN DID YOU GET A BIG CHEST?
IT WASN'T LIKE THAT BEFORE.
WAH HA HA!
BUT I ALSO GOT LOTS OF MEAT AROUND MY BELLY!!
I'M NOT PROUD TO SAY IT!!
NOT REALLY, THOUGH?
YOUR BELLY.
STARE
GYAH!! NO! DON'T LOOK!!
ばしゃ ばしゃ
SPLSH SPLSH
OH, COME ON.

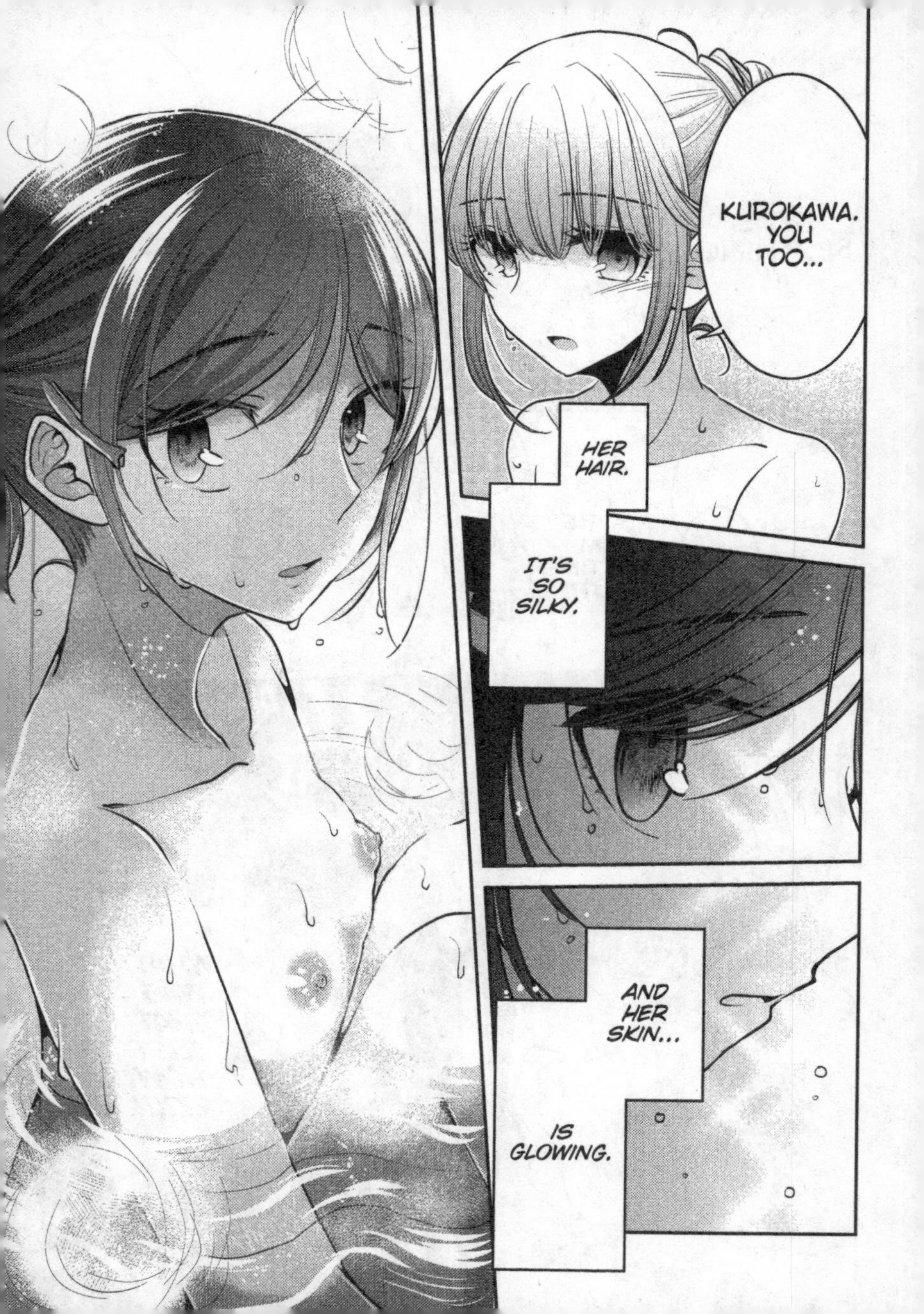
KUROKAWA. YOU TOO...
HER HAIR.
IT'S SO SILKY.
AND HER SKIN...
IS GLOWING.

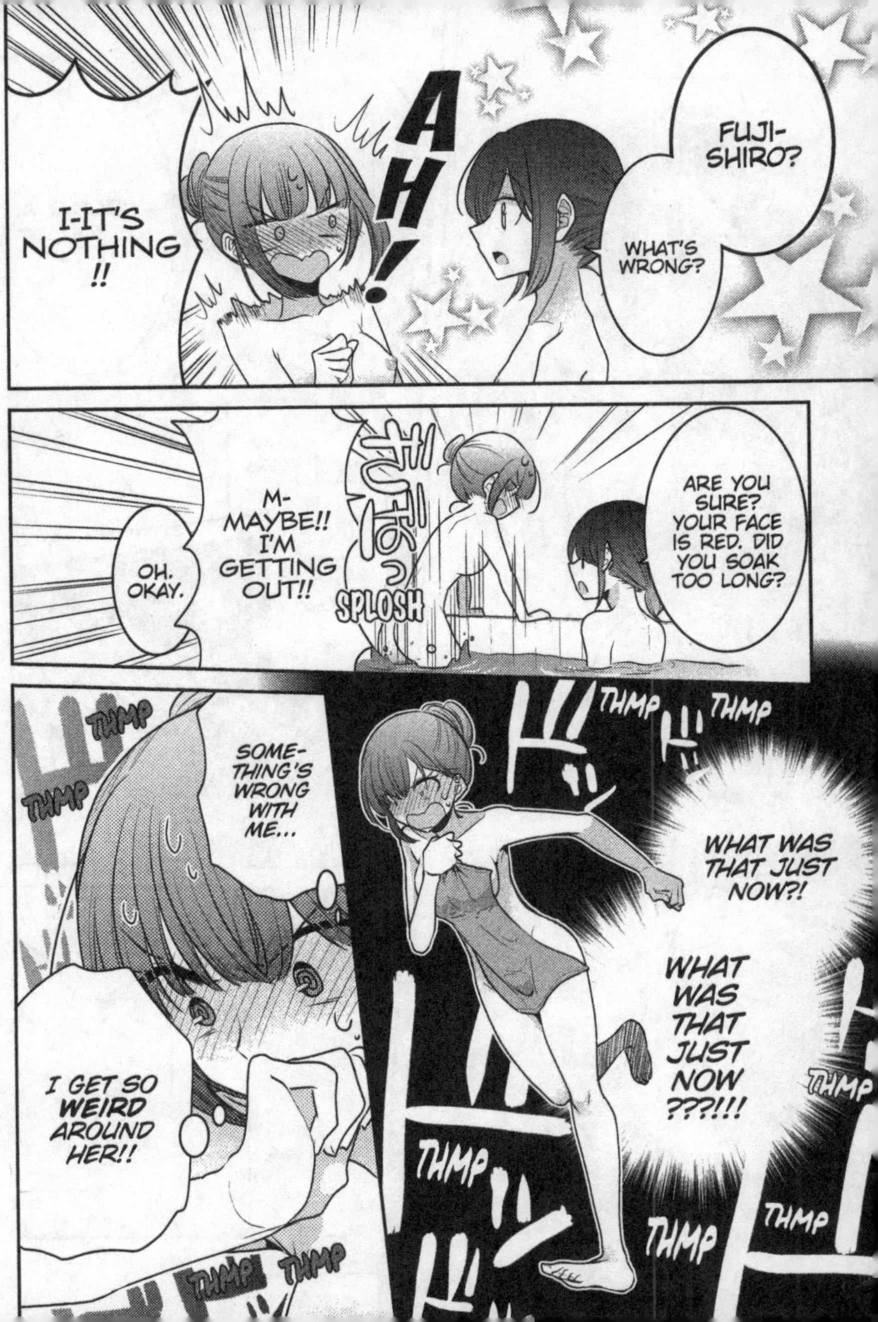
FUJI-SHIRO?
WHAT'S WRONG?
AH!
I-IT'S NOTHING!!
ARE YOU SURE? YOUR FACE IS RED. DID YOU SOAK TOO LONG?
SPLOSH
M-MAYBE!! I'M GETTING OUT!!
OH. OKAY.
THMP THMP
WHAT WAS THAT JUST NOW?!
WHAT WAS THAT JUST NOW???!!!
THMP
THMP
THMP
THMP
THMP
SOMETHING'S WRONG WITH ME...
I GET SO WEIRD AROUND HER!!
THMP
THMP
THMP THMP

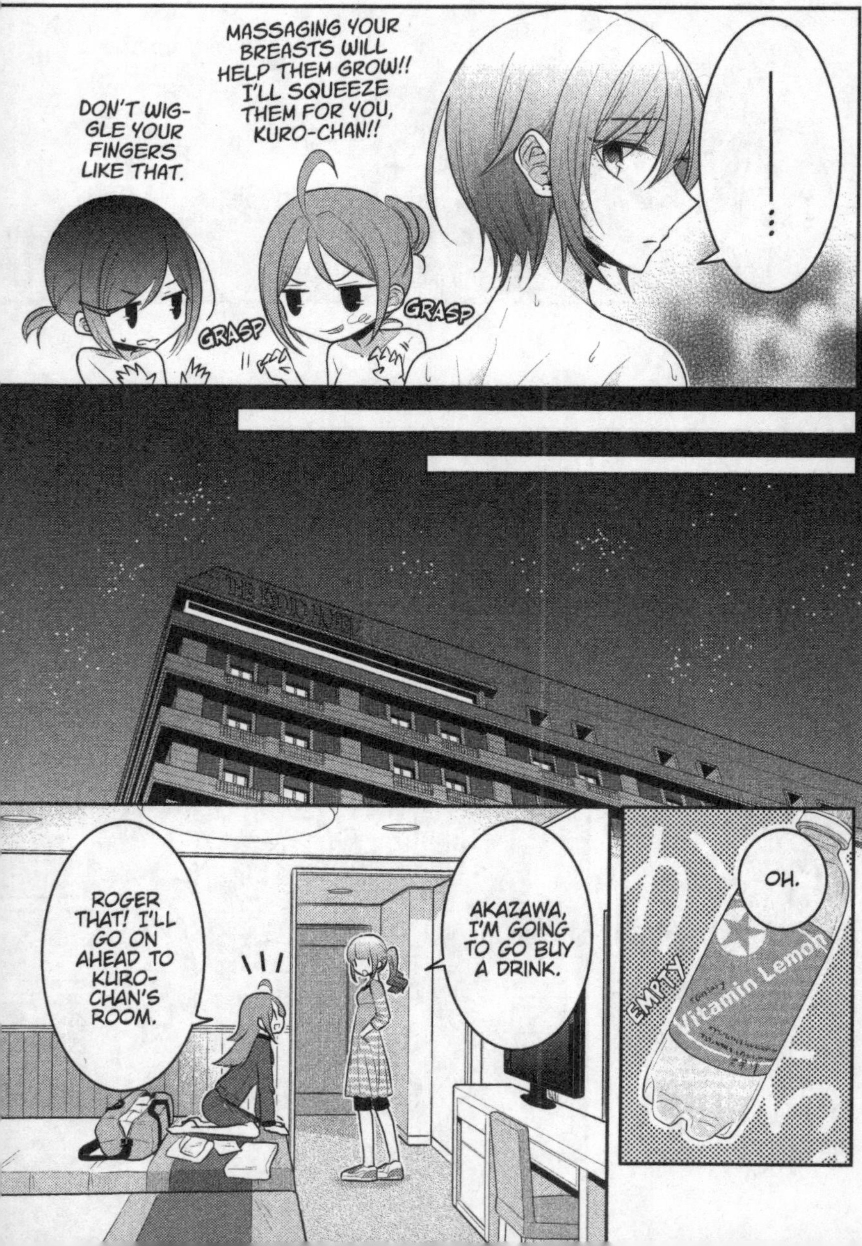
——......
MASSAGING YOUR BREASTS WILL HELP THEM GROW!! I'LL SQUEEZE THEM FOR YOU, KURO-CHAN!!
GRASP
GRASP
DON'T WIGGLE YOUR FINGERS LIKE THAT.
OH.
EMPTY
Vitamin Lemon
AKAZAWA, I'M GOING TO GO BUY A DRINK.
ROGER THAT! I'LL GO ON AHEAD TO KURO-CHAN'S ROOM.

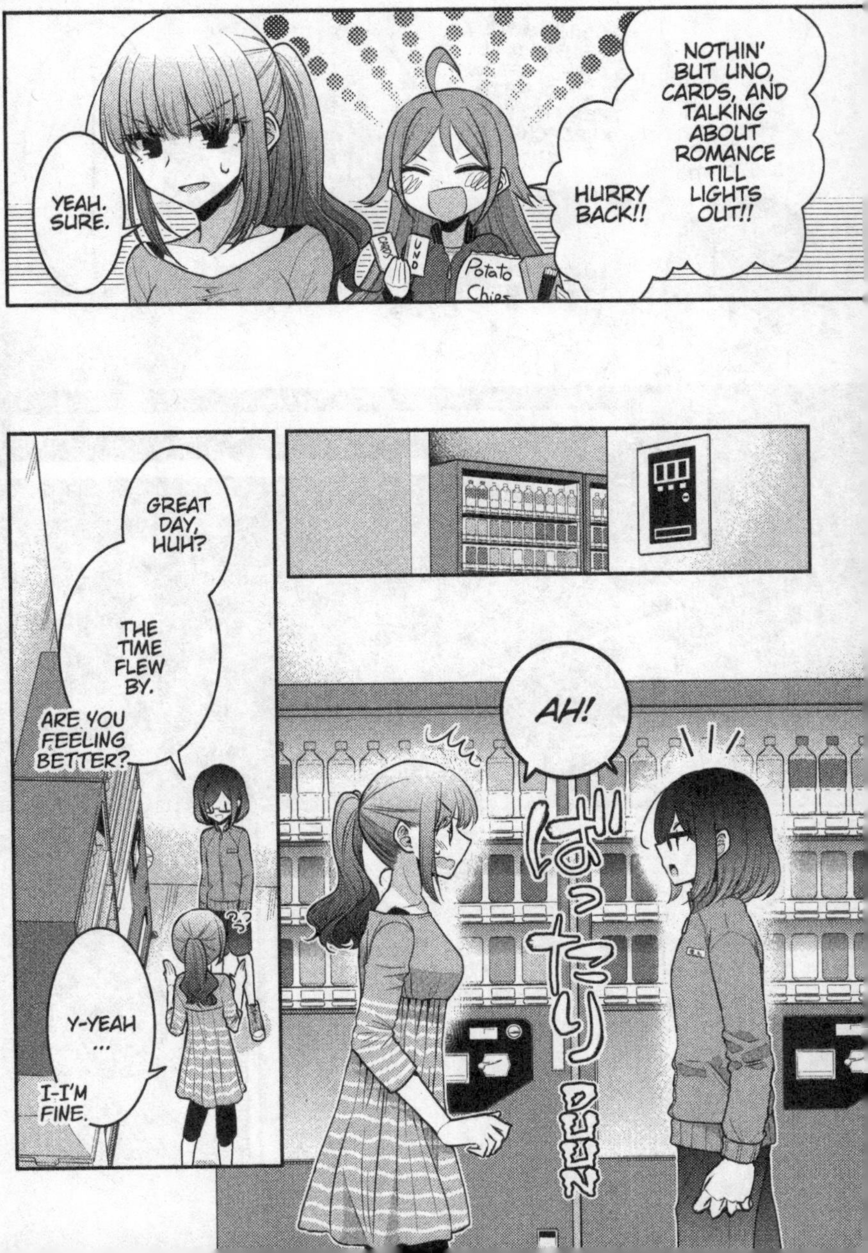
NOTHIN' BUT UNO, CARDS, AND TALKING ABOUT ROMANCE TILL LIGHTS OUT!!
HURRY BACK!!
CARDS
UNO
Potato Chips
YEAH. SURE.
AH!
ぱったり
GREAT DAY, HUH?
THE TIME FLEW BY.
ARE YOU FEELING BETTER?
Y-YEAH ...
I-I'M FINE.

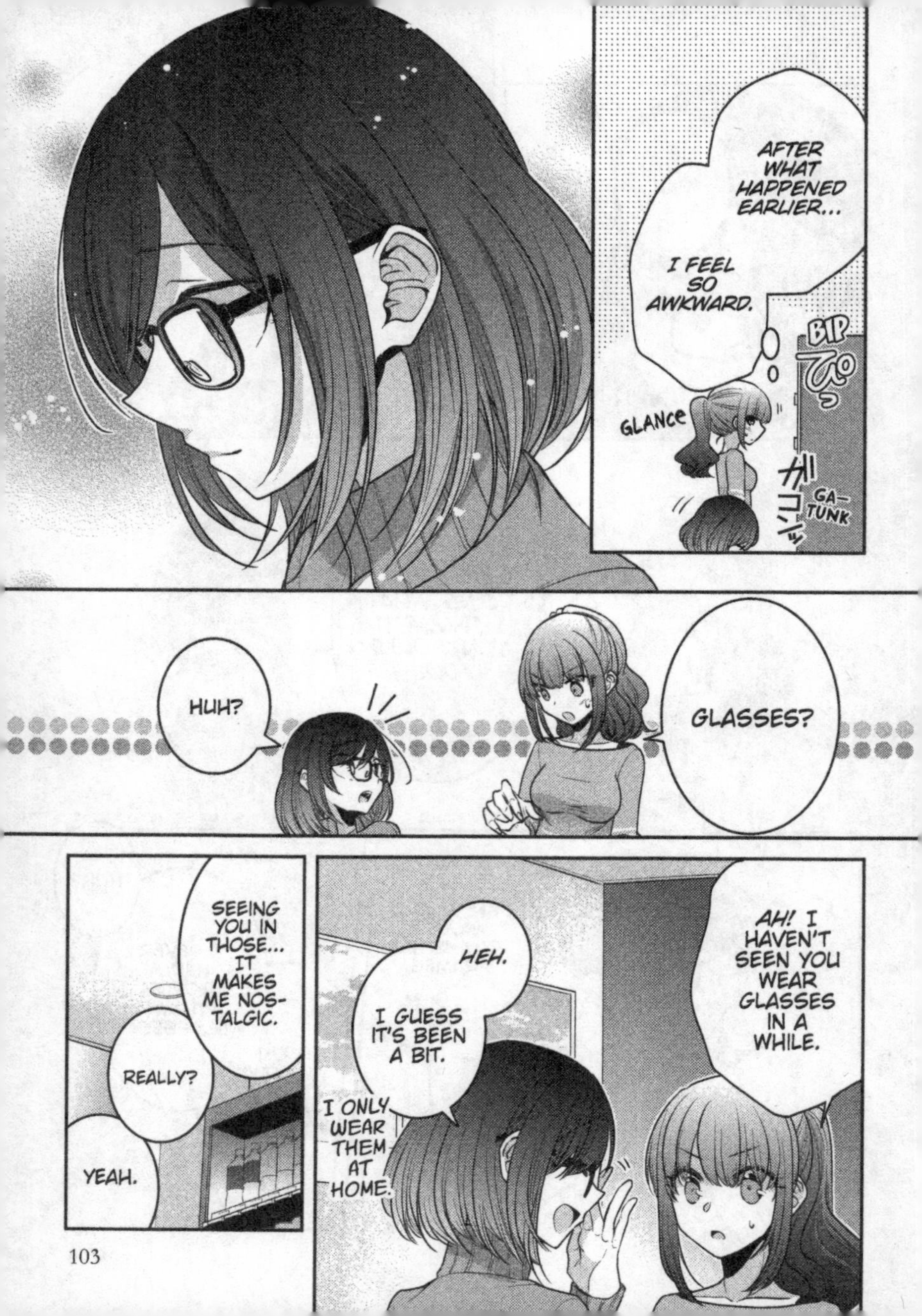
AFTER WHAT HAPPENED EARLIER...
I FEEL SO AWKWARD.
BIP
GLANCE
GA-TUNK
GLASSES?
HUH?
AH! I HAVEN'T SEEN YOU WEAR GLASSES IN A WHILE.
HEH.
I GUESS IT'S BEEN A BIT.
I ONLY WEAR THEM AT HOME.
SEEING YOU IN THOSE... IT MAKES ME NOS-TALGIC.
REALLY?
YEAH.

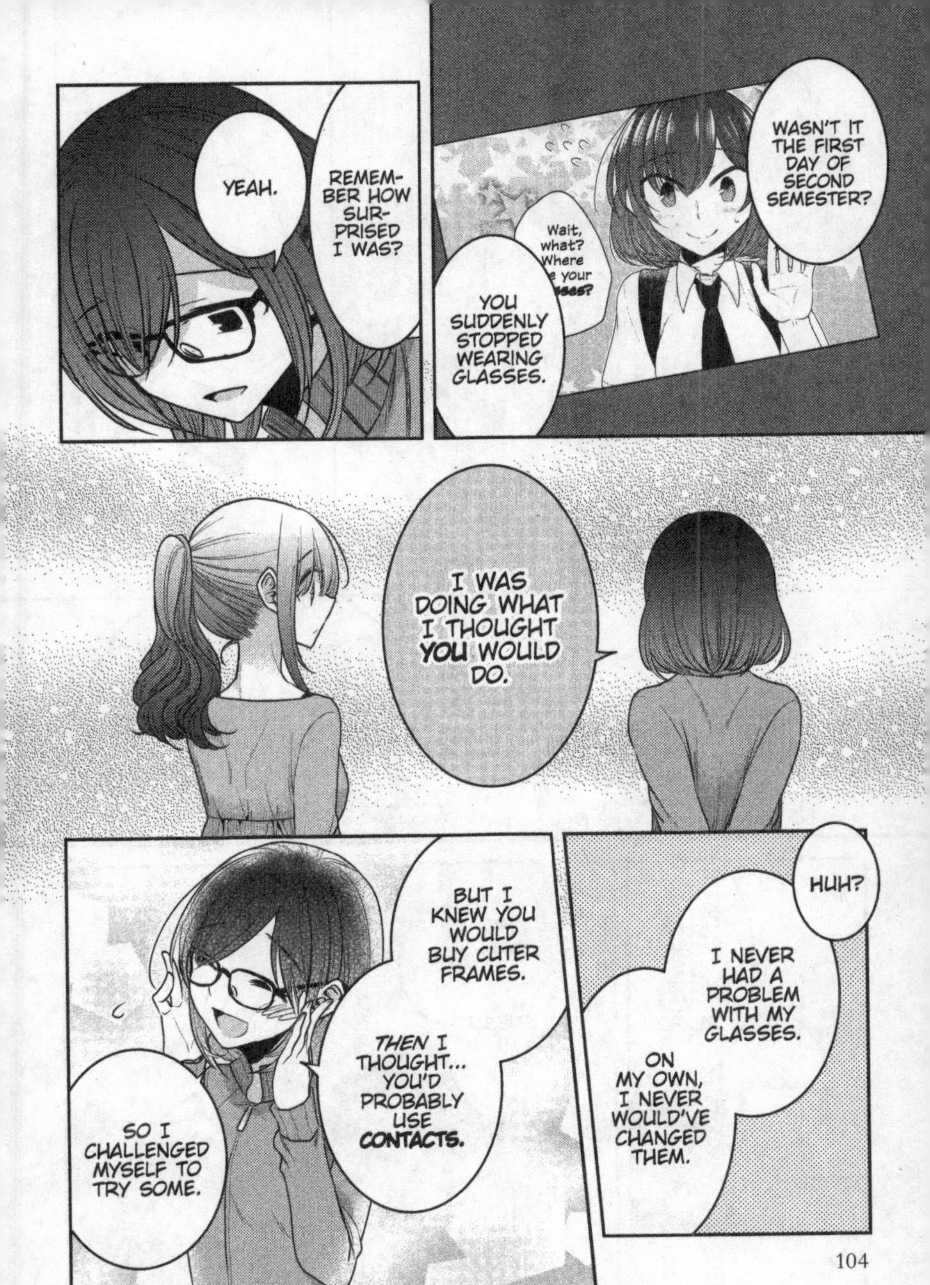
WASN'T IT THE FIRST DAY OF SECOND SEMESTER?
Wait, what? Where
YOU SUDDENLY STOPPED WEARING GLASSES.
REMEMBER HOW SURPRISED I WAS?
YEAH.
I WAS DOING WHAT I THOUGHT **YOU** WOULD DO.
HUH?
I NEVER HAD A PROBLEM WITH MY GLASSES.
ON MY OWN, I NEVER WOULD'VE CHANGED THEM.
BUT I KNEW YOU WOULD BUY CUTER FRAMES.
THEN I THOUGHT... YOU'D PROBABLY USE **CONTACTS.**
SO I CHALLENGED MYSELF TO TRY SOME.

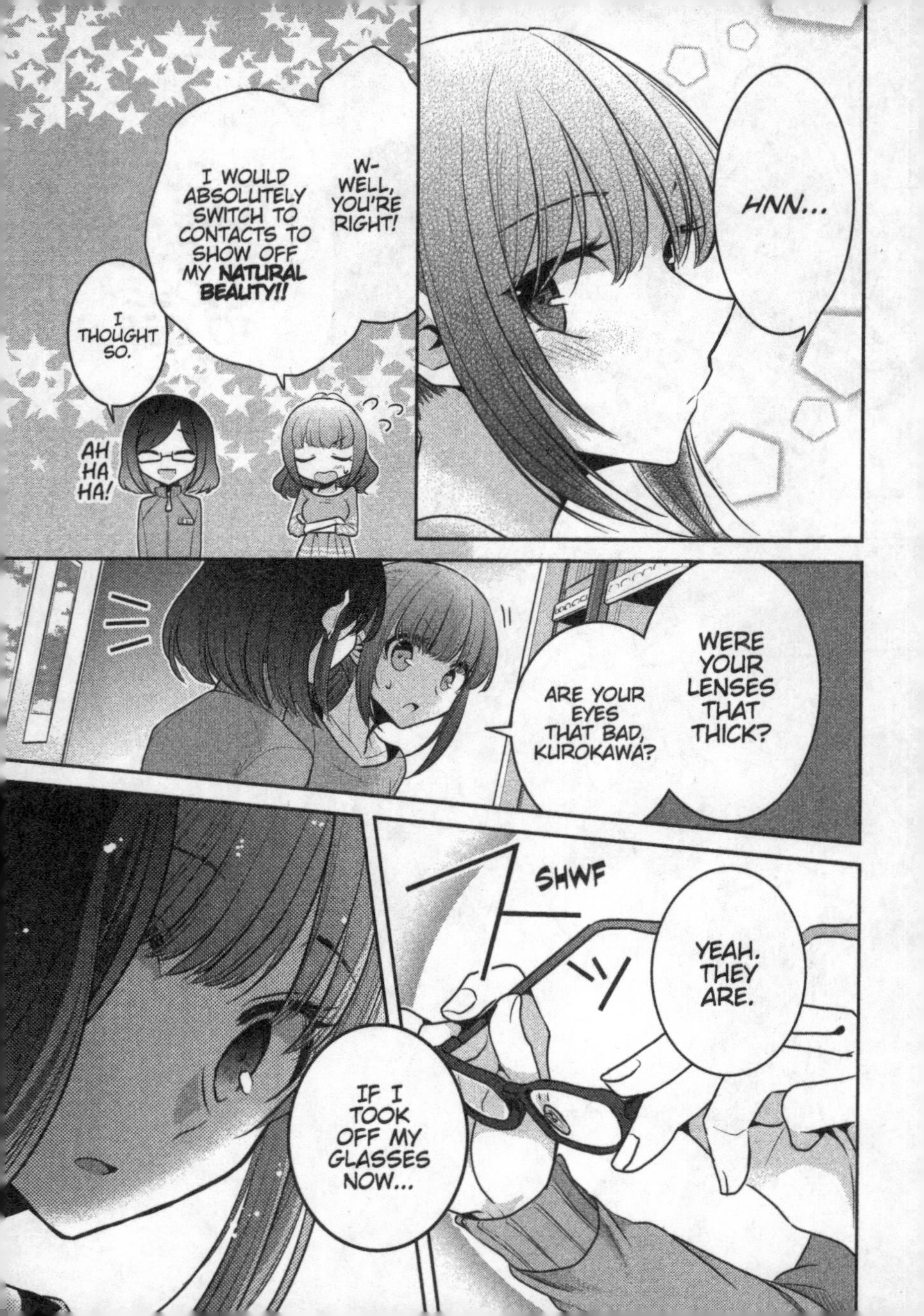
HNN...
I WOULD ABSOLUTELY SWITCH TO CONTACTS TO SHOW OFF MY **NATURAL BEAUTY!!**
W-WELL, YOU'RE RIGHT!
I THOUGHT SO.
AH HA HA!
WERE YOUR LENSES THAT THICK?
ARE YOUR EYES THAT BAD, KUROKAWA?
SHWF
YEAH. THEY ARE.
IF I TOOK OFF MY GLASSES NOW...

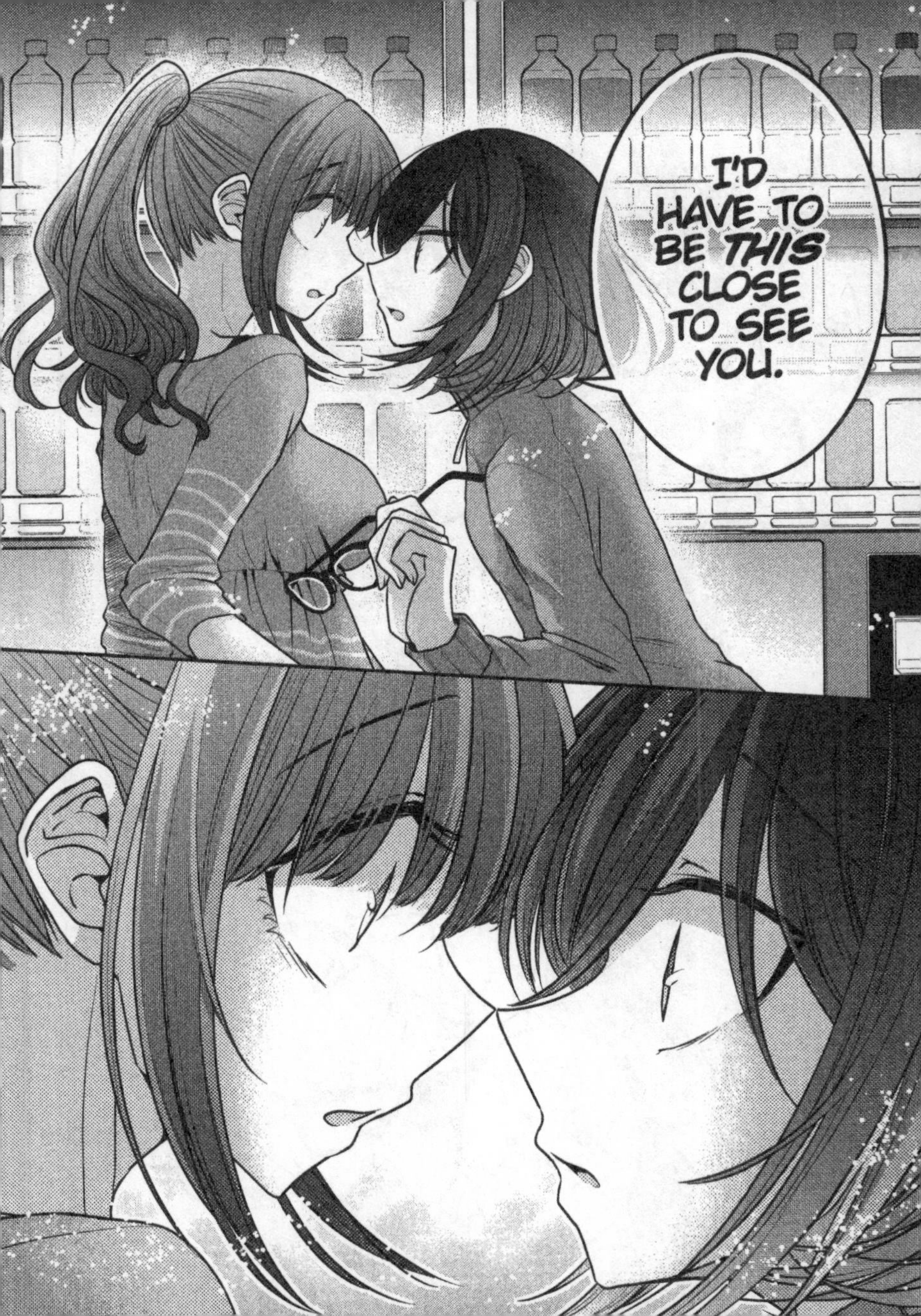
I'D HAVE TO BE *THIS* CLOSE TO SEE YOU.

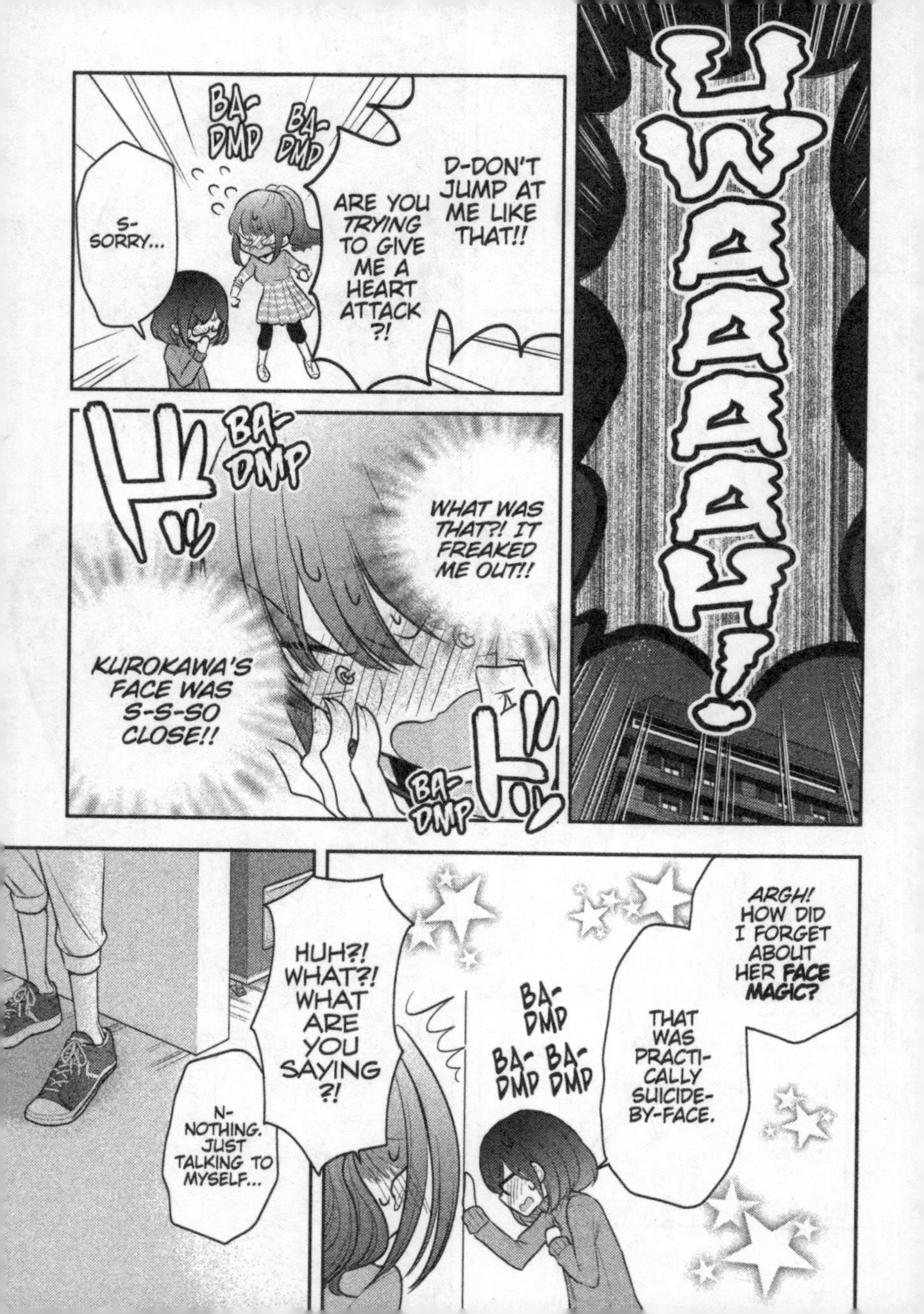

UWAAAAH!
D-DON'T JUMP AT ME LIKE THAT!!
BA-DMP BA-DMP
ARE YOU *TRYING* TO GIVE ME A HEART ATTACK?!
S-SORRY...
ドッ
BA-DMP
WHAT WAS THAT?! IT FREAKED ME OUT!!
KUROKAWA'S FACE WAS S-S-SO CLOSE!!
ドッ
BA-DMP
ARGH! HOW DID I FORGET ABOUT HER **FACE MAGIC?**
THAT WAS PRACTICALLY SUICIDE-BY-FACE.
BA-DMP
BA-DMP BA-DMP
HUH?! WHAT?! WHAT ARE YOU SAYING?!
N-NOTHING. JUST TALKING TO MYSELF...

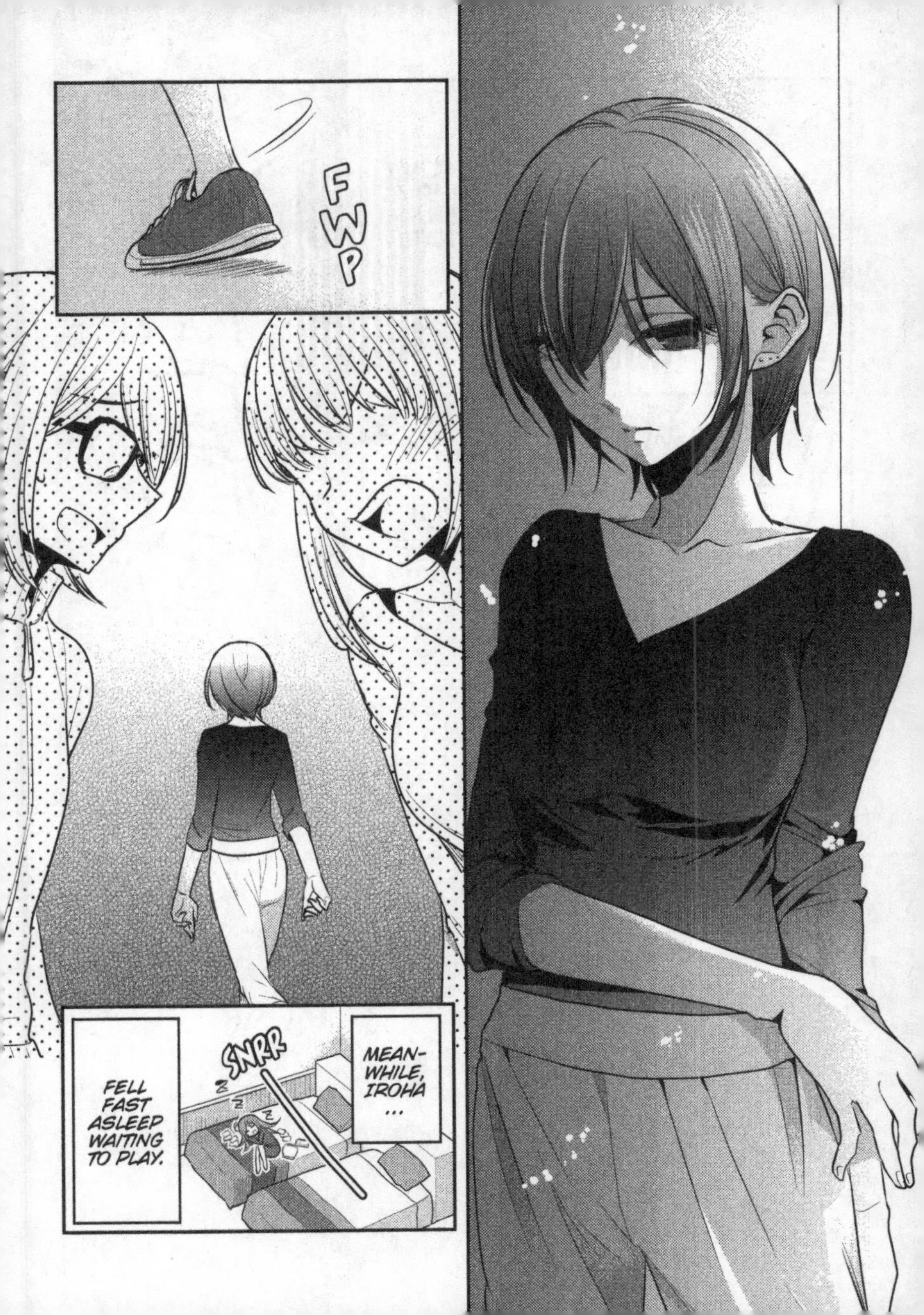
FWP
MEAN-WHILE, IROHA ...
SNRR
FELL FAST ASLEEP WAITING TO PLAY.

CHAPTER 17

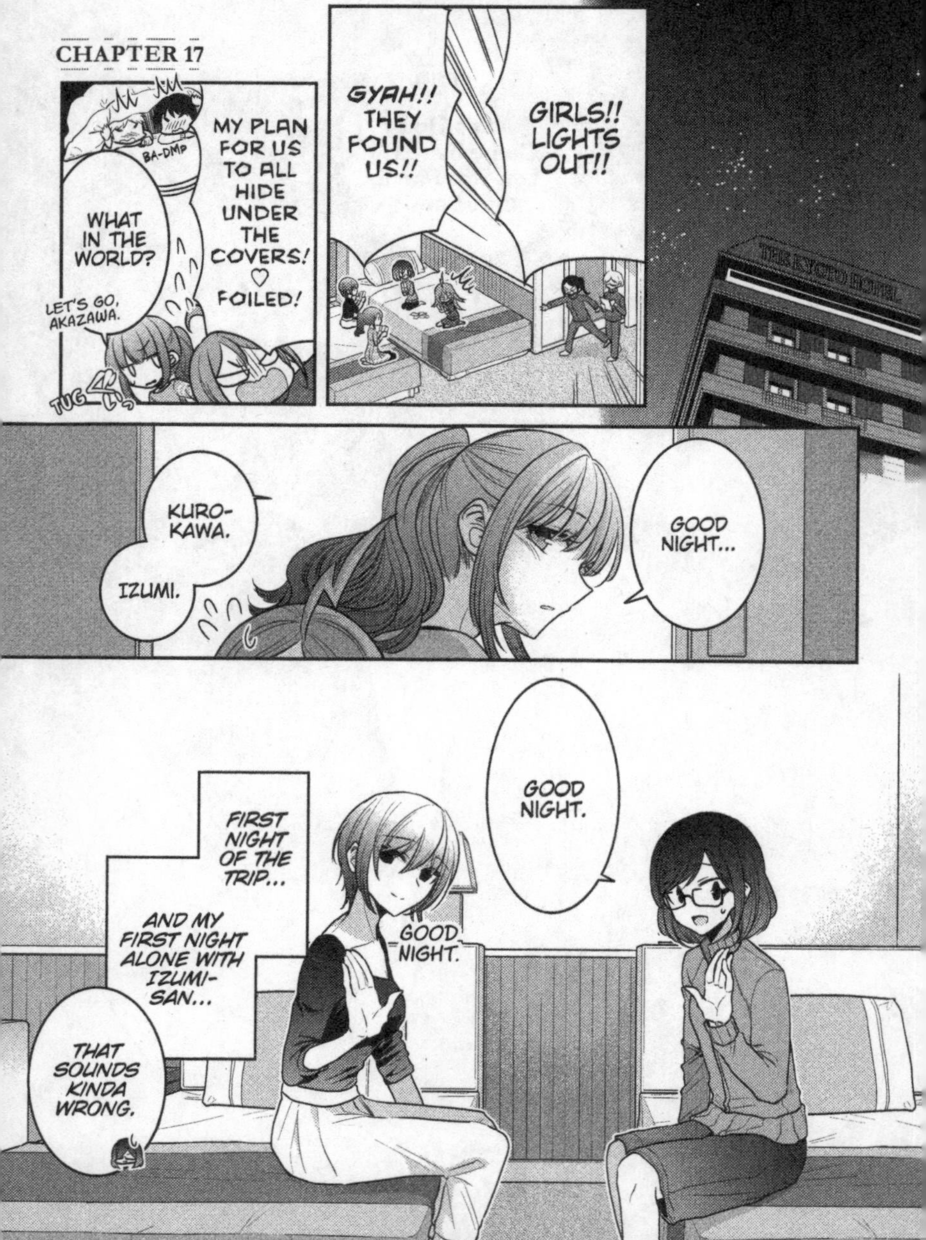
THE KYOTO HOTEL
GIRLS!! LIGHTS OUT!!
GYAH!! THEY FOUND US!!
MY PLAN FOR US TO ALL HIDE UNDER THE COVERS! ♡ FOILED!
BA-DMP
WHAT IN THE WORLD?
LET'S GO, AKAZAWA.
TUG
GOOD NIGHT...
KURO-KAWA.
IZUMI.
GOOD NIGHT.
FIRST NIGHT OF THE TRIP...
GOOD NIGHT.
AND MY FIRST NIGHT ALONE WITH IZUMI-SAN...
THAT SOUNDS KINDA WRONG.

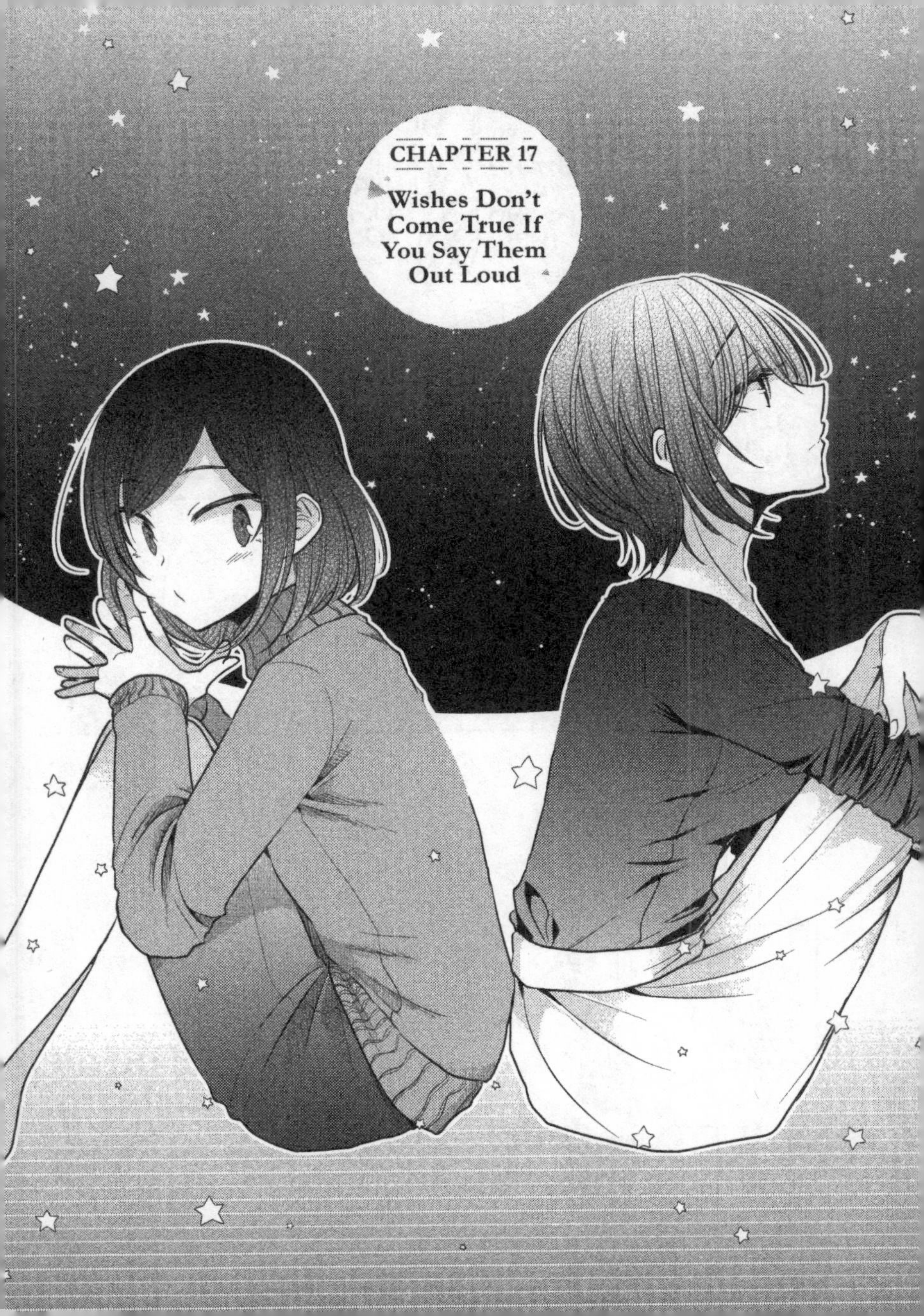
CHAPTER 17
Wishes Don't Come True If You Say Them Out Loud

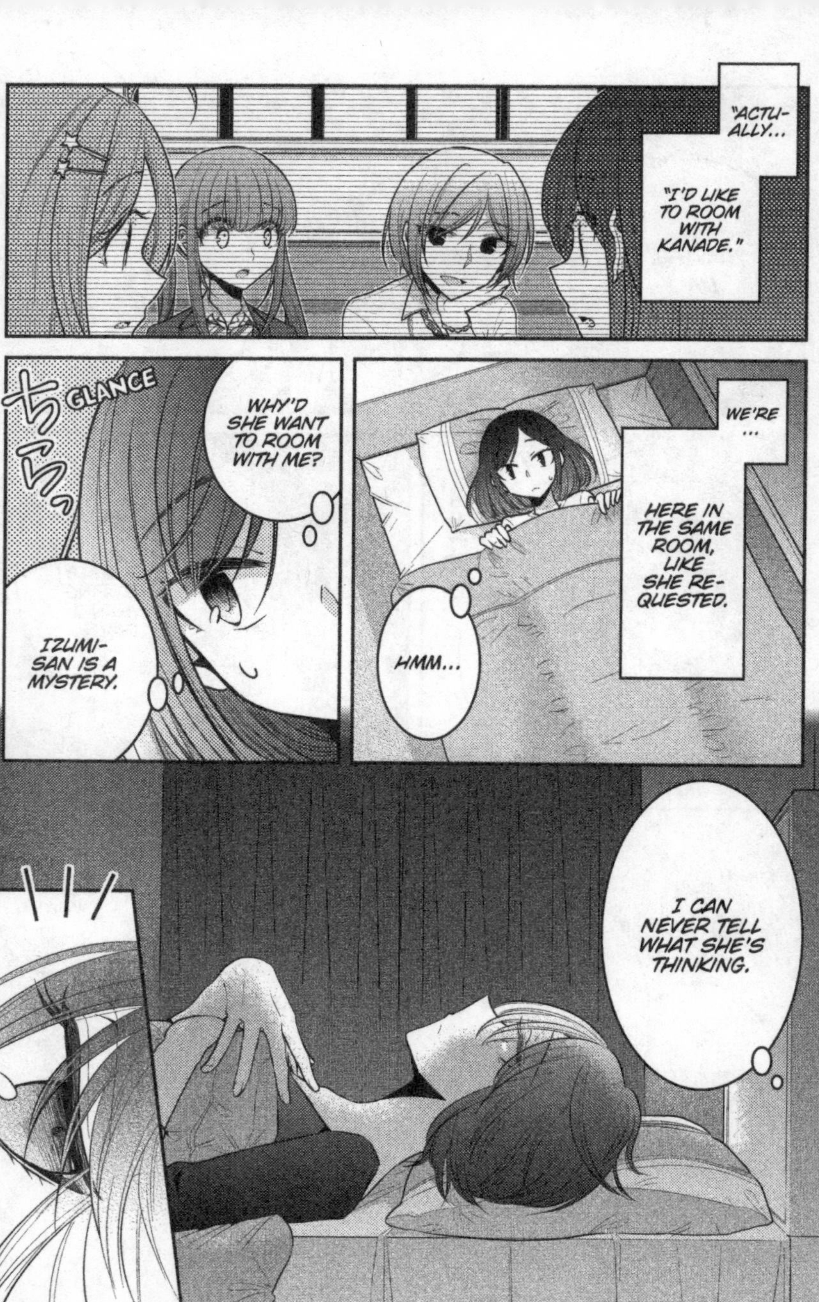
"ACTU-ALLY...
"I'D LIKE TO ROOM WITH KANADE."
WE'RE ...
HERE IN THE SAME ROOM, LIKE SHE RE-QUESTED.
HMM...
ちらっ GLANCE
WHY'D SHE WANT TO ROOM WITH ME?
IZUMI-SAN IS A MYSTERY.
I CAN NEVER TELL WHAT SHE'S THINKING.

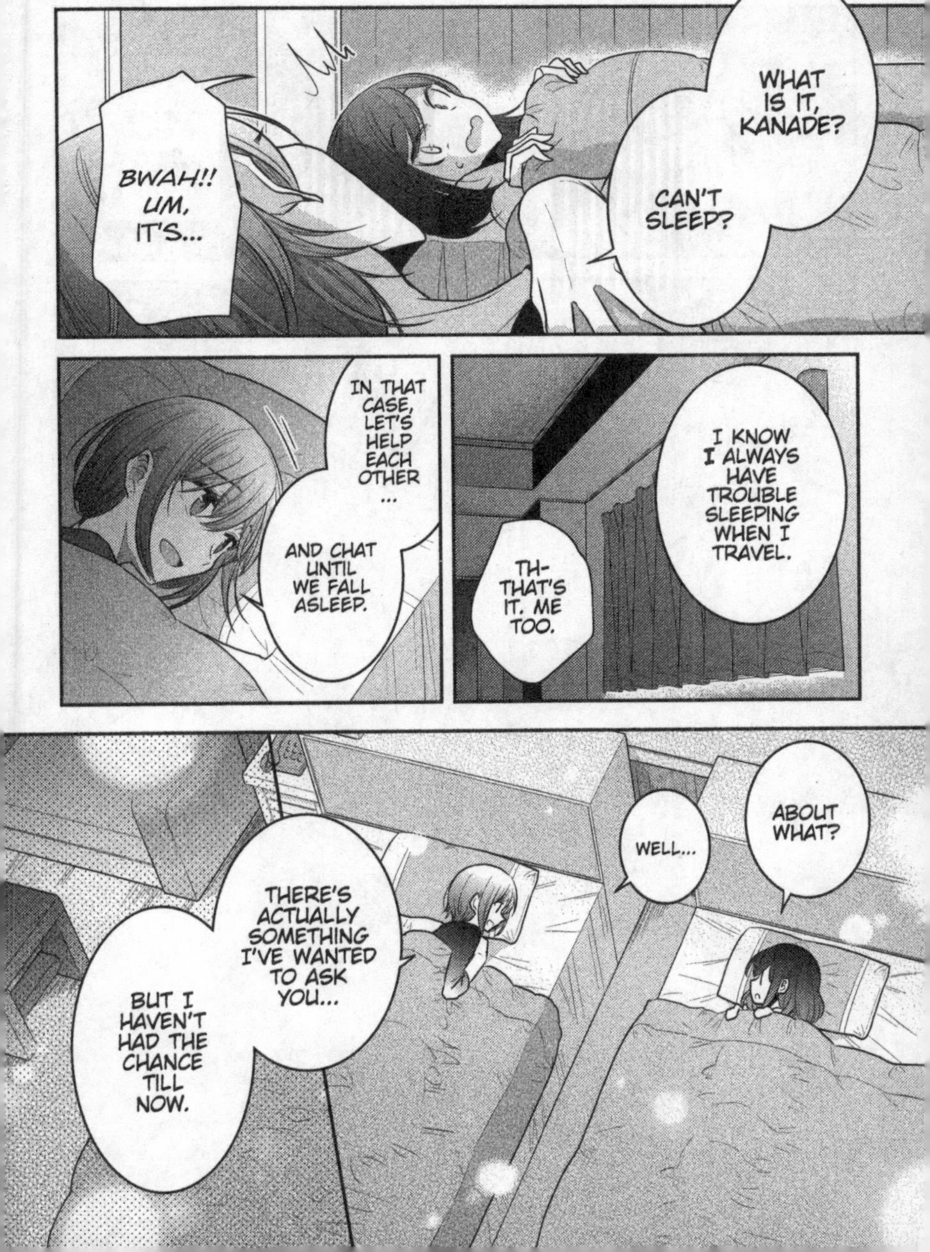
WHAT IS IT, KANADE?
CAN'T SLEEP?
BWAH!! UM, IT'S...
I KNOW I ALWAYS HAVE TROUBLE SLEEPING WHEN I TRAVEL.
TH-THAT'S IT. ME TOO.
IN THAT CASE, LET'S HELP EACH OTHER...
AND CHAT UNTIL WE FALL ASLEEP.
ABOUT WHAT?
WELL...
THERE'S ACTUALLY SOMETHING I'VE WANTED TO ASK YOU...
BUT I HAVEN'T HAD THE CHANCE TILL NOW.

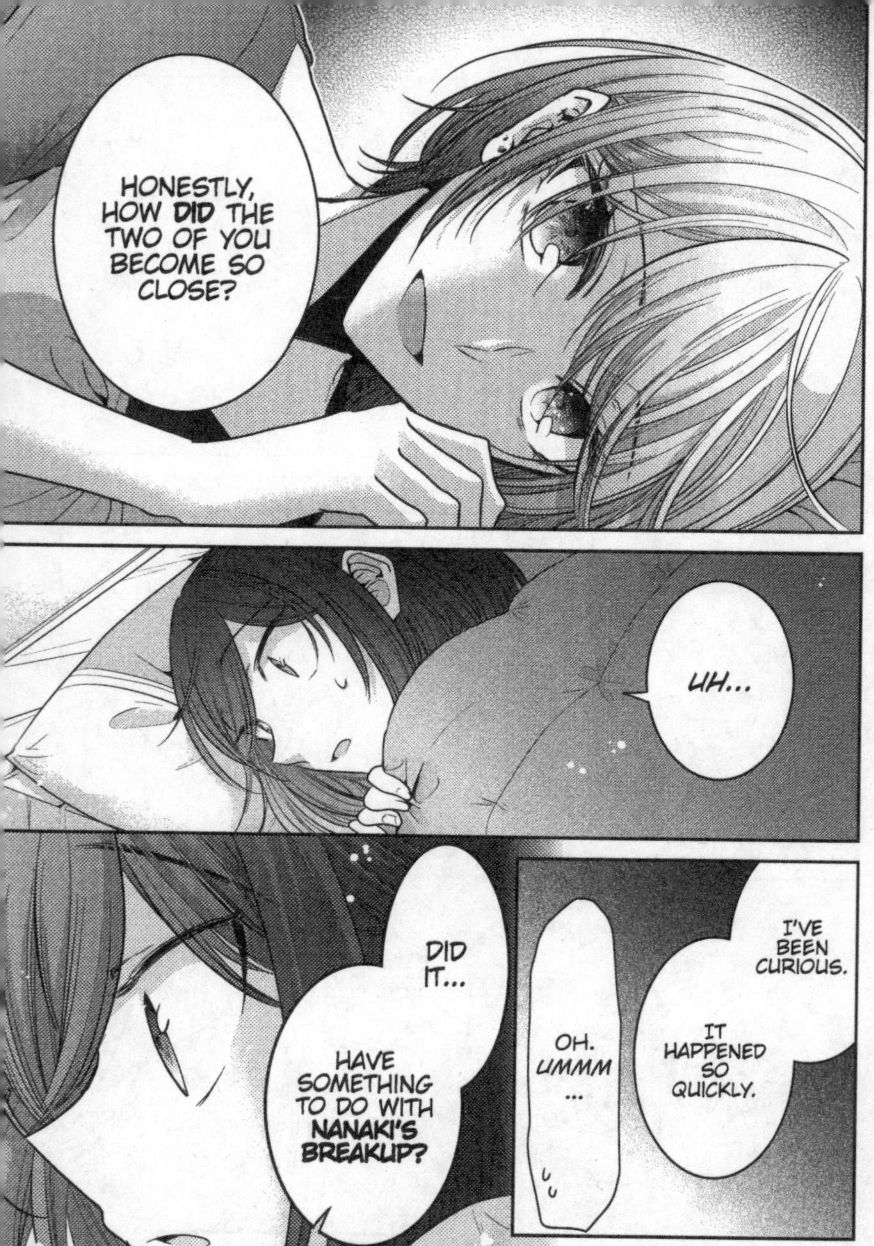
HONESTLY, HOW **DID** THE TWO OF YOU BECOME SO CLOSE?
UH...
I'VE BEEN CURIOUS.
IT HAPPENED SO QUICKLY.
OH. UMMM ...
DID IT...
HAVE SOMETHING TO DO WITH **NANAKI'S BREAKUP?**

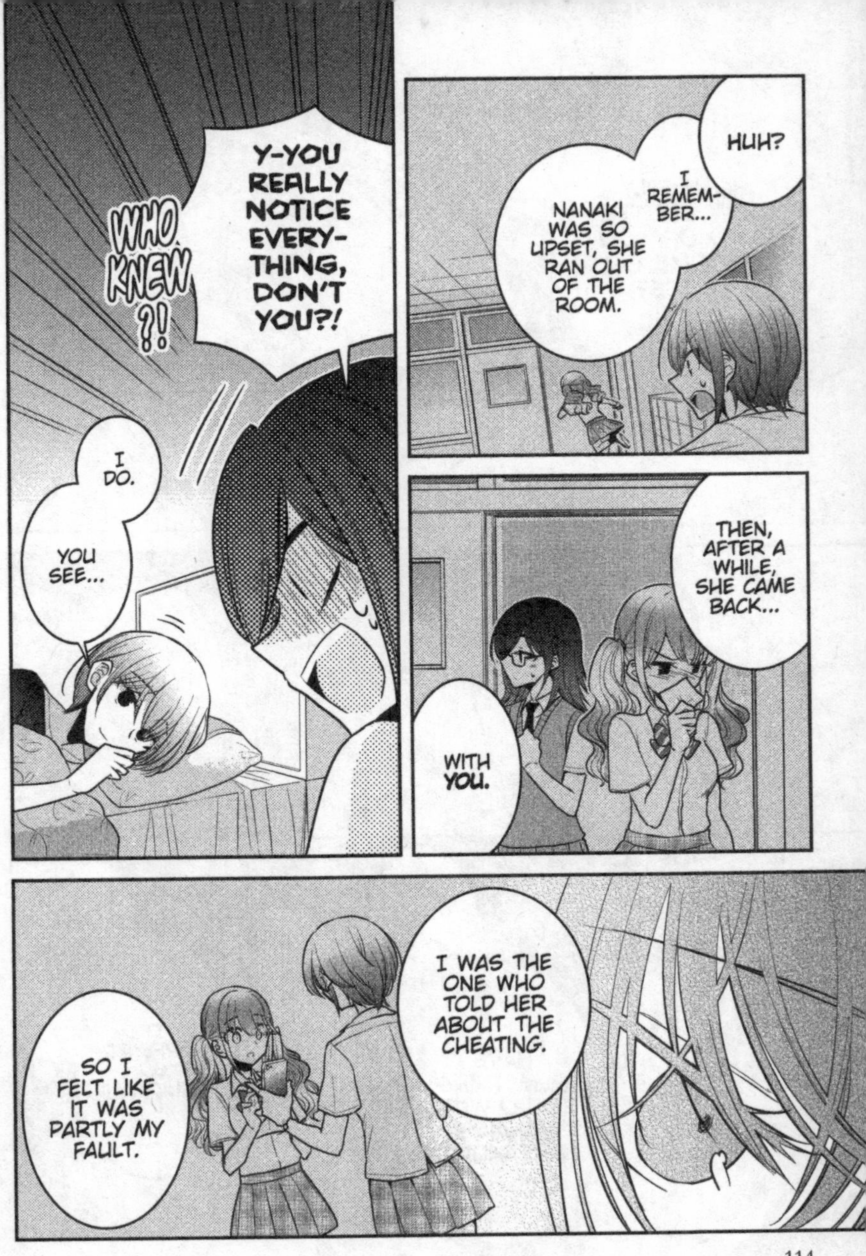
HUH?
I REMEMBER...
NANAKI WAS SO UPSET, SHE RAN OUT OF THE ROOM.
THEN, AFTER A WHILE, SHE CAME BACK...
WITH YOU.
Y-YOU REALLY NOTICE EVERYTHING, DON'T YOU?!
WHO KNEW?!
I DO.
YOU SEE...
I WAS THE ONE WHO TOLD HER ABOUT THE CHEATING.
SO I FELT LIKE IT WAS PARTLY MY FAULT.

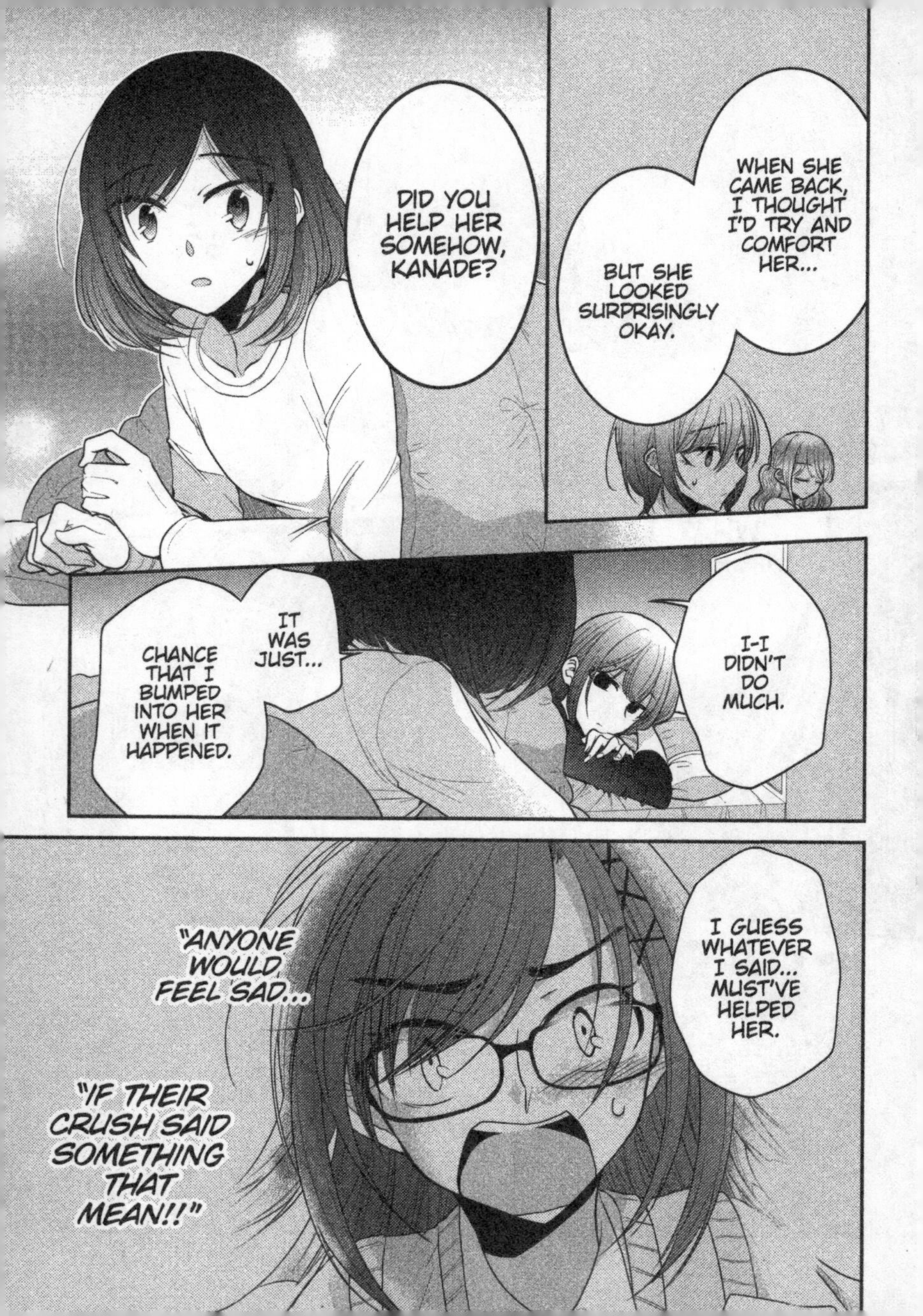
WHEN SHE CAME BACK, I THOUGHT I'D TRY AND COMFORT HER...
BUT SHE LOOKED SURPRISINGLY OKAY.
DID YOU HELP HER SOMEHOW, KANADE?
I-I DIDN'T DO MUCH.
IT WAS JUST...
CHANCE THAT I BUMPED INTO HER WHEN IT HAPPENED.
I GUESS WHATEVER I SAID... MUST'VE HELPED HER.
"ANYONE WOULD FEEL SAD...
"IF THEIR CRUSH SAID SOMETHING THAT MEAN!!"

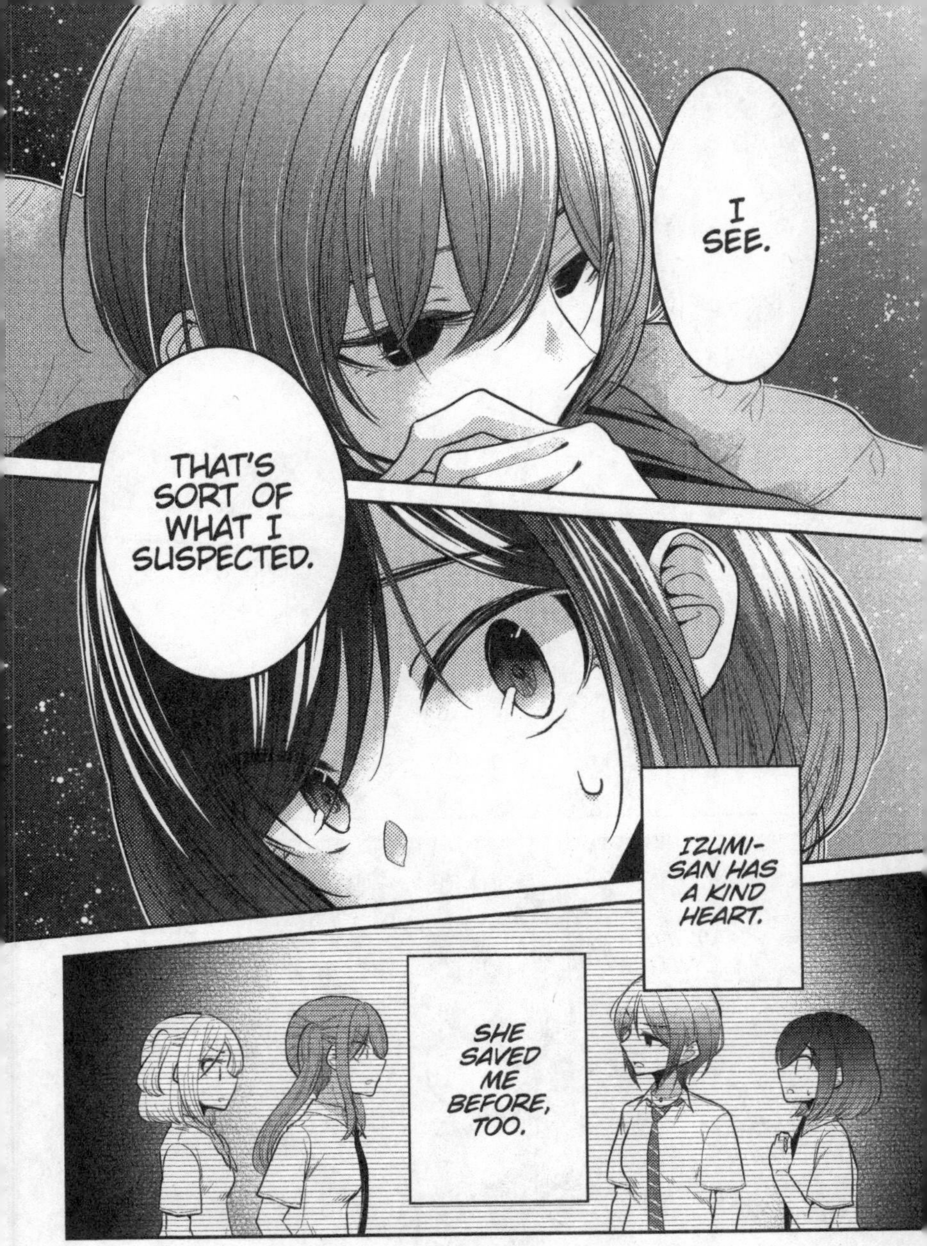

I SEE.
THAT'S SORT OF WHAT I SUSPECTED.
IZUMI-SAN HAS A KIND HEART.
SHE SAVED ME BEFORE, TOO.

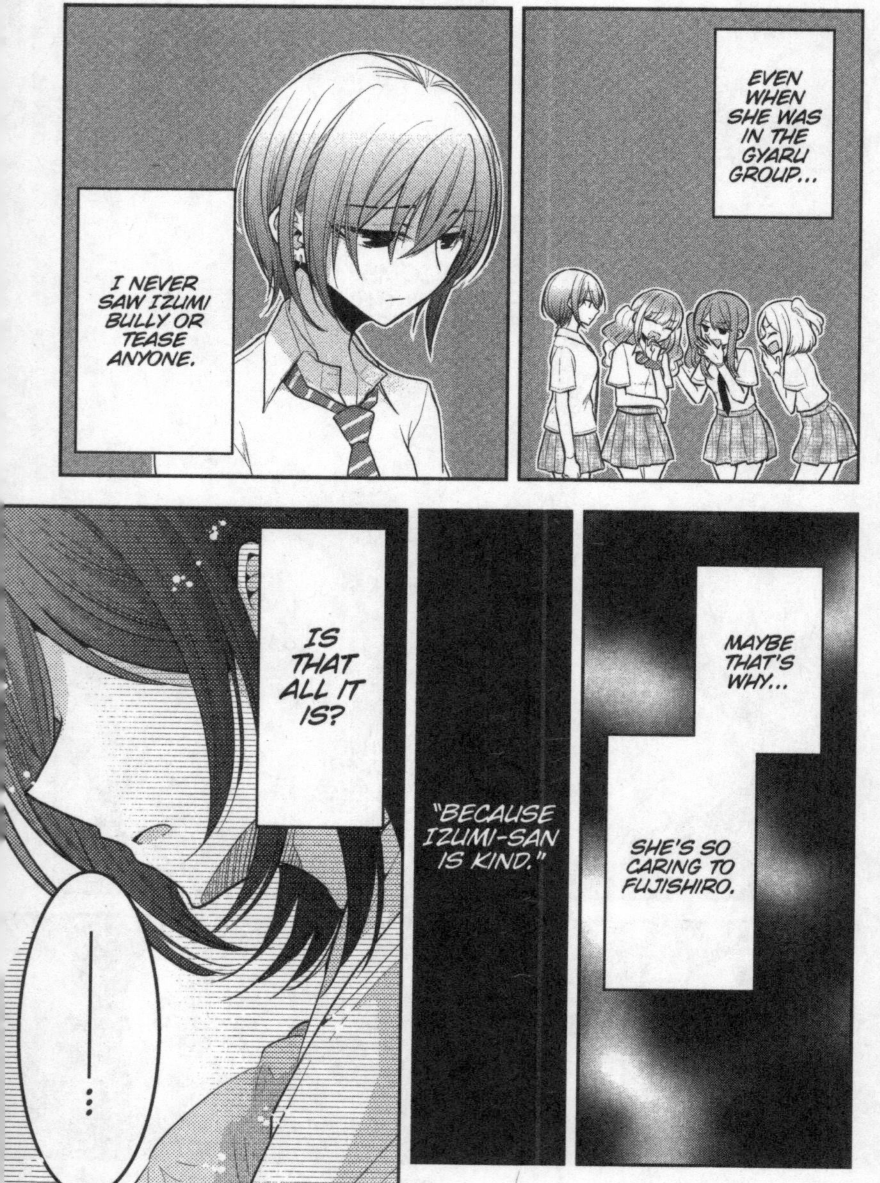
EVEN WHEN SHE WAS IN THE GYARU GROUP...
I NEVER SAW IZUMI BULLY OR TEASE ANYONE.
MAYBE THAT'S WHY...
SHE'S SO CARING TO FUJISHIRO.
"BECAUSE IZUMI-SAN IS KIND."
IS THAT ALL IT IS?
——...

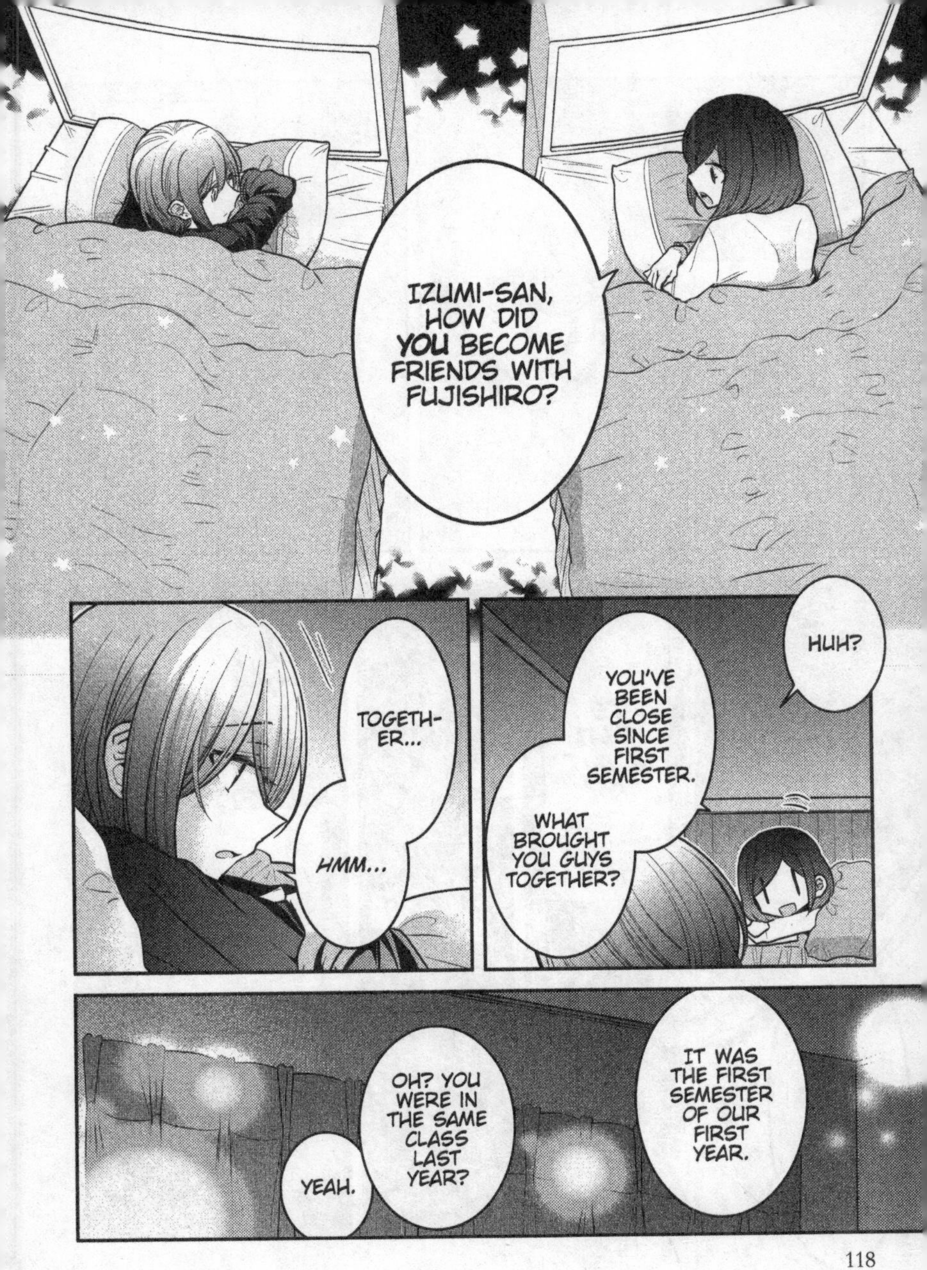
IZUMI-SAN, HOW DID **YOU** BECOME FRIENDS WITH FUJISHIRO?
HUH?
YOU'VE BEEN CLOSE SINCE FIRST SEMESTER.
WHAT BROUGHT YOU GUYS TOGETHER?
TOGETH-ER...
HMM...
IT WAS THE FIRST SEMESTER OF OUR FIRST YEAR.
OH? YOU WERE IN THE SAME CLASS LAST YEAR?
YEAH.

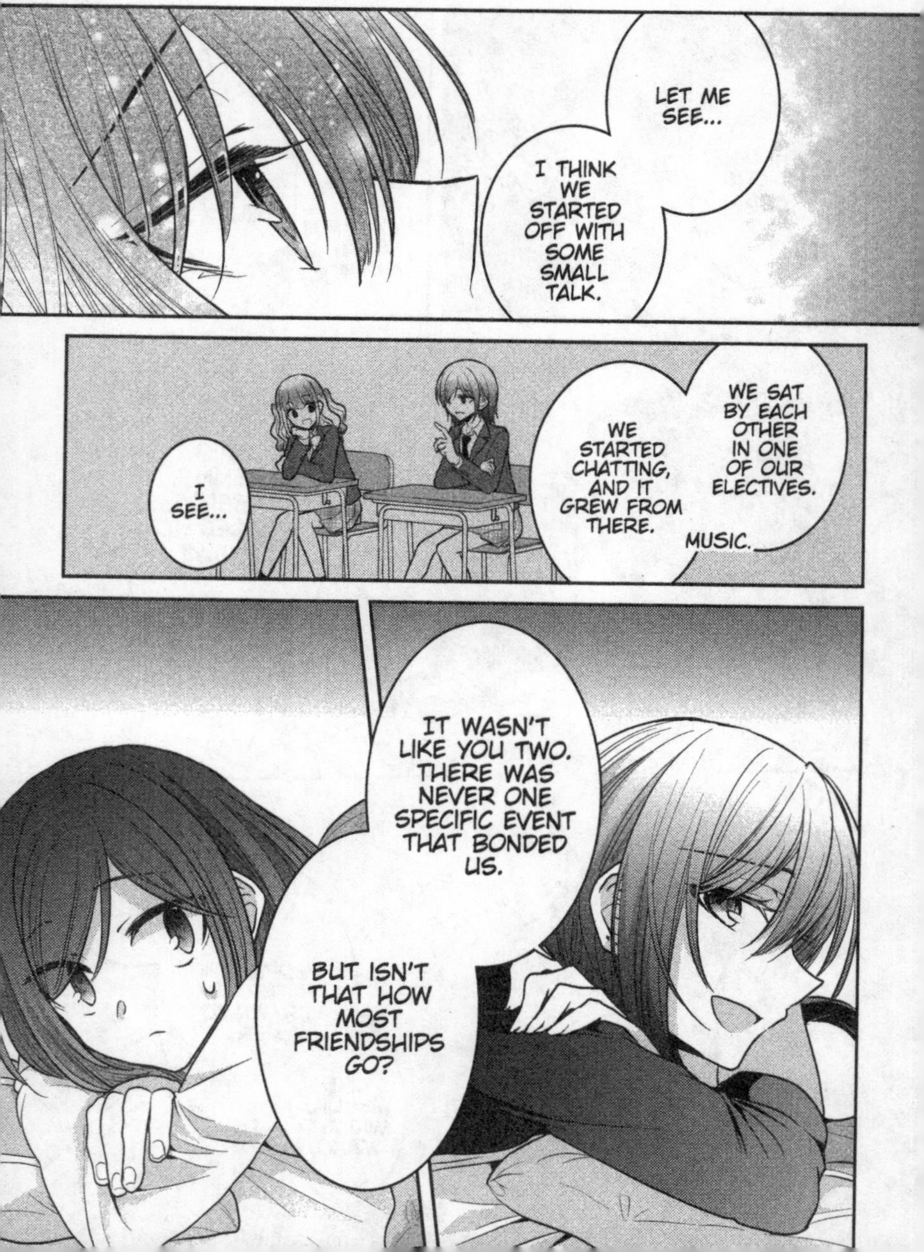
LET ME SEE...
I THINK WE STARTED OFF WITH SOME SMALL TALK.
WE SAT BY EACH OTHER IN ONE OF OUR ELECTIVES.
MUSIC.
WE STARTED CHATTING, AND IT GREW FROM THERE.
I SEE...
IT WASN'T LIKE YOU TWO. THERE WAS NEVER ONE SPECIFIC EVENT THAT BONDED US.
BUT ISN'T THAT HOW MOST FRIENDSHIPS GO?

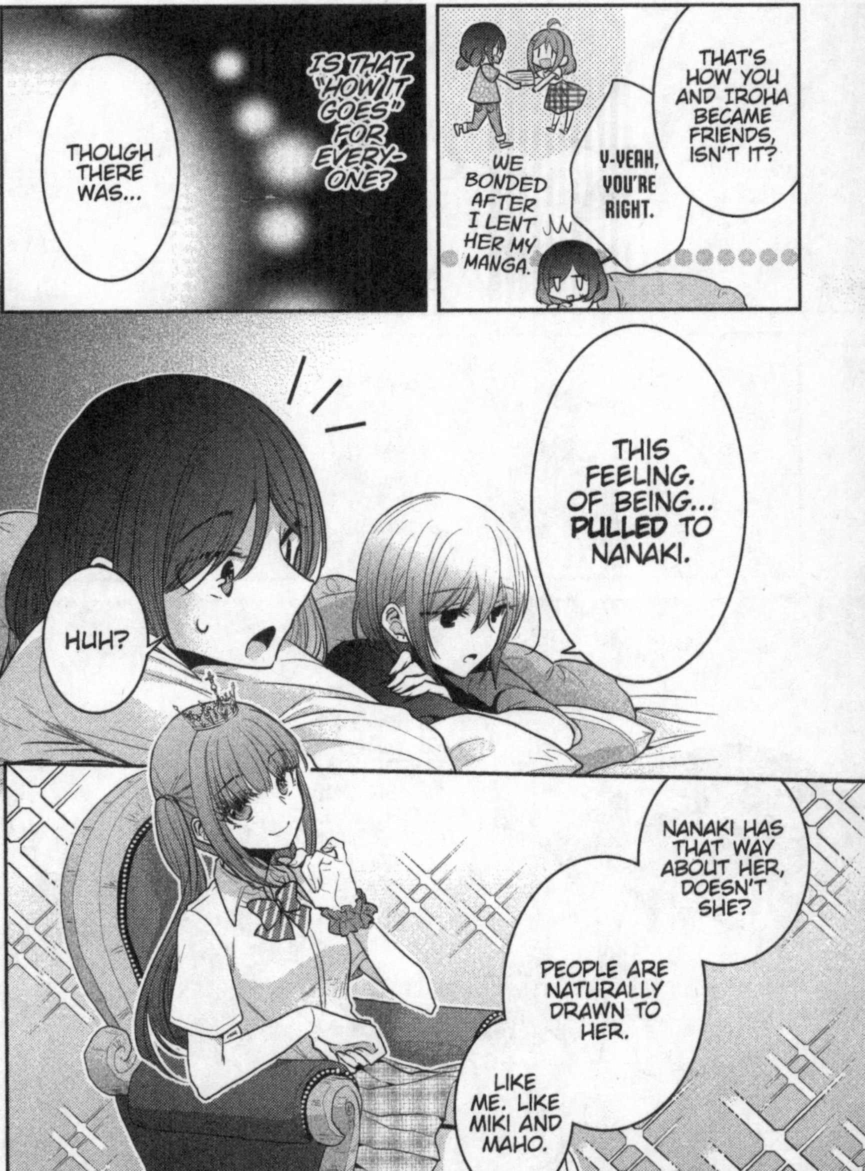
THAT'S HOW YOU AND IROHA BECAME FRIENDS, ISN'T IT?
Y-YEAH, YOU'RE RIGHT.
WE BONDED AFTER I LENT HER MY MANGA.
IS THAT "HOW IT GOES" FOR EVERY-ONE?
THOUGH THERE WAS...
THIS FEELING. OF BEING... **PULLED** TO NANAKI.
HUH?
NANAKI HAS THAT WAY ABOUT HER, DOESN'T SHE?
PEOPLE ARE NATURALLY DRAWN TO HER.
LIKE ME. LIKE MIKI AND MAHO.

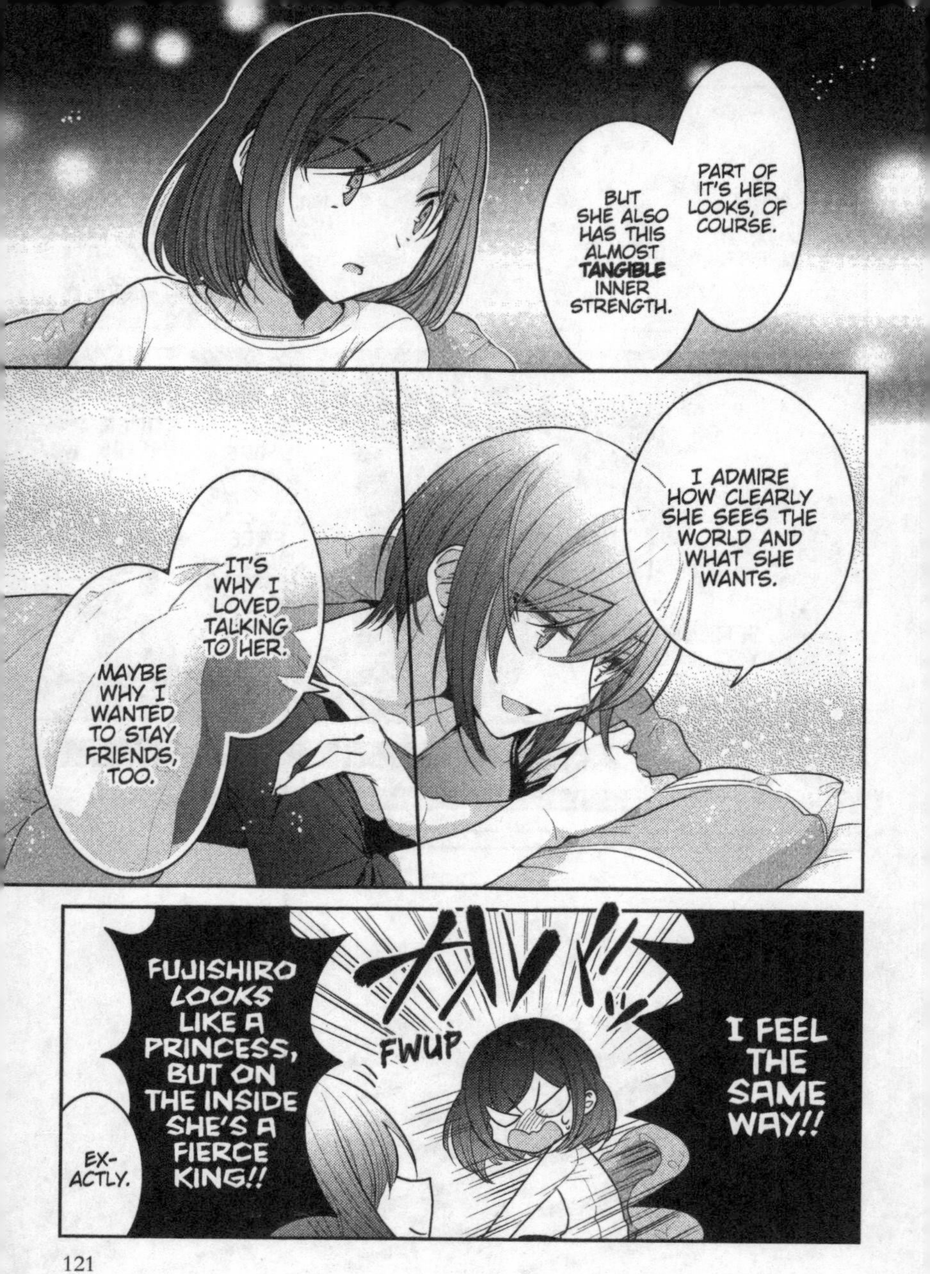
PART OF IT'S HER LOOKS, OF COURSE.
BUT SHE ALSO HAS THIS ALMOST TANGIBLE INNER STRENGTH.
I ADMIRE HOW CLEARLY SHE SEES THE WORLD AND WHAT SHE WANTS.
IT'S WHY I LOVED TALKING TO HER.
MAYBE WHY I WANTED TO STAY FRIENDS, TOO.
I FEEL THE SAME WAY!!
FWUP
FUJISHIRO LOOKS LIKE A PRINCESS, BUT ON THE INSIDE SHE'S A FIERCE KING!!
EX-ACTLY.

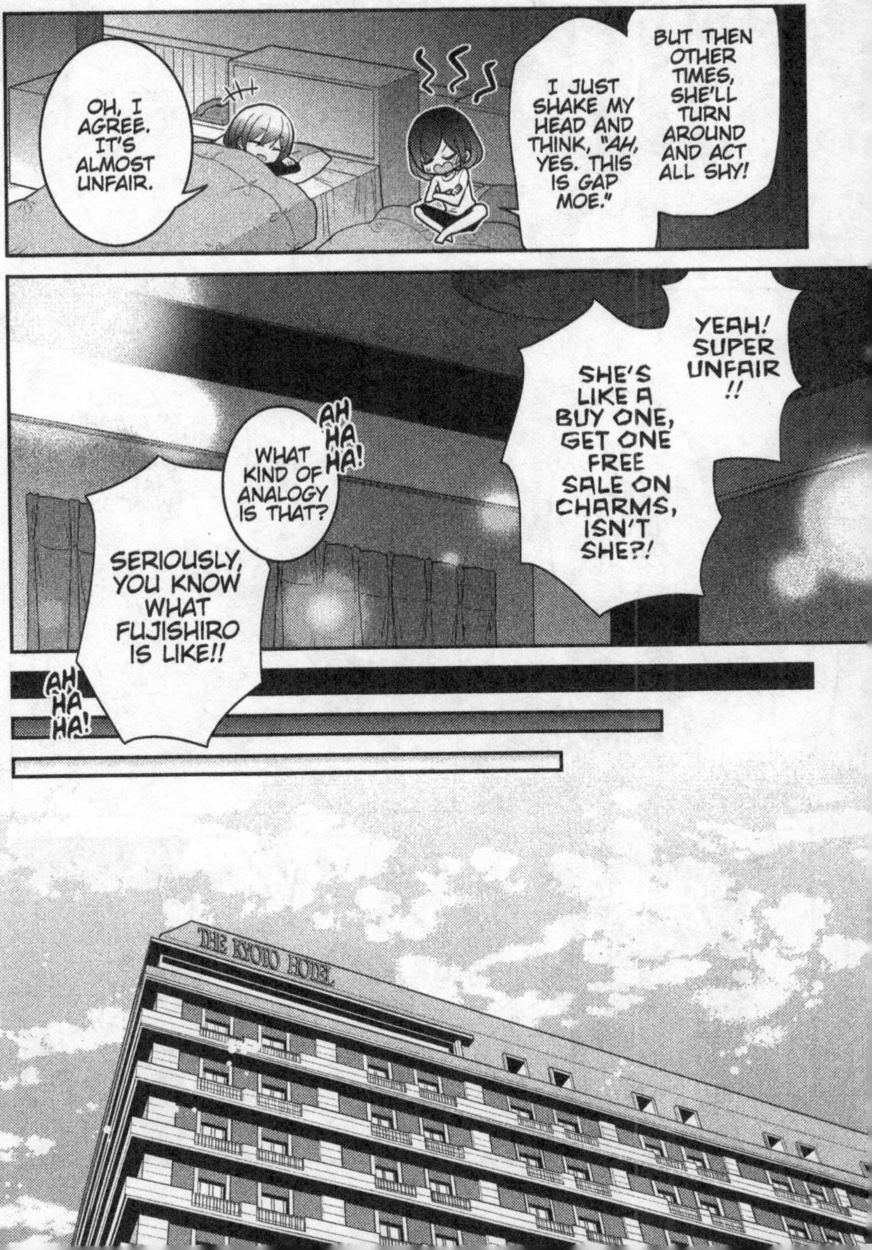
BUT THEN OTHER TIMES, SHE'LL TURN AROUND AND ACT ALL SHY!
I JUST SHAKE MY HEAD AND THINK, "AH, YES. THIS IS GAP MOE."
OH, I AGREE. IT'S ALMOST UNFAIR.
YEAH! SUPER UNFAIR!!
SHE'S LIKE A BUY ONE, GET ONE FREE SALE ON CHARMS, ISN'T SHE?!
AH HA HA!
WHAT KIND OF ANALOGY IS THAT?
SERIOUSLY, YOU KNOW WHAT FUJISHIRO IS LIKE!!
AH HA HA!
THE KYOTO HOTEL

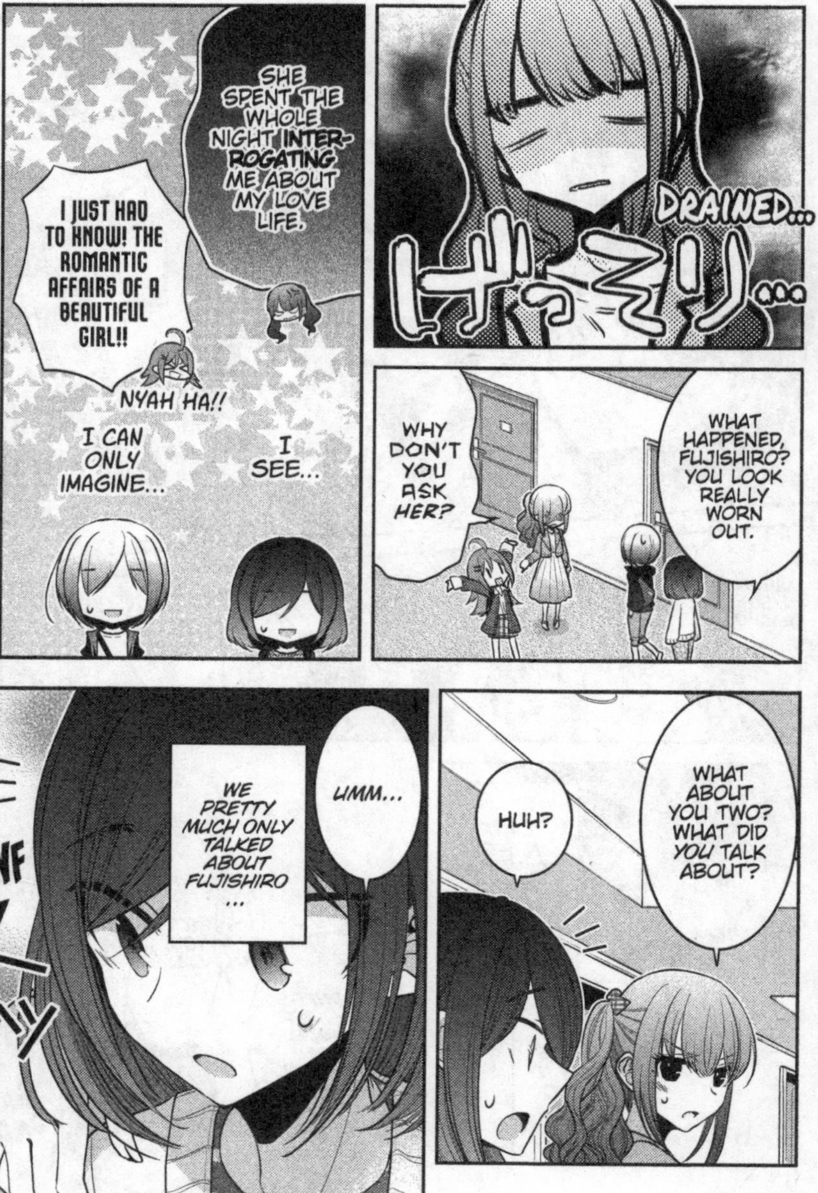
DRAINED...
げっそり...
WHAT HAPPENED, FUJISHIRO? YOU LOOK REALLY WORN OUT.
WHY DON'T YOU ASK HER?
SHE SPENT THE WHOLE NIGHT INTER-ROGATING ME ABOUT MY LOVE LIFE.
I JUST HAD TO KNOW! THE ROMANTIC AFFAIRS OF A BEAUTIFUL GIRL!!
NYAH HA!!
I SEE...
I CAN ONLY IMAGINE...
WHAT ABOUT YOU TWO? WHAT DID YOU TALK ABOUT?
HUH?
UMM...
WE PRETTY MUCH ONLY TALKED ABOUT FUJISHIRO ...
SHWF

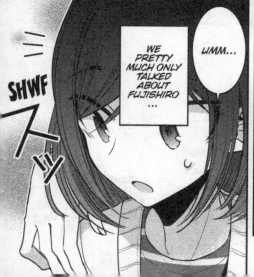

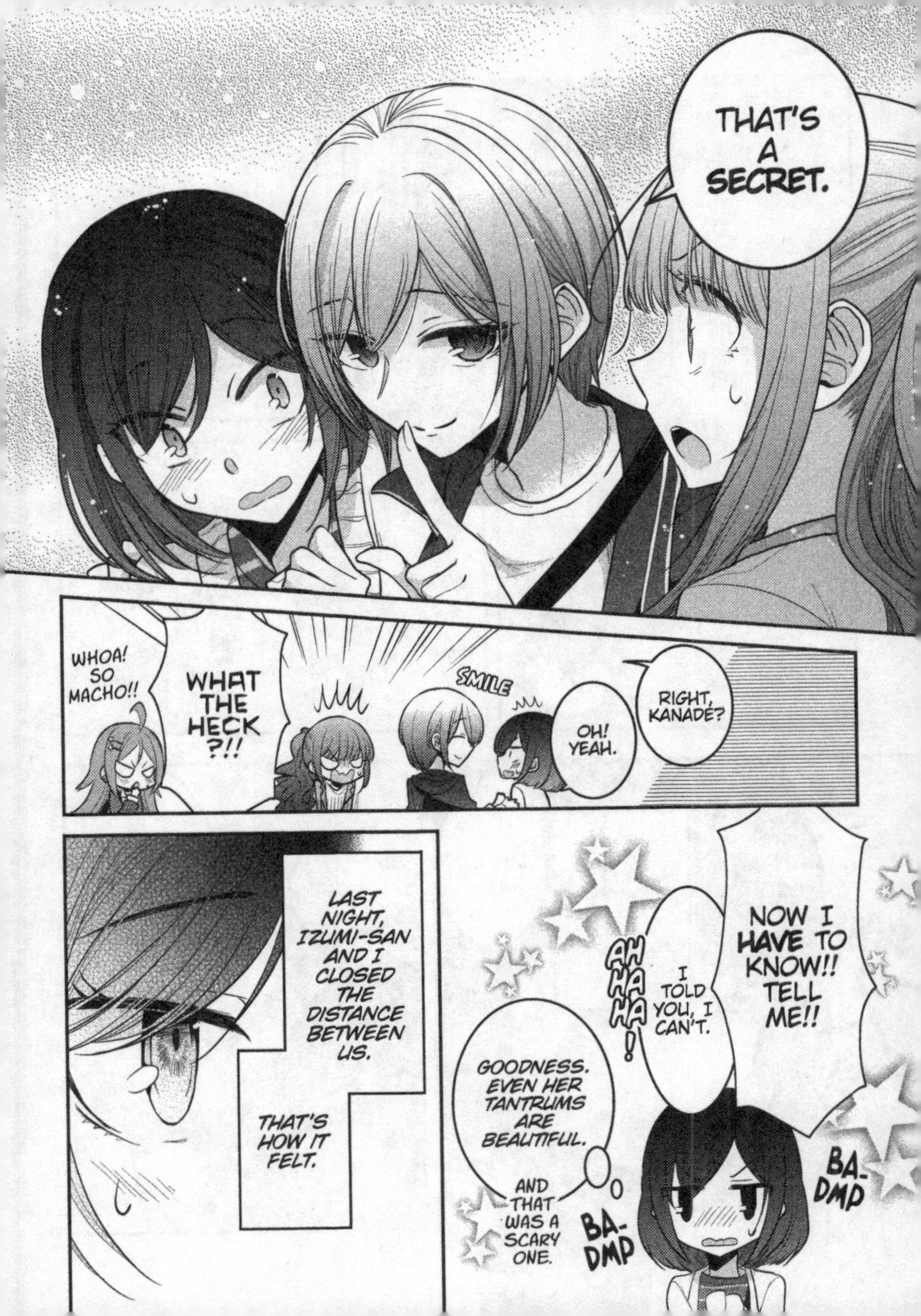
THAT'S A SECRET.
RIGHT, KANADE?
OH! YEAH.
SMILE
WHAT THE HECK ?!!
WHOA! SO MACHO!!
NOW I HAVE TO KNOW!! TELL ME!!
I TOLD YOU, I CAN'T.
AH HA HA!
GOODNESS. EVEN HER TANTRUMS ARE BEAUTIFUL.
AND THAT WAS A SCARY ONE.
BA-DMP
BA-DMP
LAST NIGHT, IZUMI-SAN AND I CLOSED THE DISTANCE BETWEEN US.
THAT'S HOW IT FELT.

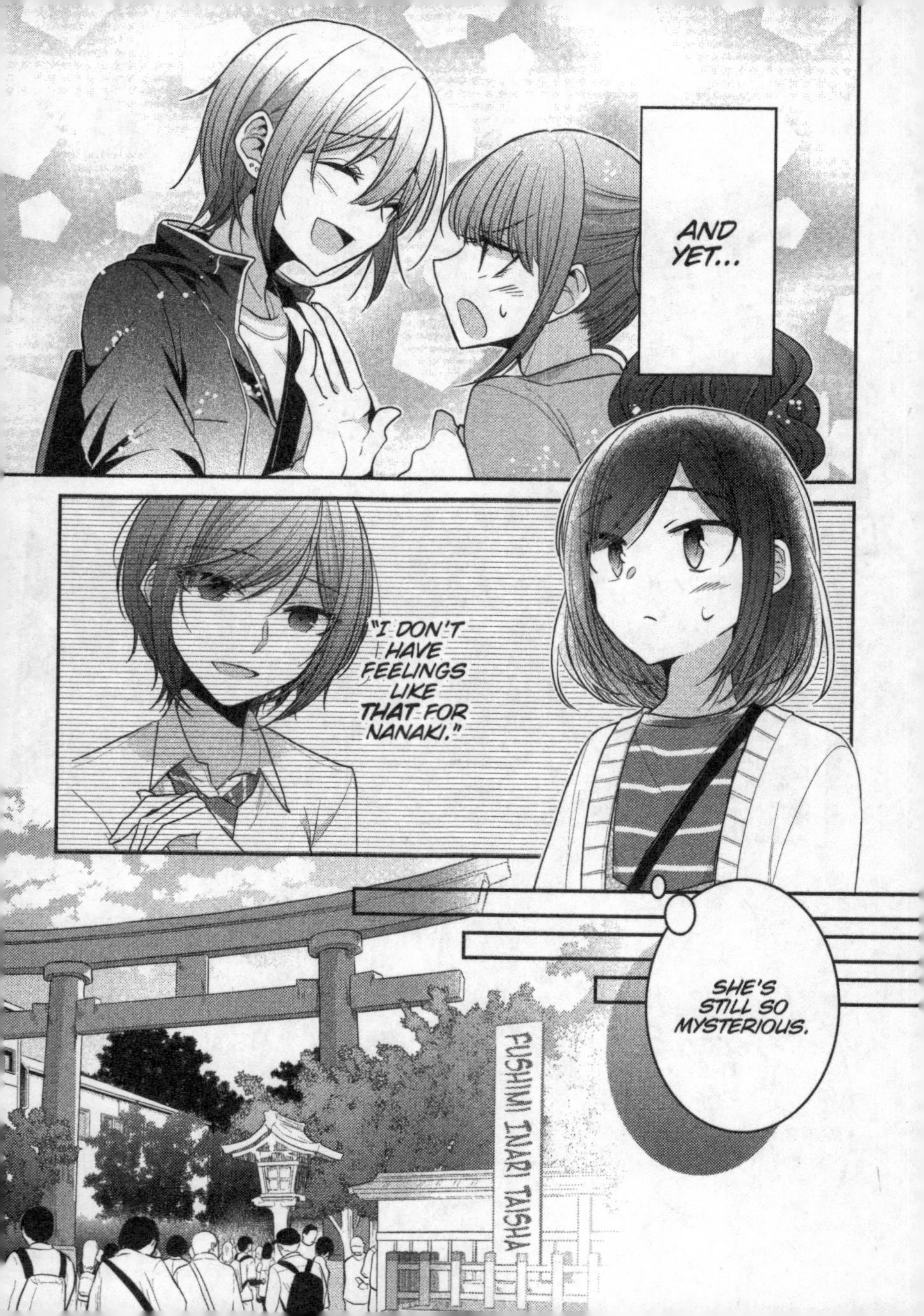
AND YET...
"I DON'T HAVE FEELINGS LIKE THAT FOR NANAKI."
SHE'S STILL SO MYSTERIOUS.
FUSHIMI INARI TAISHA

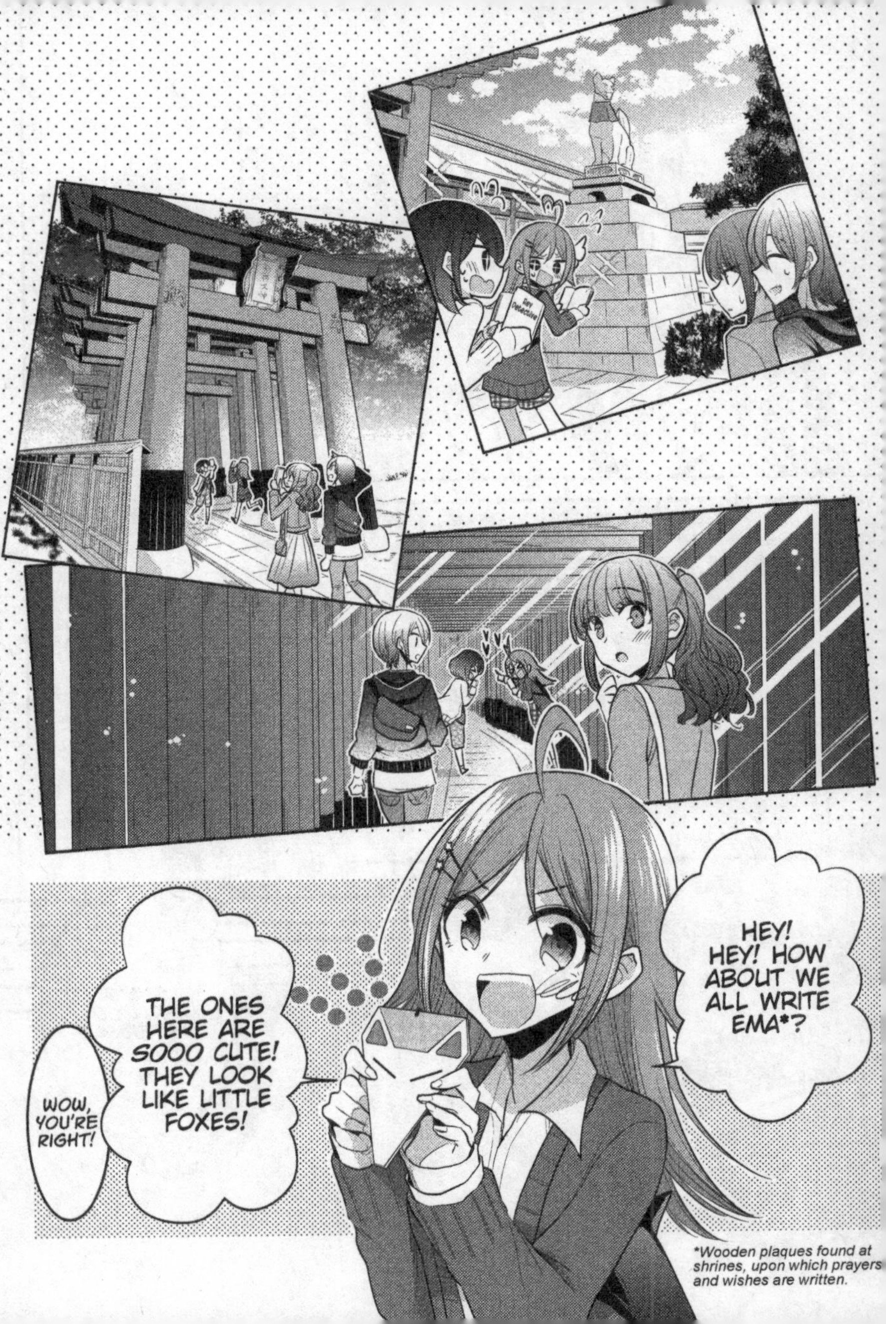
HEY! HEY! HOW ABOUT WE ALL WRITE EMA*?
THE ONES HERE ARE SOOO CUTE! THEY LOOK LIKE LITTLE FOXES!
WOW, YOU'RE RIGHT!

*Wooden plaques found at shrines, upon which prayers and wishes are written.

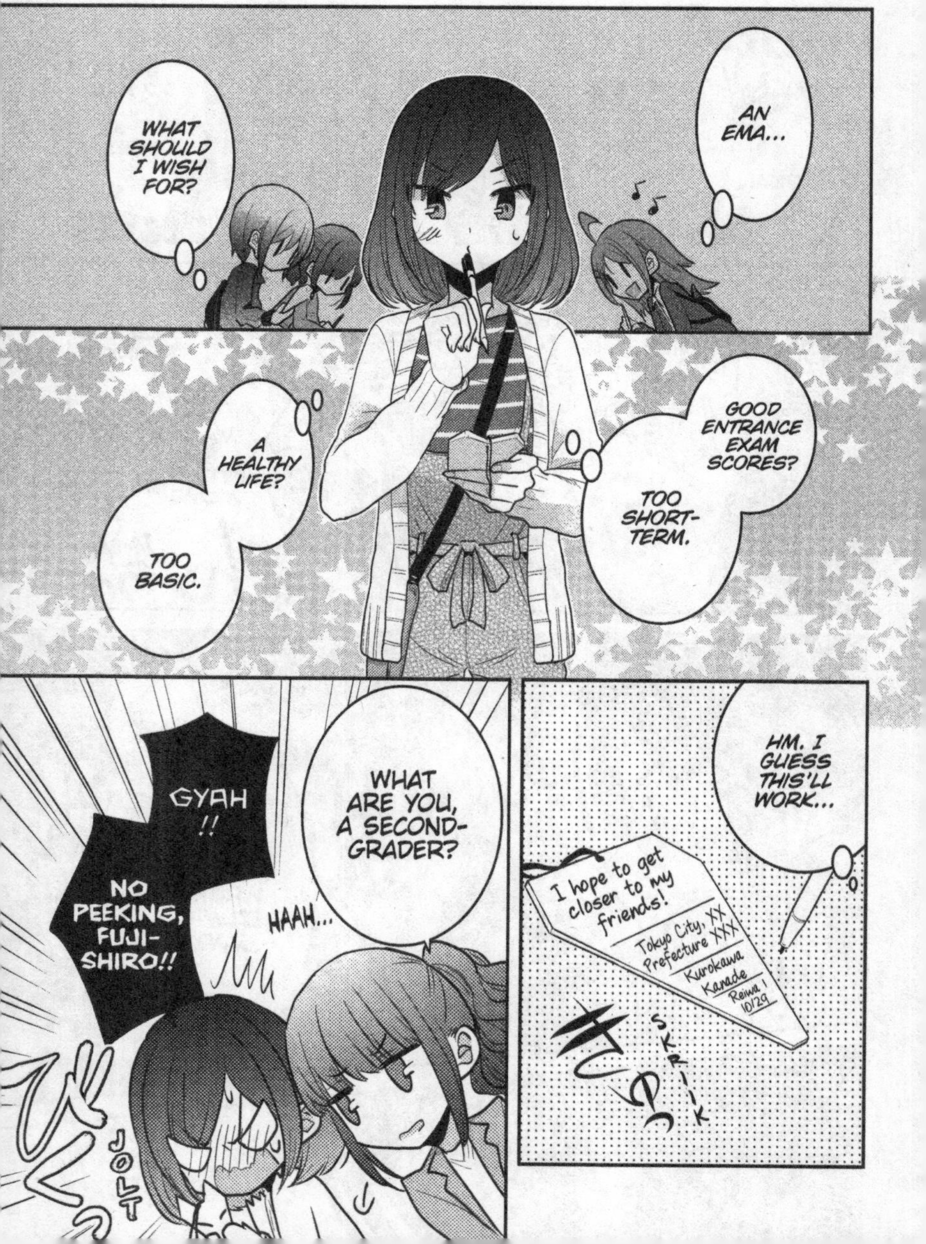
AN EMA...
WHAT SHOULD I WISH FOR?
GOOD ENTRANCE EXAM SCORES?
TOO SHORT-TERM.
A HEALTHY LIFE?
TOO BASIC.
HM. I GUESS THIS'LL WORK...
I hope to get closer to my friends!
Tokyo City, XX Prefecture XXX
Kurokawa Kanade
Reiwa 1 10/29
SKRIIK
WHAT ARE YOU, A SECOND-GRADER?
HAAH...
GYAH!!
NO PEEKING, FUJI-SHIRO!!
JOLT

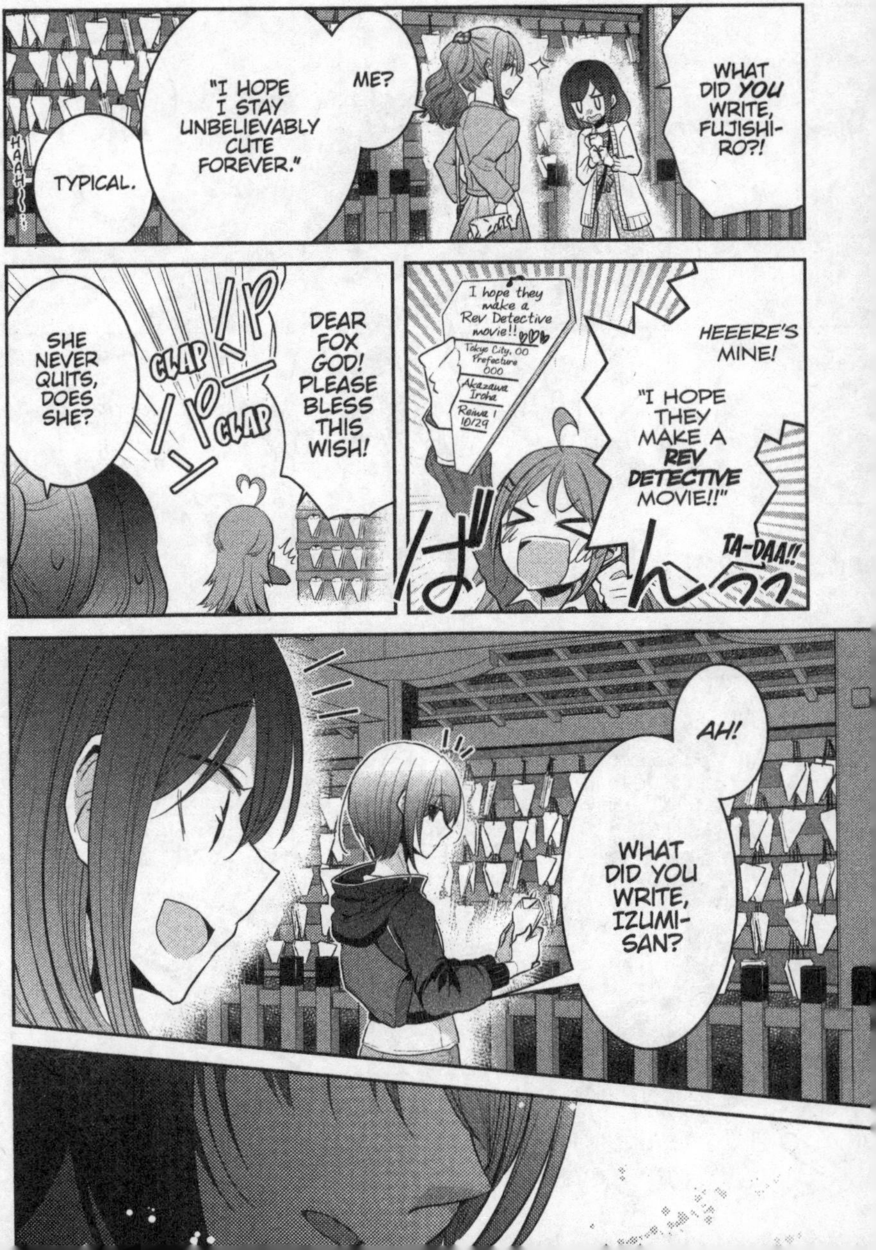
WHAT DID YOU WRITE, FUJISHIRO?!
ME?
"I HOPE I STAY UNBELIEVABLY CUTE FOREVER."
HAAAH~~
TYPICAL.
HEEERE'S MINE!
"I HOPE THEY MAKE A REV DETECTIVE MOVIE!!"
I hope they make a Rev Detective movie!!
Tokyo City, OO Prefecture OOO
Akazawa Iroha
Reiwa 1 10/29
TA-DAA!!
DEAR FOX GOD! PLEASE BLESS THIS WISH!
CLAP
CLAP
SHE NEVER QUITS, DOES SHE?
AH!
WHAT DID YOU WRITE, IZUMI-SAN?

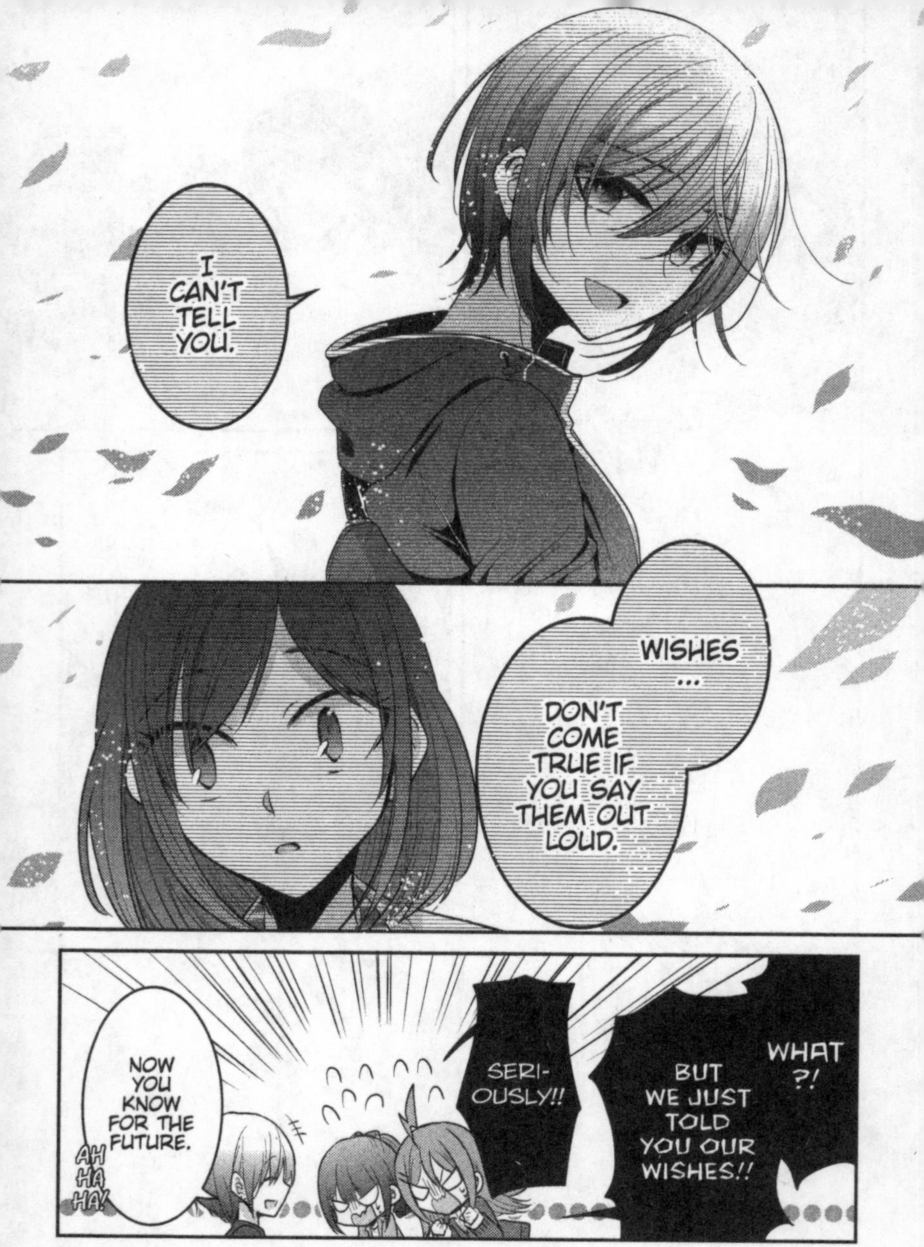
I CAN'T TELL YOU.
WISHES ... DON'T COME TRUE IF YOU SAY THEM OUT LOUD.
WHAT?!
BUT WE JUST TOLD YOU OUR WISHES!!
SERI-OUSLY!!
NOW YOU KNOW FOR THE FUTURE.
AH HA HA!

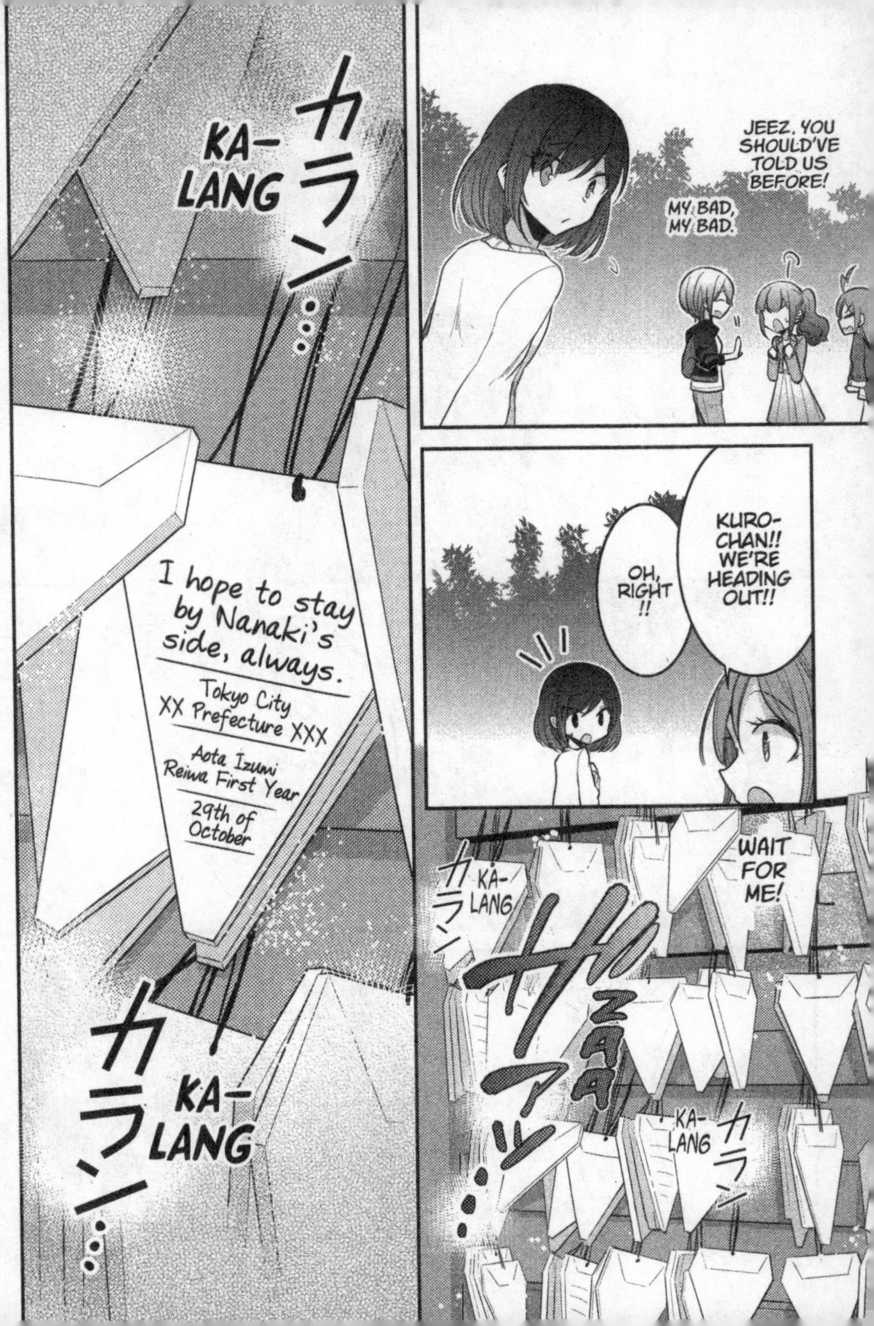
JEEZ, YOU SHOULD'VE TOLD US BEFORE!
MY BAD, MY BAD.
KURO-CHAN!! WE'RE HEADING OUT!!
OH, RIGHT!!
WAIT FOR ME!
カラン
KA-LANG
サァァッ…
カラン
KA-LANG
カラン…
KA-LANG
I hope to stay by Nanaki's side, always.
Tokyo City XX Prefecture XXX
Aota Izumi Reiwa First Year
29th of October
KA-LANG
カラン…

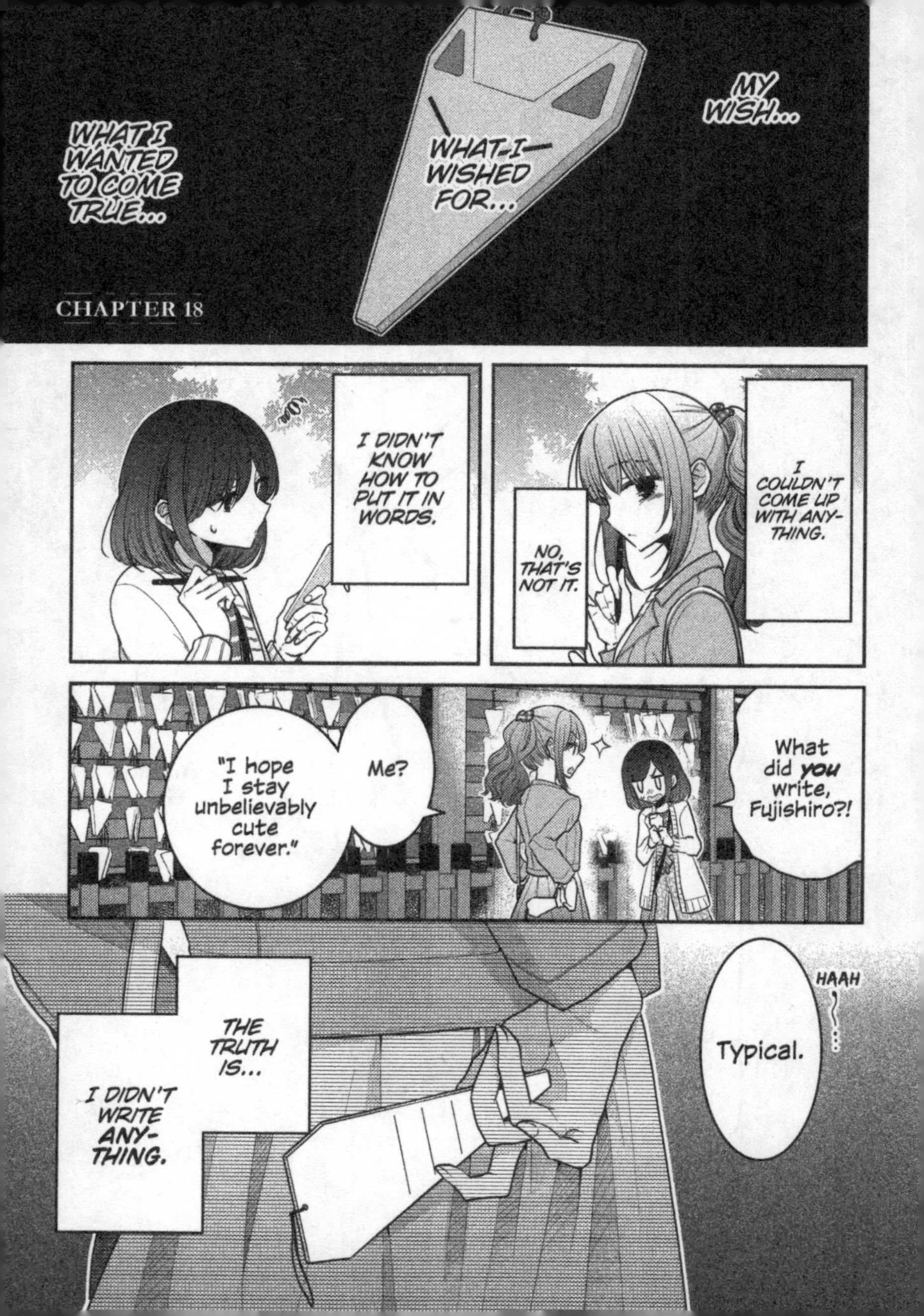
MY WISH...
WHAT-I-WISHED FOR...
WHAT I WANTED TO COME TRUE...
CHAPTER 18
I COULDN'T COME UP WITH ANY-THING.
NO, THAT'S NOT IT.
I DIDN'T KNOW HOW TO PUT IT IN WORDS.
What did you write, Fujishiro?!
Me?
"I hope I stay unbelievably cute forever."
HAAH~...
Typical.
THE TRUTH IS...
I DIDN'T WRITE ANY-THING.

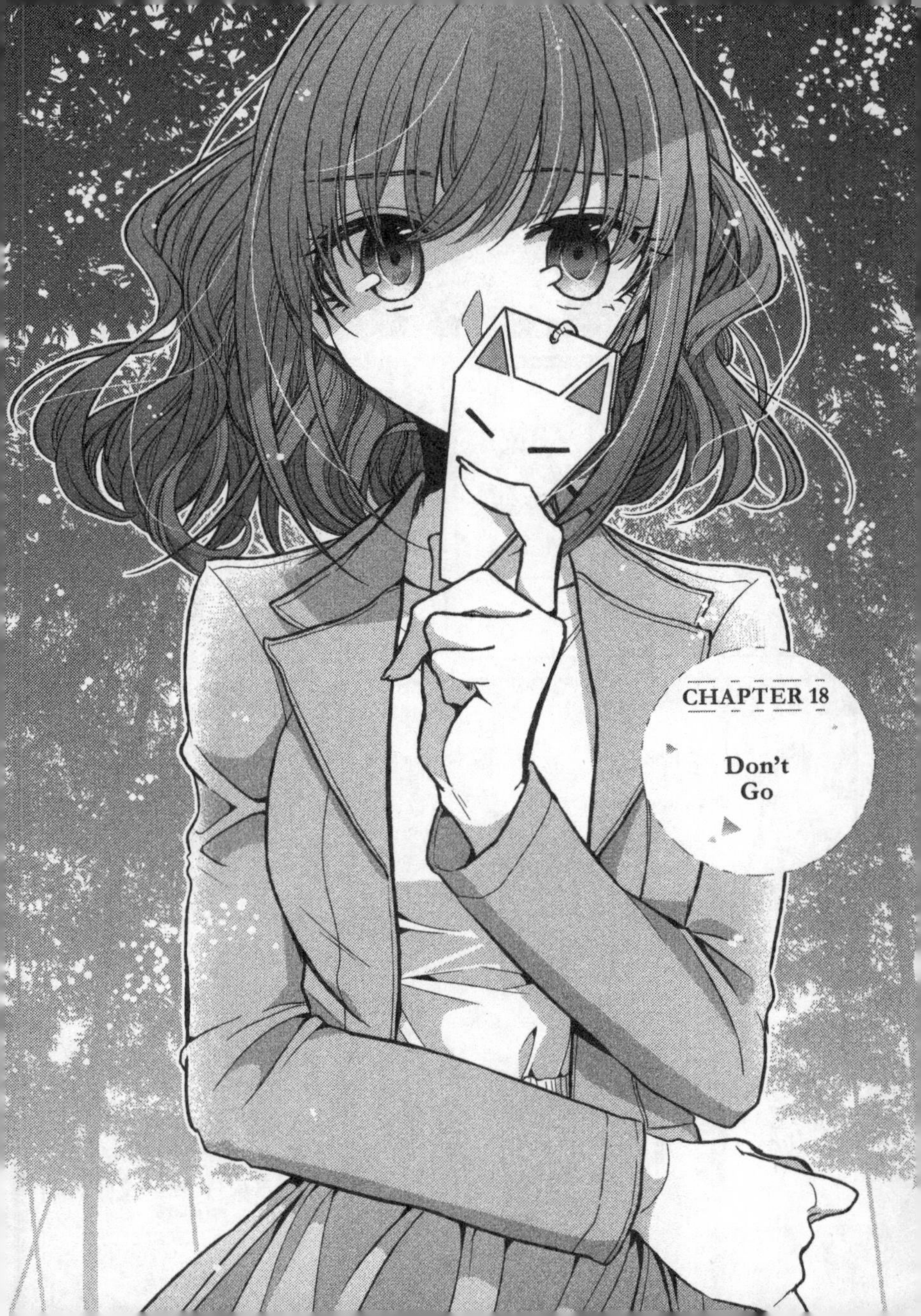
CHAPTER 18
Don't Go

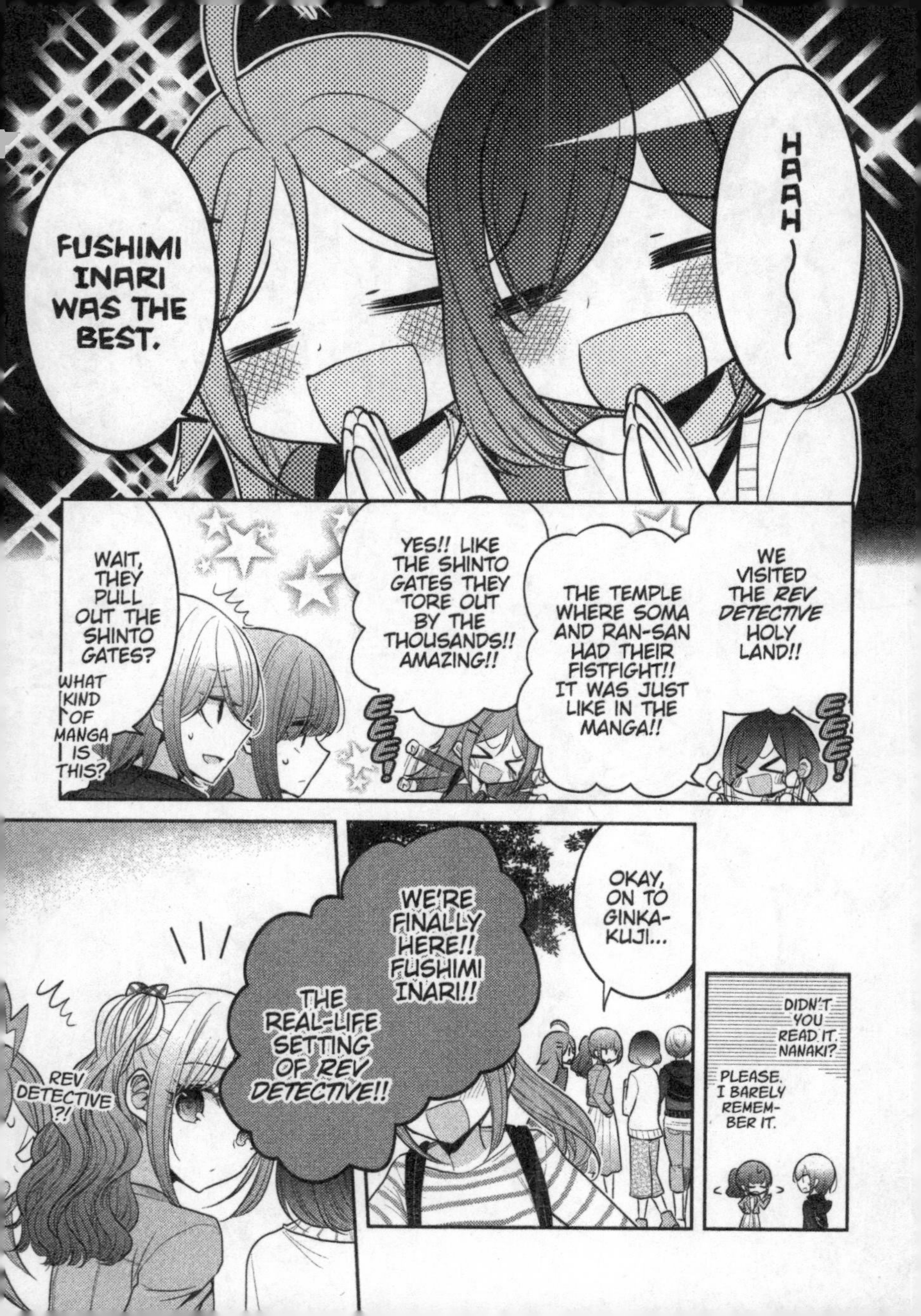

HAAH~~
FUSHIMI INARI WAS THE BEST.
WE VISITED THE *REV DETECTIVE* HOLY LAND!!
THE TEMPLE WHERE SOMA AND RAN-SAN HAD THEIR FISTFIGHT!! IT WAS JUST LIKE IN THE MANGA!!
YES!! LIKE THE SHINTO GATES THEY TORE OUT BY THE THOUSANDS!! AMAZING!!
WAIT, THEY PULL OUT THE SHINTO GATES?
WHAT KIND OF MANGA IS THIS?
OKAY, ON TO GINKA-KUJI...
DIDN'T YOU READ IT, NANAKI?
PLEASE. I BARELY REMEM-BER IT.
WE'RE FINALLY HERE!! FUSHIMI INARI!!
THE REAL-LIFE SETTING OF *REV DETECTIVE*!!
REV DETECTIVE ?!

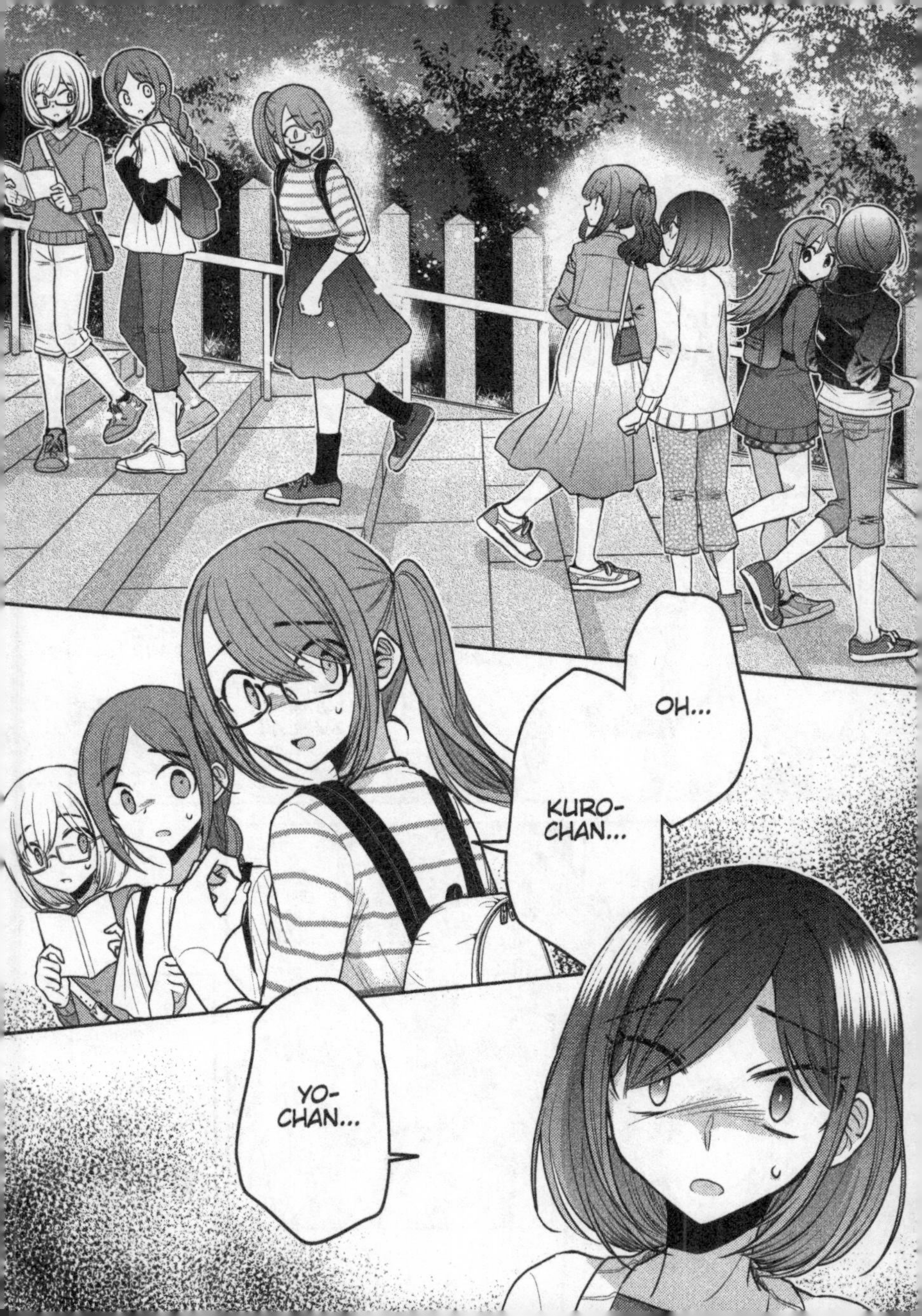
OH...
KURO-CHAN...
YO-CHAN...

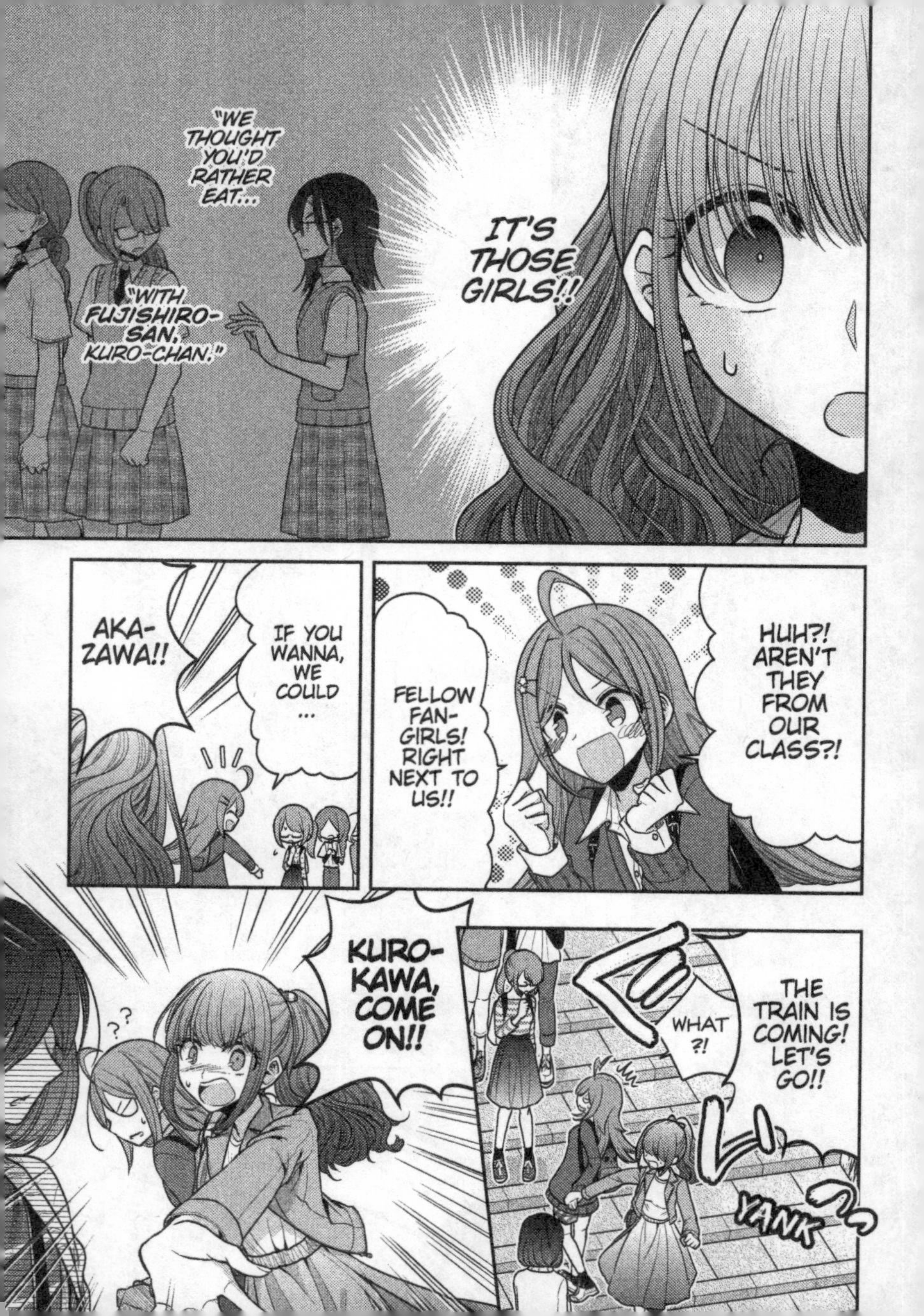
IT'S THOSE GIRLS!!
"WE THOUGHT YOU'D RATHER EAT...
"WITH FUJISHIRO-SAN, KURO-CHAN."
HUH?! AREN'T THEY FROM OUR CLASS?!
FELLOW FAN-GIRLS! RIGHT NEXT TO US!!
IF YOU WANNA, WE COULD ...
AKA-ZAWA!!
THE TRAIN IS COMING! LET'S GO!!
WHAT?!
YANK
KURO-KAWA, COME ON!!

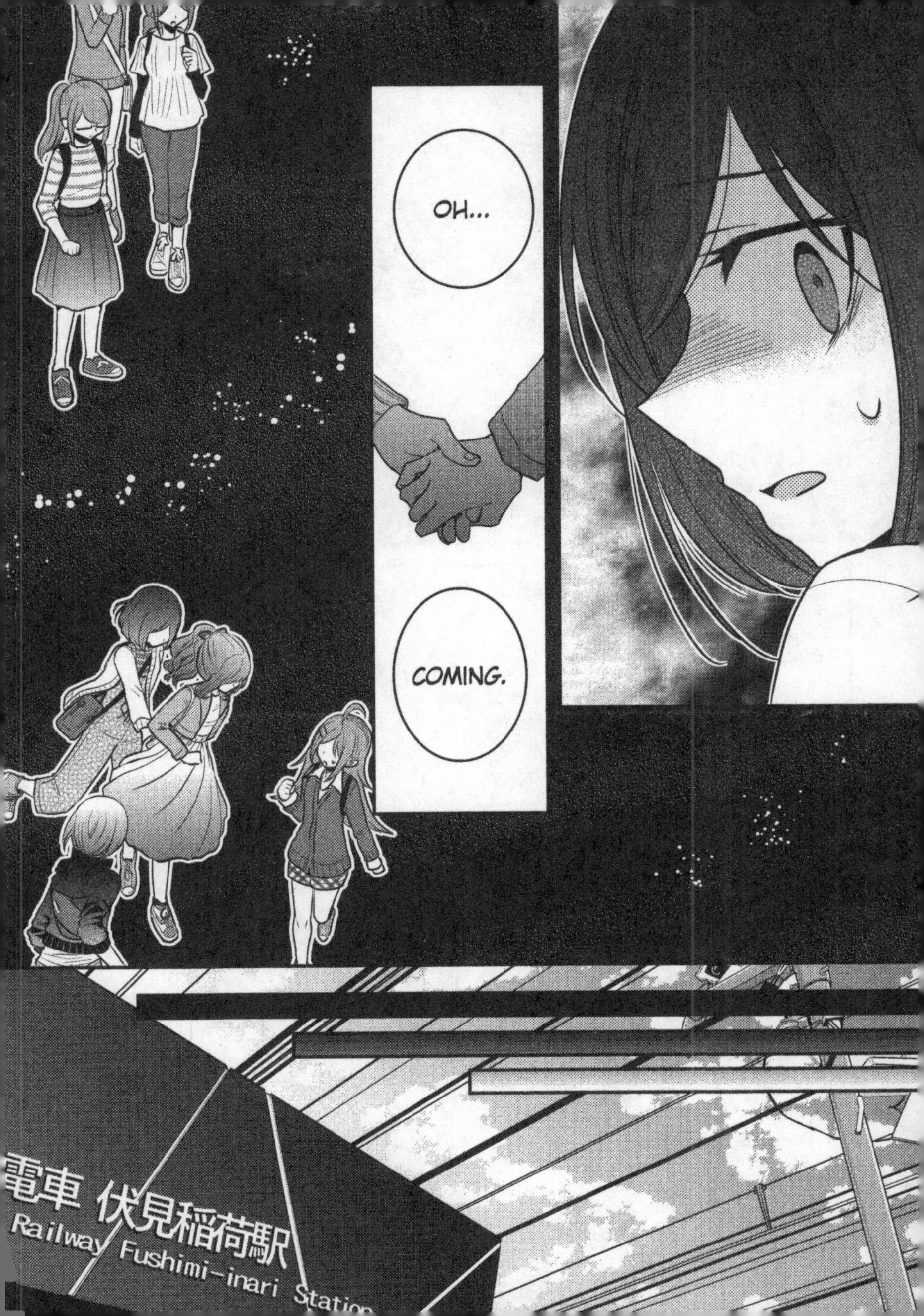
OH...
COMING.
電車 伏見稲荷駅
Railway Fushimi-inari Station

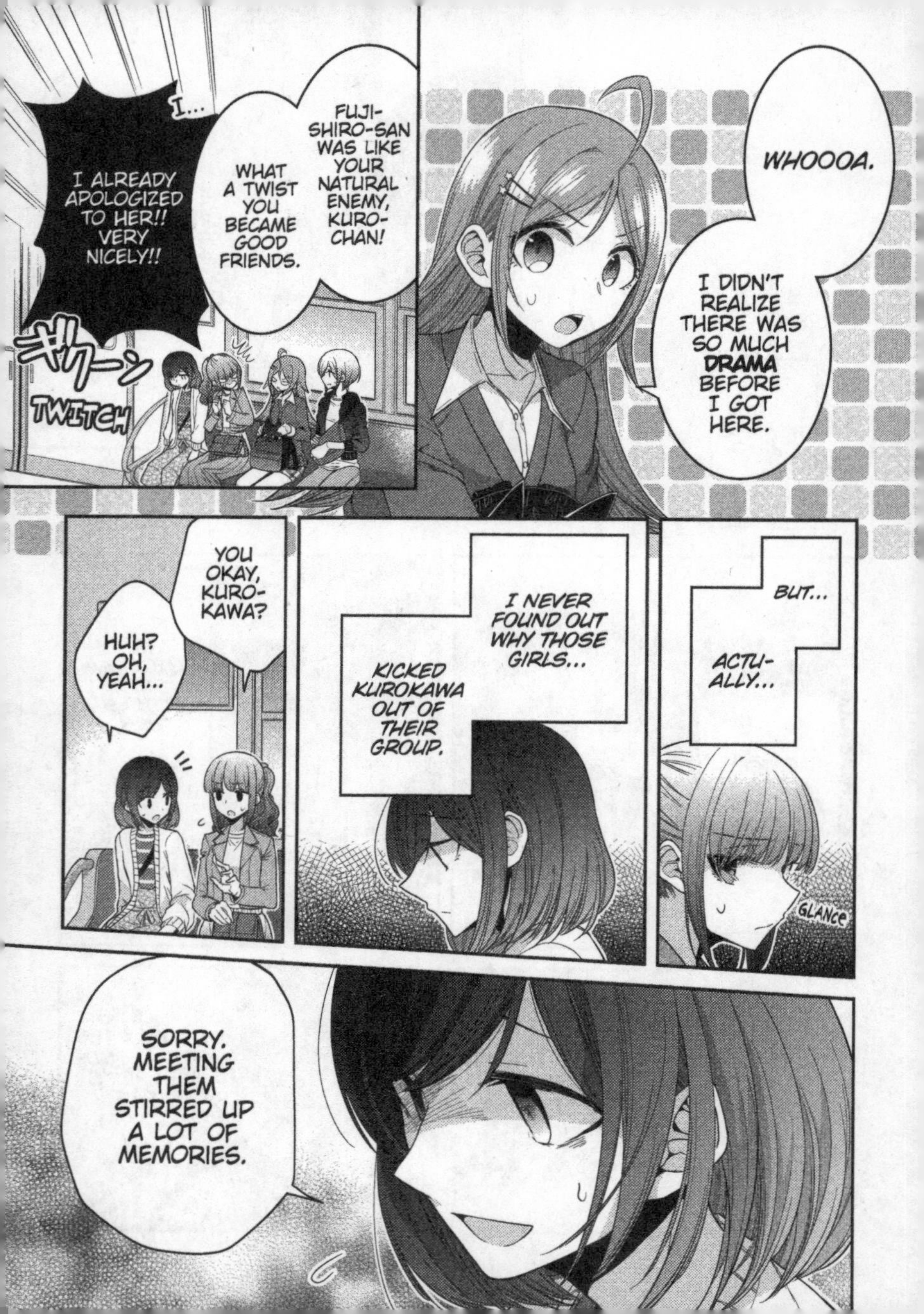
WHOOOA.
I DIDN'T REALIZE THERE WAS SO MUCH **DRAMA** BEFORE I GOT HERE.
FUJI-SHIRO-SAN WAS LIKE YOUR NATURAL ENEMY, KURO-CHAN!
WHAT A TWIST YOU BECAME GOOD FRIENDS.
I...
I ALREADY APOLOGIZED TO HER!! VERY NICELY!!
ギクーン
TWITCH
BUT...
ACTU-ALLY...
GLANCE
I NEVER FOUND OUT WHY THOSE GIRLS...
KICKED KUROKAWA OUT OF THEIR GROUP.
YOU OKAY, KUROKAWA?
HUH? OH, YEAH...
SORRY. MEETING THEM STIRRED UP A LOT OF MEMORIES.

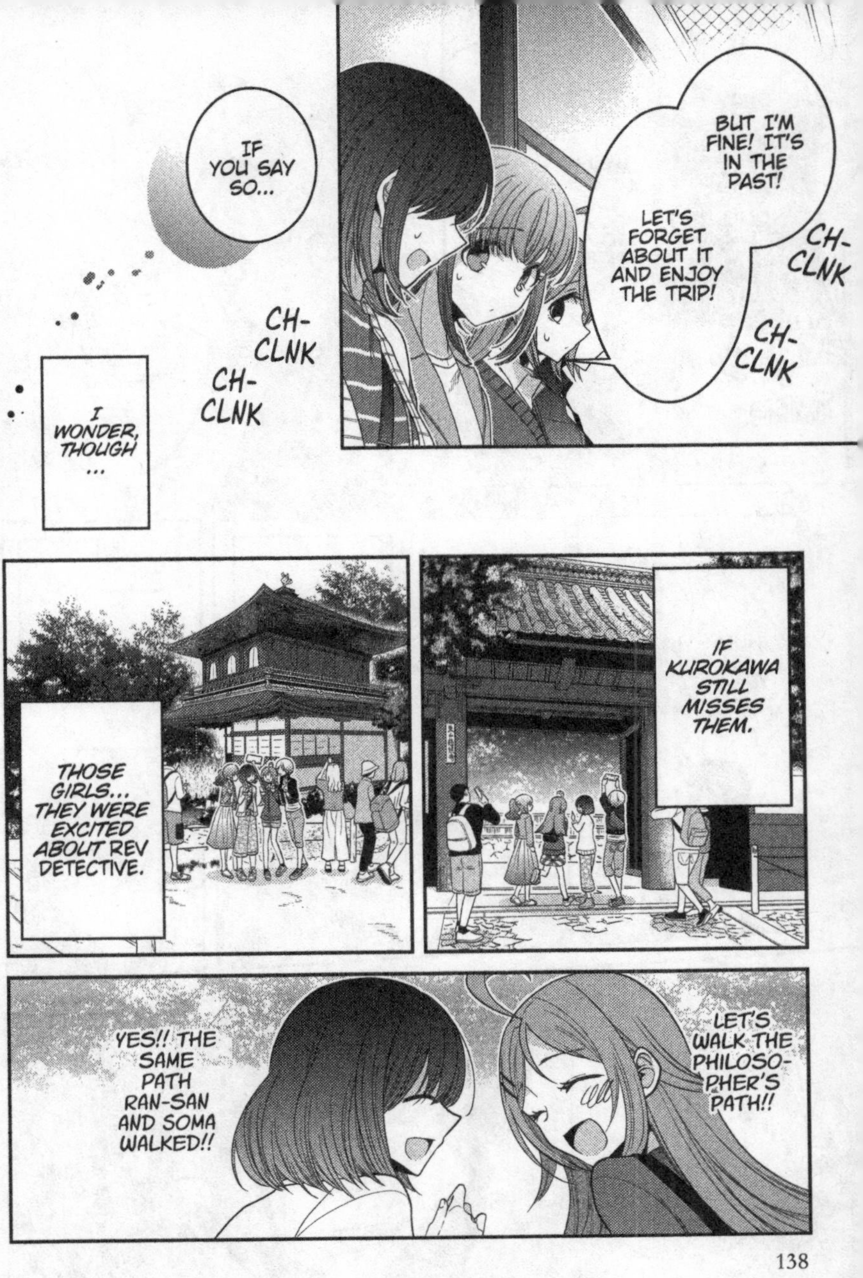
BUT I'M FINE! IT'S IN THE PAST!
LET'S FORGET ABOUT IT AND ENJOY THE TRIP!
CH-CLNK
CH-CLNK
CH-CLNK
CH-CLNK
IF YOU SAY SO...
I WONDER, THOUGH...
IF KUROKAWA STILL MISSES THEM.
THOSE GIRLS... THEY WERE EXCITED ABOUT REV DETECTIVE.
LET'S WALK THE PHILOSO-PHER'S PATH!!
YES!! THE SAME PATH RAN-SAN AND SOMA WALKED!!

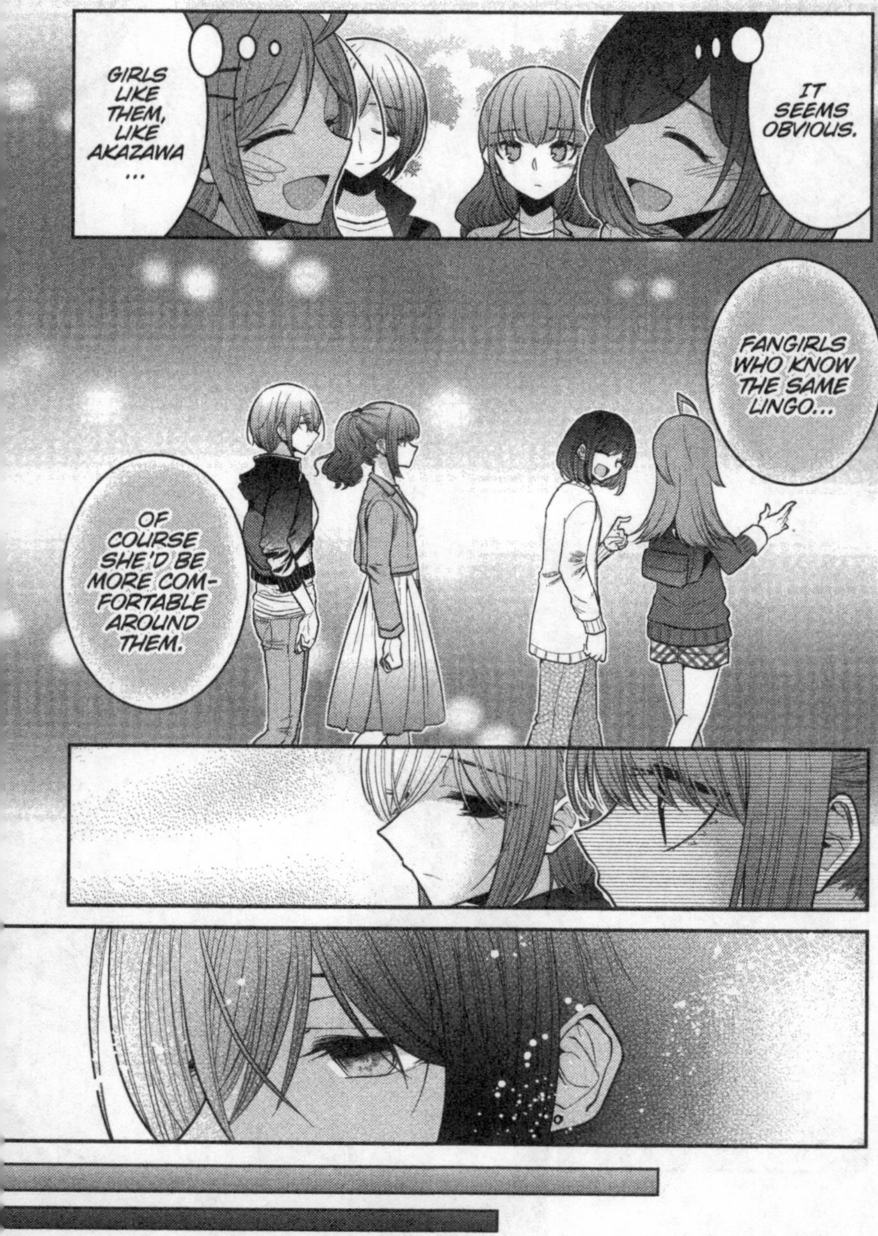
IT SEEMS OBVIOUS.
GIRLS LIKE THEM, LIKE AKAZAWA ...
FANGIRLS WHO KNOW THE SAME LINGO...
OF COURSE SHE'D BE MORE COMFORTABLE AROUND THEM.

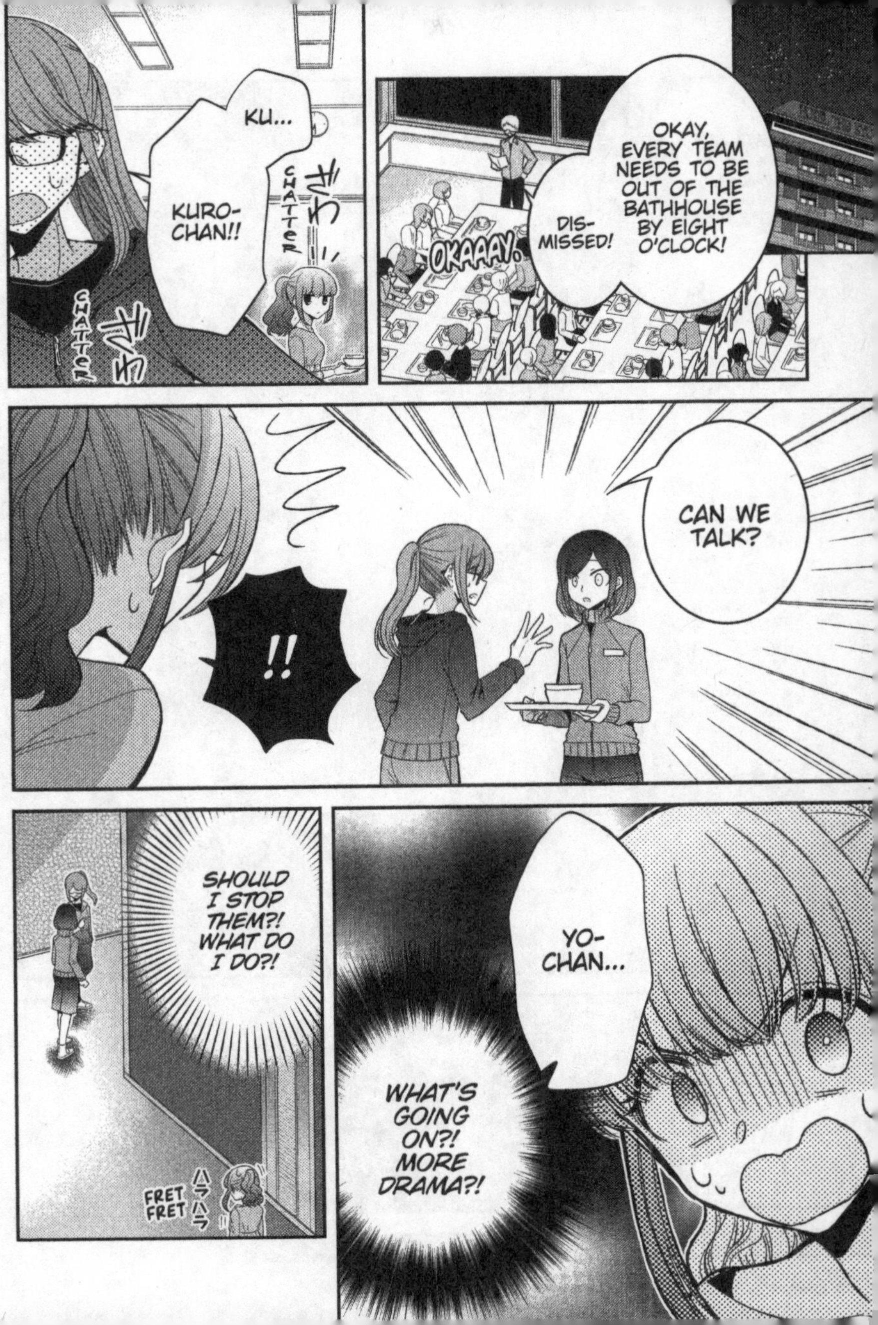
OKAY, EVERY TEAM NEEDS TO BE OUT OF THE BATHHOUSE BY EIGHT O'CLOCK!
DIS-MISSED!
OKAAAY.
KU...
KURO-CHAN!!
ざわ CHATTER
ざわ CHATTER
CAN WE TALK?
!!
YO-CHAN...
WHAT'S GOING ON?! MORE DRAMA?!
SHOULD I STOP THEM?! WHAT DO I DO?!
ハラハラ FRET FRET

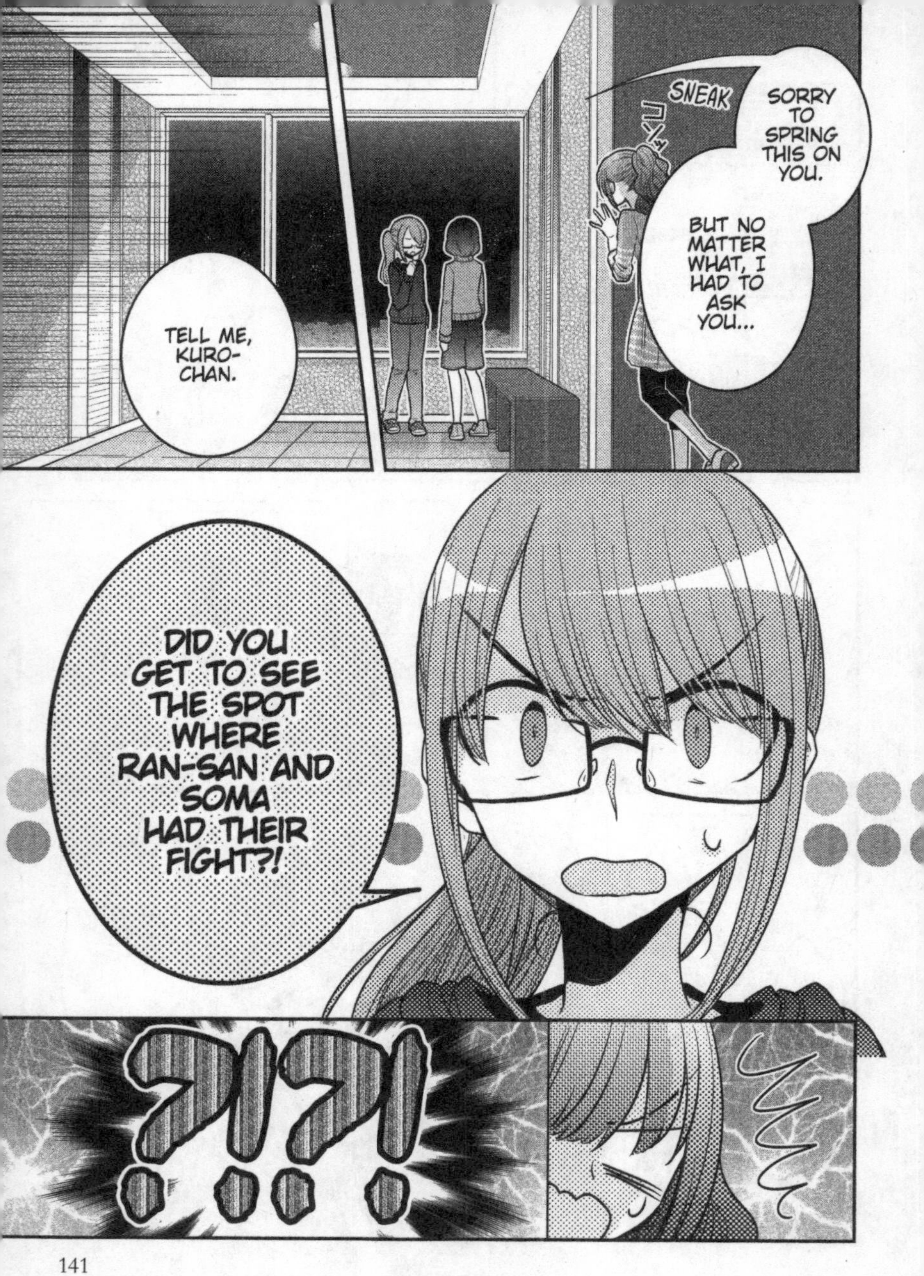
SNEAK
SORRY TO SPRING THIS ON YOU.
BUT NO MATTER WHAT, I HAD TO ASK YOU...
TELL ME, KURO-CHAN.
DID YOU GET TO SEE THE SPOT WHERE RAN-SAN AND SOMA HAD THEIR FIGHT?!
?!?!

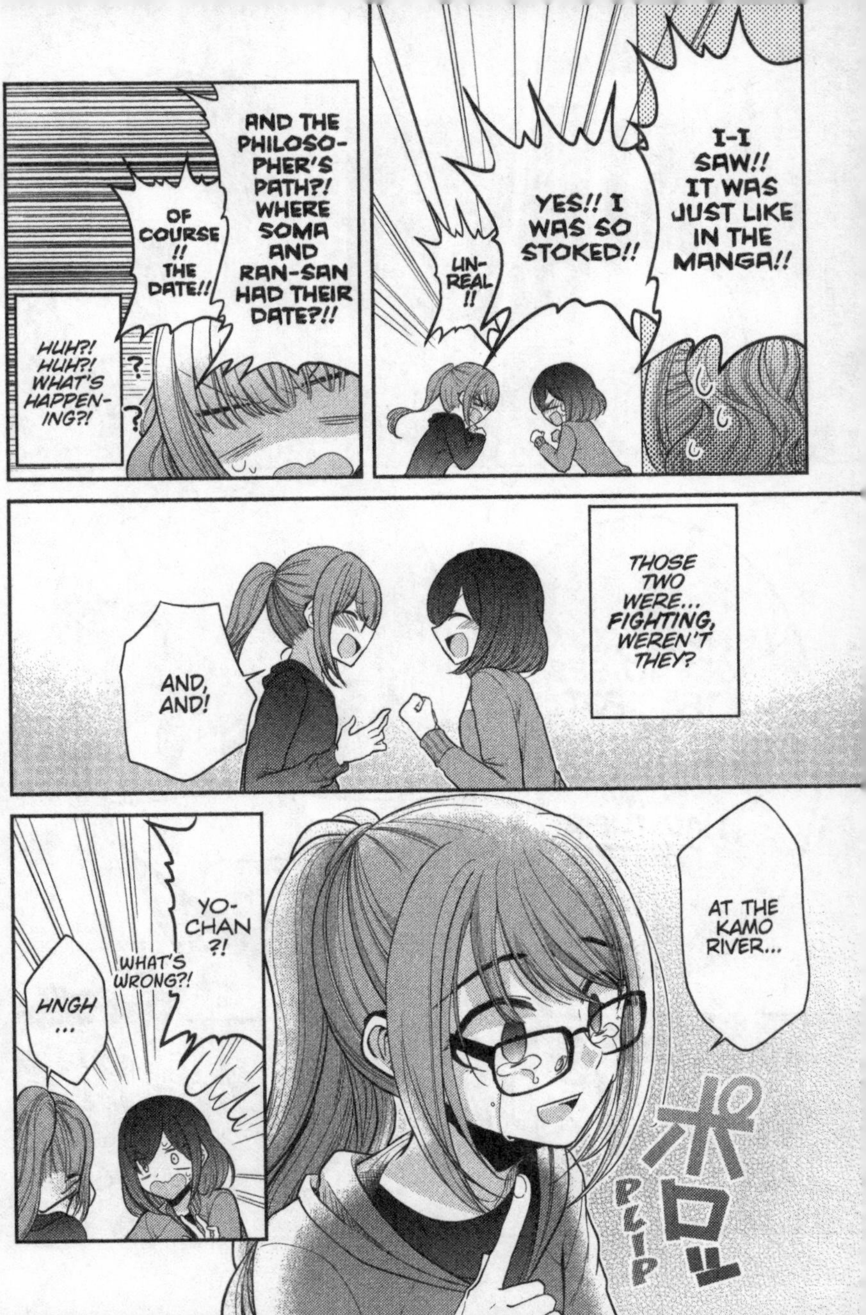
I-I SAW!! IT WAS JUST LIKE IN THE MANGA!!
YES!! I WAS SO STOKED!!
UN-REAL!!
AND THE PHILOSOPHER'S PATH?! WHERE SOMA AND RAN-SAN HAD THEIR DATE?!!
OF COURSE!! THE DATE!!
HUH?! HUH?! WHAT'S HAPPENING?!
THOSE TWO WERE... FIGHTING, WEREN'T THEY?
AND, AND!
AT THE KAMO RIVER...
ポロッ
PLIP
YO-CHAN?!
WHAT'S WRONG?!
HNGH...

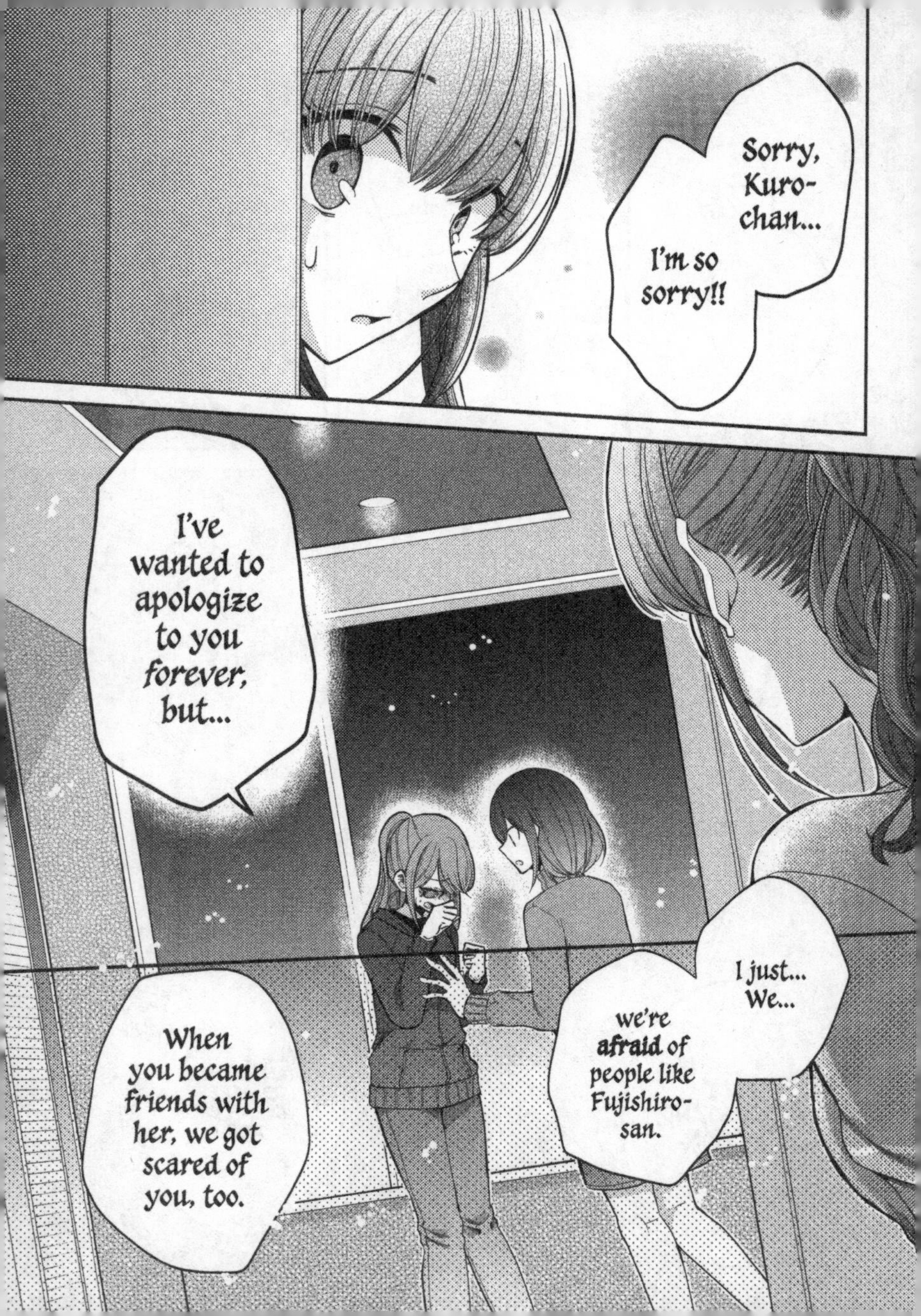
Sorry, Kuro-chan... I'm so sorry!!
I've wanted to apologize to you *forever*, but...
I just... We... we're **afraid** of people like Fujishiro-san.
When you became friends with her, we got scared of you, too.

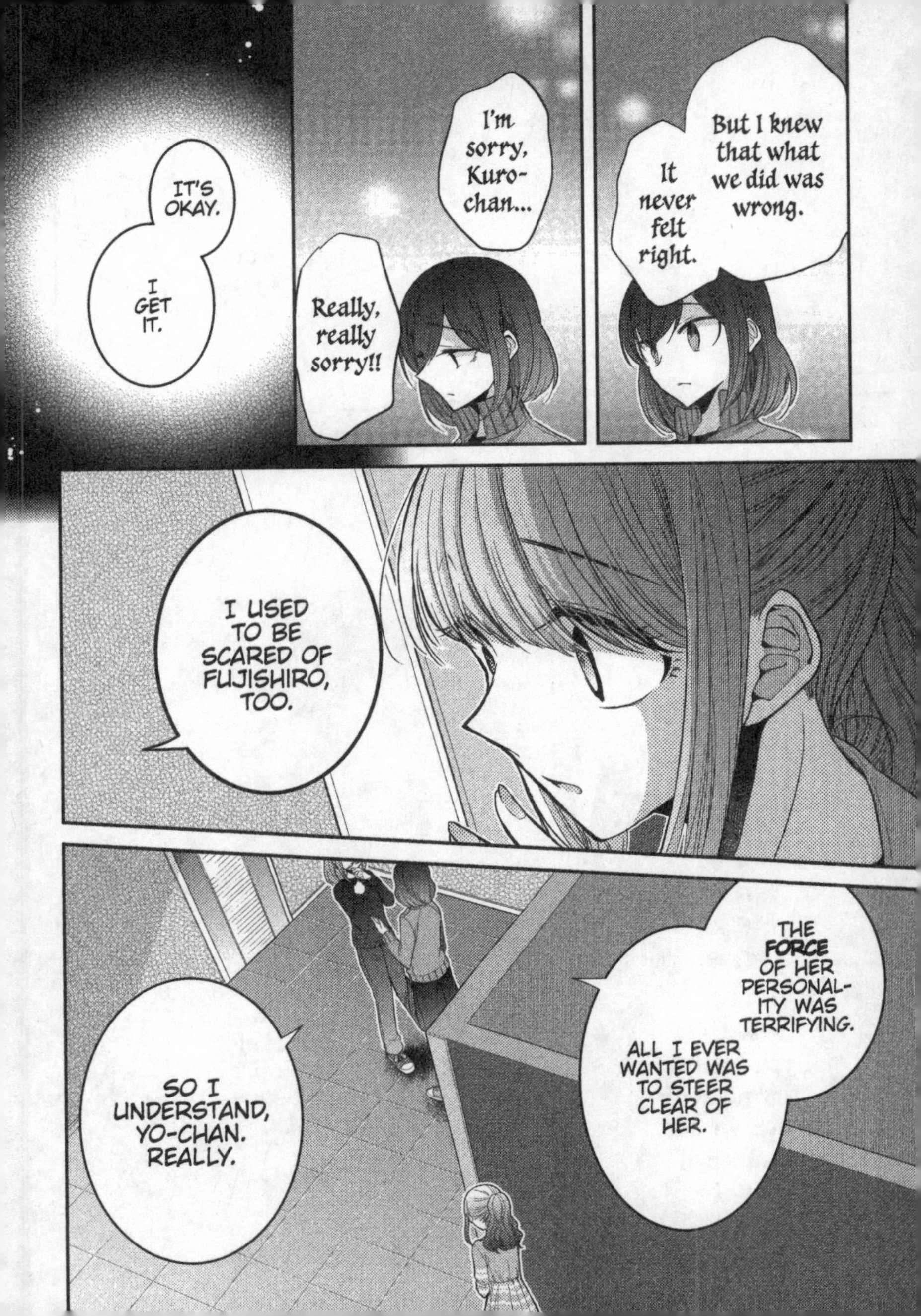
But I knew that what we did was wrong.
It never felt right.
I'm sorry, Kuro-chan...
Really, really sorry!!
IT'S OKAY.
I GET IT.
I USED TO BE SCARED OF FUJISHIRO, TOO.
THE FORCE OF HER PERSONALITY WAS TERRIFYING.
ALL I EVER WANTED WAS TO STEER CLEAR OF HER.
SO I UNDERSTAND, YO-CHAN. REALLY.

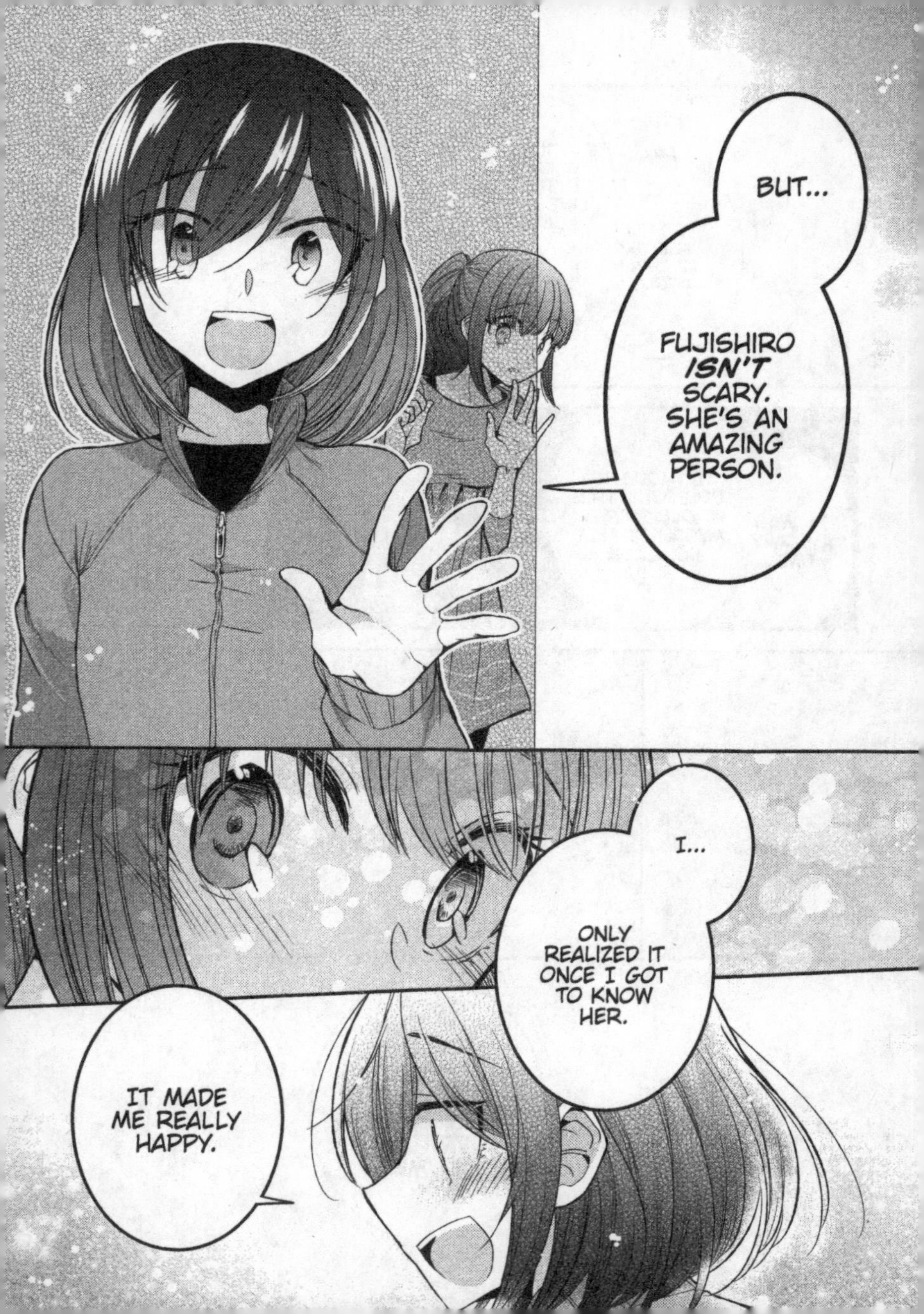
BUT...
FUJISHIRO ***ISN'T*** SCARY. SHE'S AN AMAZING PERSON.
I...
ONLY REALIZED IT ONCE I GOT TO KNOW HER.
IT MADE ME REALLY HAPPY.

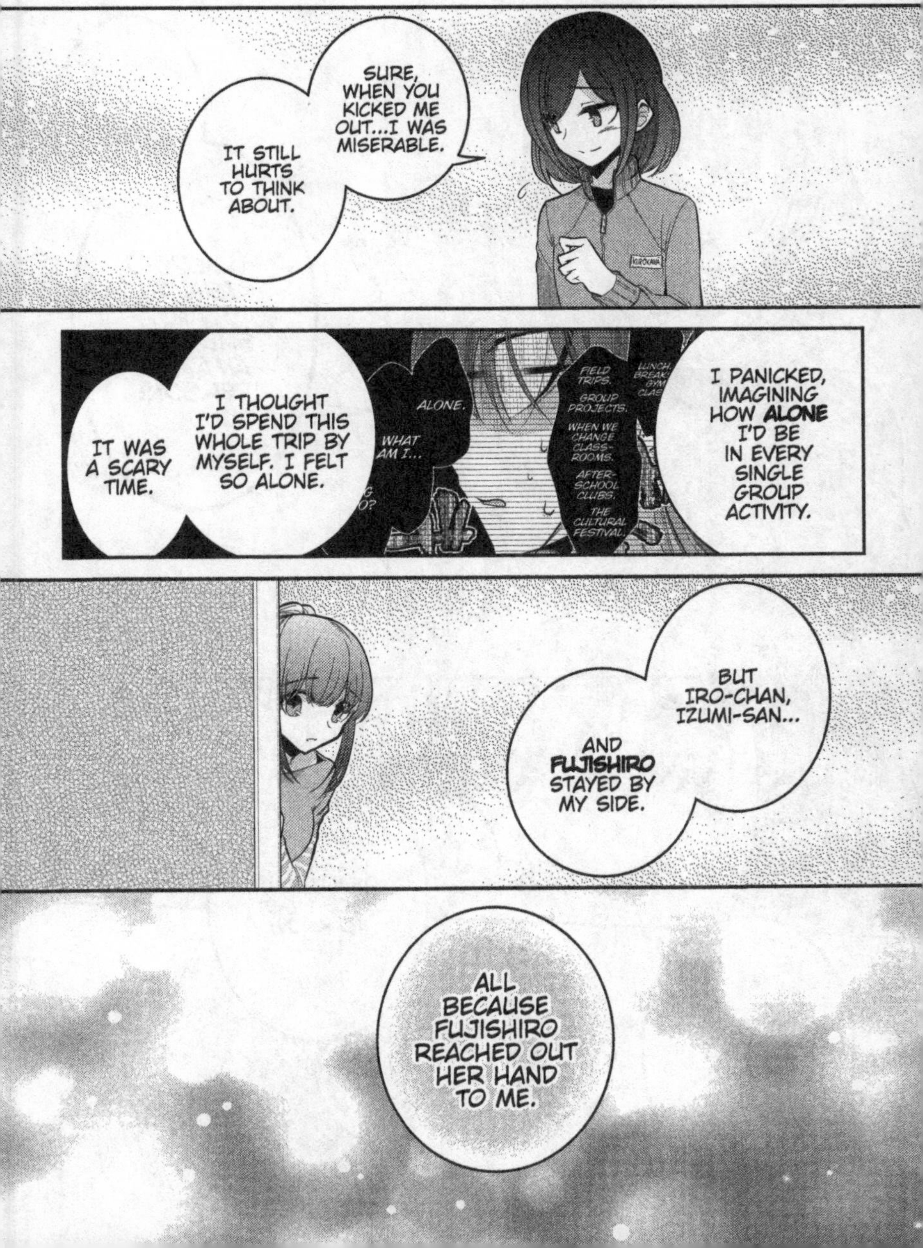
SURE, WHEN YOU KICKED ME OUT...I WAS MISERABLE.
IT STILL HURTS TO THINK ABOUT.
I PANICKED, IMAGINING HOW **ALONE** I'D BE IN EVERY SINGLE GROUP ACTIVITY.
FIELD TRIPS. GROUP PROJECTS. WHEN WE CHANGE CLASS-ROOMS. AFTER-SCHOOL CLUBS. THE CULTURAL FESTIVAL.
ALONE.
WHAT AM I...
I THOUGHT I'D SPEND THIS WHOLE TRIP BY MYSELF. I FELT SO ALONE.
IT WAS A SCARY TIME.
BUT IRO-CHAN, IZUMI-SAN...
AND **FUJISHIRO** STAYED BY MY SIDE.
ALL BECAUSE FUJISHIRO REACHED OUT HER HAND TO ME.

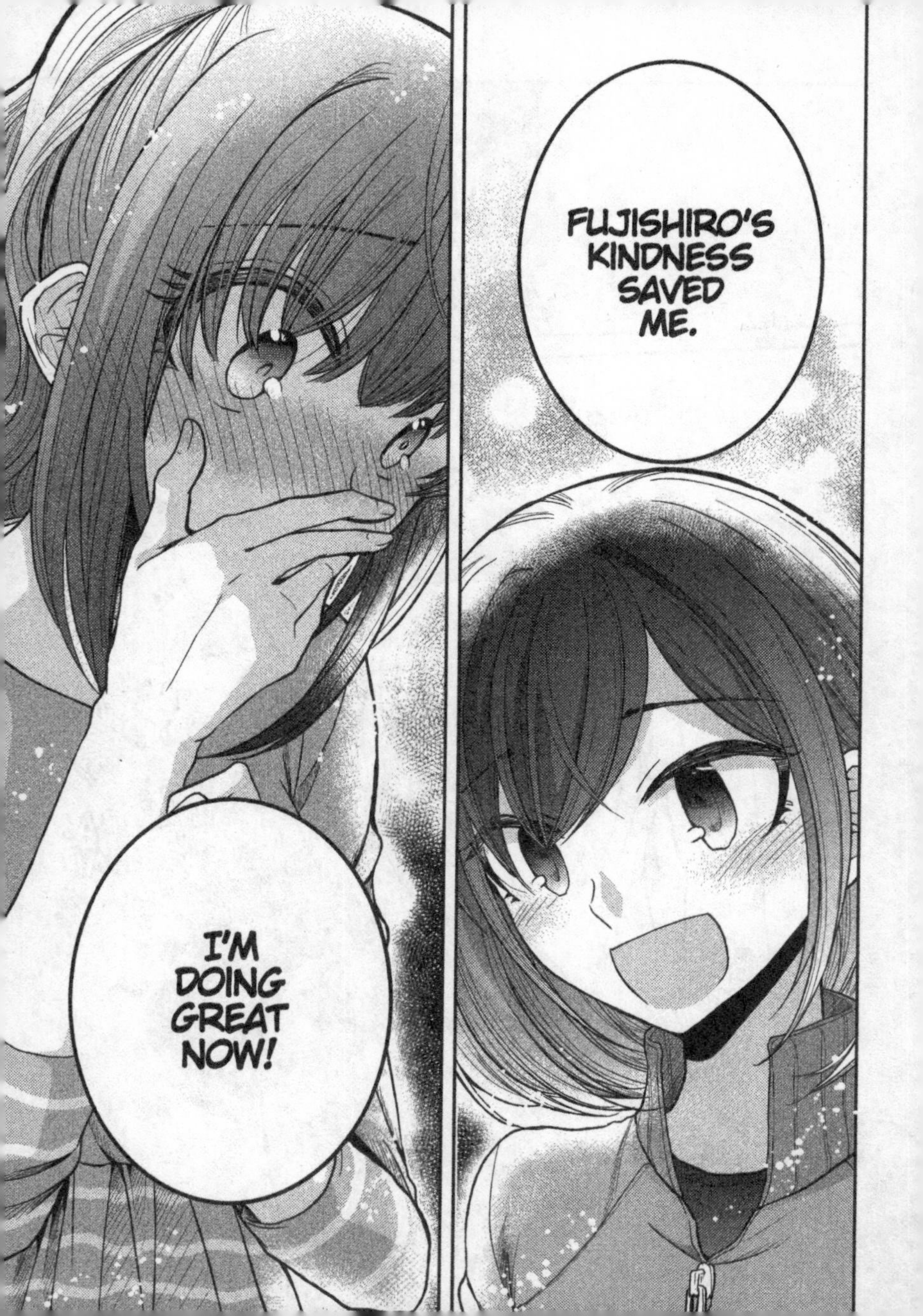
FUJISHIRO'S KINDNESS SAVED ME.
I'M DOING GREAT NOW!

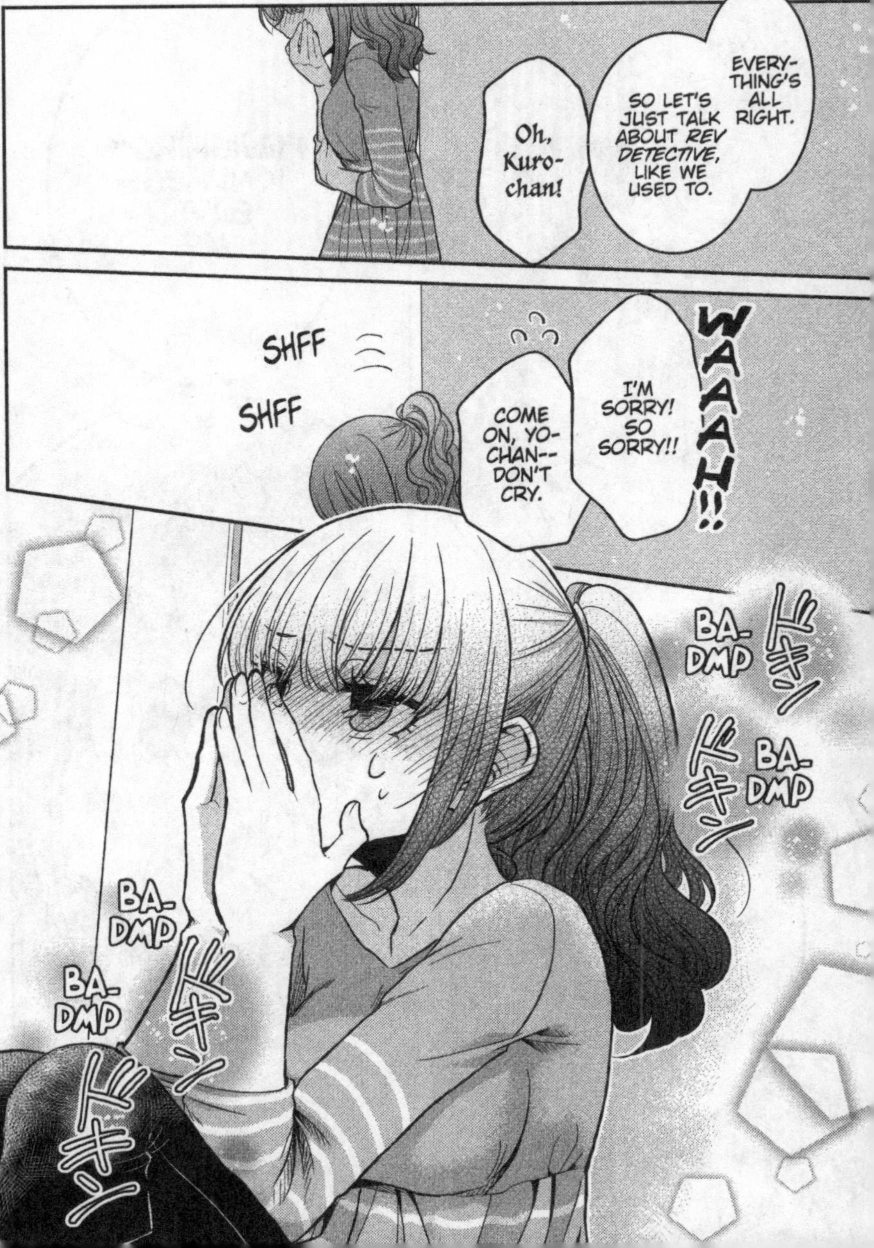
EVERY-THING'S ALL RIGHT.
SO LET'S JUST TALK ABOUT *REV DETECTIVE*, LIKE WE USED TO.
Oh, Kuro-chan!
WAAAH!!
I'M SORRY! SO SORRY!!
COME ON, YO-CHAN-- DON'T CRY.
SHFF
SHFF
ドキン
BA-DMP
ドキン
BA-DMP
BA-DMP
ドキン
BA-DMP
ドキン

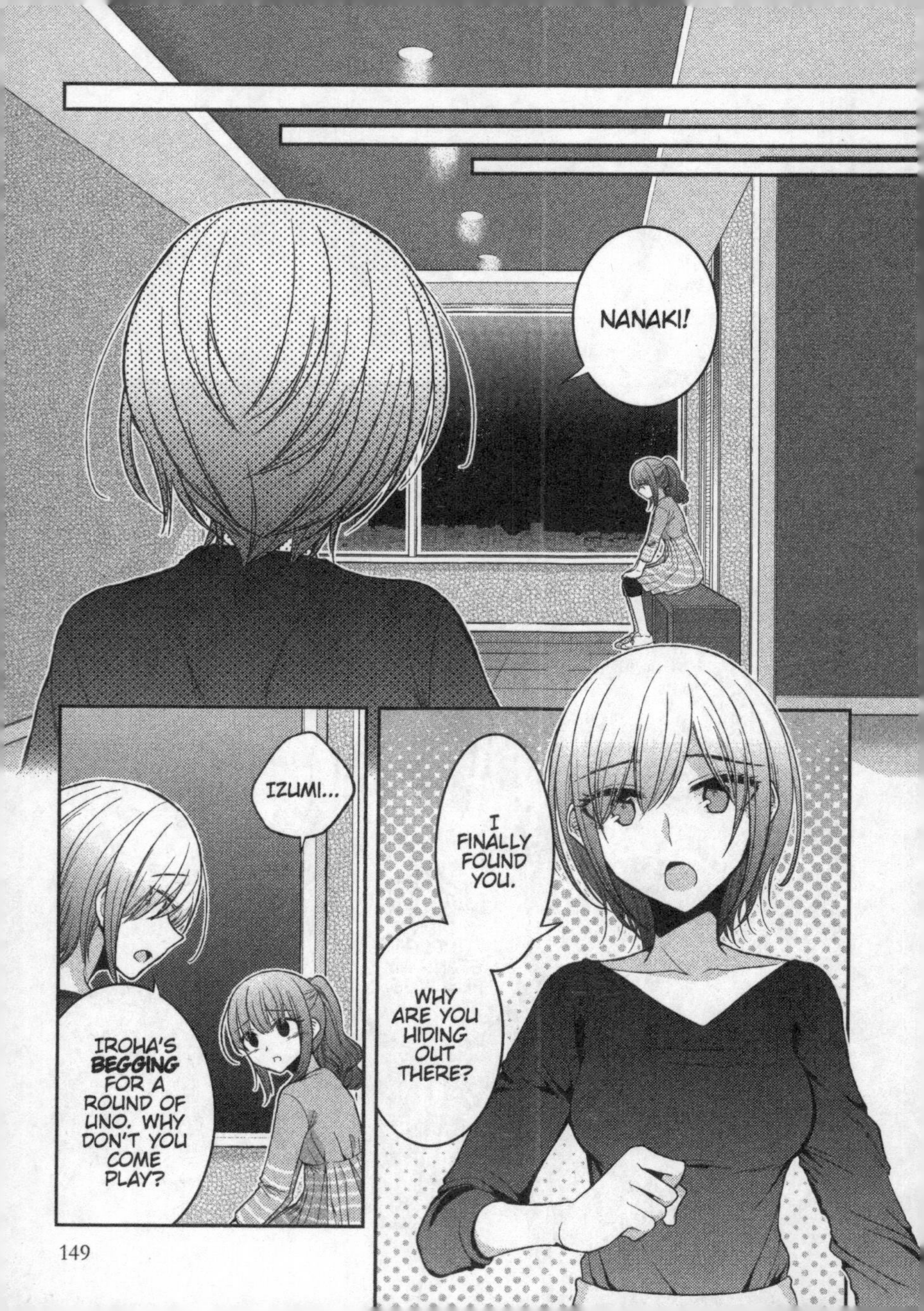
NANAKI!
I FINALLY FOUND YOU.
WHY ARE YOU HIDING OUT THERE?
IZUMI...
IROHA'S **BEGGING** FOR A ROUND OF UNO. WHY DON'T YOU COME PLAY?

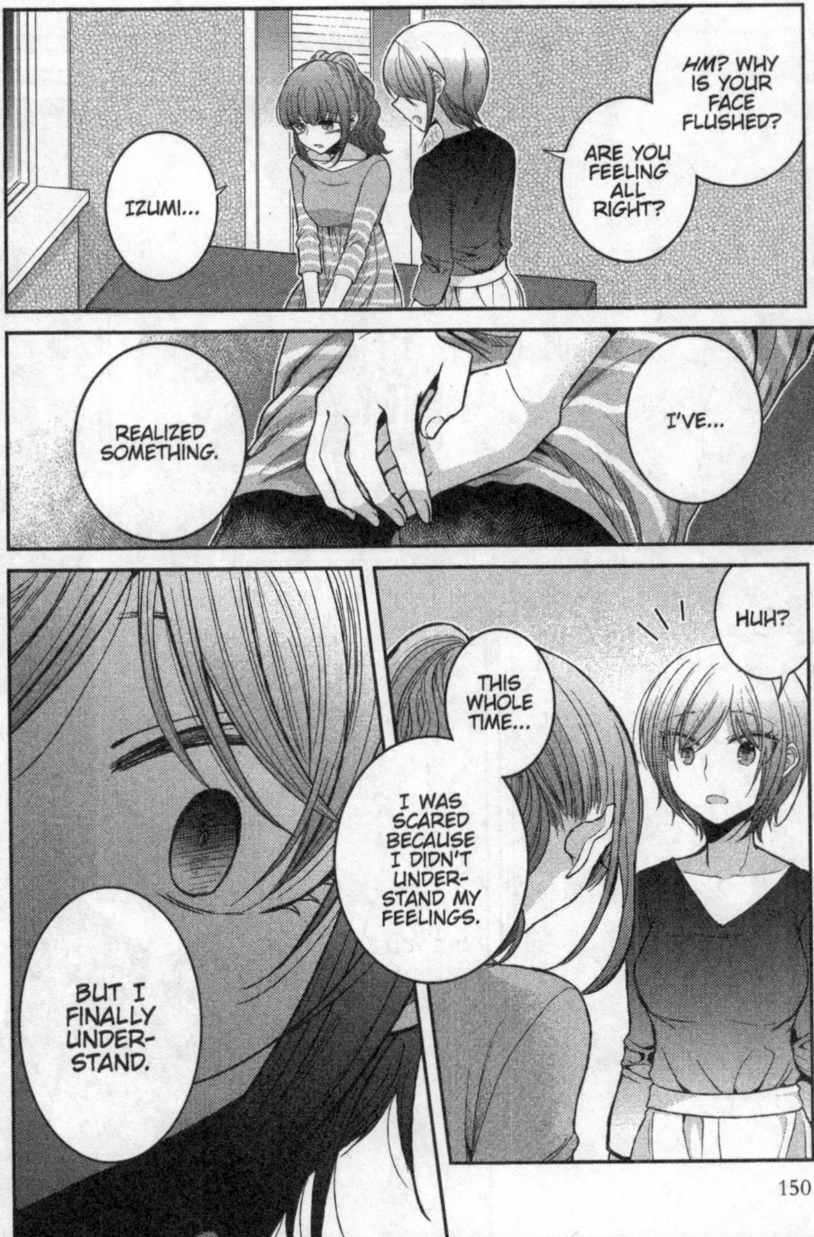
HM? WHY IS YOUR FACE FLUSHED?
ARE YOU FEELING ALL RIGHT?
IZUMI...
I'VE...
REALIZED SOMETHING.
HUH?
THIS WHOLE TIME...
I WAS SCARED BECAUSE I DIDN'T UNDER-STAND MY FEELINGS.
BUT I FINALLY UNDER-STAND.

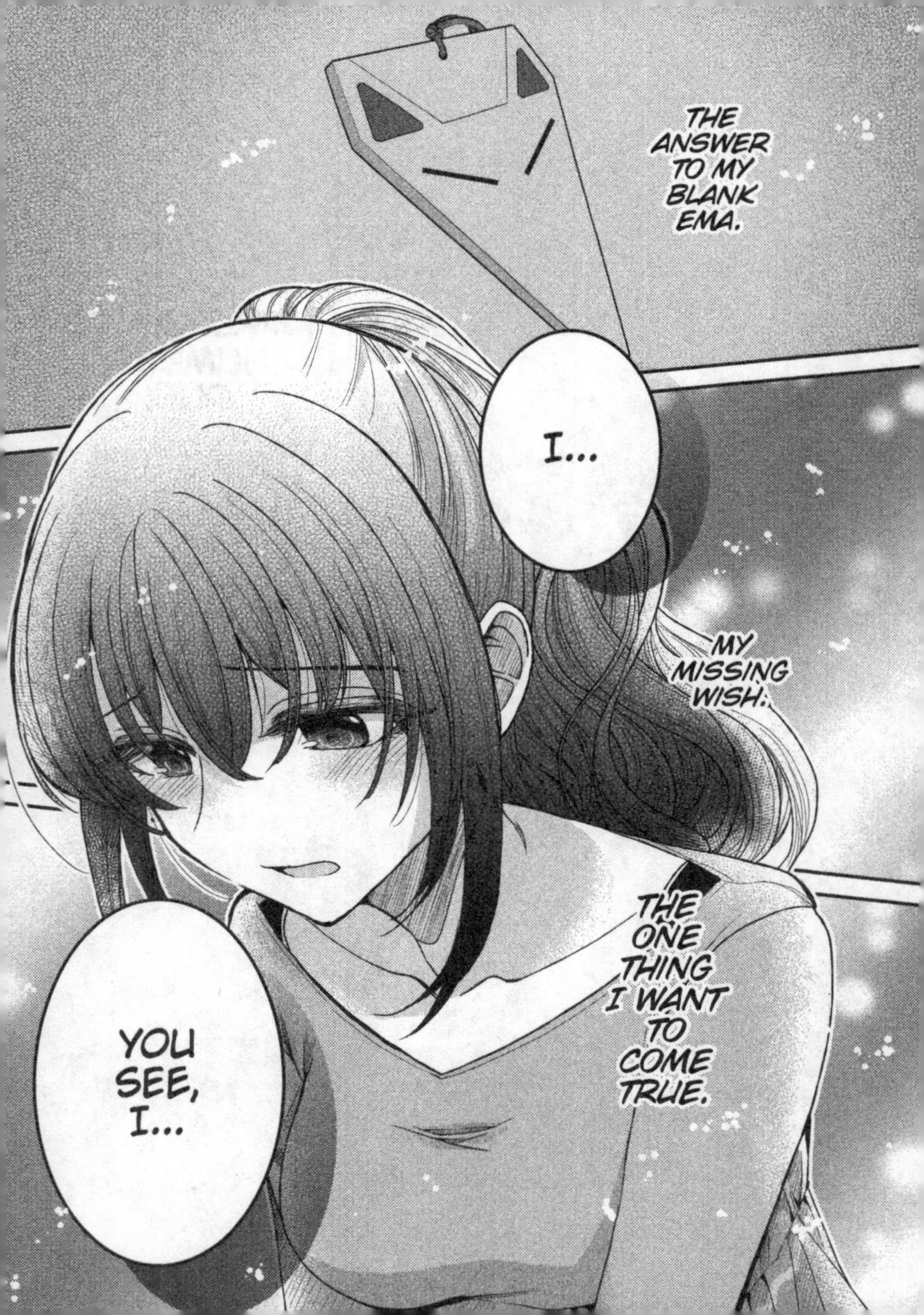
THE ANSWER TO MY BLANK EMA.
I...
MY MISSING WISH.
THE ONE THING I WANT TO COME TRUE.
YOU SEE, I...

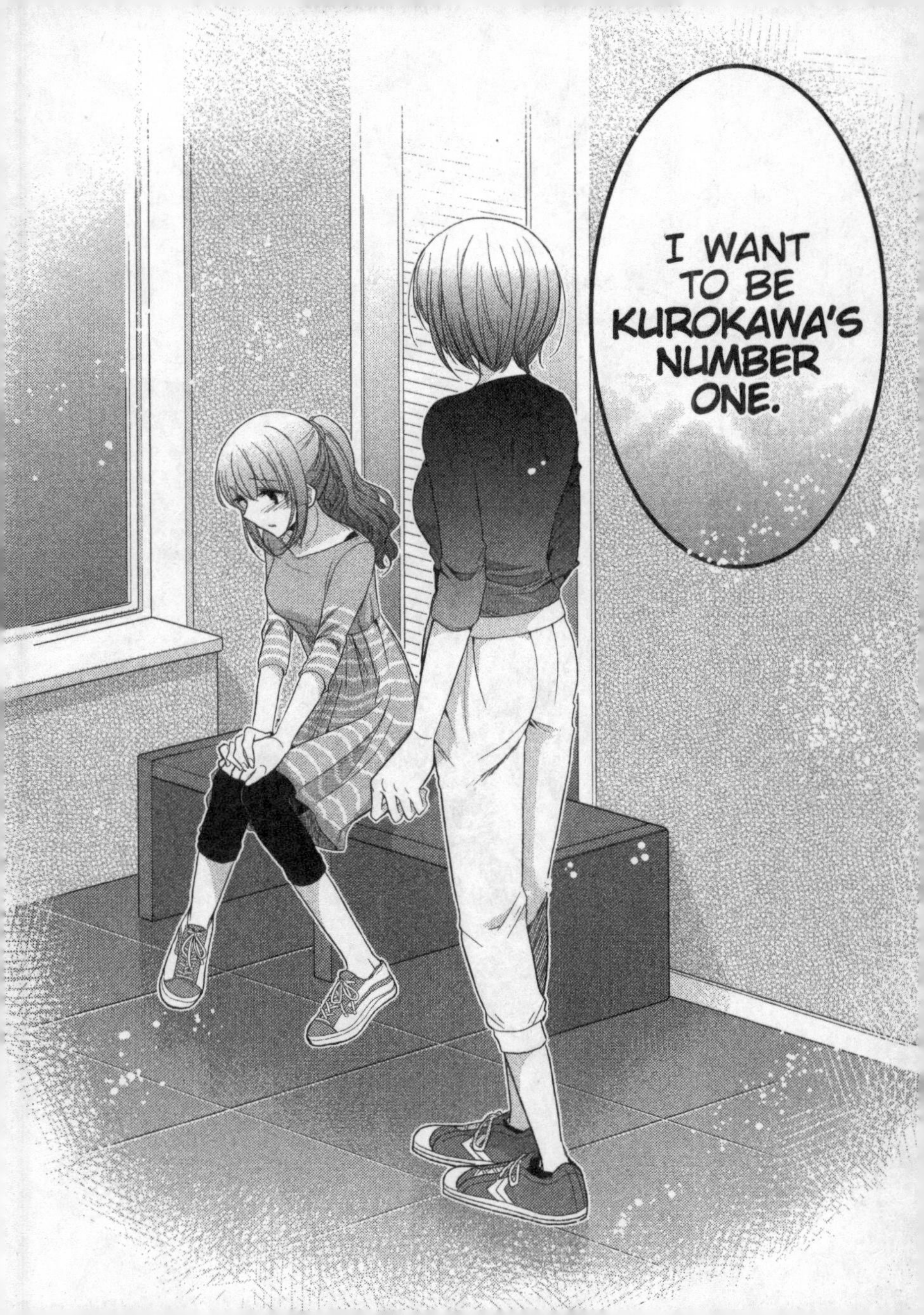
I WANT TO BE KUROKAWA'S NUMBER ONE.

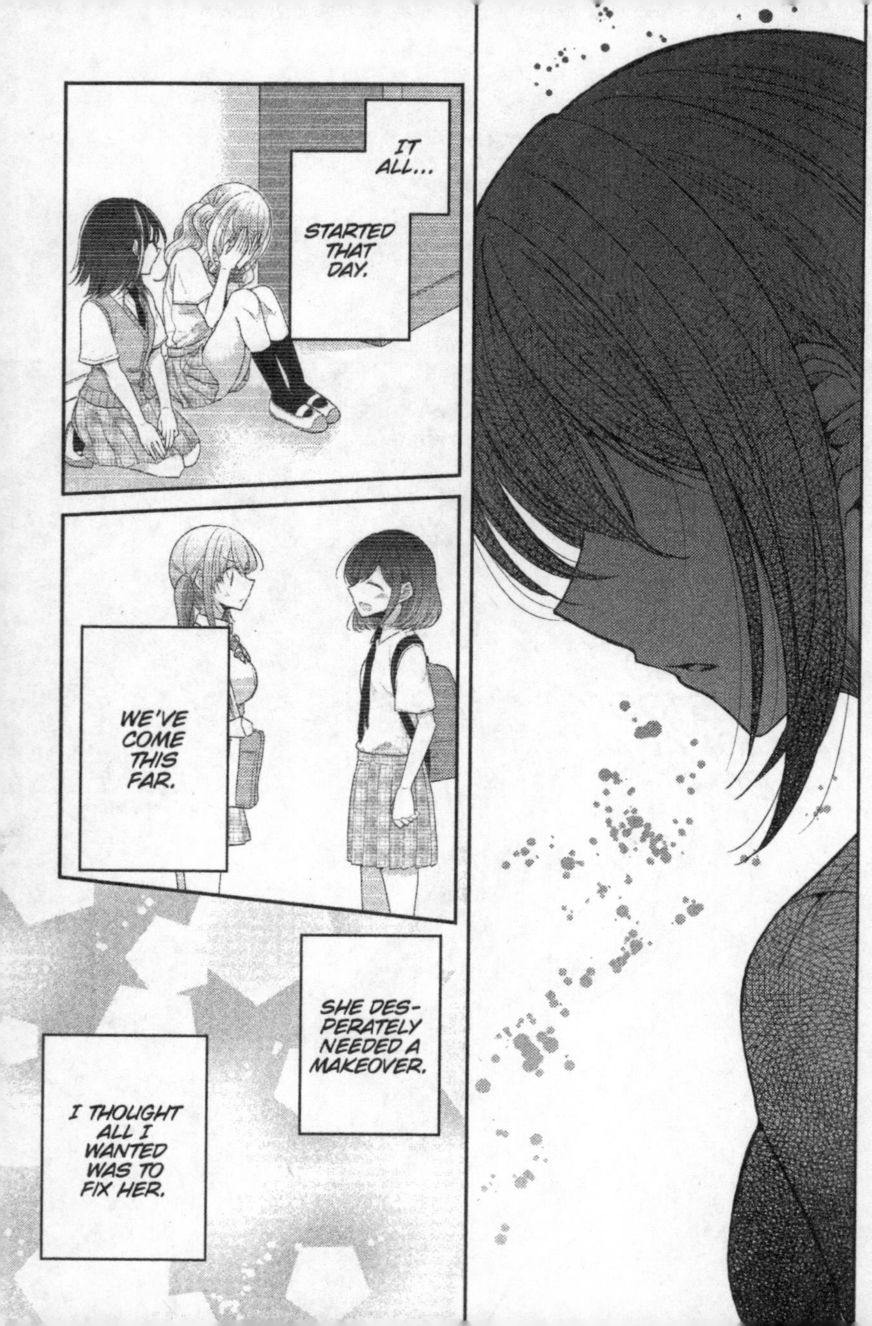
IT ALL...
STARTED THAT DAY.
WE'VE COME THIS FAR.
SHE DES-PERATELY NEEDED A MAKEOVER.
I THOUGHT ALL I WANTED WAS TO FIX HER.

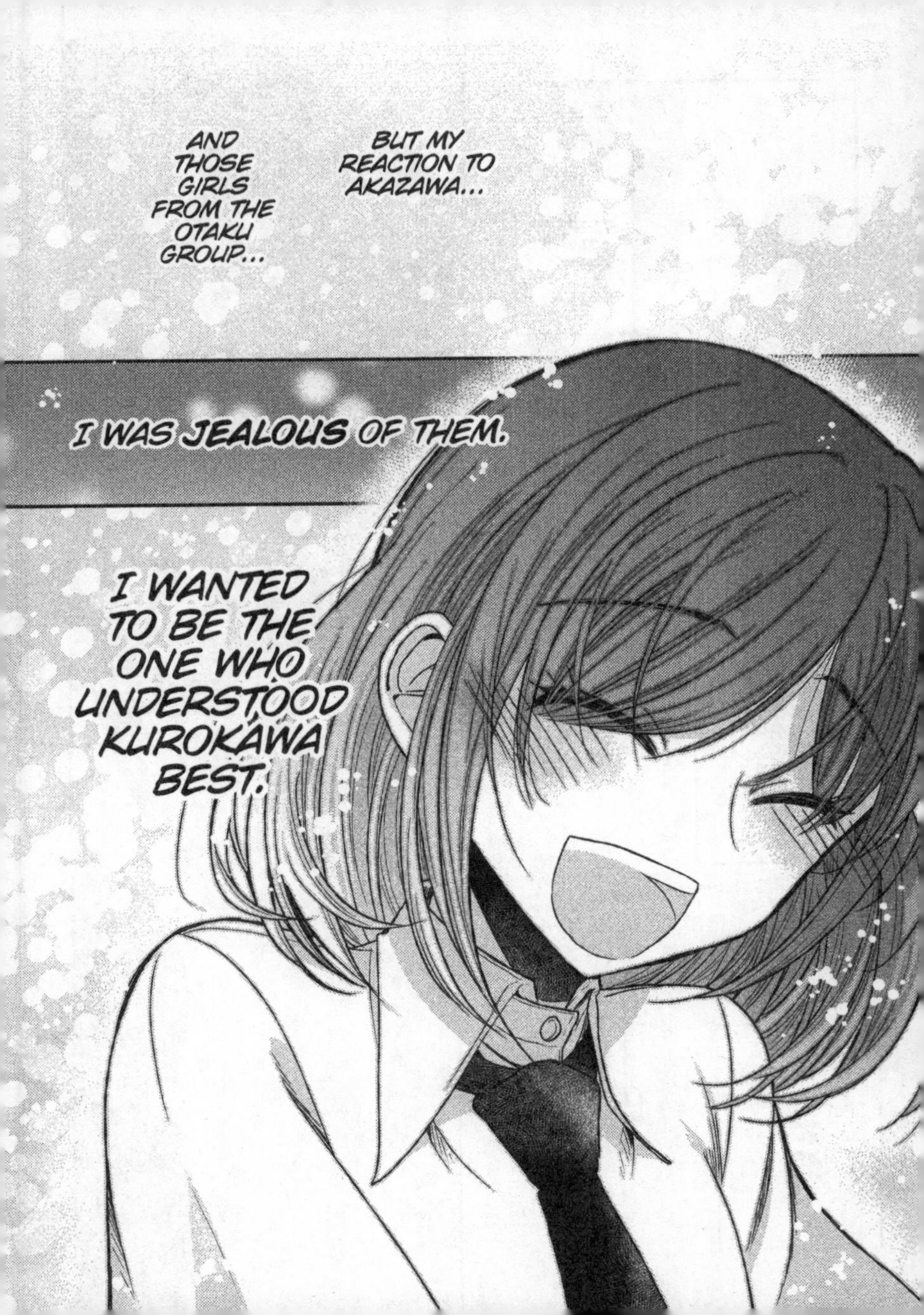
BUT MY REACTION TO AKAZAWA...
AND THOSE GIRLS FROM THE OTAKU GROUP...
I WAS JEALOUS OF THEM.
I WANTED TO BE THE ONE WHO UNDERSTOOD KUROKAWA BEST.

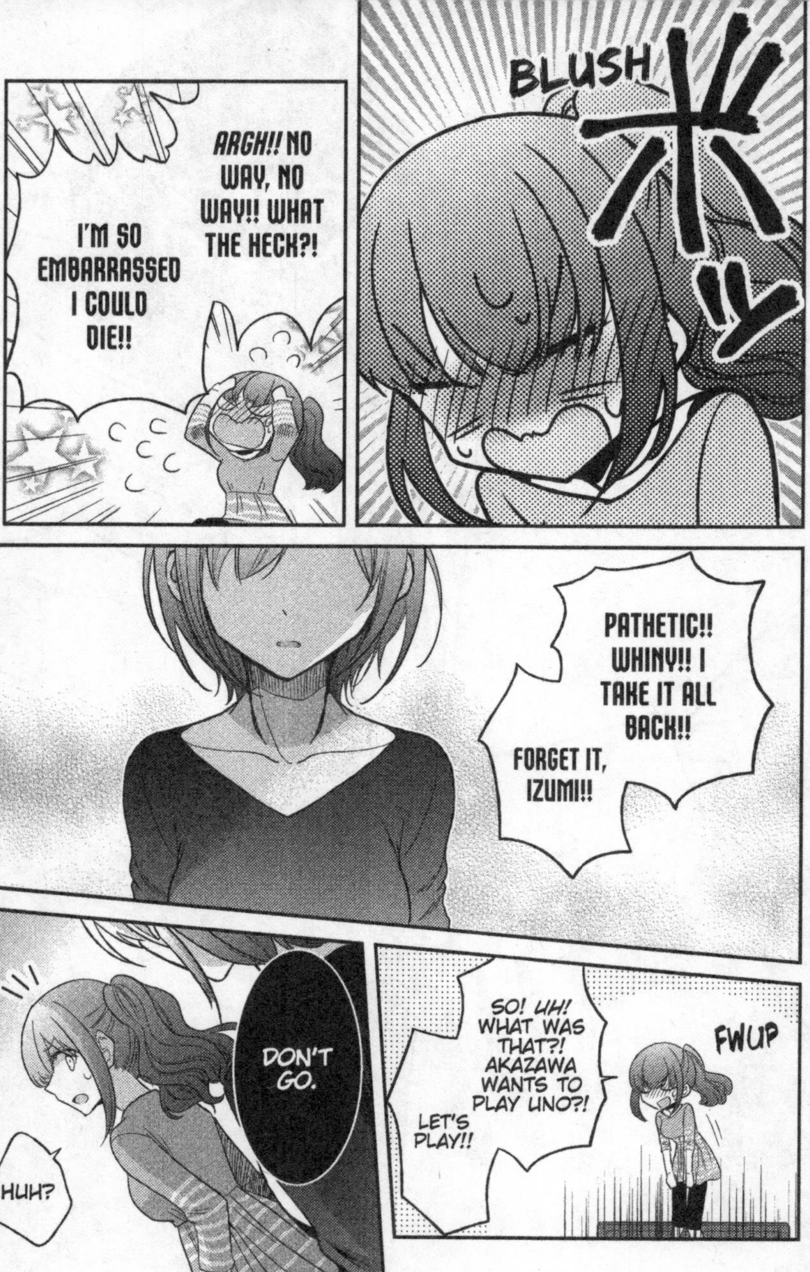
BLUSH
ARGH!! NO WAY, NO WAY!! WHAT THE HECK?!
I'M SO EMBARRASSED I COULD DIE!!
PATHETIC!! WHINY!! I TAKE IT ALL BACK!!
FORGET IT, IZUMI!!
SO! UH! WHAT WAS THAT?! AKAZAWA WANTS TO PLAY UNO?!
LET'S PLAY!!
FWUP
DON'T GO.
HUH?

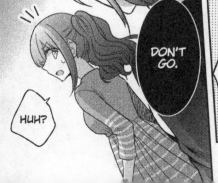

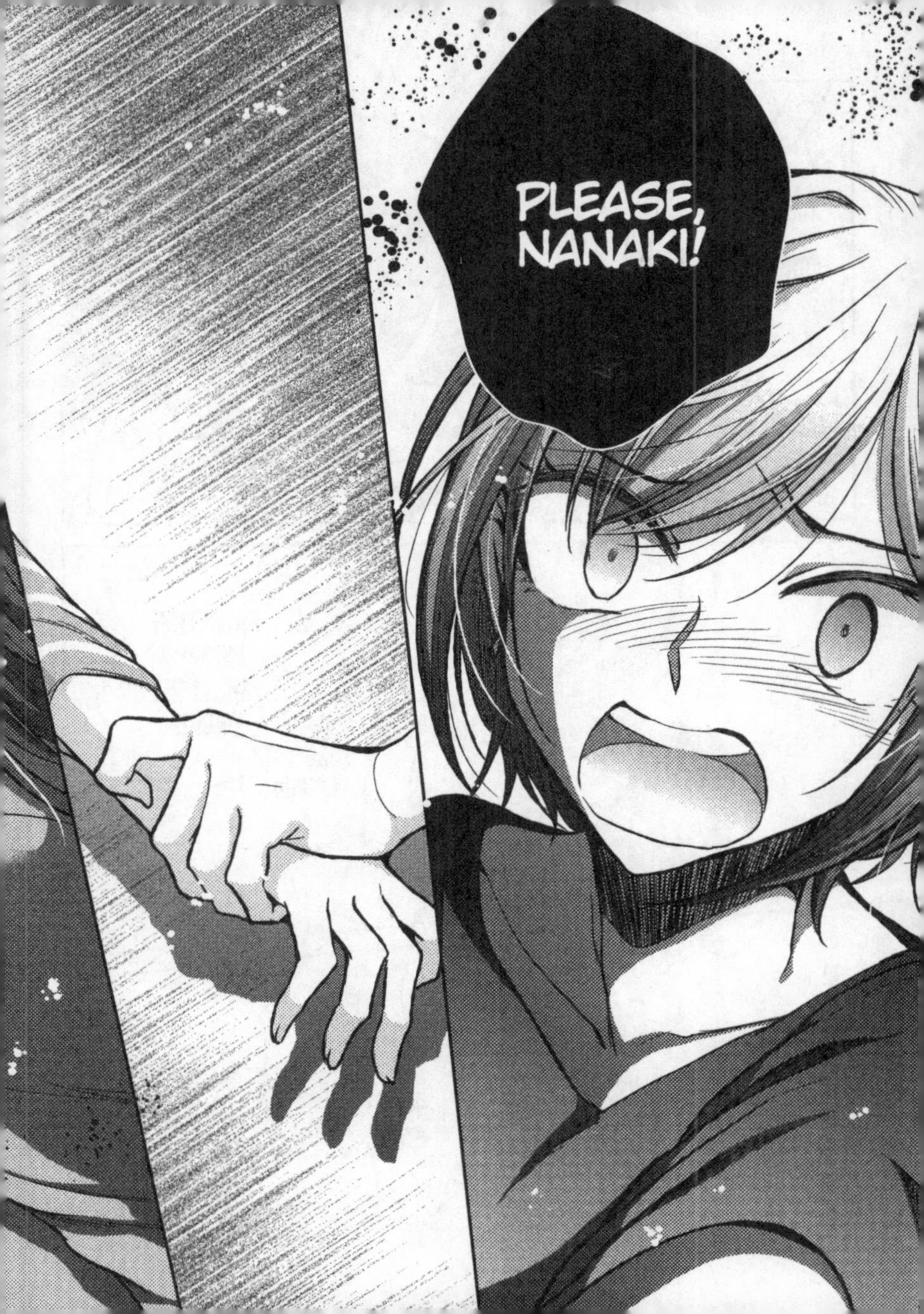
PLEASE, NANAKI!

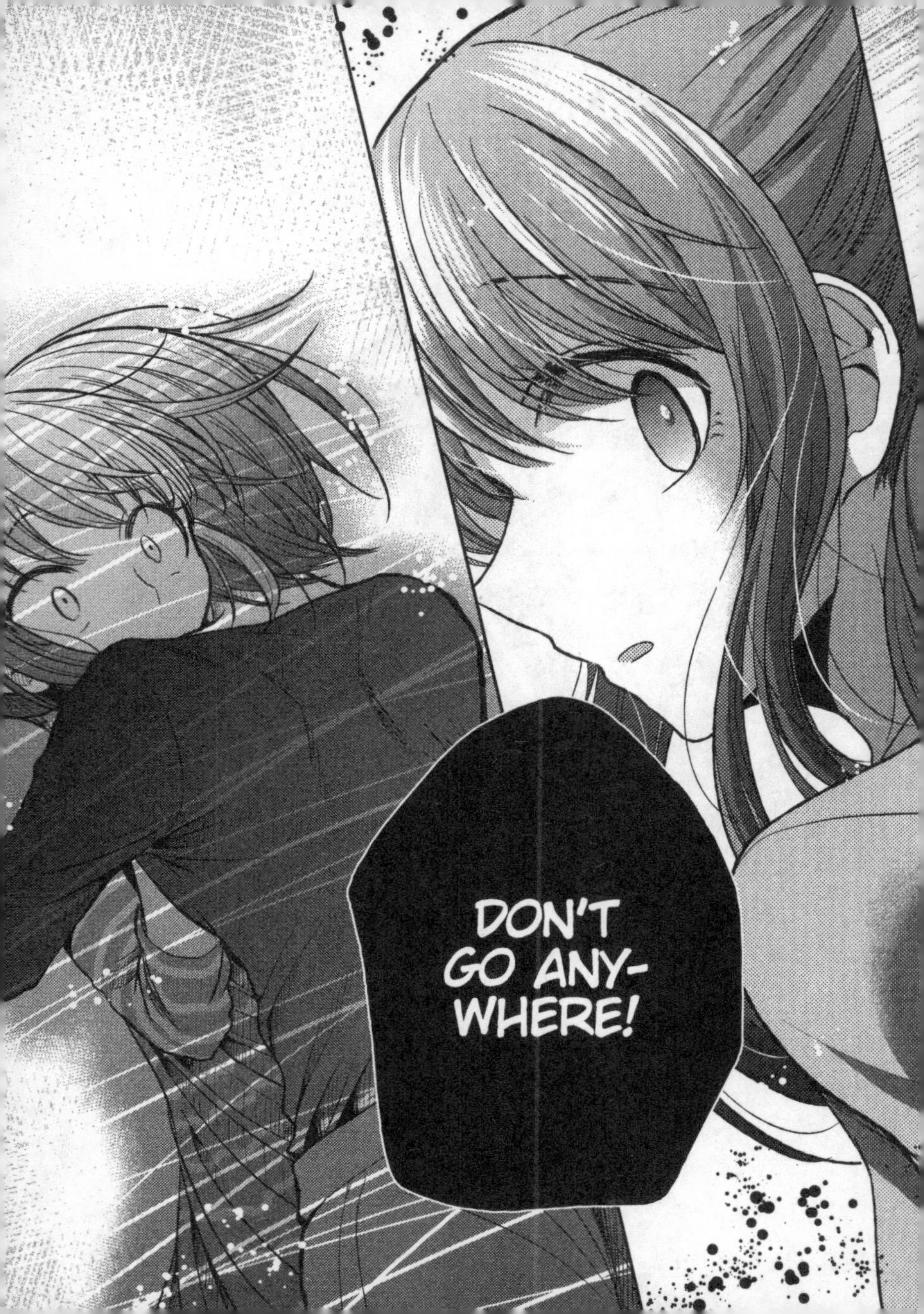
DON'T GO ANY-WHERE!

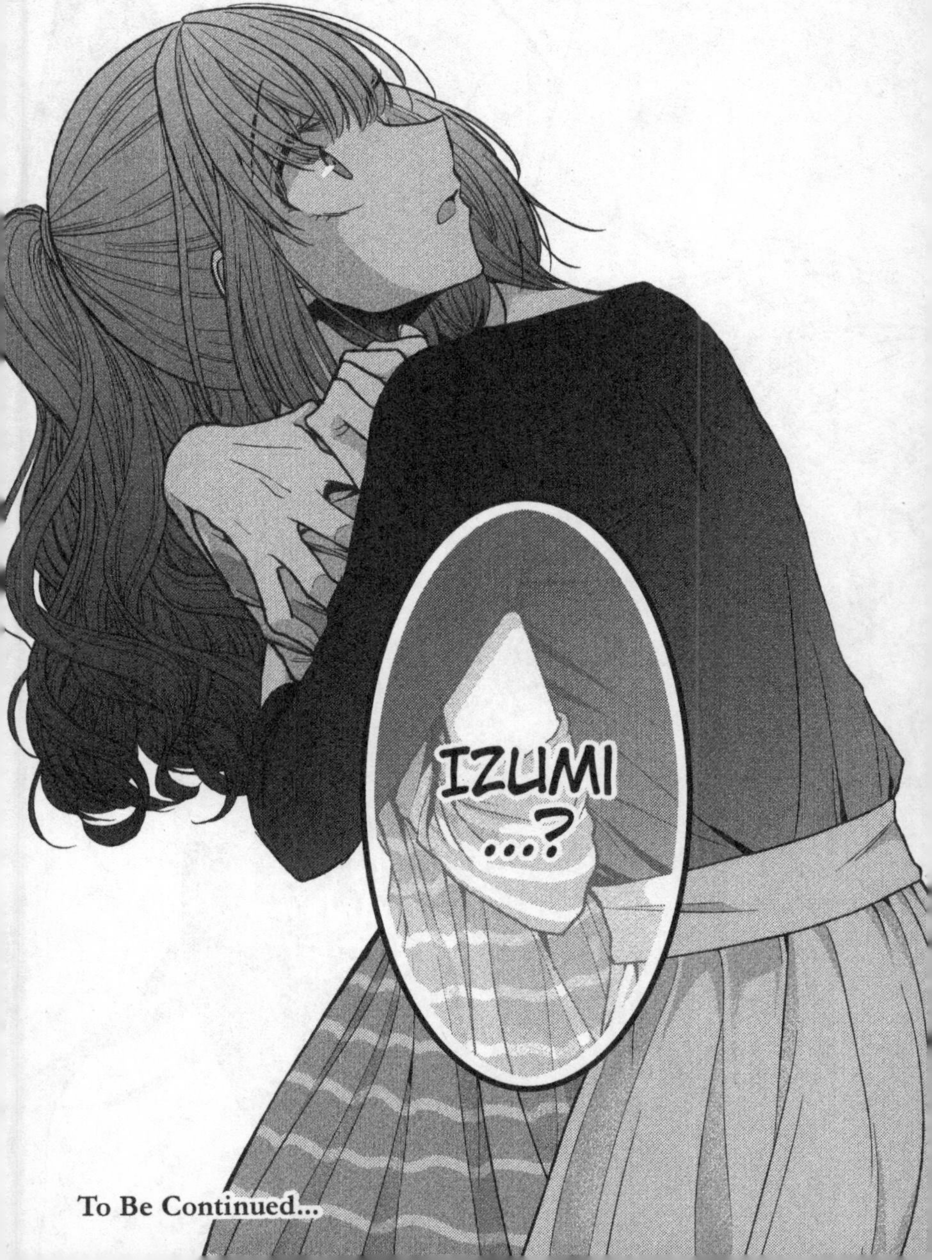
IZUMI
...?

To Be Continued...

NEXT VOLUME PREVIEW

The feelings she's desperately kept hidden have finally --?!

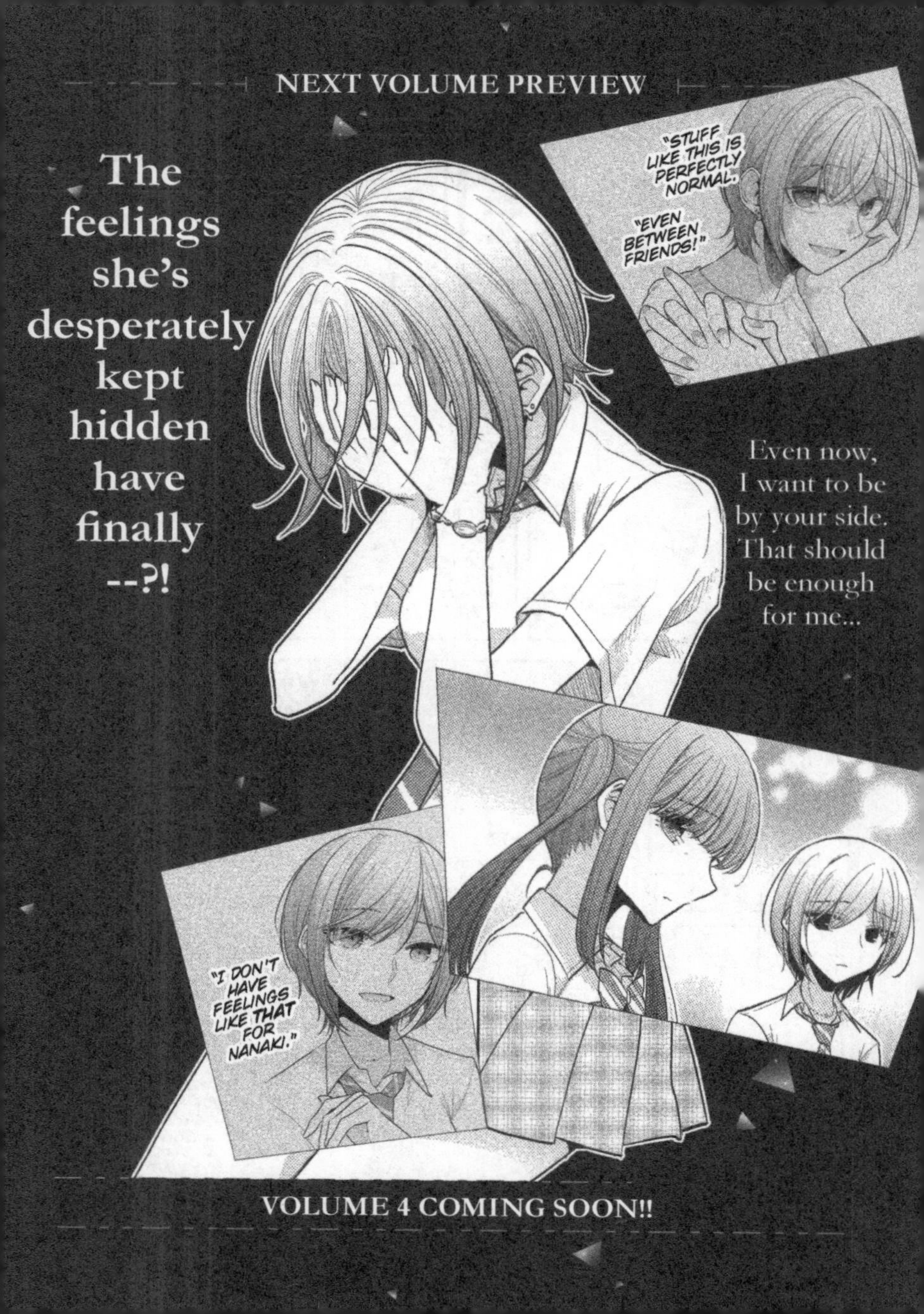
"STUFF LIKE THIS IS PERFECTLY NORMAL.
"EVEN BETWEEN FRIENDS!"
"I DON'T HAVE FEELINGS LIKE THAT FOR NANAKI."

Even now, I want to be by your side. That should be enough for me...

VOLUME 4 COMING SOON!!

AFTERWORD

EACH COMIC IS ASSIGNED A MAXIMUM NUMBER OF PAGES. (MORE PAGES MEANS A MORE EXPENSIVE COMIC.)

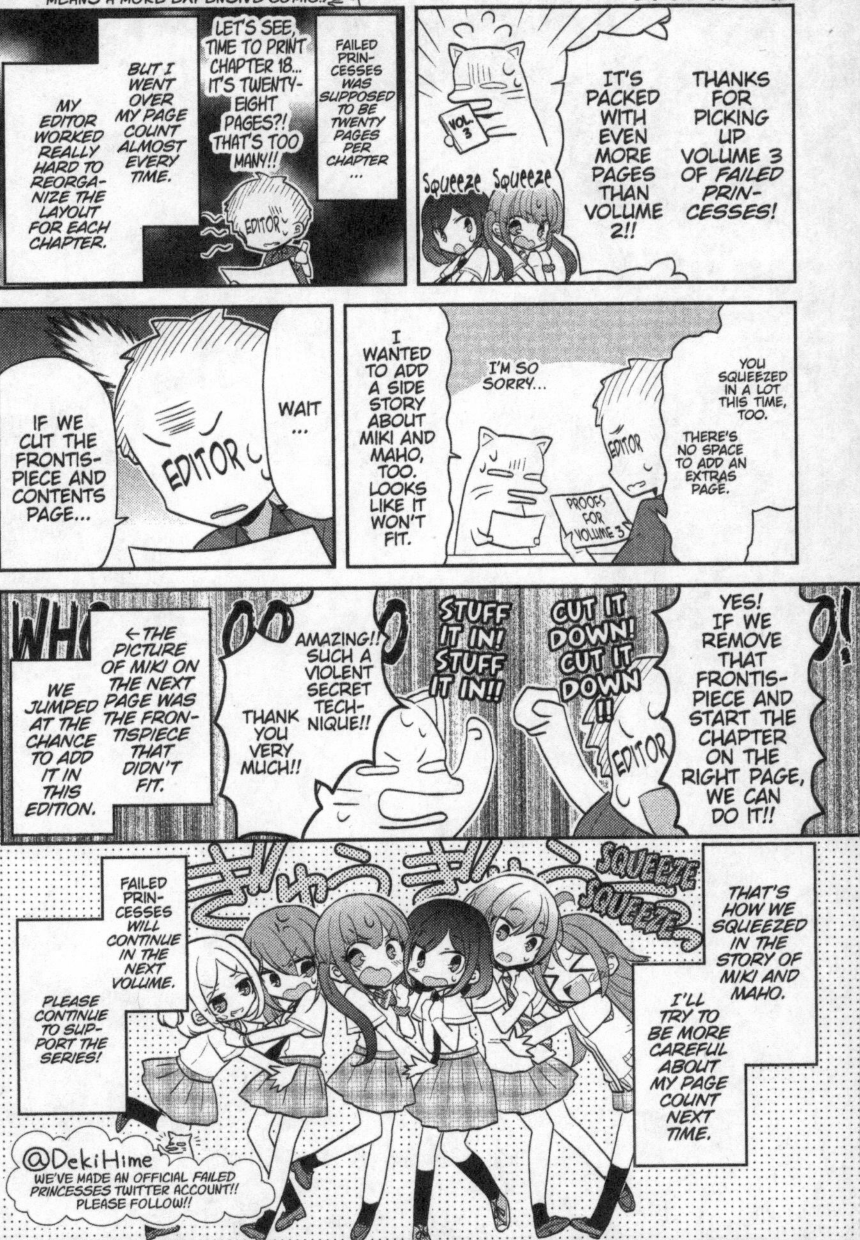
THANKS FOR PICKING UP VOLUME 3 OF FAILED PRINCESSES!
IT'S PACKED WITH EVEN MORE PAGES THAN VOLUME 2!!
VOL. 3
Squeeze
Squeeze
FAILED PRINCESSES WAS SUPPOSED TO BE TWENTY PAGES PER CHAPTER...
LET'S SEE, TIME TO PRINT CHAPTER 18... IT'S TWENTY-EIGHT PAGES?! THAT'S TOO MANY!!
BUT I WENT OVER MY PAGE COUNT ALMOST EVERY TIME.
MY EDITOR WORKED REALLY HARD TO REORGANIZE THE LAYOUT FOR EACH CHAPTER.
EDITOR
YOU SQUEEZED IN A LOT THIS TIME, TOO.
THERE'S NO SPACE TO ADD AN EXTRAS PAGE.
EDITOR
I WANTED TO ADD A SIDE STORY ABOUT MIKI AND MAHO, TOO. LOOKS LIKE IT WON'T FIT.
I'M SO SORRY...
PROOFS FOR VOLUME 3
WAIT...
IF WE CUT THE FRONTISPIECE AND CONTENTS PAGE...
EDITOR
YES! IF WE REMOVE THAT FRONTISPIECE AND START THE CHAPTER ON THE RIGHT PAGE, WE CAN DO IT!!
CUT IT DOWN! CUT IT DOWN!!
STUFF IT IN! STUFF IT IN!!
EDITOR
AMAZING!! SUCH A VIOLENT SECRET TECHNIQUE!!
THANK YOU VERY MUCH!!
←THE PICTURE OF MIKI ON THE NEXT PAGE WAS THE FRONTISPIECE THAT DIDN'T FIT.
WE JUMPED AT THE CHANCE TO ADD IT IN THIS EDITION.
THAT'S HOW WE SQUEEZED IN THE STORY OF MIKI AND MAHO.
I'LL TRY TO BE MORE CAREFUL ABOUT MY PAGE COUNT NEXT TIME.
SQUEEZE
SQUEEZE
FAILED PRINCESSES WILL CONTINUE IN THE NEXT VOLUME.
PLEASE CONTINUE TO SUPPORT THE SERIES!
@DekiHime
WE'VE MADE AN OFFICIAL FAILED PRINCESSES TWITTER ACCOUNT!! PLEASE FOLLOW!!

illustration gallery

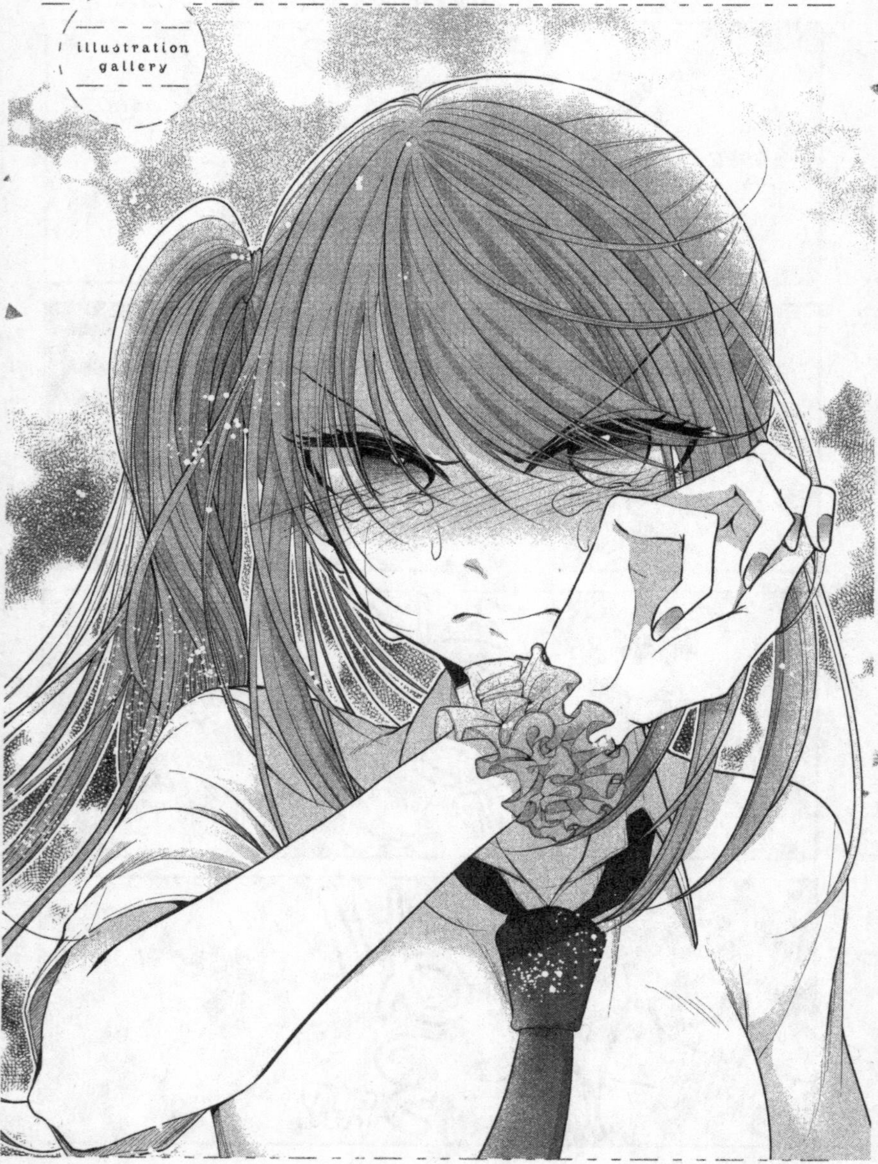

f a i l e d   p r i n c e s s e s   v o l u m e   t h r e e

[IN THE BATHHOUSE DRESSING ROOM]

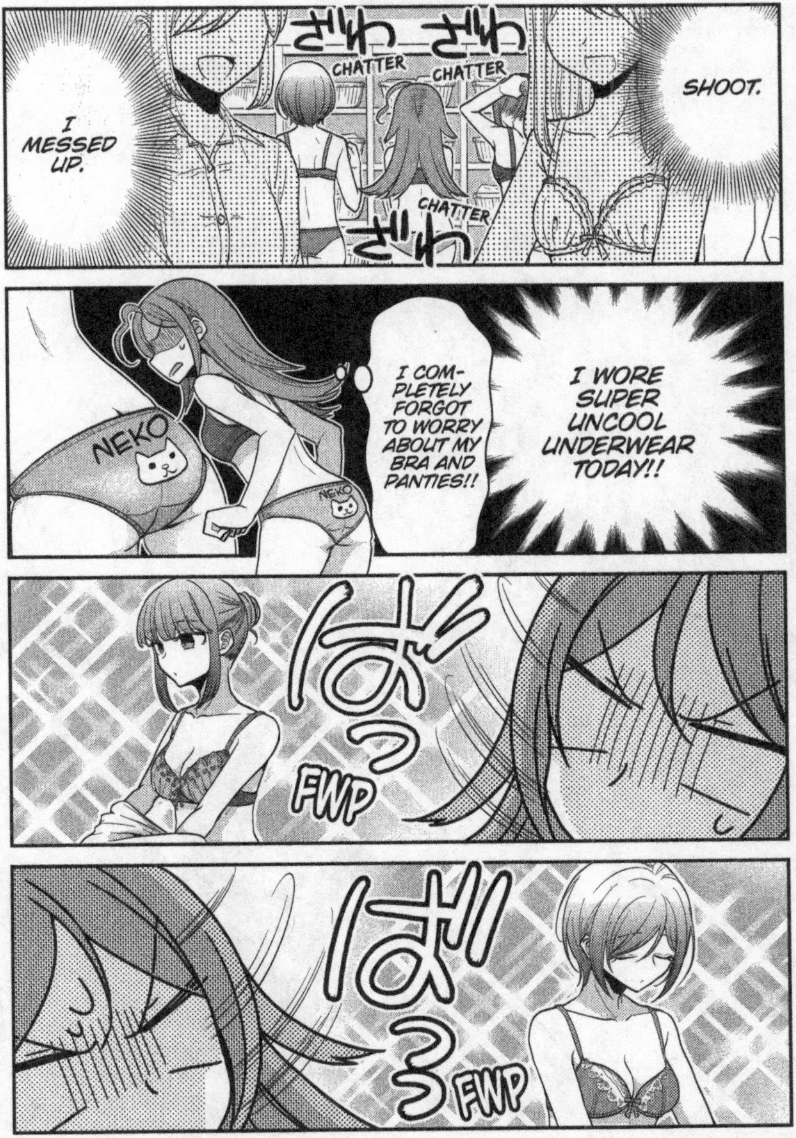
SHOOT.
ざわ ざわ
CHATTER CHATTER
I MESSED UP.
CHATTER
ざわ
I WORE SUPER UNCOOL UNDERWEAR TODAY!!
I COMPLETELY FORGOT TO WORRY ABOUT MY BRA AND PANTIES!!
NEKO
NEKO
ぱっ
FWP
ぱっ
FWP

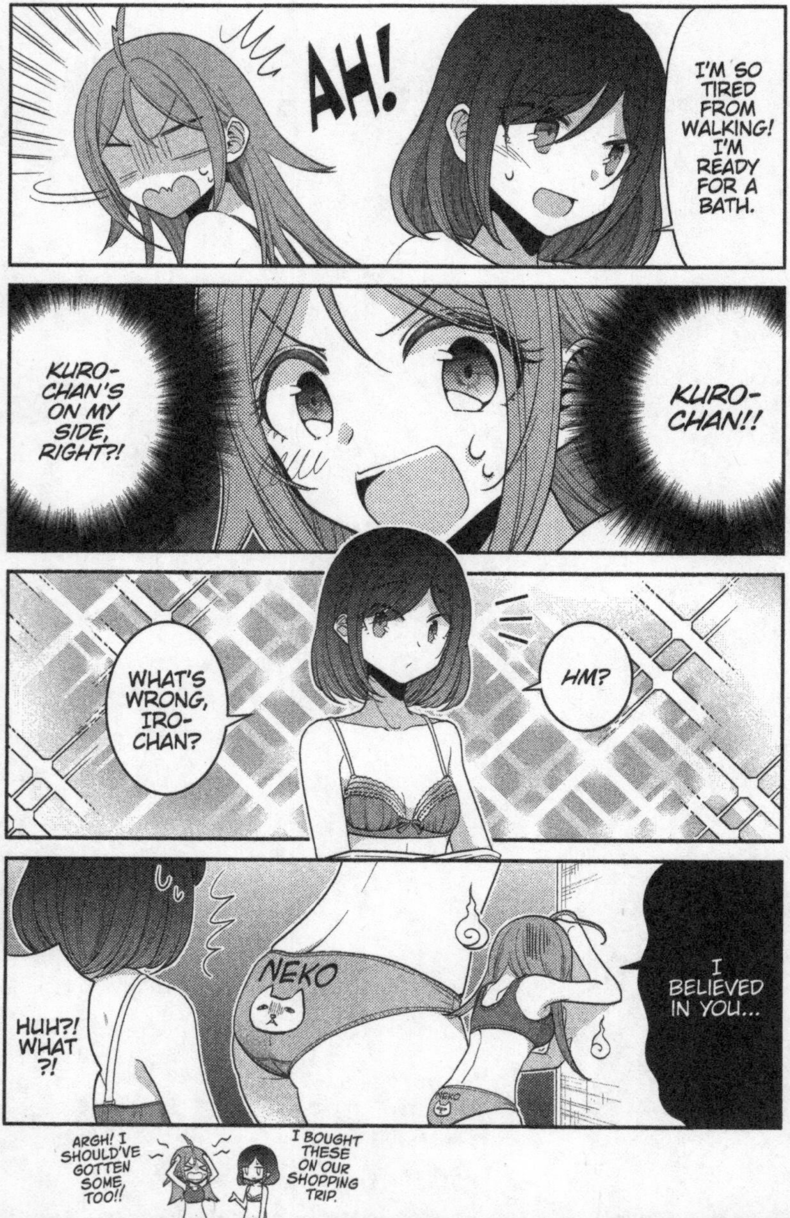
I'M SO TIRED FROM WALKING! I'M READY FOR A BATH.
AH!
KURO-CHAN!!
KURO-CHAN'S ON MY SIDE, RIGHT?!
HM?
WHAT'S WRONG, IRO-CHAN?
I BELIEVED IN YOU...
NEKO
NEKO
HUH?! WHAT?!
I BOUGHT THESE ON OUR SHOPPING TRIP.
ARGH! I SHOULD'VE GOTTEN SOME TOO!!

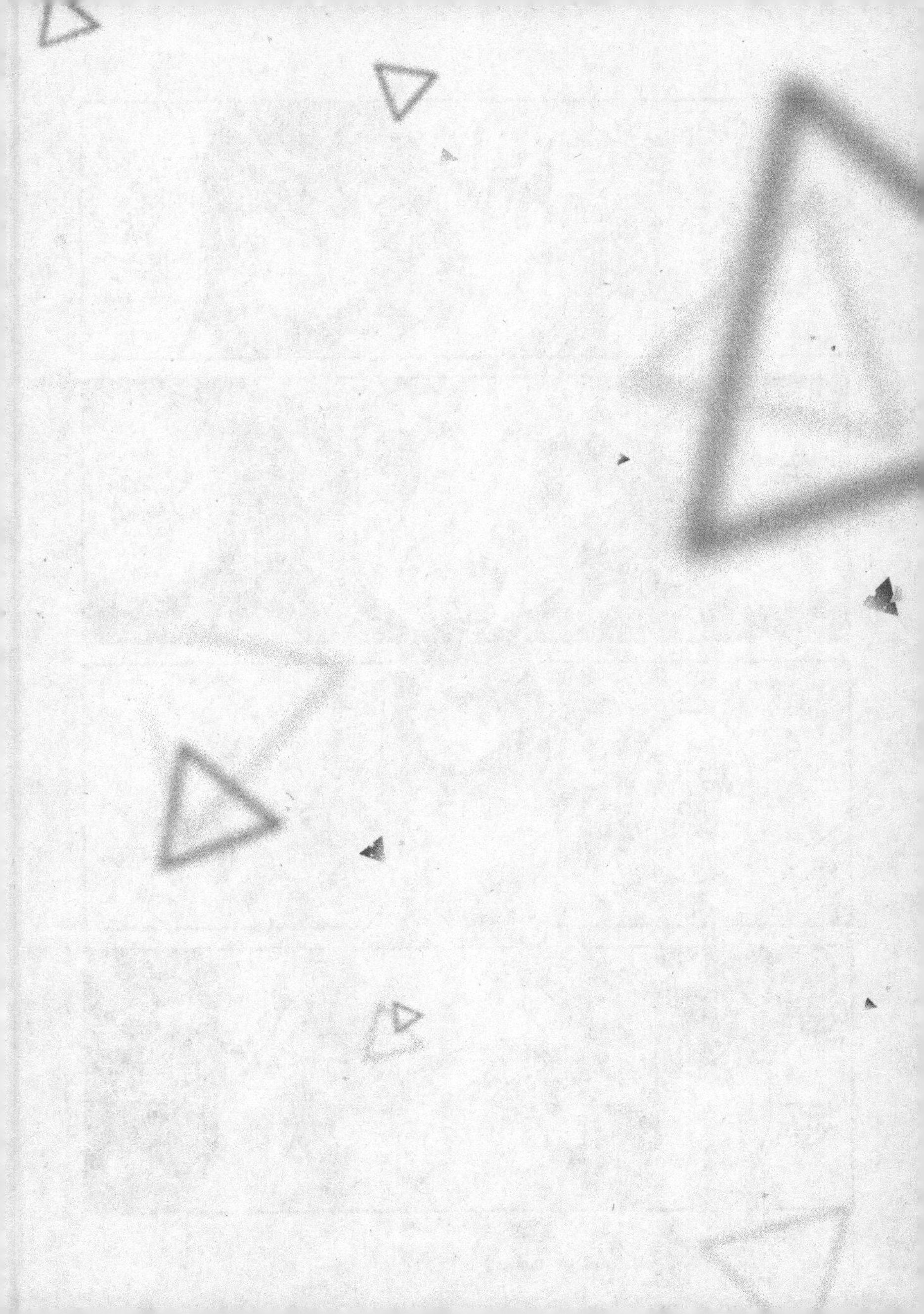

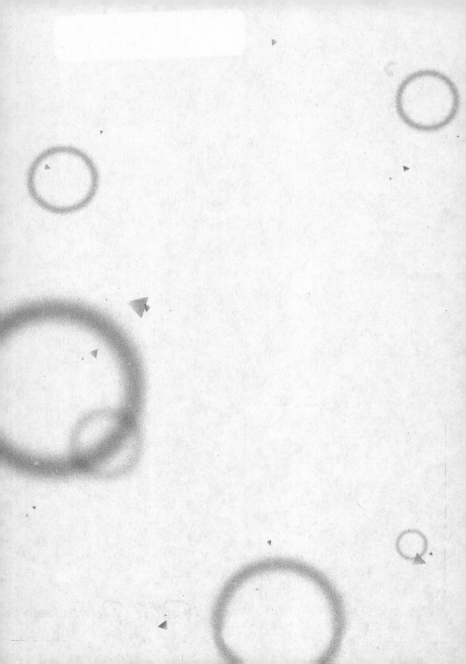

Failed Princesses